P9-AOT-891

New Designs for the Elementary School Curriculum

McGRAW-HILL SERIES IN EDUCATION

HAROLD BENJAMIN, *Consulting Editor-in-Chief*

ARNO A. BELLACK, *Teachers College, Columbia University*
Consulting Editor, Curriculum and Methods in Education

HAROLD BENJAMIN, *Emeritus Professor of Education*
George Peabody College for Teachers
Consulting Editor, Foundations in Education

HARLAN HAGMAN, *Wayne State University*
Consulting Editor, Administration in Education

WALTER F. JOHNSON, *Michigan State University*
Consulting Editor, Guidance, Counseling, and
Student Personnel in Education

CURRICULUM AND METHODS IN EDUCATION

ARNO A. BELLACK, *Consulting Editor*

JOHN U. MICHAELIS

Professor of Education, University of California, Berkeley

RUTH H. GROSSMAN

Assistant Professor of Education,
The City College of the City University of New York

LLOYD F. SCOTT

Professor of Education, University of California, Berkeley

MC GRAW-HILL BOOK COMPANY

New York, St. Louis, San Francisco, Toronto, London, Sydney

New Designs for the Elementary School Curriculum

PROVIDENCE
COLLEGE
LIBRARY

LB
1570
M5

Cover picture courtesy of Wide World Photos.

NEW DESIGNS FOR THE ELEMENTARY
SCHOOL CURRICULUM

Copyright © 1967 by McGraw-Hill, Inc. All Rights Reserved.
Printed in the United States of America. No part of this publication may be reproduced, stored in a retrieval system, or transmitted, in any form or by any means, electronic, mechanical,
photocopying, recording, or otherwise, without the prior written
permission of the publisher.
Library of Congress Catalog Card Number 67-16933

41768

1 2 3 4 5 6 7 8 9 0   M P   7 4 3 2 1 0 6 9 8 7

APR 1 9 1968

THE CURRICULUM REVOLUTION which was given impetus in the 1950s has continued to accelerate and expand. Its manifestations are conspicuously diverse, yet its direction in all curriculum areas has been guided by many common factors and viewpoints. At the present time curriculum revision is being undertaken in many school systems, increasing contributions are being made by curriculum planning centers outside the school systems, and there is continual academic and commercial production of new programs and materials. In view of this vast activity, there is a need for a clarifying focus on the essential features of the emerging modern curriculum. There is also a need for guidelines which will serve the continual examination, evaluation, and utilization of new curriculum designs and materials in the elementary school program.

In response to these needs, this volume is addressed to those who wish to improve the elementary school curriculum. Recent trends and developments in different areas of the curriculum are reviewed in detail. Special attention is given to materials prepared in curriculum project centers, recently published curriculum guides, and professional textbooks. Every effort has been made to select what the writers believe to be the dominant features of current developments as they are revealed in materials prepared for the basic curriculum areas. The intention is to present a comprehensive and timely view of what is advocated in new curriculum materials.

This book, therefore, differs markedly from the typical book on the elementary curriculum. Its central focus is on those elements of curriculum design that are dominant in the current curriculum revolution as it is actually taking place. No attention is given to peripheral matters, such as a detailed review of traditional goals of education, studies of learning done long ago, implications of child development studies conducted in out-of-school contexts, the self-contained classroom versus other forms of organization, homogeneous versus heterogeneous grouping, and the like. Rather, direct attention is given to the foundation disciplines on which areas of the curriculum are based, new objectives in each subject area, curriculum designs, prominent teaching strategies, evaluation of instructional outcomes, and evaluation of the program. An important feature is the use of the taxonomies of cognitive and affective objectives in the construction of evaluation devices. Special efforts have been made to identify the conceptual structures and modes of inquiry that are proposed in new curriculum materials and to present both substantive and process components of the curriculum.

The organization of this volume provides a framework that may be used to examine and evaluate new curriculum developments. Chapter 1 develops some understandings of the organization of knowledge basic to a balanced perspective of the total curriculum. Contributions of foundation disciplines to current curriculum planning are discussed. Chapter 2 outlines a model of components of the curriculum which are useful in reviewing developments, designs, and materials in every area. Chapters 3 through 12 utilize the model in discussing new developments and innovations in each area of the elementary school curriculum. Chapter 13 presents guidelines for continued review of new curriculum materials and designs.

This volume has been written and organized to be used in courses in elementary curriculum and in curriculum planning for graduate students in the fields of curriculum, instruction, supervision, or administration. It is also intended as a tool for in-service curriculum preparation for teachers, supervisors, administrators, and others who participate in curriculum development or who are involved with the implementation of new designs.

The task of reviewing the mass of new curriculum material has been a formidable one. Undoubtedly, some excellent examples of new developments have been overlooked. However, the authors have found the task challenging and exciting and hope that the examples presented will spur others to continue the rewarding search. The new views of structure, inquiry, content, and learning processes that can be found in a thorough review of current materials take one far beyond the perspectives that were dominant in the early 1960s. It is hoped that the theoretical framework used to organize this book will be useful to others as they review new developments and work to improve the elementary curriculum.

Acknowledgment is made of the contributions of theorists, project staffs, and elementary school teachers whose efforts to reform the elementary school curriculum have resulted in written materials. The writers are grateful for the responsive dialogue with students, elementary school teachers, and colleagues that has served to sharpen our perceptions. Special thanks are given to those who gave permission to quote material in the text.

John U. Michaelis
Ruth H. Grossman
Lloyd F. Scott

CONTENTS

Chapter One

FOUNDATIONAL ASPECTS OF NEW CURRICULUM DESIGNS

CHANGE AND INNOVATION have been hallmarks of education during the past decade. Areas of the curriculum have been revised under the direction of scholars from the academic disciplines. New instructional media, such as television, language laboratories, and programmed materials, have been introduced in many schools. Team teaching, nongraded schools, and a variety of patterns for grouping students have been explored. New designs for school buildings and equipment have been devised. And new interest has been kindled in the investigation of teaching-learning processes.

A driving force for educational change has been the desire to improve the quality of instruction. Laymen have been aroused by critics of American education. Scholars in colleges and universities have accepted the challenge to make direct contributions to curriculum development. Professional educators have become involved in a variety of studies and projects focused on the program of instruction. All who have been genuinely concerned with matters of schooling have sought to bring the instructional program to increasingly higher levels of quality.

A variety of factors have operated to produce change and to stimulate the desire for instruction of high quality. Scientific achievements, technological advances, and the knowledge explosion have been key factors. International conflicts, national needs, and disparities in educational offerings throughout states and communities have sharpened thinking about the importance of education for all children and youth. The continuing upsurge of the democratic ideal has focused attention on the needs of minority groups, the culturally different, the residents of depressed areas, the disadvantaged, and others who have not had the opportunities and responsibilities that are expected in a democratic society. These and related factors have created a new and powerful interest in education in general and in curriculum improvement in particular (National Society for the Study of Education, 1966; NEA, 1963a).

Education is viewed as a vital force in human affairs. It seems that no matter what is proposed for the improvement of individual or group welfare, for local, state, or national benefit, or for private or public interest, education is regarded as one of the essential elements for continuing progress. This recognition of the basic importance of education, coupled with social forces and changes, has stimulated a new approach to curriculum development in which the goal of improved instruction is attacked in a diversity of ways.

A central concern of many individuals and groups has been to develop new designs for the curriculum. First efforts during the curriculum reform movement of the past decade were put into new designs for high school curricula. In the past few years increasing attention has been given to the elementary school curriculum. This book has been prepared to give an overview of new designs that have been proposed for different areas of the curriculum in the elementary school.

In this chapter attention is given to selected aspects of the foundations of curriculum development. In recent years the disciplines have been moved to the forefront as the core foundation of curriculum planning. The social and philosophical foundation and the psychological foundation have been viewed in the main as supplementary or facilitating foundations of planning. For example, new programs in mathematics education, science education, and other areas have been developed without the traditional prior analysis of social change, child development, learning, and the like. However, as instructional problems have been encountered, systematic attention has by necessity been given to social and psychological considerations. The dominant view appears to be to get the subject right in terms of structural components and then to draw on other sources of knowledge to complete curriculum planning. It is reasonable, therefore, to begin with classifications of knowledge and the structure of disciplines. Next, attention is directed to other foundations of curriculum development. Third, attention is given to the procedural and organizational aspects of curriculum planning. Finally, a model of major elements to consider in studying new designs for the elementary school curriculum is outlined.

CLASSIFICATIONS OF KNOWLEDGE

Man has created many things that set him apart from other living creatures. Without doubt the most distinctive of man's creations are the domains of knowledge that deal with the natural world in which man lives, the social world that he has organized, and the spiritual world that he has contemplated. Man uses these domains of knowledge to solve problems, to make plans, to appraise action, and to create new knowledge, new techniques, new institutions, new views of the spiritual realm, and new interpretations of experience. No other earthly creatures are comparable to man in this respect. Only man creates, structures, stores, interprets, applies, and communicates concepts and generalizations. Only man has developed the ability to abstract concepts from his experience and to use symbols to express thoughts and feelings. As man emerged and developed the ability to communicate, he started the long knowledge-building trek that has resulted in the complex structuring of ideas which is our heritage of knowledge today. Beginning with bits of knowledge gained through commonsense reactions to experience, man has acquired additional knowledge at a slow and arduous pace. Bound for centuries by superstition, dogmatism, and authoritarian traditions, he achieved a breakthrough during the scientific revolution. New modes of inquiry and new concepts were created. Diverse methods of inquiry and intricate symbolic systems have been devised. New branches of knowledge and a host of specializations have been developed. The discovery of knowledge has accelerated in geometric proportions, bringing the knowledge explosion of today, which is the forerunner of greater explosions in the future.

How to classify the burgeoning domains of knowledge is a problem of long standing to philosophers and of immediate concern to scholars and educational planners. Philosophers have explored relationships among various disciplines and between the sciences and the humanities. Scholars in various domains of knowledge have classified their disciplines in terms of research activities and applications to problems. Various classifications have been reviewed recently for curriculum planners (Elam, 1964; Ford & Pugno, 1964).

Early Classifications

Great philosophers of ancient times viewed knowledge in broad classifications (Elam, 1964). Plato viewed knowledge in two large classes—the intellectual and the visible. The intellectual included pure reason (real ideas) and understanding (hypothetical ideas). The visible included belief (things) and conjecture (images). Aristotle, for a second example, used three broad classifications: (1) theoretical knowledge in such fields as mathematics and science, (2) practical knowledge in such fields as politics and ethics, and (3) productive knowledge in such fields as the arts and engineering.

Modern Classifications

Modern man has classified knowledge in a variety of ways (Elam, 1964). Comte viewed the sciences in order of complexity, beginning with the least complex and moving to the most complex: mathematics, physics, chemistry, biology, and sociology. Scheler stressed three kinds of knowledge: knowledge for control, knowledge of nonmaterial culture, and knowledge for salvation.

More recently other classifications have been suggested. An economist (Machlup, 1962) has classified knowledge as follows: *practical*—useful in one's work; *intellectual*—for curiosity and liberal education; *small-talk* and *pastime* knowledge—stories, novels, games; *spiritual* knowledge—religion and salvation; and *unwanted* knowledge—outside one's interest, incidentally acquired. A psychologist (Cronbach, 1963) has classified knowledge as: *preverbal*—ideas, attitudes, and skills from firsthand experience; *verbal*—descriptions, prescriptions, principles, and systematized knowledge. A chemist (Cassidy, 1962) has made an insightful analysis of knowledge in terms of the humanities (arts) and the sciences. This analysis merits further discussion.

Humanities and Sciences

Cassidy (1962) suggested a way of viewing different branches of knowledge that reveals interrelationships. Chart 1–1 is an adaptation of Cassidy's schematization in which groups of disciplines and specific disciplines are placed on a continuum that includes the sciences and the humanities, but at the same time shows relationships between disciplines or groups of disciplines.

Beginning at the bottom of Chart 1–1 is mathematics, a discipline in its own right with many links to other disciplines, e.g., very close links to the sciences on the right and to logic on the left and intimate links to certain areas of philosophy. Moving to the right and up are physical sciences (e.g., physics, chemistry) ; these supply fundamental ideas that are useful in the biological sciences which follow them. Next are placed those behavioral sciences (branches of psychology and anthropology) which are closely related to the biological sciences. Next are other social sciences, such as social psychology, sociology, cultural anthropology, and human geography, which focus on the behavior of people in groups. Next is economics, a social science with a special focus on both theoretical and policy-making aspects of economic activities. Political science is placed next because of its many links to economics, to other social sciences, and to philosophy and history.

Chart 1–1.   The humanities and the sciences.

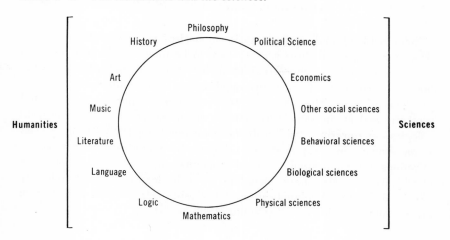

At the top is philosophy, a synoptic discipline that is linked in many ways to other disciplines. To the left and down the circle is history, a synoptic discipline that draws much material from other disciplines. Next in order are art, music, and literature, which deal with subjective expression of thoughts and feelings and have distinctive modes of expression, criticism, and underlying structures. Next is language, whose patterns are studied in detail by linguists employing systematic and rigorous modes of inquiry that are closely related to those employed by the logician.

Diversity within disciplines as well as differences between disciplines must be kept in mind when one reviews a chart of this type. For example, some material on mathematical models in economics and psychology should be placed near mathematics, some material in political science is rooted in the behavioral sciences, and some material on values, nature of man, and world view in the social sciences should be placed on the humanities side of the continuum.

Three Basic Activities

Cassidy (1962) has outlined three types of activity which are characteristic of scholars whether they be philosophers, artists, scientists, or technologists:

> *Analytic activities*: observing, collecting, naming, reporting, making distinctions, dividing, classifying

> *Synthetic activities*: seeking relationships among facts and theories, deriving trends, hypotheses, theories, and laws

> *Reduction to practice*: returning from the general to the particular or the theoretical to the practical, putting ideas to use, making applications

Some fields of study may at times emphasize one type of activity more than another, but all three activities are to be found in the disciplines as they are currently practiced. For example, philosophy is highly synthetic, but also analytic, and has many applications to other disciplines and to problems of man. The arts and the sciences are generally analytic and synthetic and at the same time have innumerable applications. The technologies—engineering, law, medicine, education, applied psychology, and so on—engage in many analytic and synthetic activities even though applications are emphasized. As Cassidy points out, research is emphasized in all university disciplines, including the technologies. And research may well be defined as "the application of analysis, synthesis, and reduction to practice in pioneering ways" (Cassidy, 1962, p. 25).

Among other points that Cassidy stresses is one that curriculum workers should not overlook. The difference between "science" and "technology" has been stressed in many recent projects, and primary attention has been given to "science." Cassidy shows that technology is important; he points out that reduction to practice, the making of applications, is a fundamental process of basic importance and that applications of mathematics, physics, jurisprudence, and other disciplines are made to a variety of situations. Involved in this process are individuals who work primarily in the basic disciplines as well as individuals in engineering, law, education, medicine, applied psychology, and other applied fields. Disciplined inquiry is brought to bear upon problems of application or reduction to practice. Scholars at work on curriculum projects should assist in identifying those aspects of reduction to practice that should be included in the curriculum. Without doubt this can be done without giving low priority to the development of fundamental concepts and ideas; it should be done in ways that contribute to a better understanding of key ideas. Certainly a judicious inclusion of material on reduction to practice should add dimensions of meaning to the *significance* of key concepts and ideas in technological development, in particular, and in human affairs, in general.

Classifications for Curriculum Planning

Classifications of knowledge have been developed in response to the need for considering the disciplines in direct relation to curriculum planning. Broudy (1954) discussed learning as an intellectual discipline and viewed methodology as a means of developing insights essential to perception, conception, and reasoning. He argued that if life is to be rational, students need knowledge of the physical and social environment and of their "psychic life," or "the life of the self." The natural sciences, the social sciences, and the humanities were suggested as the three corresponding fields of knowledge to be used in curriculum planning. Broudy made a special plea for attention to the humanities as sources of content related to the individual's integration of self.

Thelen (1960) stressed the importance of frames of reference derived from the disciplines. For example, the educated person should be able to ask fruitful questions; and this ability requires the development of frames of reference through the study of four domains of knowledge: the physical, biological, social, and subjective or humanistic. Each domain must be studied in its own terms with attention to its methods, concepts, and modes of thought. Thelen argued that students could attack social problems and issues by drawing upon frames of reference developed through the study of the disciplines.

Taking the position that the disciplines should be the primary source of curriculum content, Phenix (1964) outlined six realms of meaning that are useful in instructional planning:

> *Symbolics*: the arbitrary symbolic systems developed by man to express meaning; these systems include verbal language, mathematics, rhythmic patterns, rituals, and other nondiscursive symbolic forms
>
> *Empirics*: meanings based on observation and experimentation in the natural and social sciences; expressed as descriptions, generalizations, and theories which are recognized as probable empirical truths in accord with specified criteria for evidence, verification, and analysis
>
> *Aesthetics*: meanings derived subjectively and expressed through music, visual arts, literature, and arts of movement
>
> *Synnoetics*: personal or relational knowledge that is direct and concrete and may apply to oneself, to other people, or to things
>
> *Ethics*: moral meanings related to obligations and personal conduct
>
> *Synoptics*: integration of meanings from empirical, aesthetic, and synnoetic realms into comprehensive structures, as in history, philosophy, and religion

Phenix pointed out that every cognitive meaning has two aspects, quantity and quality. Three degrees of quantity are identified: singular—knowledge about single things; general—knowledge of a selected plurality; and comprehensive—knowledge of a totality. Three qualities of meaning are identified: fact—that which actually exists; form—imagined possibilities; and norm—the idea of what ought to be. The cartesian product of these two sets of characteristics results in nine categories of meaning (Phenix, 1964, pp. 26–28). These include the following:

> *General form*: applications of generalized symbols to express meanings—the realm of symbolics
>
> *General fact*: general forms related to the actual world—the realm of empirics
>
> *Singular fact*: self-knowledge or personalized knowledge—the realm of synnoetics

Singular form: meanings perceived through imagination and found in unique, particular objects—the realm of aesthetics

Singular norm: individual moral obligation, considerations of personal ethics

General norm: generalizations about moral conduct and principles—this category is combined with singular norm as the realm of ethics

Comprehensive fact: study of the actual world viewed as a totality—the field of history

Comprehensive form: concepts of wide generality applied to all fields of knowledge—philosophy

Comprehensive norm: religion—all three comprehensive categories are combined to form the realm of synoptics

Phenix suggested that all meanings in human experience can be classified in one of the six realms of meaning or as a combination of several realms. Human beings may be regarded essentially as creatures who are able to experience meanings. Since general education is viewed as the process of engendering essential meanings, acquisition of meaning is facilitated by the classification of the different realms. Once identified, these realms may be represented in the curriculum by content drawn from the disciplines which constitute the subrealms of each classification. Each of these disciplines contributes representative concepts and methods of inquiry which enable the learner to derive meanings in the manner characteristic of the particular realm.

Although the school is not the sole agency for the development of learning in all realms, it must make some provision for instruction in every realm at every level of schooling in order to ensure a full range of essential experiences for each learner. Phenix defined the well-educated person as one who has a high level of competence in all six realms of meaning. In addition to this provision for balance in the scope of the curriculum, he suggested that symbolics be given emphasis in the earlier school years because verbal, mathematical, and nondiscursive symbol systems are essential to expression in every other field. Learning in the synoptic fields is based upon integration of learnings in other realms and therefore would receive greater emphasis in the later years. Phenix's book provides a further discussion of ways in which an understanding of the realms of knowledge can be used in planning the scope and sequence of the curriculum and in designing learning experiences in different subjects. Appropriate reference will be made to each realm in the chapters that follow.

ACQUISITION OF KNOWLEDGE

Individuals acquire knowledge in several ways. One means is through contacts with others in which traditions, customs, and symbols are learned as a part of daily living. Another way is through instruction that is given in the home, the school, and other institutions. Another is through response to ideas that flow through mass media of communication. Still another is through individual travel, study, reflection, and contemplation. All these ways take man into the world of knowledge, but some men penetrate far more deeply than do other men.

Some individuals do not go far beyond the knowledge that is gained through elementary schooling and personal experience. Some advance beyond this through additional schooling and more varied experience. Still others push to the edge of knowledge in a given field and dedicate themselves to a lifetime of study and reflection.

Modern societies have made systematic arrangements that are designed to assure minimum levels of understanding of the realms of knowledge. The home, church, schools, and other institutions provide learning experiences that virtually take one from the cradle to the grave. Systematic programs of instruction are provided and standards have been set to guide the licensing of individuals who desire to work in various occupations and professions. Care is taken to establish minimum levels of competence that are deemed essential to the general welfare.

Schooling has assumed increasing importance as a means of providing systematic entry into the realms of knowledge. All levels of education have been given fundamental responsibilities; when linked together, the various levels provide an introduction in depth to organized branches of knowledge. Yet it is recognized that schooling is only an introduction, for the pursuit of knowledge is a lifelong task.

The realization that the pursuit of knowledge is a lifelong task has spurred recent changes in schooling. One of the most significant changes is the emphasis on competence in using conceptual schemes and methods of inquiry so that the individual can "go it on his own" and thus continue to learn throughout his lifetime. The goal is to develop the understandings and learning strategies that will enable the individual to reap greater benefits from personal experience, mass media, schooling, and other means of penetrating the domains of knowledge more deeply. Indeed, a further goal is to begin the development of the ability to extend man's knowledge far beyond the present horizon.

This new emphasis on developing the ability to inquire has forced a reconsideration of schooling as a systematic means of introducing individuals to domains of knowledge. The nature of knowledge has been restudied in order to get clues that might facilitate curriculum planning. The systematic ways in which man acquires, organizes, and uses knowledge have been examined to identify conceptual structures and methods of inquiry that should be used as foundations of instruction. High value has been placed on developing programs of instruction that are consistent in approach, methods, and styles of thought with those employed by scholars in the basic disciplines.

THE DISCIPLINES AS SOURCES OF STRUCTURE

Out of the discussion, study, and planning of ways to improve instruction has come a mode of curriculum development that relies heavily on basic disciplines. In current approaches, direct attention is given to a critical review of the disciplines on which the school subjects are based. The nature of knowledge and the structure of the disciplines are viewed in new ways. Fundamental elements of knowledge and modes of inquiry are discussed in terms that are directly related to curriculum planning (Elam, 1964). Ways of extending and structuring knowledge are being analyzed in order to derive implications for organizing instruction.

The search for knowledge of greatest worth has also taken a new turn. No longer is it merely a quest for new information. Rather, efforts are being made to specify structural components of disciplines that can be used to design areas of the curriculum. The specified structure is used to select content and to plan units of instruction. The intent is to develop curricula that are logically organized around those concepts, key ideas, and methods of inquiry which scholars believe to be most fundamental and powerful in their fields of specialization. In addition, attention is given to those disciplines which shed light on social and psychological foundations of the curriculum. Thus the disciplines are viewed as primary sources of data for curriculum planning.

Persuasive arguments have been advanced in support of building the curriculum on structural components derived from the disciplines (Bruner, 1960; Heath, 1964; Phenix, 1964; Rosenbloom, 1964). Economy of learning is enhanced by the focus on fundamental ideas and the use of content to develop key ideas. Relationships among ideas are highlighted as a sense of structure emerges through the use of concepts and generalizations in active inquiry. Fundamental ideas are brought to bear upon the solution of problems, and current problems are used to extend understanding of key ideas. Transfer of learning is facilitated as concepts and generalizations of broad applicability are stressed. Curricula may be kept up-to-date because of the close liaison with scholars in the basic disciplines. Teaching strategies and basic study skills may be closely linked with methods of inquiry drawn from the disciplines. Motivation may be heightened as the lure of discovery characteristic of the work of inquirers is made a part of instruction. By using techniques that are tested and yet are being continually improved, students can get a grasp of fundamental approaches to knowing and to the means by which knowledge is extended. Better articulation can be achieved between instruction in the schools and institutions of higher learning. The role of the school can be kept in sharper focus as emphasis is given to the cognitive and affective outcomes to be attained through the pursuit of knowledge via disciplined modes of inquiry.

Identifying the Structures of Disciplines

A key problem for curriculum builders is to specify the structures of the basic disciplines that are used to develop curricula in different school subjects. What is needed is an outline that can be used to identify the fundamental aspects of those disciplines which are used as a basis for structuring the curriculum.

Broudy (1954) has outlined the elements of a discipline that students should understand if they are to master it: (1) basic entities or units, such as events in history, atoms in physics; (2) relationships among the entities or units, such as chronology in history; (3) established facts or data; (4) tentative hypotheses formulated to account for facts not yet established; (5) hypotheses generally accepted by scholars in the field. Broudy argues that the mastery of these elements should be pursued in a manner that clarifies the total structure of the discipline.

Bruner's report (1960) on the conference of scholars of Woods Hole stresses the importance of relationships in defining structure. Concepts and principles are viewed as focal points which students can use to get a grasp of the structure of a subject, to guide inquiry, and to organize and retrieve information. Bruner stresses the importance of guiding students to discover how ideas are related. He insists that methods of inquiry used by the student should be the same as those used by scholars, for "it is easier for him to learn physics behaving like a physicist than doing something else" (Bruner, 1960, p. 120).

Foshay (1961) has proposed that direct attention be given to the disciplines in curriculum planning. He suggests that structure be defined in terms of the domain of study of each discipline, the methods, rules, and concepts used to handle data, and the history or traditions of the discipline. Foshay also urges that attention be given to basic social problems of current importance, pointing out that we must "have it both ways"—learning based on the disciplines and on problems.

Schwab (Elam, 1964) has discussed the syntactical and conceptual structures of disciplines. Syntactical structure includes the kinds of evidence, the techniques used to obtain data, the interpretation of data, and other processes of inquiry important in a discipline. Conceptual structure includes the concepts, principles, themes, generalizations, and other constructs that guide inquiry. Both structures are intimately intertwined in actual inquiry.

Bellack (1963) has also emphasized the importance of examining both the conceptual and the methodological dimensions of the disciplines. Key concepts are used to pose questions, frame hypotheses, and draw conclusions. There is a hierarchy of ideas in a discipline; some ideas are more explanatory than others. A variety of methods are used to investigate problems within the domain of a discipline; these should be examined to determine the styles of thought, logical processes, and other procedures that are employed. Also stressed by Bellack is the fact that there is a plurality of structures in most disciplines. This plurality is clearly evident in the diverse definitions of structure that have appeared in current curriculum materials.

A review of conceptions of the structure of disciplines has been prepared by King and Brownell (1966). In summary, they point out that a discipline may be viewed as a domain, a tradition, an expression of human imagination, and a community of persons. The major structural components are substantive, or conceptual, and methodological, or syntactical. A discipline is marked by specialized language, it has a heritage of literature and a network of communication, and scholars within a discipline take a valuative and affective stance.

An Operational Approach to Structure

The approach to structure in this book may be characterized as operational in the sense that examples are given of the actual ways in which structure is outlined in new curriculum materials. A search has been made of ways in which the substantive and inquiry dimensions of structure have been embedded in programs of instruction. In short, an attempt has been made to identify the varying interpretations of the concept "structure" and to give concrete examples of ways in which the concept has been implemented in curriculum development.

By way of introduction it may be pointed out that sets of concepts and generalizations are widely used to outline the substantive base of areas of the curriculum. Throughout the text the expression "concept clusters" is used to refer to illustrative sets of concepts in different subjects. A more detailed discussion of concept clusters is presented in the next chapter.

The methodological or inquiry dimensions of structure include a variety of methods and processes, ranging from observation and experimentation in the natural sciences to criticism and evaluation of human expression in the arts. From the wide array of methods and techniques extant in the disciplines have been selected those adjudged by curriculum developers in mathematics, the sciences, and other fields to be most useful in instruction. The examples included in different chapters vary from models of inquiry to specific techniques such as interviewing.

SOCIAL AND PHILOSOPHICAL FOUNDATIONS

Specialists in philosophy of education have made significant contributions to clarifying the relationships between the nature of knowledge and curriculum development. In fact, much of the material in the preceding section has been drawn from the writings of educational philosophers. Other aspects of the social and philosophical foundations need to be considered as new designs for the curriculum are studied.

A fairly consistent philosophical point of view underlies many new curriculum developments. High premium is placed on the role of knowledge in human affairs, the increasing need for depth of education in the disciplines, the changing nature of society and knowledge, and the importance of both scientific and humanistic approaches to the extension of knowledge. There is an emphasis on ways in which man creates conceptions of reality, builds structures of knowledge about reality, and makes interpretations of experience. Knowledge is viewed as dynamic and changing, and high value is placed on invention, discovery, and restructuring of knowledge in new patterns. Openness to experience and logical consistency are brought together and focused on the use of concepts to build knowledge out of interpreted experience.

An aspect of social change that has been given great attention is scientific advancement—the explosion of knowledge—and its impact on human affairs. Scientific literacy is regarded as essential to an understanding of contemporary issues and problems. Economic, political, and social problems are intimately related to scientific and technological developments. And the scientific study of human problems—local, national, and international—is gaining recognition as a critical need that must be given increasing emphasis at all levels of instruction (Educational Policies Commission, 1966).

At the same time, thoughtful consideration is given to other ways of knowing and studying, not only to the scientific. Insights, feelings, aspirations, and viewpoints expressed through humanistic studies and writings and through art and music are a part of a complete curriculum. The narrative of history and the changing and differing interpretations of events and processes provide understandings and appreciations that can be attained only in a complete curriculum, which includes the humanities and the arts. The humanities add dimensions to human understanding and are viewed as an important component of the disciplines foundation of curriculum planning.

The importance of *learning to live intelligently* in a rapidly changing world has been emphasized with a new look at what is most significant both for now and for the future. The search for the most significant learnings has led to the identification of durable ideas, durable in the sense of having lasting value in promoting continuing learning. A basic assumption is that the key concepts, themes, generalizations, models, and theories that form the structure of disciplines are the durable ideas that should be emphasized. And they should be emphasized in the context of how they are produced, how they have changed, and how they will continue to change. The goal is to enable students to develop the competencies needed to learn on their own in a self-directive manner. Significant knowledge for living in our times, therefore, consists in key concepts and generalizations supported by critically selected content and in a grasp of rational processes of inquiry that facilitate independent learning.

Isolated problems of students, life situations, incidents that arise in the community, and the like are not used as the basis for planning. Nor is first consideration given to technological issues and problems, life-adjustment needs of students, consumer problems, and trouble spots here and there throughout the world. Rather, the fundamentals of the disciplines, the elements that are basic to a grasp of the structure of disciplines, are given first consideration. As was pointed out earlier, practical applications of knowledge (reduction to practice) may well be included, but not as a starting point for curriculum planning.

Social conditions, values, and changes are included in some projects in the context of current issues and problems, such as population changes, urbanization, conservation problems, democratic values and processes, ideological conflicts, and international problems. Although one can find in proposed programs some topics and units that deal with vital social problems and issues, these are usually embedded in the context of the supporting disciplines; they are not approached as isolated problems and issues; they are considered in relation to concepts and key ideas drawn from the disciplines.

Still another way in which the social setting is utilized as a source of content may be found in the illustrations of contemporary situations that are selected to illumine concepts and main ideas from the disciplines. For example, in mathematics programs there may be problems of social significance in which students can use mathematical concepts that are being developed. Or in science and social science programs, socially significant situations may be used to extend and deepen concepts and generalizations.

But here again, primary emphasis is given to the basic concepts and generalizations, and socially significant situations are selected to extend the student's understanding of them.

PSYCHOLOGICAL FOUNDATIONS

Knowledge of child development and learning has not been used in traditional ways in recent curriculum development activities. For example, reviews of developmental characteristics with related implications for curriculum planning have not been made. The fact has forcibly been pointed out by psychologists that there is little in existing learning theories which is of help to curriculum builders (King & Brownell, 1966, pp. 106–107). And the critical need for a theory of instruction has been presented by a psychologist (Bruner, 1966b).

Scholars involved in projects have taken an experimental approach to the study of what and how students learn under various conditions. New materials have been devised, tried out in the classroom, and then revised in terms of findings gleaned from an analysis of teaching and learning problems. Thus, rather than serving as a source of authority regarding what should or should not be done in the instructional program, knowledge of child development and learning has been put to use in actual classroom studies of learning.

Certain notions or ideas about learning and how to promote it have emerged. The following appear to be reflected in the materials produced at several different centers:

1. **The traditional readiness concept of deferment of instruction until children mature is rejected in favor of the principle that pupils can be introduced to a subject as early as desired, provided it is presented properly and the pupils have the prerequisite background of experience.**

2. **Transfer of learning and future learning are enhanced when emphasis is given to basic concepts, generalizations, and processes of inquiry of wide applicability.**

3. **The guided discovery of relationships by the student results in more efficient and permanent learning than do didactic approaches in which children learn about the conclusions reached by others.**

4. **Interest and motivation may be generated through the lure of discovery within the subject itself, not in peripheral matters, as students are guided to raise questions, discover relationships, interpret findings, formulate principles, and engage in other aspects of inquiry.**

5. **Meaningful verbal learning involves the organizing or structuring of facts into conceptual schemes or systems that can be used to generate ideas, raise questions, or make new interpretations.**
6. **Inductive approaches are favored because of their value in promoting discovery through inquiry and in giving experience in formulating generalizations, but deductive approaches are evident in experiences designed to develop skill in explaining new facts, formulating hypotheses, making inferences, and interpreting information.**
7. **The study of selected topics in depth is more conducive to the discovery of relationships than is superficial coverage of masses of material.**
8. **Depth and breadth of learning are attained through recurring encounters with concepts, processes, theories, models, and generalizations on higher cognitive levels and in new contexts.**
9. **Learning is enhanced when there is conceptual and process continuity from unit to unit and throughout a program of instruction.**
10. **The solving of problems by students aids concept development, develops the ability to put principles to use, and leads to the development of higher-order principles.**
11. **Emphasis on the organizing or structuring of ideas helps students to develop a grasp of relationships, improves their ability to remember and retrieve ideas, provides a basis for generating new ideas, and promotes transfer of learning.**

A cognitive field theory is dominant in some materials; emphasis is given to a clear goal for the learner, the learner's perception of the problem, action and reinterpretation on the part of the learner, and continuing action, reinterpretation, and evaluation by the learner (Snygg, 1963). Thus goal, action, reaction, interpretation, subsequent action and reaction, and evaluation are stressed from the learner's point of view as he is guided to make discoveries. To be sure, there are many exceptions to this view of learning, especially in foreign language programs and in programmed materials in which a stimulus-response-reinforcement theory is dominant. However, in most programs there is agreement on the fundamental idea that, in order to learn, the student must act, react, and organize experience. Such an active and dynamic concept of learning is clearly evident even though there may be different explanations of motivation, conditions of learning, and behavior of the learner.

New interest has been shown in the work of Piaget (Bruner, 1960; Ripple & Rockcastle, 1964). In a few projects attention has been given to Piaget's stages of intellectual development that begin with sensory-motor and intuitive processes, move to concrete operations, and move on to formal operations. Although the age levels for various operations reported by Piaget have not been fully accepted, some programs in mathematics and science education stress intuitive approaches and concrete operations prior to formal operations. For example, intuitive approaches are typically used to develop concepts of sets and geometric figures in the primary grades. In general, however, Piaget's work seems to be more helpful as a source of ideas for investigation of intellectual development than as a source of ideas for curriculum planning.

Types of Learning

One of the most helpful developments has been the ordering of types of learning into a hierarchy which can be used to plan sequences of instruction directly related to the nature of teaching-learning tasks that confront curriculum planners. Rejecting the view that there is one type of learning such as stimulus-response or problem-solving learning, Gagné (1965) has outlined eight types and arranged them in a hierarchy as follows:

> *Signal learning*: development of a reflexive response to a signal by repeating a signal or stimulus in close proximity to an unconditioned stimulus; illustrated by responses to bells, automobile horns, and clap of hands to get children to pay attention
>
> *Stimulus-response learning*: referred to as trial-and-error, operant, or instrumental learning by some writers; illustrated by the initial learning of words
>
> *Motor chaining*: connection of a set of stimulus-response learnings; illustrated by printing letters, using science equipment, operating a model
>
> *Verbal chaining or association*: learning of chains of verbal associates as in oral language activities; illustrated by learning sequences of sentence patterns, memorizing verbal expressions, reciting a poem
>
> *Multiple-discrimination learning*: learning to make different responses to objects and events or to distinguish among them; illustrated by learning distinctions among shapes, colors, solids, liquids, and gases, or sets of words in a foreign language
>
> *Concept learning*: learning to put objects or events into a class and responding to them as a group; illustrated by learning such concepts as cell, striated muscle, family, or legislature

The learning of principles: learning to link concepts together to show relationships as in generalizations and formulas; illustrated by "Round things roll," "Resources are used to provide food, shelter, and clothing," and "Find the area of a rectangle by multiplying length times width"

Problem solving: using principles to attain a goal and thereby learning a higher-order principle that changes the learner's capability; illustrated by using principles of addition, subtraction, or other processes to solve arithmetical problems, principles of line, space, form, color, and texture to solve art problems, or principles of supply and demand to solve economic problems

Gagné stresses the point that learning is cumulative; prerequisite conditions within the learner and external to the learner must be considered. Sequences of instruction should be planned in hierarchies to provide for the attainment of specified terminal behavior. For example, if problem solving in science is to be developed, prerequisite principles, concepts basic to the principles, and so on back to prerequisite verbal associations and chains must be given attention in the sequence of instruction. Examples of how this may be done are presented in Gagné's book on *Conditions of Learning*. The chapter on Science Education in this volume contains illustrations of hierarchies of science processes drawn from a current project.

Cognitive Processes

New interest has been shown in the study of cognitive processes and their relationships to learning and teaching in different areas of the curriculum. General models of the structure of intellectual processes, cognitive processes in relation to teaching strategies, and cognitive tasks faced by students have been reviewed in an effort to improve instructional planning (LaGrone, 1964). Selected examples follow.

Guilford and Merrifield (1960) have proposed a model that includes processes or operations that range from cognition and memory to convergent production, divergent production, and evaluation. The ideas of convergent and divergent thinking have sparked interest in giving greater attention to the planning of learning experiences that lead to divergent thinking, when diversity and originality are prime objectives, and convergent thinking, when the objective is to focus on a key learning of central importance to a group of students. For example, divergent thinking may be emphasized in preliminary exploration of a problem and in various types of expressive activities in language and artistic expression. Convergent thinking may be emphasized in developing and extending key concepts and principles and in drawing conclusions from a set of data.

Taba (1965) has reported a study of three cognitive tasks: concept formation, the making of inferences and generalizations, and the use of generalizations or principles to provide explanations and to make predictions. Taba argues that concrete operations are essential to the attainment of high levels of cognition and that some students need far more concrete experience than do others. It is reported that less able students can develop high levels of abstract thinking if enough concrete experience is provided.

One of the most complete analyses of processes has been made in a current science project (AAAS, 1965). Basic processes emphasized in the primary grades are observing, classifying, using space/time relations, using numbers, communicating, measuring, inferring, and predicting. Integrated processes emphasized in the intermediate grades are formulating hypotheses, controlling variables, interpreting data, defining operationally, formulating models, and experimenting. All the processes are viewed as basic activities for the learning of science. A discussion of each of the processes is included in the chapter on Science Education. These processes have many applications to other subjects that should be explored by curriculum builders.

DEVELOPMENT AND ORGANIZATION OF NEW CURRICULA

The process of developing new curricula may be viewed in terms of two broad phases—development and implementation (Frazier, 1964). The development phase may be characterized as the basic planning and design stage of curriculum development. Points of view are clarified and assumptions are made about the role of the school, teaching, and learning; purposes are clarified; structure is defined in terms of key ideas and methods of inquiry; and content is selected in accord with the structure, purposes, and assumptions. The implementation phase may be characterized as completion and refinement of the instructional program. A critical review is made of available materials of instruction, new materials are prepared if available materials are inadequate, strategies of teaching are selected and tested, and principles and techniques of evaluation are designed and used to assess outcomes. These phases are interlinked, and the steps within them are not followed in an exact order. For example, consideration may be given to problems of teaching and evaluation at many points in both phases.

General Procedures

The overall steps of procedure seem to flow somewhat as follows in complete curriculum development programs that begin with original development of materials and conclude with adoption at the local level:

> **Staking out a domain of study to be given primary attention**
>
> **Identifying the underlying structure of content and processes and selecting elements to include in instructional materials**
>
> **Planning sequences of instruction for presenting content and processes**
>
> **Preparing blocks or units of instruction in which to present the planned sequences of instruction and devising means of assessing instructional outcomes**
>
> **Preparing related teacher's guides that include teaching strategies which are consistent with methods of inquiry stressed in the materials**
>
> **Engaging in a pilot tryout of materials and providing related in-service education of teachers**
>
> **Revising units, evaluation devices, and guides as a result of feedback from the pilot tryout**
>
> **Engaging in further tryout on a broader scale and providing related in-service education**
>
> **Revising of materials followed by commercial publication for wide-scale adoption at the local level**
>
> **Providing in-service education and supervision at the local level to promote effective use of the new program**

Several feedback loops and a variety of assessment procedures may be used to get a flow of evaluative data that can be used to improve instructional materials. Preliminary evaluation may be obtained by setting up a feedback loop in which experts—scholars, teachers, curriculum specialists, psychologists—examine materials and make suggestions for improvement. A major feedback loop may be set up to get a flow of suggestions from schools in which teachers, pupils, and curriculum workers try out the materials. A third feedback loop, a subsystem within the preceding one, includes the teacher and students and is used to modify and adapt materials as they are used in the instructional program. Motion pictures, tape recordings, detailed records, and the observation of teachers' problems and students' difficulties may be made as materials are used in the classroom. Tests, check lists, and other evaluative devices are designed and used to assess achievement of students after completion of individual exercises, units of instruction, and the overall program.

Roles

The roles of the many individuals involved in preparing new designs for the curriculum can be characterized in general terms even though there is considerable variation from project to project. A new development of special significance is the involvement of scholars in all phases of development from initial planning through in-service education. Specialists in the disciplines from colleges and universities play a dominant role in identifying the structural components of the curriculum and in organizing logical sequences of instruction. A common practice of scholars in several projects is to devise units of instruction, observe as the units are tried out in the classroom (some actually teach), and revise the units as feedback is obtained. Scholars also make contributions to the design of teaching strategies, the development of new instructional media, the preparation of evaluative devices, and the in-service education of teachers.

School personnel play a central role in the tryout of materials. Teachers carry the primary responsibility for testing materials in the classroom and providing feedback that can be used to revise materials. Curriculum coordinators and supervisors assume varied roles ranging from informing the staff about new materials to the coordination of classroom tryouts and the provision of in-service education.

Psychologists and specialists in education play varied roles ranging from sharing reviews of relevant studies on child development and learning to actual participation in the various phases of program development. They may contribute directly to the specification of objectives, organization of instructional sequences, design of teaching strategies, development of programs of evaluation, and education of teachers.

Principles and Patterns of Organization

A major difference between traditional and newer patterns of organization is in the degree of flexibility and latitude left to the teacher. In many current programs a definite sequence of instruction is proposed to develop the concepts, main ideas, modes of inquiry, and attitudes selected for study. The sequence is arranged in an order believed to be most efficient for promoting cumulative learning and the attainment of overall objectives of the program. Teachers at each level and for each unit of instruction are provided with guides and materials that are designed as part of a cohesive program of instruction. Training programs have been provided in some projects so that the teachers will use the materials properly. While optional or supplementary units may be suggested, provisions are made for basic units of instruction related to defined objectives, and optional units provide for the extension or enrichment of basic ideas. In short, a clear-cut pattern of organization is typical of many new curricula.

Another major difference in patterns of organization is to be found in the underlying rationale. In most new programs a direct analysis of the disciplines is made to identify the essentials to include in the curriculum. A pattern of organization is then structured in terms of the essential elements selected from the disciplines. It is not deemed necessary to devise a pattern of instruction around contemporary situations in which mathematics, natural sciences, or the social sciences are significant. Nor is it deemed necessary to devise a pattern in which current questions, interests, and problems of students are used as the basis for organization. Nor are community conditions, social functions, or persistent life situations used as a basis for organization. Rather the curriculum is organized to give direct attention to concepts, main ideas, and generalizations that are to be developed. A plan of organization based on such secondary analyses as are represented by the social functions, basic human activities, or day-to-day needs of the students diverts attention from the basic objectives of instruction. Furthermore, students may not obtain a grasp of the defined conceptual and inquiry components of structure when patterns of organization are based on secondary analyses. In summary, it appears to the authors that the following principles of organization are emphasized:

1. **The scope of instruction is defined in terms of the concepts, main ideas, processes, or generalizations to be developed.**
2. **The sequence of instruction is organized in a logical-psychological order found through the tryout of units in the classroom to be effective in providing for cumulative learning of key ideas, methods of inquiry, skills, and attitudes.**
3. **Required units of instruction are designed to facilitate the attainment of objectives, and optional or supplementary units for enrichment of learning may be provided.**

A variety of patterns of organization may be noted in the descriptions of programs presented in the following chapters. First, some are *predisciplinary* in that concepts and methods of inquiry are emphasized in general contexts, not in the context of a discipline or group of disciplines. For example, some units in science education include concepts of interaction, system, and measurement without reference to specific disciplines. Second, some programs are based primarily on a *single discipline*; this is true in mathematics, in some science programs, in the arts, and in social studies programs in which history, geography, or other fields are singled out for emphasis. Third, some programs are *multidisciplinary* in that topics or problems are approached from the view of several disciplines. For example, in the social studies a given country or region may be studied in terms of geographic conditions, historical development, economic activities, and cultural achievements. Fourth, some programs are *interdisciplinary* in that several specific disciplines may be fused around key topics, concepts, ideas, themes, or problems. For example, some science units draw from several basic sciences and some units in the social studies draw from several social sciences in an effort to relate content and methods of inquiry to selected key ideas.

A MODEL FOR STUDYING NEW DESIGNS FOR THE CURRICULUM

What is needed by curriculum workers is a model that can be used to study new developments. Such a model should include each of the major elements with which curriculum builders deal as they seek to improve instructional programs. Attention should be given to the following:

> **Foundation disciplines on which each area of the curriculum is based**
>
> **Examples of content and methods of inquiry drawn from the disciplines and structured for curriculum development**
>
> **Consideration of developmental characteristics of importance to instructional planning**
>
> **Objectives of instruction as viewed by curriculum developers**
>
> **Components of a complete program of instruction including major strands or scope of the program and sequences of instruction**
>
> **Teaching strategies suggested for implementing the program of instruction**
>
> **Basic guidelines for teachers to use in developing the program**
>
> **Guidelines for evaluating outcomes of instruction in both the cognitive and affective domains**
>
> **Guidelines for evaluating the instructional program in terms of each of the foregoing elements**

The model outlined above is proposed for use in analyzing new designs for the elementary school curriculum. Chapter 2 deals with each element in the model in detail. In subsequent chapters the model is used as a framework for presenting a review of new designs for areas of the curriculum.

REFERENCES

AAAS, Commission on Science Education. *Science: a process approach.* (3d experimental ed.) Washington, D.C.: American Association for the Advancement of Science, 1965. Hierarchies of processes charted in *An evaluation model and its applications.*

Almy, Millie. *Young Children's Thinking.* New York: Teachers College Press, Columbia University, 1966. Studies of selected aspects of Piaget's theories.

Association for Supervision and Curriculum Development. *Learning and mental health in the school.* Yearbook. Washington, D.C.: National Education Association, 1966. Chapters on mental health, learning and development, cognitive field theory, self-actualization, and related topics.

Ausubel, David P. *The psychology of meaningful verbal learning.* New York: Grune & Stratton, 1963. Discussion of psychological aspects of verbal learning in school.

Bellack, A. Structure in the social sciences. In G. Wesley Sowards (Ed.), *The social studies: curriculum proposals for the future.* Chicago: Scott, Foresman, 1963. A discussion of structure that is applicable to several subjects.

Broudy, Harry S. *Building a philosophy of education.* Englewood Cliffs, N.J.: Prentice-Hall, 1954. Pp. 144–196. Sections on elements to be mastered in any logically organized field or discipline.

Bruner, Jerome. *The process of education.* Cambridge, Mass.: Harvard, 1960. Views on structure and inquiry formulated after a conference on new curriculum developments.

Bruner, Jerome. (Ed.) *Learning about learning.* Washington, D.C.: Office of Education, OE–12019, 1966. (a) Report of a conference on attitudinal and affective, cognitive, and related aspects of learning.

Bruner, Jerome. *Toward a theory of instruction.* Cambridge, Mass.: Harvard, 1966. (b) Discussion of elements in a theory of instruction.

Cassidy, Harold C. *The sciences and the arts.* New York: Harper, 1962. Discussion of relationships between sciences and humanities.

Cronbach, Lee J. *Educational psychology.* New York: Harcourt, Brace, 1963. Pp. 58–63. Discussion of kinds of knowledge.

Educational Policies Commission. *The central purpose of American education.* Washington, D.C.: National Education Association, 1961. A review of earlier statements of purposes and a discussion of thinking ability as the central purpose.

Educational Policies Commission. *The spirit of science.* Washington, D.C.: National Education Association, 1966. A presentation of values that underlie rational inquiry.

Elam, Stanley. (Ed.) *Education and the structure of knowledge.* Chicago: Rand McNally, 1964. Essays on logical and psychological aspects of the structure of knowledge.

Ford, G. W., & Pugno, Lawrence. (Eds.) *The structure of knowledge and the curriculum.* Chicago: Rand McNally, 1964. Essays on structure in various disciplines.

Foshay, Arthur W. A modest proposal for the improvement of education, *Educ. Leadership,* May, 1961, **18**, 500–514. A review of values to be obtained by analyzing the disciplines.

Frazier, Alexander. Making use of national curriculum studies, *Educ. Leadership*, November, 1964, **22**, 101–106. Analysis of steps in developing new curriculum materials.

Gagné, Robert M. *The conditions of learning.* New York: Holt, 1965. Review of conditions for promoting eight types of learning.

Goodlad, John I. *School curriculum reform in the United States.* New York: Fund for the Advancement of Education, 1964. Review of early tendencies in the current reform of the curriculum.

Guilford, J. P., & Merrifield, P. R. *The structure of intellect model.* Los Angeles: University of Southern California Press, 1960. A model of contents, operations, and products with suggestions for uses of the model.

Heath, Robert W. (Ed.) *New curricula.* New York: Harper, 1964. Reviews and discussions of new curricula and curriculum change.

Jenkins, Gladys G., Schacter, Helen S., & Bauer, William W. *These are your children.* (2d ed.) Chicago: Scott, Foresman, 1966. Review of developmental characteristics from the earliest years through adolescence.

King, Arthur R., Jr., & Brownell, John A. *The curriculum and the disciplines of knowledge.* New York: Wiley, 1966. A theory of curriculum development in which the disciplines are viewed as of central importance.

LaGrone, Herbert F. (Dir.) *A proposal for the revision of the pre-service professional component of a program of teacher education.* Washington, D.C.: American Association of Colleges of Teacher Education, 1964. A review of teaching strategies, cognitive processes, and related matters.

Machlup, Fritz. *The production and distribution of knowledge in the United States.* Princeton, N.J.: Princeton, 1962. Analysis of knowledge and knowledge production by an economist.

National Society for the Study of Education. *Theories of learning and instruction.* Sixty-third Yearbook, Part I. Chicago: University of Chicago Press, 1964. Chapters on theories, verbal learning, motivation, creative thinking and problem solving, readiness, teaching, and instructional problems.

National Society for the Study of Education. *The changing American school.* Sixty-fifth Yearbook, Part II. Chicago: University of Chicago Press, 1966. Chapters on changing role of the teacher, the curriculum, guidance, instructional resources, school organization, and foundational aspects of education.

NEA Project on Instruction. *The scholars look at the schools.* Washington, D.C.: National Education Association, 1962. Review of structural components of disciplines.

NEA Project on Instruction. *Education in a changing society.* Washington, D.C.: National Education Association, 1963. (a) This and the following two booklets present principles and procedures for instructional planning.

NEA Project on Instruction. *Deciding what to teach.* Washington, D.C.: National Education Association, 1963. (b)

NEA Project on Instruction. *Planning and organizing for teaching.* Washington, D.C.: National Education Association, 1963. (c)

NEA Project on Instruction. *Schools for the 60's.* New York: McGraw-Hill, 1963. (d) Summary of recommendations for improving education in decision-making areas ranging from who should make them to improvement of materials.

Phenix, Philip H. Key concepts and the crisis of learning, *Teach. Coll. Rec.*, December, 1956, **57**, 137–143. Discussion of the need to focus on key concepts.

Phenix, Philip H. *Realms of meaning.* New York: McGraw-Hill, 1964. A philosophy of curriculum development for general education.

Ripple, Richard E., & Rockcastle, Verne N. (Eds.) *Piaget rediscovered.* Ithaca, N.Y.: School of Education, Cornell University, 1964. A report on the Piaget conferences at Cornell and the University of California, Berkeley.

Rosenbloom, Paul D. (Ed.) *Modern viewpoints in the curriculum.* New York: McGraw-Hill, 1964. Report of a conference on new curriculum developments.

Snygg, Donald. A learning theory for curriculum change. *Using current curriculum developments.* Washington, D.C.: Association for Supervision and Curriculum Development, 1963. Pp. 109–115. A cognitive field approach to learning with implications for curriculum planning.

Taba, Hilda. The teaching of thinking, *Elem. English*, May, 1965, **42**, 534–542. Report on a study of cognitive tasks faced by students in elementary schools.

Thelen, Herbert. *Education and the human quest.* New York: Harper, 1960. Pp. 31–75. Discussion of domains of knowledge.

Chapter Two

KEY COMPONENTS OF
NEW CURRICULUM DESIGNS

CHAPTERS 3 THROUGH 12 of this volume outline new designs in all areas of the elementary school curriculum. In the contemporary and emerging elementary curriculum, attention is devoted primarily to the realms of symbolics, empirics, and aesthetics. Language arts, reading, foreign language, and elementary mathematics represent the realm of symbolics. Science education and social sciences education are in the realm of empirics. Health education falls within two realms, empirics because of its forms of inquiry and aesthetics because of its close relation to physical education, which is firmly in the latter realm because it is concerned with the arts of movement (Phenix, 1964, p. 166). Art and music education are within the aesthetic realm, and, as if to close the circle, creative written expression and the study of literature are also classified within aesthetics.

However, the other three realms of meaning are also represented in the curriculum. Health education and physical education contribute understandings which are within the realm of synnoetics. So too, in a less direct manner, fall understandings in social sciences education which are derived from studies related to considerations of psychology and social psychology. Of course, as Phenix (1964, p. 277) suggests, the school contributes to synnoetic knowledge primarily through social activities and guidance counseling. Ethics, while not represented in a formal study of moral problems in the elementary school, is nonetheless a pervasive concern in the curriculum, as the child is involved daily in processes of value formation and decision making in every area of his studies, as well as in his co-curricular activities. The realm of synoptics is represented by studies of history within social sciences education.

The preceding chapter presented a model for studying new designs for the curriculum. The sequence of elements in the model is the same (with occasional minor variations) as the order of sections in each curriculum area chapter. By discussing each element of the curriculum-study model, this chapter provides an introduction to the chapters that follow.

FOUNDATION DISCIPLINES

In the preceding chapter, particularly in the section on "The Disciplines as Sources of Structure," the authors have indicated the increasing emphasis today upon the disciplines as basic sources for the content, scope, sequence, and teaching-learning strategies of new curriculum designs for the elementary school.

In some areas, certain disciplines contribute content and modes of inquiry from a broad range within the scope of the discipline. Such are the contributions of the various branches of mathematics to elementary mathematics; the physical and life sciences to science education; geography, history, and the social sciences to social sciences education; linguistics to learnings in foreign language and English language arts; and knowledge from the visual and musical arts to art and music education.

Other disciplines provide content and modes of inquiry less directly, or to a more limited extent, but are nonetheless foundational. Examples are the contributions of mathematics to science education; mechanics and optics (branches of physics) to art education; mechanics and physiology to physical education; medical sciences and public health to health education; and rhetoric, calligraphy, and etymology to the language arts.

Disciplines such as history, sociology, and anthropology may be considered foundational to many of the curriculum areas because they can provide historical and contemporary perspective in regard to the place and function of the curriculum area in other societies, as well as in our own.

It will be noted that a particular discipline or an applied field of knowledge may be foundational to more than one curriculum area, although not necessarily to the same extent in each case. Exceptions to this are a discipline and an applied field which contribute substantially to every curriculum area: psychology and education. Psychology contributes knowledge of child growth and development and theories of learning. Education provides instructional theory and the curriculum-planning strategies which constitute the means whereby all the other foundational disciplines are drawn upon, and drawn together, to create the elementary curriculum.

Three basic activities suggested by Cassidy are outlined in the preceding chapter in the section on "Classifications of Knowledge." Teachers and curriculum workers should note, in descriptions in the following chapters, the many ways in which new curriculum projects and designs provide experiences for children in analytic and synthetic activities and in activities in the category of reduction to practice. Indeed, these three categories of activities are basic, not only to the foundational disciplines, but to every area of the elementary curriculum.

Concepts, Concept Clusters, and Generalizations

The basic building blocks of the substantive aspects of structure include concepts, concept clusters, and generalizations. Concepts and generalizations have been used for years by curriculum workers, and they are used extensively in newly developed materials, because they constitute the essence or basic substance of what is taught. Concepts are categories or classifications, abstractions that apply to a class or group of objects or activities that have certain qualities in common. Generalizations are statements of broad applicability that indicate the relationships between concepts (Brownell & Hendrickson, 1950). Concepts and generalizations serve as centers for organizing facts and data in a form that sets forth relationships. They also serve as tools of inquiry, used to formulate questions and hypotheses to guide problem solving, experimentation, or the analysis of source materials. These functions are enhanced when concept clusters are utilized.

In between concepts and generalizations may be noted *sets* or *groupings* of concepts which the authors call *concept clusters*. A concept cluster is a set consisting of a basic or root concept and the concepts that are related to it and are needed to give the root depth and breadth of meaning.

Scholars in the various disciplines use concept clusters as a means of bringing related concepts together. For example, an earth scientist uses the concept cluster, "types of rock": metamorphic, sedimentary, igneous. Economists typically use "functions of money": medium of exchange, standard of value, store of value, standard for deferred payments. A music critic uses "elements of music": rhythm, melody, harmony. The way in which concepts are clustered or grouped together in curriculum project materials and courses of study indicates the relationships of basic ideas. Therefore, clusters help to indicate the scope of the teaching task in a given teaching episode. For example, a basic concept, such as "major landforms" or "factors in production," is almost always linked with related concepts as shown in the following examples:

> *Major landforms*: **plains, hills, plateaus, mountains**
>
> *Factors of production*: **land, labor, capital, management, government**

The authors believe that curriculum planning and teaching are greatly improved as concepts are brought together into clusters and used to devise instructional materials and teaching guides. In fact, a hallmark of the current movement is the manner in which sets of related concepts are used to structure materials for both teachers and students. Teachers and curriculum planners who make note of clusters of concepts will be alerted to the various dimensions of basic concepts that must be taught. Incomplete relationships of concepts, which the authors have found in some teaching materials, can lead to incomplete or erroneous learnings. For example, each of the concepts related to "factors of production" needs to be learned if the total concept is to be understood. If even one important factor of production is omitted, the root concept will be lacking in essential meaning.

This consideration brings up another key point: concept clusters enable one to examine the most important or essential factors or aspects of a problem, question, or situation. New project materials, current textbooks, units of study, and courses of study contain the concept clusters that the producers believed to be most important. To take the example cited above, if a student is led to consider only two of the factors of production, say, labor and capital, he will obviously only examine a segment of the problem in contrast to the student who considers all factors. With this point in mind, curriculum workers should identify, in source materials, the clusters that are most important in designing the instructional program.

Concept clusters can facilitate completeness of learning in another way as well. It should be borne in mind that although an essential cluster may be clearly identified, it may not be feasible or even possible for the learner to encounter the total set of concepts all at the same time. If attention is given to clusters, it is possible to design sequences of instruction that include basic components of key concepts in an order that is eventually productive of complete learning. For example, the cluster of factors in "climate" may begin with temperature and precipitation as fundamental factors. Later as various land areas are studied, such factors as elevation, latitude, mountain systems, winds, and ocean currents may be considered to round out the cluster and provide a model for studying the climate of different regions. By sequencing instruction, one can begin with simple models that fit a given situation and add dimensions as they are needed for more complex situations.

In fact, concept clusters are used by scholars and students alike as conceptual models for studying a variety of topics in every discipline and curriculum area, as will be illustrated in the chapters that follow. The use of concept clusters as a teaching-learning strategy is further discussed in this chapter in the section on "Teaching Strategies." A key point here is that concept clusters are not absolutes to be memorized and treasured for their own sake. They are sets of concepts which are selected and used to guide study and inquiry, and they are adapted and changed to serve changing purposes of inquiry.

As defined by the authors, concept clusters consist of two or more concepts at the same level of generality or inclusiveness which combine to define a basic concept at a higher level of inclusiveness. Ausubel (1964) described relationships of concepts in a hierarchical sequence, beginning with those at the most generalized and inclusive level, moving forward to less inclusive subconcepts, and ultimately extending to specific factual data. He suggested that the teacher may present concepts to the learner which are at a more inclusive level than the learning material he is about to encounter. These concepts, presented in an expository manner, serve as organizers of new material and constitute a conceptual framework within which the more specific data may be subsumed. Ausubel points out that this expository and deductive strategy for introduction and use of concepts promotes efficiency of learning effort and facilitates both initial learning and retention by providing a meaningful framework for new learning material. Both concept clusters and hierarchies of concepts serve as organizers for knowledge in the manner described by Ausubel.

In the discussion by Ausubel, attention was concentrated on the use of concepts in an expository strategy for receptive learning. In addition, concept clusters and hierarchies can serve to organize knowledge when they are built up by the learner on an inductive basis and are encountered in a sequence that progresses from specific data to more and more inclusive concepts. Teaching strategies described as "discovery" procedures develop clusters as inquiry tools in a primarily inductive manner. Other strategies may combine expository presentation and discovery encounters by providing exploration experiences that precede and application experiences that follow the expository introduction of the "invention" or relevant concepts. Examples of these types of strategies will be found in the following chapters.

Because sets of concepts are selected as inquiry tools in differing situations and by different scholars, one may find differences in clusters chosen by scholars in a particular field. Some economists define "factors of production" as land, labor, and capital, whereas others add entrepreneurship, and still others add government. Furthermore, clusters may be changed from situation to situation in order to provide the analytical tools that are useful in exploring questions or analyzing problems. A sociologist may use values, norms, and sanctions in one situation and norms, sanctions, and roles in another. Teachers should recognize this fluidity and flexibility of concept clustering and should provide students with opportunities to discover the reasoning behind such changes.

In addition to serving as organizers of understandings and tools of inquiry, some clusters, such as those given in the chapters on foreign language and physical education, serve to guide the teacher by indicating sequences of learning experiences or relationships of activities.

Generalizations drawn from the disciplines are also used in these ways. The generalization "Living things are adapted by structure and function to their environment" serves to organize content in science education, while the generalization "The sentence is the smallest unit of full expression" guides the language arts teacher's development of learning activities. In the chapters that follow, both concept clusters and generalizations from different disciplines are presented. These are given as examples to alert curriculum workers to the need to search out others in current materials.

Modes of Inquiry

The syntactic aspects of a discipline are its characteristic modes of inquiry. These may be described in terms of the nature and sources of data, techniques of data gathering, processing, and recording, and the instruments and conceptual models used. The scientist uses controlled experiments as one of his inquiry modes; the historian uses internal and external analysis of documents; the geographer records his data in maps, globes, and charts; the painter combines elements of visual art into unique forms of expression. While each discipline has its own set of inquiry modes, some specific techniques may be utilized by several disciplines. The scientist, mathematician, and geographer all use forms of measurement to gather and classify data. Social scientists, scientists, mathematicians, and linguists may use charts and graphs to organize and examine relationships of data.

Instruction in some elementary school subjects is carried out in a manner that is close to the structure of the foundational discipline. In the field of visual arts, for example, the child develops his interests and skills in the same manner as the adult artist—by actual practice, exploration of art elements, and development of refined standards based on principles of good design. There is no other way for the child to "learn art" than to act like an artist. In many other subject areas, the child all too often is not given the opportunity to use characterisic modes of inquiry to reach his own conclusions. Instead, he is given facts and information; he is told, or reads, conclusions. New curriculum designs are drawn upon the premise that the modes of inquiry of a discipline may be utilized by elementary school students both as a means of acquiring important understandings in a particular field and as a means of acquiring learning techniques that enable the student to extend his understanding in new situations. The curriculum designs described in the following chapters encourage children to practice thinking skills, engage in various inquiry activities, and develop independence in learning; they do this by incorporating into curriculum materials guidelines for appropriate learning experiences drawn from the modes of inquiry of relevant disciplines.

CONTENT AND INQUIRY STRUCTURED FOR CURRICULUM DEVELOPMENT

An important characteristic of new curriculum designs is that they draw upon the substantive and syntactic structure of foundational disciplines for the framework and implementation of the elementary curriculum. However, much variation will be found in the structural scope of different projects and designs, as well as in the level of structure represented in curriculum materials.

Some projects and units of study utilize a structure at the level of clusters of concepts drawn from the disciplines. Examples include the project of the *Syracuse Social Studies Curriculum Center* found in Chapter 8, and the *Unit on Human Physiology* in Chapter 7.

Selected generalizations from foundational disciplines provide another level of structure. The health education project outlined by Sliepcevich (Chapter 9) is one example. Others include the social studies programs of California, New York City, and Wisconsin found in Chapter 8. Each generalization includes, or is built upon, concepts and concept clusters.

In some cases, structure is reflected in the definition of broad strands which run through the total program. These strands serve as a third level of organization, and relevant generalizations are grouped within each strand. The California proposals in science and programs in mathematics education, Chapters 6 and 7, exemplify this approach.

At still another level, proposed programs reflect a more completely defined structure of a foundational discipline. For example, the structures diagramed in Chapters 3, 11, and 12 describe not only the structures of language, visual arts, and music, but the content and inquiry-based learning experiences of the elementary curriculum as well.

Although described in the preceding paragraphs in terms of their levels of substantive structure or content organization, the curriculum designs cited above and the others given in the following chapters do, of course, include syntactic aspects in their materials. A program that, unlike most others, uses syntactic structure to organize both content and learning experiences is exemplified by *Science: A Process Approach*, described in Chapter 7.

DEVELOPMENTAL STAGES AND THE CURRICULUM

Considerations of child growth and development are essential to curriculum planning in every area. Educators distinguish, however, between developmental stages which are primarily a function of physiological and psychological maturity and those which are primarily cognitive and experiential and may be a function of planned educational experiences.

The more completely stages of physiological and psychological development are described and the more accurately teachers are able to note the developmental characteristics of their pupils, the more effectively can provision be made for learning experiences suitable to the child's needs at a particular level and his needs for growth toward successive stages. It should be recognized that such stages or levels are only descriptive points that reflect changes in a continuum of growth and behavior patterns. While a given stage may be descriptive of the general characteristics of a group of children, not all individuals in the group will be at the same point in the continuum.

Chapter 10 on Physical Education outlines developmental characteristics of children relevant to the elementary program. Developmental stages of perception and expression in the visual arts have been defined by several experts and are outlined in Chapter 11 on Art Education.

Physical and psychological growth are factors which have an influence on the child's early language-learning experiences. In addition, the child's readiness for specific language learnings is affected by his prior language experience and conceptual understandings. Today readiness for language learnings, as well as readiness in other subject areas, is not regarded as a fixed condition to be awaited, but as succeeding stages of learning ability to be developed through appropriate curricular and co-curricular experiences.

It is also recognized that language learnings, as skills, must be acquired in a developmental sequence, as is the case with physical skills. Therefore, experts in language learning have outlined sequential stages of language development which are described in Chapters 3 and 4 on Language Arts and Reading.

In most of the areas of the elementary curriculum, educators believe that readiness for specific learnings is primarily a function of the curriculum, not of the child's growth. They suggest that almost any concept or topic can be taught at any grade level, provided that it is conveyed in terms appropriate to the child's level of understanding and that instruction is paced in accord with his attention and comprehension span. In foreign language instruction, elementary mathematics, music, social sciences, science, and health education, it is becoming increasingly more tenuous to assert that a specific topic must be deferred to a specific grade level on the basis of knowledge of physiological and mental growth. Instead, the trend is to explore instructional possibilities. This is frequently done through the use of new curriculum projects. In new curriculum designs, almost any topic may appear at any grade level, but the complexity of understandings developed, the amount of time allotted, and the specific learning activities employed vary in accord with the general learning characteristics of children at each level.

In place of the developmental stages outlined in the chapters on language arts, reading, mathematics, physical education, and art, examples of curriculum sequences given in the other curriculum chapters are based on the logical-psychological structure of content and inquiry skills as these have been worked out by scholars and curriculum producers. While charts of these sequences indicate suggested or practiced grade-level placements, it should be borne in mind that these are merely illustrative. Although the sequential order of related skills and topics may be fixed, the length of time for a sequence to be completed depends upon the grade level at which it is begun. As an illustration, the California foreign language program (1962) is described in terms of four successive phases of learning. Phase 1, the preliminary and primarily audio-lingual stage, may require three or four years if begun in the intermediate grades of the elementary school, but is completed within a year if begun in the first year of high school.

OBJECTIVES OF INSTRUCTION

The preceding chapter, in discussing the foundations of the curriculum, highlights underlying conditions provoking changes in education today. The knowledge explosion and the increased expression of needs for "literacy" in science, mathematics, foreign language, and the arts have created problems of curriculum priorities and content selection. One attempt to cope with these problems is reflected in an objective that is receiving increasing attention: learning how to learn. To implement this objective in every area of the elementary curriculum, emphasis is being placed on the use of learning techniques that have always been effective and are now augmented by the use of inquiry procedures adapted from the inquiry modes of the disciplines. Related to this is another important objective: the development of understandings consistent with the structure of foundation disciplines.

These two comparatively new objectives have been added to long-standing objectives relating to the development of effective citizenship, vocational and academic competence, ethical character, and mental and physical health. In many statements of purposes in new curriculum designs, emphasis is weighted toward the newer goals, although the others are not neglected.

But perhaps greatest prominence is being given to an objective which is considered fundamental to all the others. The primary purpose of education, the development of man's rational power, as expressed by the Educational Policies Commission (1961), is a central objective in many recent curriculum designs. The emphasis placed on this objective is the result of recognition that attainment of all the other goals of education is enhanced and facilitated when the child's rational powers are developed to the fullest extent of his capacity.

Statements of instructional objectives in recent curriculum designs emphasize the following purposes:

> **To develop concepts, main ideas, and generalizations identified by scholars as basic to understanding the structure of the disciplines**
>
> **To develop insight into processes of investigation used by scholars in the various disciplines**
>
> **To develop attitudes and appreciations related to the styles of thought and rational methods employed by scholars in the disciplines**
>
> **To develop independent study skills in order to promote lifelong learning**

Notice that content, processes, skills, and attitudes are included, but in each instance they are primarily related to the disciplines, not to utilitarian applications or to current issues and problems outside the disciplines. The underlying principle is that the study of selected units in depth gives students a grasp of fundamental learning that promotes future learning in a field of study and can be put to use in a variety of situations. In contrast, emphasis on applications and other peripheral elements results in the learning of isolated bits of knowledge without a grasp of basic ideas in a given field of study. Furthermore, if purposes such as those listed above are kept in view at each level of instruction, understandings, skills, and attitudes are brought to higher levels of development in a cohesive program of instruction. Thus, objectives become useful in planning developmental programs of instruction and teachers do not become sidetracked by objectives unrelated to the central core of instruction.

Specific objectives are identified in each curriculum area in the chapters that follow. Teachers and curriculum workers should be alert to statements of objectives in courses of study, curriculum projects, units of instruction, and sets of teaching materials.

COMPONENTS OF THE COMPLETE PROGRAM OF INSTRUCTION

The complete program of instruction is described in terms of its scope and sequence; the topics, problems, and skills included as its content and activities; and the sequential development and grade placement of learning experiences.

New curriculum designs tend to draw their structure from that of foundational disciplines. Therefore, descriptions of the scope of new programs are often synonymous with their organizational frameworks, as described above in the section on "Content and Inquiry Structured for Curriculum Development." In addition to programs previously cited for their use of concept clusters, generalizations, or strands as structural frameworks, some programs describe their scope in the form of broad categories. For example, a suggested language arts program is described in terms of language, literature, and composition (California, 1966). Many art education programs provide for development of expression, understanding of design concepts, art in daily living, art in other subjects, and art history and development of taste. Within each of these broad categories, scope may be more specifically described in terms of a number of strands, such as those outlined in the chapters on language arts, reading, and art education.

Scholars from the foundational disciplines have played a dominant role in curriculum design and the selection of content. Criteria for content selection are directly related to the objectives of the proposed program. Social utility in an everyday, practical sense, a major criterion in traditional programs, has not been used in newer programs. Rather, emphasis has been given to the following considerations:

1. **What concepts, main ideas, generalizations, and themes are essential to an understanding of the structure of this field of knowledge?**

2. **What content is needed to develop a logical and cohesive view of this field?**

3. **What content and activities are needed to develop insight into modes of inquiry that are used?**

4. **What content is needed to reveal limitations of existing knowledge, unsolved issues and problems, and topics in need of study?**

5. **What content and materials are needed to develop independent study skills, laboratory techniques, and critical-creative thinking abilities?**

6. **What content is needed to develop the attitudes, styles of thought, and appreciations characteristic of scholars in this field?**

The application of criteria such as these has led to the elimination of trivial material. Depth of understanding has been stressed rather than the coverage of material. Attempts have been made to provide a logical and cohesive view of the disciplines in a psychologically sound sequence. Processes of inquiry have been blended with concepts, models, and generalizations. The doubts, mistakes, false starts, and difficulties experienced by scholars have been included in some materials. Facts and ideas have been patterned into conceptual schemes or systems to highlight structure. Limitations of existing knowledge and processes of investigation also have been included in some curricula. Of special significance is the emphasis on the diversity and variety of inquiry methods used to discover knowledge, an emphasis in sharp contrast to that in which a single "scientific" method has been stressed. Most new curriculum designs are planned in a K-12 sequence. Primary purposes of this strategy are consistency of learnings, balance in content covered, and provision of sequential development of concepts, understandings, and skills at increasing levels of complexity from grade to grade. Rationales for the sequences of various programs are indicated above in the section on "Developmental Stages and the Curriculum." Bases for sequence determination may vary considerably within a curriculum area. One science sequence is based on the inherent relationships and complexity of inquiry processes (AAAS, 1965), while another sequence is related to stages of the child's intellectual development (Karplus & Thier, 1967).

TEACHING STRATEGIES

Changing objectives of education and development of new forms of instructional materials have brought attention to the techniques of instruction most effective in the implementation of new curriculum designs. Emphasis on dynamic instructional strategies that promote the development of thinking processes, creativity, use of inquiry techniques derived from the disciplines, and higher-level cognitive outcomes may be found in new curriculum designs. The intent in many programs is to provide experiences in which the students investigate, analyze, organize, synthesize, interpret, and formulate conclusions. Finding pat answers, following routine directions, memorizing facts and conclusions, and other dogmatic procedures are replaced by working to formulate one's own answer, devising procedures to solve problems, relating facts to concepts and theories, and using techniques of inquiry. The slavish following of a textbook is avoided and provision is made for the use of multiple materials especially designed to achieve stated objectives. The classroom is a laboratory for learning and the teacher's role is to guide learning in ways that are consistent with the production and discovery of knowledge in the disciplines.

A second instructional emphasis may be found in the increased use of independent learning activities. Although this emphasis is closely related to the use of modes of inquiry, attention should be called to certain skills that cut across the boundaries of the disciplines. For example, reading-study skills involved in locating, summarizing, organizing, and evaluating information are important in all areas of instruction. Similarly, skills in making observations, keeping records, using library resources, interpreting visual materials, evaluating sources of information, and reporting data are put to use in different subjects. Also important are the basic skills involved in defining problems, suggesting hypotheses, deciding on procedures to use, gathering and interpreting data, and formulating conclusions. Individual and small-group study are used to an increasing extent, particularly as materials are devised to facilitate such activities in the classroom and the school library or instructional materials center.

The methods recommended for use in many of the new programs are embedded in a mood or style that includes a spirit of inquiry, creativity, and discovery. Active questioning, hypothesizing, searching, structuring, interpreting, and generalizing are given high priority. Facts are related to key ideas, and generalizations are formulated by students as they organize and reorganize data which they have gathered to test hypotheses or answer critical questions.

The teacher's role is to stimulate and guide inquiry along the lines actually employed by scholars themselves. The difficulties, questions, mistakes, and problems that inevitably arise in making investigations are an important part of learning, and the teacher's role is to utilize these "set-backs" constructively, not to smooth the way or set up procedures to assure the correct answer or conclusion.

Instructional materials for teachers and students have been designed as interrelated elements of a coherent program. Multimedia approaches that include films, reports of original studies, programmed materials, documents, artifacts, pamphlets, monographs, readings, and other resources are used to take students far beyond the textbook. The intent is to organize materials in a system that is supportive of the rationale underlying the program of instruction. Materials and bibliographies that can be used in independent study are features of some programs and are used to extend learning in a variety of ways. Original source materials, such as documents, artifacts, and reports of investigations, are essential to the development of insight into modes of investigation. Special emphasis has been given to the production of materials that are truly reflective of scholars' views of the discipline.

Current efforts to analyze and classify teaching processes have resulted in differing proposals for descriptions of instructional activity. A broad distinction much discussed in recent years is the dichotomy of expository and hypothetical teaching styles (Bruner, 1962). The expository mode is one in which the instructor provides information or demonstrates skills and procedures while the learner responds by listening, following directions, or questioning the instructor in order to obtain further information along lines determined by the instructor. The hypothetical mode, sometimes referred to as the "discovery mode," is one in which the learner initiates more of the learning episodes while the instructor responds by providing needed information and directions and encouraging the learner's discovery by stimulating him to question and explore.

However, these distinctions are too broad to be descriptive of specific teaching-learning procedures. The terms "expository" and "discovery" are not definitive descriptions of single procedures, but rather characteristics which may be applied to a number of specific procedures. For example, the "telling" demonstration described in Chapter 7 on Science Education is an expository technique, whereas the "questing" demonstration is a discovery activity. Furthermore, exposition by the instructor and discovery by the learner may be elements of the same unified instructional episode or teaching strategy.

A more productive approach to definition of instructional procedures is to identify categories of educational objectives and then to group the procedures according to the objectives they implement. One such suggestion is the identification of four categories of objectives: acquisition of basic knowledge; development of thinking skills; development of attitudes, feelings, and sensitivities; and attainment of academic and social skills (Taba & Hills, 1965). In the category of thinking skills, three strategies for elementary social sciences education are described in detail: concept formation; interpreting, inferring, and generalizing; and application of principles. Taba and Hills also outline discussion techniques to be used in each of these strategies.

To be of use to curriculum workers and classroom teachers, such an approach needs to be expanded to include the full range of strategies used in all areas of the elementary curriculum. The authors find the following categories of objectives useful in relating and describing teaching strategies:

> *Problem solving*: objectives related to acquisition of understandings and development of requisite thinking and data-handling skills, as needed especially in areas of science, mathematics, social science, and health education
>
> *Skill development*: objectives related to attainment of specific skills such as reading, use of native and foreign languages, mathematical computation, and athletic skills
>
> *Creative expression*: objectives related to development of divergent expressive abilities in such areas as written and oral expression, visual arts, and music
>
> *Analytical and appreciative response*: objectives related to development of evaluative criteria for use by the pupil as a "consumer" of art, music, literature, and other expressive forms

In each of these categories of objectives, groups of related strategies may be described in terms of the specific outcomes they are designed to achieve, the patterns of teacher-pupil interactions involved, and the combinations of learning activities employed.

In some cases, distinctions between strategies and activities may seem difficult to draw, but this presents no problem if strategies are considered a unified set of selected activities designed to achieve specific cognitive and behavioral outcomes. Since a set sometimes has a single element, an activity such as a demonstration may be conducted as part of a broader strategy or it may constitute the total procedure of the learning episode.

Strategies identified in new curriculum designs include the following. Examples of these strategies are discussed in greater detail in the curriculum area chapters.

> *Problem-solving strategies*
> Using inquiry techniques: using concept clusters; using direct and primary data sources; using verbal data sources; using graphic and pictorial data sources; using simulated data sources
> Concept formation
> Generalizing

>   Hypothesizing
>   Using programmed materials
>
>   *Skill-development strategies*
>   Habituating a response
>   Guided exploration of skill alternatives
>   Using programmed materials
>
>   *Creative expression strategies*
>   Exploration of expressional elements
>   Production of creative work
>
>   *Analytical and appreciative response strategies*
>   Concept or criteria formation
>   Application of evaluative skills

GUIDELINES FOR IMPLEMENTING PROGRAMS OF INSTRUCTION

While teaching strategies provide guidance in specific teaching situations, new curriculum materials also give attention to the broader range of the classroom teacher's responsibilities. In each of the following chapters, these suggestions have been gathered into a section on "Guidelines for the Teacher." Although appropriate guidelines vary for each curriculum area, the following suggestions are found, in more specific terms, in all areas.

Be cognizant of new developments in the disciplines.   Teachers will understand the rationale of a new program and will be able to implement it more effectively if they keep abreast of developments in foundation disciplines as well as in the field of education.

Focus on important ideas.   It is helpful to be aware of all aspects of the structure or organization of the instructional program and to focus attention on the basic ideas that will serve to facilitate the learners' grasp of structure.

Try to recognize and meet individual learning needs.   Be alert to possibilities for modification of the amount of content or pace of experiences suitable to the differing needs of pupils within each class.

Stimulate pupils' independence in learning.   Encourage active and independent thinking by providing inductive learning experiences and varieties of investigative techniques.

Use questions to raise levels of thinking.   Promote active inquiry and higher levels of thought by using questions based on taxonomies of objectives.

Use inquiry techniques appropriate to each field.   Utilize suggestions in new curriculum designs for learning experiences and materials based on the inquiry modes of relevant disciplines.

Use a variety of appropriate materials.   Make selections and re-
quests well in advance to be sure of adequate instructional materials when
they are needed. Provide appropriate work space in the classroom as needed
for inquiry activities.

*Provide for continuous and cooperative evaluation of pupil
progress.*   Use evaluative instruments appropriate to the range of behavior implied in the program's objectives.

Develop positive attitudes.   Provide a classroom atmosphere that
encourages and values the participation and contributions of each pupil
and promotes the development of positive attitudes toward self, peers,
school experiences, and learning in general.

GUIDELINES FOR EVALUATION
OF INSTRUCTIONAL OUTCOMES

Shifts in objectives have impelled changes in the evaluation of students'
learning. Greater attention is given to higher-level cognitive outcomes,
such as the ability to formulate questions, the ability to conceptualize and
categorize data, make inferences, and interpret data, the ability to use
concepts as tools of inquiry, and the ability to use methods of inquiry. A
critical problem that has not yet been solved is the development of adequate measures of the ability to use methods of inquiry.

An approach which the authors believe to be valuable is the use of taxonomies of cognitive and affective objectives (Bloom, 1956; Krathwohl,
Bloom, & Masia, 1964) as guides for the development of questions and activities to be used in oral, written, or performance tests. The full descriptions of cognitive levels in the first taxonomy provide sample questions
and activities which involve appraisal of higher-level cognitive outcomes
and in some cases suggest items for evaluation of inquiry skills. To facilitate the teacher's use of this approach, examples of the use of the taxonomies are included in each of the following chapters. For ease of reference,
the taxonomy categories are briefly outlined below. However, utilization
of these categories in classroom evaluation will be more easily undertaken after examining the full taxonomy publications cited above.

Cognitive Domain

The categories are arranged according to level of increasing complexity,
with each category dependent on the preceding ones.

> *Knowledge*: specific terms and facts, conventions, trends, classi-
> fication and categories, criteria, methodologies, principles and
> generalizations, theories and structures; emphasis on knowl-
> edge but *not* application of knowledge

Comprehension: translation from one level of abstraction to another, from one symbolic form to another, from one verbal form to another; interpretation by relating parts, reordering ideas, making qualifications, and recognizing essentials; extrapolation by extension to past and future situations

Application: applying terms and concepts, generalizations, laws, models, criteria to new situations

Analysis: identifying elements, relationships, organizational principles

Synthesis: producing a unique communication, a plan or set of operations, a set of abstract relations

Evaluation: judgments in terms of internal evidence, judgments in terms of external criteria

Affective Domain

The categories are arranged in hierarchical order in terms of degree of internalization.

Receiving (attending): awareness, willingness to receive, controlled or selective attention

Responding: acquiescence in responding (compliance), willingness to respond, satisfaction in responding

Valueing: acceptance of a value, preference of a value, commitment (conviction)

Organization: conceptualization of a value, organization of a value system

Characterization by a value or value complex: generalized value set, characterization of the individual

Examples of these categories are given in each of the curriculum chapters.

Three important trends in evaluation are found in all curriculum areas. First, new programs stress the need for continuous evaluation of instructional outcomes to be integrated with long-term and daily instructional planning. Second, provision is urged for cooperative evaluation between teacher and pupil and for development of the pupil's skill in self-evaluation. Third, teachers are urged to obtain or devise evaluative instruments capable of measuring the broad range of outcomes beyond the level of acquisition of factual knowledge.

GUIDELINES FOR EVALUATION
OF THE INSTRUCTIONAL PROGRAM

In order to plan instructional programs and incorporate or adapt new curriculum designs and materials, teachers and curriculum workers will find it useful to develop evaluative criteria for the assessment of programs and projects in their proposed or implemented forms.

The following framework is suggested as a guide to elements of the program which should be given evaluative attention. In the curriculum chapters, more specific questions are provided for each category in the framework.

Foundations

Does the program draw upon relevant disciplines for content and instructional procedures?

Are appropriate developmental characteristics used to provide effective instruction and sequence of learnings?

Structure

Are content and inquiry methods consistent with the structure of relevant disciplines?

Is the conceptual structure outlined in a form suitable to students' comprehension?

Inquiry

Are appropriate inquiry techniques emphasized?

Objectives

Are objectives comprehensive, realistic, and clearly defined?

Complete program

Is the program planned and balanced in terms of the overall K-12 sequence?

Is the program designed to meet all appropriate objectives?

Teaching strategies

Are teaching strategies consistent with inquiry procedures of related disciplines?

Are opportunities provided for inductive development of understandings?

Pupil evaluation

Are provisions made for continuous, cooperative, and comprehensive evaluation of instructional outcomes?

Is constructive self-evaluation encouraged?

Program evaluation

Is provision made for continuous evaluation of the program and revision in the light of relevant developments in foundation disciplines as well as educational procedures?

Teacher education
Are pre-service and in-service programs suited to instructional procedures of new curriculum designs?
Are specialists available to assist teachers in planning instruction?
Are teachers involved in curriculum planning and evaluation?

REFERENCES

AAAS, Commission on Science Education. *Science: a process approach.* (3d experimental ed.) Washington, D.C.: American Association for the Advancement of Science, 1965. Outline of curriculum proposals.

Association for Supervision and Curriculum Development. *Theories of instruction.* Washington, D.C.: National Education Association, 1965. Brief summary of viewpoints on instruction.

Association for Supervision and Curriculum Development. *Evaluation as feedback and guide.* Yearbook. Washington, D.C.: National Education Association, 1967. Suggestions for replacement of grades, marks, tests, and credits with ongoing evaluation that encompasses all objectives and facilitates self-evaluation, effective teaching and learning, and curriculum decisions.

Ausubel, David P. Some psychological aspects of the structure of knowledge. *Education and the structure of knowledge.* Chicago: Rand McNally, 1964. A discussion of the hierarchical structure of the concepts of a discipline in a sequence of increasing inclusiveness or generality.

Bloom, Benjamin S. (Ed.) *The taxonomy of educational objectives: cognitive domain.* New York: McKay, 1956. Classification of objectives and examples of test items.

Brownell, William A., & Hendrickson, G. How children learn information, concepts, and generalizations. *Learning and instruction.* Forty-ninth Yearbook, Part I, National Society for the Study of Education. Chicago: University of Chicago Press, 1950. Definitions of "words," "concepts," "generalizations."

Bruner, Jerome S. *On knowing: essays for the left hand.* Cambridge, Mass.: Harvard, 1962. Chapter on "The Act of Discovery" discusses discovery in the learning process.

Buros, Oscar K. *The sixth mental measurements yearbook.* Highland Park, N.J.: Gryphon Press, 1965. Information on tests published between 1959 and 1964; reviews of earlier tests in preceding volumes. Reviews of intelligence and achievement tests.

California. *French: listening, speaking, reading, writing.* Sacramento: State Department of Education, Bulletin 31, No. 4, 1962. Description of sequential phases of foreign language learning.

California. State Advisory Committee for an English Framework. *Preliminary reports.* Sacramento: State Department of Education, 1966. Suggestions for a K-12 program of instruction.

Educational Policies Commission. *The central purpose of American education.* Washington, D.C.: National Education Association, 1961. Discussion of the development of thinking ability as the central purpose.

Karplus, Robert, & Thier, Herbert D. *A new look at elementary science.* Chicago: Rand McNally, 1967. Discussion of theory, procedures, and instructional materials in the Science Curriculum Improvement Study.

Krathwohl, David R., Bloom, Benjamin S., & Masia, Bertram S. *Taxonomy of educational objectives: affective domain.* New York: McKay, 1964. A classification of objectives and sample test items in the area of attitude and value development.

National Society for the Study of Education. *Theories of learning and instruction.* Sixty-third Yearbook, Part I. Chicago: University of Chicago Press, 1964. Chapters on theories, verbal learning, motivation, creative thinking and problem solving, readiness, teaching, and instructional problems.

Phenix, Philip H. *Realms of meaning.* New York: McGraw-Hill, 1964. A philosophy of curriculum development.

Taba, Hilda, & Hills, James L. *Teacher handbook for Contra Costa social studies, grades 1–6.* Hayward, Calif.: Rapid Printers and Lithographers, Inc., 1965. Descriptions of teaching strategies, including concept formation, generalizing and inferring, and application.

Chapter Three

LANGUAGE ARTS

L ANGUAGE IS DEFINED as a structured system of arbitrary vocal sounds and symbols used as communication. Language is human speech in both oral and written forms.

The language arts are the four modes of communication through human speech: speaking, listening, reading, and writing. These arts are part of the broad realm of symbolics in which there is a focus on general form (Phenix, 1964). Important concepts and generalizations that underlie language study are derived by scholars in the various foundation disciplines of language.

The structure of current language arts programs in the elementary school is defined in terms of three major aspects: the study of language structure, oral and written composition, and literature. The first two areas are considered in this chapter. Literature is considered in Chapter 4.

FOUNDATION DISCIPLINES

The fundamental discipline underlying the language arts is linguistics, the field of knowledge concerned with the nature and functioning of human language. Linguistics provides understanding of the structure of language, key concepts and generalizations about language, and modes of inquiry for the study of language. Two major branches of this discipline, semantics and psycholinguistics, contribute knowledge about word meanings and human language behavior. Other related language disciplines are etymology, the origins of word meanings; philology, a study of linguistic aspects of literature and of cultural and social documents; paleography, a study of origins of language; rhetoric and calligraphy, concerned respectively with the arts of verbal and graphic expression; and comparative literature, a study of written expression.

In addition to these linguistic disciplines, which contribute to the structure of the language arts, other disciplines, such as anthropology and history, contribute an understanding of the development of language; psychology and physiology contribute to an understanding of language-learning processes and the functions of sensory organs involved in communication; and the science of communication engineering applies its findings to the improvement of efficiency in communication. All these disciplines contribute to instructional aspects of the language arts curriculum.

Concepts and Concept Clusters

Linguistics, as the fundamental language discipline, is the source of many concepts and concept clusters germane to all areas of the language arts.

The fields of literary analysis, rhetoric, and calligraphy contribute to the areas of reading, speaking, and writing, respectively.

Examples of concept clusters in the various aspects of the language arts are as follows:

Reading and literature

myths	drama	fiction	reading for:
folktales	prose	nonfiction	information
fantasy	poetry	biography	directions
		autobiography	inferences

Reading and creative writing

metaphor	rhyme	synonym
simile	alliteration	homonym
imagery	meter	antonym
symbol		

Grammar

structure:	sentence	levels of usage:
phoneme	noun phrase	regional variations
morpheme	verb phrase	informal standard
tagmeme	clause	formal standard
		literary forms

article	subject	slots	preposition
adjective	predicate	movables	auxiliary
noun	object		modifier
verb			determiner
adverb			conjunction

Speech

dialect	pitch	modulation
accent	stress	enunciation
pronunciation	juncture	expression

Written language

letter	creative	originality
outline	functional	fluency
report		style

Spelling

phoneme	root	silent letters
morpheme	affix	diphthongs
grapheme	prefix	digraphs
	suffix	
	inflectional changes	

Handwriting

manuscript	slant
cursive	spacing
roman type	alignment
italics	letter form

Listening

purposes:	hearing
informational	listening
critical	auding
recreational	

Generalizations

Generalizations from foundation disciplines which are essential to language arts education include the following:

> Language is man's instrument for thinking and for social intercourse.
>
> Language is an arbitrary system of vocal symbols.
>
> Because it is an arbitrary system, language is subject to change.
>
> Written language is a secondary system of signs and symbols formed to represent vocal symbols.
>
> English is a structured language and must be described in terms of its system, which includes its phonology, morphology, and syntax.
>
> Pitch, stress, and juncture are part of the sound system of the language and help to convey meaning.
>
> Environment affects language habits and levels of language usage.
>
> Language is interwoven with all phases of thinking and learning processes.

INTERRELATIONSHIPS OF THE LANGUAGE ARTS

Comprehension of language structure underlies all four language arts. Skill in each area depends upon understanding of phoneme-grapheme correspondence, lexicon, and syntactical structure of the language.

The language arts are interrelated in developmental sequence, reciprocity of communication, and relationship to mental processes and behavior.

In developmental sequence, the infant first acquires language understanding through listening, and next begins to speak. Later, the child recognizes and utilizes the written representation of his oral language, as he learns to read and, soon after, to write. The primacy of use and comprehension of language in its spoken form continues throughout the child's successive language-learning experiences. He learns to speak by listening and imitating. The extent of his grasp of spoken language affects his ability to acquire skill in recognition, interpretation, and use of language in its graphic form. Throughout life, he is likely to deal with spoken language to a far greater extent than with written language. This implies a need for considerable attention to the development and application of listening and speaking skills in all the elementary grades.

Listening and speaking have a reciprocal relationship. In language communication, speakers address listeners, and listeners become listeners when they are attentive to speakers. Both listening and speaking are phonological skills; both are based on the phonological structure of language: meaningful sound patterns and sequences, lexicon, and syntax. Understanding of this structure enhances one's ability to listen and speak effectively. Auditory acuity, clarity of enunciation, accuracy of pronunciation, comprehension of sentence structure, organization of ideas, etc., are requisite to competence in both listening and speaking. This reciprocal relationship implies the desirability of providing instruction or practice in both skills simultaneously.

Reading and writing are commonly based on the graphological structure of language and are reciprocal as communication skills, although, unlike listening and speaking, the activities involved are not always simultaneous. Recognition of phoneme-grapheme correspondence, knowledge of written word formation (spelling), comprehension of sentence structure, and ability to organize ideas in paragraph, outline, and more complex literary forms are requisite to competence in both reading and writing.

The language arts are also interrelated in accordance with the child's behavioral and mental processes. Listening and reading are receptive forms of communication. Through these means, the child gains information. Similar comprehension skills are required of the child both as a listener and as a reader. In addition, much of the child's instruction in reading requires him to listen to directions, instructions, questions, and the oral reading of others. These two receptive language arts differ in pace. The child sets his own pace for reading, but must listen at the pace set by the speaker.

Speaking and writing are the expressive modes of language. Both areas require skill in organizing a meaningful sequence of words and ideas. Speech is the more fluid form of expression, with less structure of formal patterns than written expression. However, the communicative purposes of speech and writing are similar. Instruction in the common elements of the expressive or the receptive form will benefit both language arts in that form.

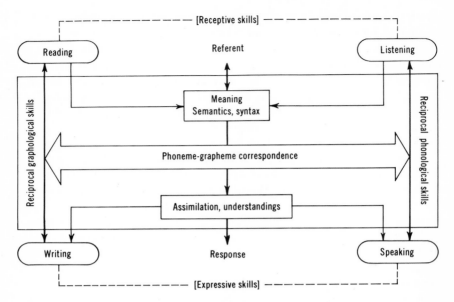

Chart 3–1.   A structure of the language arts.

Receptive language skills and referent objects or ideas provide information and meaning. Assimilation of ideas and understandings leads to response in thought and in expressive language skills. Processes within the rectangle (Chart 3–1) refer to the individual's mental processes in language activity.

An important area of difference in the four language arts is the child's command of vocabulary. In his preschool years the child has an extensive listening vocabulary. He understands far more words and sentence forms than he can utilize in his own oral expression. In the primary grades his speaking vocabulary is extended and exceeds his slowly developing vocabulary of recognized written words. As the child attains greater skill in reading, at the level of the upper elementary grades, his reading vocabulary becomes second in extent to his listening vocabulary, and both exceed his expressive vocabulary. In the early grades, experience with oral vocabulary leads to comprehension of written vocabulary. In the upper elementary grades, the child's oral and written vocabulary may be extended by words and meanings encountered in reading.

The child's progress in any language art depends upon his growth in the others, because of the many foundational elements, skills, and purposes common to all and because of the interrelationships outlined above. Instruction that facilitates improvement in one language art is likely to benefit the other three and to enhance the child's understanding of his language.

THE STRUCTURE OF LANGUAGE AND STRUCTURE IN THE LANGUAGE ARTS

Structure of Language

Linguistic scholars outline the structure of language in terms of the basic sound elements, meaning or conceptual elements, and structural principles of the language. This structure is illustrated in Chart 3–2.

Sound elements are the basis of a language, the recognizable sounds that convey meaning when expressed in specific patterns or sequences. Linguists identify between forty-three and forty-six distinct sound elements, or phonemes, in English. The twenty-six letters of the alphabet, certain letter combinations, and punctuation marks constitute the graphemes used to represent the phonemes of the English language.

Morphemes are basic elements of meaning in word structure. Roots, affixes, and inflectional changes are classes of morphemes. Morphemes may be described as expressing concepts on a continuum from concrete to abstract. Concrete concepts refer to objects, actions, and qualities, and are often expressed by roots of words. More abstract relational concepts may be expressed by affixes, inflectional changes, word sequence, or separate words.

Chart 3–2. A structure of language.

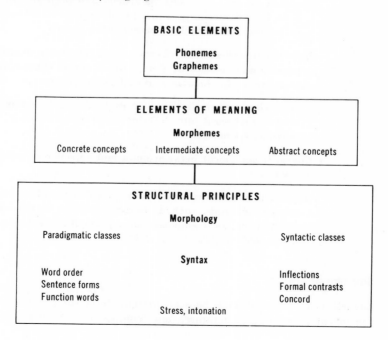

The structural principles of English are the essence of the language (Phenix, 1964, p. 66). These principles pertain to morphology, a classification of words according to their function and structural relationships, and syntax, conventional word patterns and relationships.

Current morphological classifications are not based on lexigraphic meanings of words, but rather on the basis of their function. Sapir (1921) suggests the division of words into two major classes. The paradigmatic classes include words that change inflectionally or by means of affix alterations, such as nouns (singular or plural), forms of personal pronouns, verbs, and adjectives. Other parts of speech which are not subject to change in form, such as adverbs, prepositions, and conjunctions, fall into syntactic classes on the basis of their use in the organization of word sequence, phrases, and sentences.

Syntax is the structure of word relationships, sets of principles which indicate conventional relationships that convey meaning, in such categories as the following:

> *Word order*: **meaningful sequences of words in phrases or clauses**
>
> *Sentence patterns*: **characteristic patterns of word sequence and varying levels of complexity of each pattern**
>
> *Function words*: **words such as articles and prepositions, having little lexical meaning, which in phrases and sentences serve to indicate relationships between other words**
>
> *Inflections*: **inflectional changes, such as those described in paradigmatic classes of words, which signal changes in word meaning, as in singular or plural nouns or cases of verbs**
>
> *Formal contrasts*: **inflectional or root-affix modifications which alter a root word into differing parts of speech, e.g., friend, friendly, friendless**
>
> *Concord*: **agreement between noun and adjective or subject and predicate**
>
> *Stress and intonation*: **sound patterns which signal meanings for groups of words, such as rising inflection at the end of a question or vocal emphasis on a particular word (e.g., "The boy is sick" or "The boy is sick")**

Structure of English

English as a discipline may be structured in terms of three interrelated components: language, literature, and composition (California, 1966;

	Language	Literature	Composition
Speaking	Developing effective skills in expression	Choral speaking, poetry, drama	Original oral and written expression
Writing		Literature as models for pupils' work	
Reading	Developing skill in comprehending written and oral language	Content for interest, taste; analysis of form, meaning	
Listening		Listening to poetry, drama	

Chart 3–3.   Relationships of structural components and processes of English.

Commission on English, 1965). The language component includes the sounds, the structural patterns, the symbols for representing sounds, and other elements. Literature includes nursery rhymes, folktales, legends, poems, prose fiction, drama, essays, biographies, and autobiographies. Composition includes thoughtful expression in oral and written form. These three components are intertwined in the instructional program that gives direct attention to the four basic communication processes: listening, speaking, reading, and writing.

Instruction in listening includes the experiences designed to develop the full spectrum of abilities ranging from informal to critical listening. Speaking includes conversation, discussion, oral reports, and other modes of oral expression. Reading includes experiences that range from the interpretation of symbols to critical analysis of literary works. Writing includes handwriting, spelling, and a variety of activities ranging from the composing of notes and reports to the creating of poems and other forms of literature. One way of showing the relationships among the structural components and the four processes is given in Chart 3–3.

Structure in the Language Arts

The structure of English may be conveyed to the pupil in two ways—as he learns *about* language and as he learns *to use* language. Oral and written language experiences in the curriculum provide practice in use of language and will be discussed later in this section. Oral and written use of language is primarily achieved through development of expressive skills, with comparatively little standardization of content. The oral and written aspects of language use are augmented in the instructional program by the more content-oriented aspects that enable the child to study his language

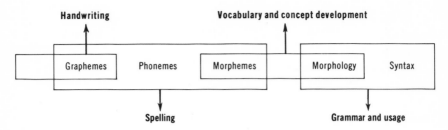

Chart 3–4. Relationships of language structure and instruction.

as a language—handwriting, spelling, vocabulary and concept development, and usage. Language structure may be conveyed through these instructional means as suggested in Chart 3–4.

Handwriting. Handwriting instruction enables the child to form conventional graphemes according to standards of legibility for effective communication. Graphological structure, as conveyed in the language arts curriculum, may be outlined in terms of the following:

Letter form		*Letter relationships*
vertical strokes	**circles**	**size: uniformity**
horizontal strokes	**curves**	**proportion**
slanted strokes	**loops**	**spacing**
compound curves		**slant**
clockwise strokes		**alignment**
counterclockwise strokes		**regular line quality**

These structural elements are foci of instruction. Specific attention is given to letter forms in the preliminary stages of handwriting instruction. In the next stages, attention is given to practice in meeting standards for each element in the formation of manuscript letters and numerals and in the formation and connection of cursive letters. Letters and numerals with similar form elements are usually grouped for instructional purposes, going from the simpler to the more complex or difficult forms.

Instruction in handwriting proceeds on the basis of such principles or generalizations as the following:

> **All letters and numerals in manuscript writing are made with straight lines, circles, or parts of circles.**
> **Writing of manuscript letters begins from the top of each letter.**
> **All letters are formed from left to right.**
> **Letter size is always uniform and proportionate; the lowercase a is the basic size unit.**

Inquiry and skill development make use of such modes as observation, analysis of model forms, comparison, deductive application of principles, and practice.

Spelling. Spelling instruction enables the child to group letters according to standard usage for efficient communication. The structural elements of language that pertain to spelling skill include concepts of phonemes, graphemes, and morphemes and generalizations relevant to phoneme-grapheme correspondence, letter combinations and sequences, regular inflectional or derivative changes in words, and syllabication.

Examples of generalizations are as follows:

> **The letter q is always followed by u in common English words.**
> **Proper nouns and most adjectives formed from proper nouns should begin with capital letters.**
> **Plurals of most nouns are formed by adding s to the singular. When the noun ends in s, x, sh, and ch, the plural is generally formed by adding es.**
> **Words of one syllable that end in a single consonant preceded by a single vowel double the final consonant when adding a suffix beginning with a vowel.**

Pupils may be guided toward discovery of generalizations on the basis of inductive analysis of several words that are already part of their reading vocabulary. Deductive application of generalizations may then be made to additional words. Other methods of inquiry and skill development include visual observation of word forms, analysis of model forms, comparison, visualization, writing, and memorization.

Vocabulary. Continuous vocabulary and concept development from the earliest elementary grades enables the child to understand and utilize the meaning of an increasing number of words and to acquire higher or more complex meanings and connotations of words and verbal concepts. These meanings are based upon concepts and generalizations of etymological and morphological structure.

Inquiry is conducted through such means as recall of experience, reference to word context, analysis of the morphemic elements and morphological function of words, application of definitions, and comparison with words in other languages.

Grammar and usage. The term *grammar* is most appropriately applied to the structural principles of language in the areas of morphology and syntax. Instruction in grammar in the elementary school is concerned with the teaching of the form and structure of sentences. Instruction in usage is the teaching of correctness and use of acceptable forms of words and phrases. Accepted levels or patterns of usage vary from one region or locale to another. The elements and idioms in usage instruction therefore tend to vary from one school situation to another. Grammatical instruction also varies in accordance with the referent grammatical structure —traditional (based on Latin grammatical forms), structural, or generative transformational grammar.

References containing linguists' descriptions of structural grammar and generative transformational grammar are listed at the end of the chapter. Both grammars are descriptive of English as it is expressed, primarily according to oral forms, and not in comparison with Latin models. Both grammars emphasize the primacy of the spoken form of English, and both identify model sentence forms which indicate the word-order patterns that convey meaning in English.

Structural grammar classifies words into two broad categories: the four open classes—nouns, verbs, adjectives, adverbs—which contain most of the words of the language, and several small, closed classes containing a limited number of words—articles, pronouns, connectors, determiners, and so on. Generative transformational grammar has a similar approach, but utilizes a larger number of classifications. Structural grammar describes six or seven basic sentence patterns which, with some modifications, constitute the patterns of meaningful word order for almost all possible sentences in English. A common pattern is that of noun/verb/noun, as in the sentence "The boy threw the ball." Generative transformational grammar identifies similar patterns as kernel sentences, which through specified transformational procedures can generate all other sentence forms. For example, "The boy threw the ball" can become "The ball was thrown by the boy" or "The boys threw the balls" or "Did the boy throw the ball?" or "The short, chubby boy quickly threw the red ball."

New curriculum proposals and materials focus on familiarizing the elementary pupil with kernel sentences which he is to use as models to help him to understand new sentences or utterances and to engage in effective oral and written expression (California, 1966; Roberts, 1966). Children are encouraged to explore the generative possibilities of kernel sentences and to discover for themselves the patterns of word order that convey meaning in English. Emphasis is not on labeling and classifying, but rather on practice and use of correct patterns that will become habitual.

Oral and written expression. The structure of English is, of course, the foundational structure of all the language arts. The child's skill in speech, listening, and written expression grows with his increasing understanding of the structure of his language. Skill development in oral and written expression builds upon language structure as conveyed through instruction in spelling, handwriting, vocabulary development, grammar, and usage.

Oral and written expression are based not only upon the concepts and

Functional writing		Creative writing	
Note	Outline	Anecdote	Story
Letter	Summary		Novel
Message	Report	Narration	Description
Direction	Précis	Dramatic forms	
Recipe	Essay	Poetic forms	

Chart 3–5.   Examples of expressive forms.

generalizations that constitute language structure, but also upon the structures of various modes of expression and upon differentiated methods of inquiry, skill development, and organization of knowledge. In delineating these structural aspects, distinctions may be drawn between oral expression, functional writing, and creative writing.

Oral expression, both listening and speaking, can take such forms as conversation, discussion, debate, formal speech or lecture, report, announcement, directions, mass media programs, and various dramatic modes. Each form has its own set of rules or standards, and each utilizes syntactic principles at varying levels of usage. In addition, meaning in oral expression is conveyed through utilization and comprehension of appropriate styles of vocal expression derived from the art or discipline of rhetoric. The development of auditory acuity and of articulation, enunciation, and accurate pronunciation is included under the physiological aspects of the structure of instruction in oral expression.

Learning and skill development in oral language require participation and practice in listening and speaking. Underlying participation and practice are such activities as imitating sounds and sound patterns, observing (listening) and comparing forms of oral expression, and developing standards for clarity of speech and accuracy of listening in accordance with specific purposes in each oral language situation.

Written expression is usually divided, for instructional purposes, into the areas of functional and creative writing. These areas are differentiated in terms of specific forms of expression and appropriate activities of inquiry and practice.

The several forms of written expression are distinguished by differences in their overall structure and in their appropriate patterns of thought organization, such as types of sentences, types of poetic lines, and use of paragraphs, stanzas, or scenes. Examples are listed in Chart 3–5.

The examples of inquiry and practice methods given in Chart 3–6 are comparable, though not identical, for both areas of written expression. (See p. 64.) In addition, creative writing involves, to a greater extent than functional writing, the use of imagination and the discovery of unique associations of verbal symbols.

Functional writing	Creative writing
Construction	Construction
Guided rediscovery of forms appropriate to standard situations	Discovery of variations of the general forms for use in unique situations
Critical evaluation	Critical evaluation
Validation, verification	Comparison
Synthesis and organization of ideas	Synthesis and organization of ideas

Chart 3–6. Examples of inquiry and practice.

Functional writing is employed in expressive situations which are not unique for each writer. Most functional writing employs words at a literal level of meaning, while creative writing utilizes words at levels of more subjective connotations. There is, of course, an area between these extremes in which objective, functional forms of expression employ connotative language. Examples are personal letters, reports which veer toward subjectivity, and essays. Creative writing is expressed in literary forms. Therefore, references to literature in the chapter on reading instruction have relevance to learning activities in creative writing.

OBJECTIVES OF INSTRUCTION

Objectives of language arts instruction, as expressed in courses of study and professional publications, reflect concern for the development of communication skills, the provision of experiences designed to stimulate adequate expression, and the inculcation of an appreciation of language and a lifelong desire to learn. Examples of such objectives, broadly stated, include the following:

> To help the individual live effectively in a democratic society and scientific-industrial culture by providing him with skills for effective communication
>
> To teach pupils to organize and express ideas and to develop skillful study habits
>
> To teach pupils to listen with understanding and to speak effectively
>
> To develop correct spelling and legible handwriting for effective written communication
>
> To broaden children's experiences through mass media and to teach the discriminating and intelligent use of these media
>
> To help children acquire poise and self-confidence through use of language and observation of social amenities
>
> To provide enriching experiences that stimulate children's thought and expression

> To encourage the natural enthusiasm, vitality, spontaneity, and originality of children in their oral and written expression
>
> To develop in children a permanent interest in language, an appreciation of the significance of man's languages as tools of learning and media of communication, and an appreciation of the development, power, and beauty of language

In addition to these objectives, which are common to all programs of elementary language arts instruction, curriculum projects state objectives in terms related to their design and approach. An example is a program (Nebraska, 1963), organized around language, literature, and composition, which sets forth the following fundamental objectives:

> To teach students to comprehend the more frequent grammatical conventions
>
> To teach students to comprehend the more frequent conventions of literature composed for young children—formal or generic conventions and simple rhetorical conventions
>
> To teach students to control these linguistic and literary conventions in their own writing

A COMPLETE LANGUAGE ARTS PROGRAM

The language arts curriculum consists of school-directed activities in which children communicate by listening, speaking, reading, or writing. Thus, a complete language arts program includes four phases: (1) direct and sequential instruction in language knowledge and skills, (2) specific instruction in language skills needed for other subject areas, (3) experiences that provide ideas and stimulation for oral and written expression, and (4) application and utilization of language skills throughout the school day.

Phases 3 and 4, idea-building experiences and day-long application, are continuous and too varied to reduce to any prescribed list. The competent teacher recognizes their place in the language program and plans their inclusion accordingly. The phase of formal language instruction relevant to subject areas (phase 2, above) is often provided for in time allotted to the particular subjects. Such instruction deals with specialized vocabulary, reading of textbooks and reference materials which may utilize a specialized syntax, study skills such as analyzing data and making notes or outlines, and oral and written communication skills relevant to modes of inquiry during lessons as well as modes of reporting or sharing understandings.

Phase 1 of the language program is designed to carry out the broad objectives outlined in the preceding section and is found in courses of study and guidelines used by teachers to provide for sequential development of specific language skills. Current courses of study tend to incorporate in their organization and directions for teachers such trends as the following:

> **Recognition of the interrelationships of the language arts; inclusion of reading and literature**
> **Greater emphasis on oral language; simultaneous instruction in listening and speaking**
> **Development of skills in thinking, independent learning, and self-evaluation**
> **Emphasis on creative expression**

Spelling and handwriting are areas of language learning in which content is clearly defined in terms of finite graphological language elements, graphemes, and words. Each area requires practice of specific skills within the context of its content. Therefore, current courses of study continue to provide specific instructional frameworks for each area. At the same time, teachers are directed to provide instruction that meets the specific spelling and handwriting needs that may arise as their pupils engage in written expression.

Vocabulary and concept development is a continuous process that receives attention in every area of the language arts program and, indeed, in every area of the elementary curriculum. In courses of study, reference to vocabulary development is often made in directions regarding instruction in reading, oral and written expression, and spelling.

While there is much consistency in regard to spelling, handwriting, and vocabulary development, courses of study differ in the emphasis placed on language usage. In some programs, it is a distinct aspect of the instructional program, although application is made in all language areas. In other programs, it is integrated with oral and written expression.

Growth in thinking develops with mastery of language. Thinking processes involved in language communication and the organization of thought in oral and written expression receive attention as teachers are guided in developing thinking skills as part of the language program.

In addition to the components of the program listed above, a few courses of study include a foreign language as part of language arts instruction. Even when foreign language is considered a separate subject, it is usually taught in a listen-speak-read-write sequence, and linguistic comparisons, for the purpose of understanding and appreciation, are made with English. Few, if any, elementary programs presently include any study of the history of the English language or of language as a tool of civilization, although these areas may be explored as part of the social sciences program. Chart 3–7 outlines examples of representative programs.

The curriculum project example (Nebraska, 1963) is based on the three

Curriculum project	State proposal	School system prog am
Literature	Reading	Reading
	Literature	Oral English
Language	Language	Listening
Composition	Composition	Speaking
Oral	Listening and	Usage
Written	speaking	Written English
		Spelling
		Handwriting

Chart 3–7. **Examples of language arts programs.**

interrelated components of the structure of English. Reading instruction is not a part of this project. Primary attention is focused on presentation of stories which are intended to provide examples that will lead to eventual inductive recognition of the nature of some conventional literary forms and themes. The patterns of the stories provide models to guide children's attempts to create their own oral and written compositions. Instruction in important grammatical conventions supports the program in literature and composition. The state-proposed program (New York State, 1964) integrates listening and speaking and includes reading instruction in the language arts program. The Los Angeles program (1964) is representative of the organization of many recent programs in school system courses of study.

DEVELOPMENTAL STAGES IN THE LANGUAGE ARTS

The child's development in language maturity depends upon such factors as physical and mental maturity and language-related experiences during preschool years. The observed tendency of girls to develop greater language facility than boys in the elementary grades may be attributed to their differing rates of physical maturity, different social expectations for each sex, and the greater amount of verbal expression involved in the family associations and play activities of girls.

Oral Language

Listening and speaking constitute virtually the total language activity of the preschool child. He comes to kindergarten or the first grade with an extensive comprehension vocabulary and an ability to speak in a variety of sentence patterns, although not all his utterances are complete sentences. The level of language maturity varies from child to child, depending upon physical and mental maturity and experience. However, in general, the child in the kindergarten and in grades 1 and 2 tends to be eager to speak, though his speech is more a matter of personal expression than social interchange; he is rarely at a loss for questions. He tends to be spontaneous in his expression, and he participates easily in dramatic play and creative dramatics. During the time he is in kindergarten and first grade, he develops the ability to articulate consonants and digraphs, despite setbacks occasioned by the temporary loss of his front teeth.

In view of the developmental levels of children of five, six, and seven years of age, the language program in kindergarten and grades 1 and 2 places emphasis on oral communication. Attention is given to development of auditory acuity and discrimination and to correct articulation and pronunciation. Children are given opportunities to participate in conversations, discussions, observing social courtesies, dramatic play, making announcements, giving simple directions and explanations, storytelling, and reporting. Frequent trips are recommended to familiarize the child with the school, neighborhood, and facilities of the larger community in order to increase his fund of concepts, sharpen his observation skills, and stimulate his expression. At the end of grade 2, according to expected levels of language development, the child:

> **Understands and uses common words**
> **Acquires and uses new action, descriptive, picture, and sensory words**
> **Recognizes rhyming words**
> **Speaks spontaneously, freely, naturally**
> **Has facility in using American intonation**
> **Uses the telephone competently**
> **Begins to pronounce accurately and speak audibly**
> **Begins to contribute to group conversation, discussion**
> **Organizes ideas in sequence to develop a topic or story**
> **Keeps to the subject in speaking and responding**
> **Gives sustained attention for longer periods**
> **Listens to others courteously, attentively, and purposefully**
> **Follows verbal directions**
> **Listens to gain information and form judgments**
> **Begins to distinguish between fact and fantasy**

The child of eight and nine is developing better organization of thought. He is becoming more interested in communication and interaction with others. Experience and instruction have brought him to levels of greater independence in expression. Distinctions are made between fact and fantasy, and critical thinking skills are brought into play.

The oral language program in grades 3 and 4 builds upon the child's growth in the earlier grades. Activities are similar, but require increased skill in oral expression and refinement of listening abilities. Expected language development at the end of grade 4 includes extension of earlier levels and such additional outcomes as the following. At this time, the child:

> **Uses qualifying words, similes, metaphors for clarification**
> **Eliminates unnecessary use of "and," "so," "then," or "well" to connect sentences**
> **Develops poise and confidence in speaking**
> **Develops simple standards for use of voice, intonation, and tempo in differing situations**
> **Observes social amenities**
> **Shows increased ability to plan and carry out dramatizations**
> **Uses opening and closing sentences in well-planned reports**
> **Relates what he says to contributions of others**
> **Increases his span of attention and speed of perception of ideas when listening**
> **Gains sensitivity to correct and pleasing qualities of speech**
> **Notes how phrases, pauses, and transitional words punctuate speech and aid listening comprehension**
> **Listens to recognize relevant and irrelevant details**
> **Listens to make inferences and to raise questions**

The child of ten and eleven is interested in peer-group relationships and is conscious of the opinions of others. At this level of development he is able to enjoy suitable intellectual activities, to recognize the need for improvement of language skills, and to evaluate his own progress in skill development. He is aware of many needs and applications of language skill in classroom and noncurricular activities. He is capable of greater independence in setting goals, planning, and selecting forms of expression.

The language program of grades 5 and 6 provides the child with opportunities for an increasing variety of forms of oral expression. Greater independence is encouraged through pupil planning of activities and pupil responsibilities in giving directions, relaying messages, planning and presenting plays, reports, debates, panel discussions, and interviews.

Outcomes representative of the level of language development at the end of grade 6 include refinement of all the abilities listed above as well as the following. At this stage, the child:

> **Is aware of the interest value of variety in vocabulary and uses more vivid words**
> **Expresses thoughts clearly in more complex sentences**
> **Maintains poise in speaking in a variety of situations**
> **Takes an active part in group discussion**
> **Summarizes during and after discussions**
> **Uses transitional phrases**
> **Engages in simple club procedures**

Speaks from notes or outlines

Increases span of attention and concentration on content

Uses contextual clues effectively in listening

Compares several broadcasts of news stories

Recognizes some forms of propaganda, bias, and emotional appeal in listening to speakers, radio, television, films

Exercises critical judgment

Written Language

The child's development in written expression depends upon his level of mental maturity, reading ability, and spelling skill and upon his fund of idea-producing experiences. In general, the kindergarten child and first grader will dictate stories to the teacher. As mastery of reading and spelling increases, the child in grades 1 and 2 copies stories composed by the class as a whole. He usually makes a start at independent composition, both functional and creative, in grades 2 and 3 and grows in skill, independence, and ability to utilize more complex expressive forms as he progresses to grades 4, 5, and 6.

Expected developmental outcomes in written expression include the following. The child:

After grade 2

Understands such terms as "salutation," "closing," "margin," "indent"

Writes picture stories

Puts ideas into words

Begins to dictate and write ideas in sequence

Begins to be selective as to what is appropriate for inclusion in letters, stories

Understands the need for capitalization in proper names, days, months, holidays, titles, and first word of sentence

Understands the need for punctuation—periods, question marks, commas, apostrophes

Begins to write sentences, short paragraphs, and simple stories independently

After grade 4

Continues to improve previously developed skills

Uses synonyms, action and descriptive words in place of overworked words

Uses more initiative in selecting a topic and begins to develop ideas around a plot or topic

Recognizes a sequence of action and rearranges ideas in order

States his own ideas, reactions, opinions

Writes paragraphs with suitable opening and closing sentences

Shows independence in creative writing

After grade 6

Begins to create mood and imagery through rich vocabulary and figurative language

Develops more complex plot and story design and writes longer compositions

Suits style of writing to interest and comprehension level of intended audience

Senses and creates rhythm in poetry

Increases ability to express ideas clearly, forcefully, concisely

Takes pertinent notes in classroom and individual study

Outlines and summarizes

Begins to use direct quotations

Begins to support factual statements by evidence

Recognizes the purposes of business and social letters and adapts his style to these purposes

Uses varieties of increasingly complex sentences

Uses correct paragraphing in writing conversation

Although these descriptions of developmental levels of language ability are stated in terms of grade levels, they do not represent expectations for *all* children at those grade levels. Children enter school at different stages of language maturity and progress at different rates. Therefore, grade-level placement of instruction in written expression varies among school systems, schools, and classes within a school.

Spelling

Ability to read and write are a prerequisite to learning to spell. Therefore, instruction in spelling is deferred until the middle or end of the first grade. The child is considered ready to begin spelling when he is able to listen attentively, has developed auditory and visual discrimination, speaks clearly, has attained a broad vocabulary suitable to his language level, reads a first reader fluently, forms letters correctly, is able to write words from memory.

Spelling instruction begins informally as the child needs to write particular words. Early experiences often include copying group stories and developing spelling skills as the child checks to see that he has written the words correctly. Words are suggested for particular grade levels on the basis of their level of complexity and frequency of use in children's expression.

In grades 1 and 2, the child may be expected to copy words correctly, learn to use an alphabetical word list and picture dictionary, learn a word-study method, and write spelling words from memory.

In grades 3 and 4, the child may be expected to develop a sense of responsibility to spell correctly whatever is written for others to read. He learns proofreading skills; he may keep an individual word list; and he increases his dictionary skills. He applies a word-study method to the learning of new words and is able to draw and apply generalizations as an aid in spelling.

In addition to expanding the skills learned at earlier levels, the child in grades 5 and 6 may be expected to increase his power in word-analysis techniques, generalizations, mnemonic devices, and study methods as an aid in spelling words from a basic list and rarer words he may have occasion to use. He is able to proofread accurately, and he uses a dictionary to understand pronunciation aids, find synonyms, check syllabication, and check doubtful spellings.

Handwriting

Readiness for handwriting instruction depends upon the child's motor coordination, visual acuity, and reading ability. The child in grade 1 is unable to focus on very fine print. His smaller muscles are not well developed. Therefore, his writing experiences utilize manuscript printing, which involves short, simple, unconnected strokes. Early practice at the chalkboard enables the young child to work with easily formed large letter sizes. Later, he uses 1-inch ruled paper making capital letters and numerals 2 inches high.

At about the time he is in grade 2, he is able to reduce capitals to 1 inch and lowercase letters to half an inch. As his motor coordination and visual acuity improve and his earlier tendency toward farsightedness disappears, he is able to reduce the size of his writing.

Most children are physiologically ready for cursive writing in grade 3. Those who have reading difficulties, however, may need to raise the level of their reading ability before they are ready to read cursive forms.

After the transition to cursive writing, the child in grades 4, 5, and 6 may be expected to improve in style, fluency, and speed of writing and to maintain his skills in manuscript printing. As his competency increases, he may be able, in the upper grades, to explore varieties of letter forms for posters, charts, and special purposes.

Grammar and Usage

Pooley (1957) defines grammar as the form and structure of sentences and usage as correctness and propriety in words and phrases. Instruction in grammar and usage in the elementary school is based to a great extent upon children's specific language needs, rather than their developmental levels.

The child comes to kindergarten or grade 1 with speech patterns that include every part of speech and almost every type of sentence. His language patterns may conform to standard English usage, in which case he may require very little direct instruction, or his speech may follow a different level of usage.

Instruction in appropriate usage is based upon currently acceptable informal standard English in its oral form. Usage instruction is a matter of identifying errors in word use and substituting acceptable forms in the manner of habit replacement. Since the language patterns of children may vary far more from school to school, or even among members of the same class, than the variance from grade 1 to grade 6 in a given school, it is virtually impossible to list standard usage errors for a specific grade. Identification and instruction must be carried on by each teacher according to the needs of a particular class, regardless of grade level.

Although practice with varying sentence forms is appropriate in many areas of language arts instruction at all grade levels, linguists and educators suggest that *formal* study of grammar is a waste of time in the elementary school. Numerous studies in past years have shown that formal instruction based on *traditional* grammar is ineffective in correcting usage errors or improving the quality of children's written expression. However, there may be some promise in instruction based on generative transformational grammar. A noted linguist (Roberts, 1966) has developed an instructional program for grades 3 through 6 in the form of textbooks, workbooks, and coordinated records. To meet the objective of improving children's written expression by teaching the main features of the written language system, the textbooks present sequential lessons in spelling, form and procedure in written composition, reading of literary selections, and transformational grammar. Lessons on grammar are developed with the introduction of simple kernel sentences and the sequential addition of transformations of these sentences by such means as word order, possessive word forms, and changes of tense, as well as the generation of expanded forms of a basic sentence.

STRANDS IN THE LANGUAGE ARTS PROGRAM

Reading, literature, and foreign language, although closely related to other language arts in most programs, will be discussed in other chapters. The other major strands of the elementary language program, from kindergarten readiness to sixth-grade levels of competence, include:

Listening	**Handwriting**
Speaking	**Grammar and usage**
Creative writing	**Vocabulary development**
Functional writing	**Thinking skills**
Spelling	**Idea-building experiences**

Most of these strands are defined by specific activities which are listed below. Vocabulary is developed in many ways, both within and beyond the language program. Thinking skills are developed in the drawing of appropriate generalizations, in the critical evaluation of what is heard or read, and in the organization of ideas for oral and written expression. Idea-building experiences permeate the curriculum and are so varied and numerous as to evade any attempt to form a list.

Charts 3–8 and 3–9 list oral and written language activities and indicate the grades at which current courses of study show that these activities

Chart 3–8. Sequence of learning experiences in oral language.

	K	1	2	3	4	5	6
Auditory discrimination	×	×					
Appreciative or recreational listening	×	×	×	×	×	×	×
Informational listening							
To develop correct speech	×	×	×	×	×	×	×
To follow directions	×	×	×	×	×	×	×
To find out "why"	×	×	×	×	×	×	×
To answer specific questions	×	×	×	×	×	×	×
To find new interests, information			×	×	×	×	×
Critical listening							
To determine accuracy		×	×	×	×	×	×
To determine authenticity			×	×	×	×	×
To detect bias					×	×	×
Conducting interviews					×	×	×
Use of voice, articulation, pronunciation	×	×	×	×	×	×	×
Language usage	×	×	×	×	×	×	×
Conversation	×	×	×	×	×	×	×
Discussion	×	×	×	×	×	×	×
Relaying messages, announcements	×	×	×	×	×	×	×
Giving directions and explanations	×	×	×	×	×	×	×
Social courtesies	×	×	×	×	×	×	×
Telephoning		×	×	×	×		
News reporting		×	×	×	×	×	×
Other reporting		×	×	×	×	×	×
Storytelling		×	×	×	×	×	×
Choral speaking		×	×	×	×	×	×
Dramatic play	×	×					
Creative dramatics		×	×	×	×	×	×
Formal dramatization				×	×	×	×
Appraising oral expression				×	×	×	×

should be introduced, practiced, and mastered. Most activities are introduced at appropriately simple levels in the primary grades and are carried through grade 6. Mastery of skills at the levels shown in the charts provides readiness for language activity in junior and senior high school.

Written language experiences offer opportunities for skill development in spelling, creative and functional writing, and handwriting.

TEACHING STRATEGIES

Curriculum Organization

Most current courses of study have a separate program of language arts instruction. Specific language activities are suggested, and guidelines are provided for sequential skill development through the grades. Differences in pupils' preschool language backgrounds and rates of learning through the elementary school necessitate modifications of suggested programs to

Chart 3–9. *Sequence of learning experiences in written language.*

	K	1	2	3	4	5	6
Alphabet and alphabetizing skills	×	×	×	×	×	×	×
Dictionary use		×	×	×	×	×	×
Spelling		×	×	×	×	×	×
Capitalization and punctuation		×	×	×	×	×	×
Use of abbreviations			×	×	×	×	×
Syllabication			×	×	×	×	×
Learning parts of speech			×	×	×	×	×
Proofreading, using correction symbols				×	×	×	×
Writing names, labels	×	×	×				
Recognizing and writing sentences		×	×	×	×	×	×
Writing paragraphs				×	×	×	×
Dictating creative expression to teacher	×	×					
Writing composite (cooperative) stories		×	×				
Informal and creative writing		×	×	×	×	×	×
Letter writing		×	×	×	×	×	×
Recording information		×	×	×	×	×	×
Other functional writing		×	×	×	×	×	×
Outlining					×	×	×
Reference activities, note-taking					×	×	×
Handwriting							
Manuscript printing	×	×	×				
Cursive writing				×	×	×	×

suit the needs of particular classes. When language textbooks or work-books are employed, teachers are advised to use their contents selectively, omitting whatever is not suitable to the needs of the class or of groups of pupils.

Language activity permeates the entire curriculum. There are innumerable opportunities for teachers to correlate language skill development with learnings in other subject areas beyond the specific language skills required for study of particular subjects. This provides the meaningful application of language skills that is called for in courses of study and professional publications. Integration of language arts with other subjects is rarely recommended, as it tends to produce language instruction which is incidental and inadequate.

Classroom Organization

In the graded and multigraded vertical classroom organization, most instruction is carried on in groups. Typically, new skills are introduced to the class as a whole or to the appropriate group within the multigraded class. After an initial period of practice, the class or group is further subdivided according to pupils' needs and rates of learning. Instruction is individualized as the special problems, errors, or interests of pupils are identified by the teacher. Individualized spelling lists, correction of individual handwriting and usage errors, and freedom of choice in form and topic in creative writing are examples of individualized instruction recommended in courses of study.

In the nongraded classroom, most instruction is on an individual basis as pupils progress through sequentially developed skills at their own rates. However, in all three types of classroom organization, many language activities, including most forms of oral communication, are most appropriately conducted with the entire class.

In the self-contained classroom, the teacher will follow instructional patterns in accordance with the type of vertical organization. In a horizontal organization utilizing departmentalization, rare in the elementary school, pupils may be grouped homogeneously with respect to specific language achievement levels, with a resultant emphasis on group instruction.

When team teaching is utilized, one teacher responsible for instruction in some or all areas of language arts introduces skills in large-group lectures or demonstrations. Individual teachers follow up such lessons in classes or smaller groups. A pupil may be assigned to different follow-up groups for practice in spelling, handwriting, composition, or dramatics, depending upon his ability or interest without regard to his grade level.

Instructional Strategies

Current courses of study and recent professional publications recommend two instructional strategies which differ more in emphasis than in form. Each is appropriate for certain aspects of language learning, and both should be utilized in a complete instructional program, as they are interwoven and mutually supplementary.

One strategy emphasizes discovery and inductive learning; the other is a pattern for habit formation. In the first children observe, examine, or analyze several examples or instances and are guided to discover, by inductive thinking, relationships or common elements that lead them to derive principles or generalizations. Children's understandings are strengthened as they provide their own further illustrations or applications of their inductively derived understandings. By this means, children develop understandings of spelling rules, syntactic principles, and forms of oral or written expression suitable for particular purposes. They also utilize this procedure in recognizing and formulating standards or guidelines for effective listening, speaking, and writing. Application of generalizations is made in their subsequent expression.

This strategy of guided exploration and discovery is illustrated by the following example—determination of appropriate forms for an informal letter at the second-grade level:

1. **The problem is presented in a meaningful context: the students will be writing to children in another school or engaged in some other purposeful activity.**
2. **The children are encouraged to think about the kind of information that should be included in the letters they will write: "What else will we need, in addition to the message?" "Why should the date be included?" etc.**
3. **The children suggest appropriate sequences and placement of heading, salutation, and other elements. Suggestions are discussed and evaluated, and those selected are recorded for reference.**
4. **Using agreed-upon elements and sequence, the class may practice by writing a cooperative letter, or the children may move directly to writing indivdual letters.**
5. **Self-evaluation and teacher-pupil evaluation are made by comparing children's letters with the standards the class has devised.**

The second strategy provides for skill development in spelling, handwriting, speaking, and correct usage through habituation of an appropriate response. Motivation involves recognition of the need for skills in the context of meaningful situations. An example of correct form or pattern is presented to the children by means of demonstration by the classroom teacher or by film, television, or tape recording. The children practice the example in a drill, repeating the appropriate response to make it habitual. This initial practice is followed by application of the skill in meaningful language activities. Evaluation by teacher and pupil may proceed concurrently with drill and application. The following example is adapted from a recent language textbook for grade 4 (Roberts, 1966):

1. **The children are presented with a generalization: "Every simple English sentence has a subject and a predicate." This is followed by an expansion: "In a simple sentence the subject always comes first and the predicate follows it."**
2. **An example is given: "The girl reads a poem." The subject is identified, and children are asked to infer which words make up the predicate. Similar examples are presented and identified by the class.**
3. **The habit is strengthened through practice with fourteen sentences of similar form: "I read a poem," "The class reads a poem," etc.**
4. **The skill is applied to a few other sentences of greater variety, such as "His house is in the village," "The horse stopped in the woods," etc.**
5. **The children encounter and practice only correct examples. They are not confronted with erroneous forms, especially during initial stages of learning an example or grammatical pattern.**

Concept clusters such as those identified earlier in this chapter may be used by the children to facilitate learning. For example, during handwriting lessons early in the school year, the teacher helps the children to become aware of such concepts in the analysis of handwriting as letter form, slant, alignment, and spacing. As the children become familiar with these concepts, they are able to recognize standards for each and develop independence in using the entire cluster to analyze and improve their own writing.

Materials of Instruction

Elementary school language textbooks of former years tended to emphasize grammatical rules and standard forms for written expression. Although one of the most recent textbook series emphasizes written language, it is based on generative transformational grammar, rather than traditional grammar based on Latin models, and begins instruction at the third-grade level on the assumption that children will have much prior as well as concurrent oral language practice (Roberts, 1966). In conformity with current views that learnings in all the language arts are interdependent, many recently published textbooks provide lessons for skill development in listening and speaking as well as writing.

A multiplicity of audio-visual and manipulative materials are utilized by effective teachers in a variety of ways too numerous and familiar to require repetition. However, some mention should be made of such comparatively newer media as tape recorders, programmed instruction, and linguistic blocks.

Increasing emphasis upon oral language has added to the use of tape recorders in the classroom. Children's discussions and reports may be recorded so that the activity serves its intended purpose when carried on, while evaluation of effectiveness or analysis of speech patterns may be conducted at a later time. Tapes of children's oral expression may be used for subsequent listening lessons, or they may be evaluated by the class for voice control and correct usage. Dictation of creative expression on a tape enables children to engage in constructive evaluation before ideas are put in written form. This aids the children in relating oral and written language.

Areas of language instruction that deal with clearly defined language structure may be effectively presented, at least in part, by means of programmed instruction in machine and workbook forms. Some programs are available in spelling, handwriting, and grammar.

The Edison Responsive Environment, the so-called "talking typewriter," is used in some schools for alphabet and beginning reading instruction. The machine's potential for the language arts program has not yet been fully explored, but its provision for teacher-made programs may offer a variety of applications.

The sets of linguistic blocks produced by Scott, Foresman, and Company are primarily intended for instruction in reading and language usage. The "Rolling Reader" sets contain blocks with words of a particular part of speech on all six sides. Words on a single block are mutually interchangeable in a sentence. Children manipulate the blocks to construct increasingly more complex sentences. This type of activity may also facilitate the child's expression. Blocks in the "Rolling Phonics" sets can be utilized for spelling study and for practice in articulation and pronunciation.

Guidelines for the Teacher

Instructional guidelines provided in curriculum outlines and statements by language educators reflect current emphases on structural and generative linguistic analyses of English, the importance of effective communication, encouragement of creativity in expression, provision for individual differences, and meaningful contexts for language learnings.

General guidelines, applicable to all areas of language arts instruction, include the following suggestions to teachers:

> **Be conversant with developments in linguistics, understand the structure of language and the primacy of its oral form, and develop language learnings for pupils that are consistent with this understanding.**
>
> **Recognize the interrelationships of the language arts and relate classroom language activities so that pupils grasp the unity of their varied language experiences and learnings.**
>
> **Provide varied experiences that stimulate children's thinking and provide guidance, through group evaluation and discussion, in the organization of thought, in order to motivate expression and improve the quality of pupils' work.**
>
> **Teach skills in connection with realistic and purposeful occasions that require their use. Provide meaningful, rather than contrived, occasions and opportunities for language communication.**
>
> **Recognize the need for language skills in all areas of the curriculum and be consistent in language expectations and skill applications in all activities of the school day.**
>
> **Employ inductive procedures in helping children to develop concepts and derive generalizations.**
>
> **Group children for instruction in specific skills according to their needs and language levels. Recognize individual differences in rates of learning, and provide individual guidance and correction.**
>
> **Help children to develop their own suitable standards and guidelines for oral and written expression, and guide them to acquire the skill and habit of evaluating, correcting, improving, and appreciating their own work.**

Guidelines in specific language arts instructional areas are extensive. The following represent a selection of current suggestions.

Grammar. Utilize descriptive, rather than prescriptive, language teaching based on characteristic contemporary speech and writing. Begin instruction with study and use of entire sentences, and then work down to structural parts, in order to help children to understand the structural relationships of words and phrases. Teach children to use varieties of simple sentences, to vary sentences by substitution of words in appropriate slots, and to expand kernel sentences into more complex and expressive forms.

Usage. Recognize that different levels of language usage are appropriate under differing circumstances. Accept nonstandard forms in children's speech that reflect other levels of usage, and build skill in standard usage in addition to other forms. Concentrate corrections on common errors that are unacceptable in standard usage. Be positive in making corrections: motivate pupils to learn correct forms, provide clear examples and instruction, repeat the correct form without the intervening use of incorrect forms, and consistently put correct forms to use.

Spelling. Group spelling words which have the same phonetic patterns or which conform to a particular rule in order to enable children to see similarities and to inductively derive generalizations for use in learning new words. Use a natural language sequence in introducing new words: have children listen to words, say them, read them, and then write them. Use individualized spelling lists and encourage independent study in patterns suitable to individual pupils. Incorporate words needed by children in daily classroom activities to supplement words drawn from basic lists.

Handwriting. Allow children to write with the hand that is most comfortable. Provide appropriate directions for left-handed pupils. Allow pupils to adopt hand motions and postures that are comfortable if there is no detriment to their writing. Uniform procedures are not appropriate for all. Practice in handwriting should be in meaningful contexts, with words, phrases, and sentences rather than single letters.

Listening and speaking. Recognize that the teacher's own speech patterns greatly influence those of the pupils, and provide appropriate examples of pronunciation and voice modulation. Help children to sense specific purposes for listening. Provide experiences in which they talk and listen to each other. Emphasize the importance of clarity of communication by encouraging careful speaking and listening in all classroom activities.

Written expression. Provide experiences that stimulate imagination, sharpen observation, and provoke children's interest in writing. Help children to set their own reasonable standards for written expression. Encourage expression by minimizing corrections in creative writing. Allow children to explore a variety of expressive forms.

EVALUATION OF PUPIL PROGRESS

Evaluation of pupil progress in language skills is characterized by emphasis on the pupil's self-evaluation and by constructive guidance. In all areas of language activities, pupils are encouraged to discuss, analyze, and determine appropriate standards for skill attainment. These standards may be used by the child as a check list to measure his own progress, or they may form the basis for group evaluation. In other instances, evaluation may be conducted by the teacher alone, by teacher and pupil, or by groups of pupils. In both oral and written expression, there is more emphasis on the *production* of correct forms than on the *correction* of forms. This results in greater integration of continuous evaluation with all phases of instruction, rather than evaluation as a terminating activity for the purpose of reporting achievement levels.

In all areas of language arts instruction, standardized tests and teacher-made check lists and tests are used early in the academic year to evaluate learning needs. Oral language evaluation may involve diagnosis of speech or hearing difficulties. Charts, check lists, and recorded tests are available to enable teachers to detect indications of speech pathology or hearing loss. Minor difficulties may be overcome in classroom learning activities, while more serious problems may be identified for treatment by specialists.

Teacher and pupils may engage in continuous evaluation of speaking skills as these are practiced in all areas of the school program. More detailed and comprehensive evaluation for each pupil may be done by means of check lists, rating scales, teacher-pupil conferences, and tape recordings of pupils' speech. All these techniques lend themselves to cooperative evaluation between teacher and pupils. Listening comprehension may be evaluated in all these ways. In addition, teachers may devise tests based on check lists of listening skills, using oral games that also serve instructional purposes. A few standardized tests are available, but teachers must take into account the fact that responses on these tests involve some reading as well.

Just as pupils devise standards for oral skills in storytelling, discussion, and news reporting, so too they may devise standards for writing letters, announcements, reports, and other forms of functional writing. Specific assignments may be kept in pupil folders for evaluation of progress. Written work in other subject areas is also evaluated in accordance with appropriate standards of written expression skills. In creative writing, evaluation tends to be more subjective and individualized. Certain general questions may be used as guidelines to determine such qualities as originality, appropriate sequence of ideas or events, effective communication of intended meaning, and use of descriptive or colorful words. Evaluation is individualized as each example of creative expression is examined in the light of its author's purposes and is considered in terms of his own level of expressive skill. Folders of work are kept to evaluate individual growth. Intraclass comparison and evaluation may be based on check lists prepared by the class. Some commercial rating scales are available, but are not of recent publication, and are based on limited-time essay tests. Cooperative evaluation of creative expression by teacher and pupil, encouraged in professional publications and recent courses of study, is an integral part of instruction and is considered most effective when the focus is on the quality of the content, rather than form. Teachers are advised to limit corrections and to concentrate instead on the adequate expression of ideas through selection of appropriate content and extension of vocabulary.

Grammar and usage may be evaluated directly through standardized diagnostic or achievement tests, teacher-made tests, essays, or workbook activities. Evaluation of skills in grammar and usage also extends to all of the child's daily language activities in oral and written expression. Spelling achievement is evaluated by means of formal tests, but teacher check lists of spelling study skills, extent of pupils' vocabularies, and awareness of their own needs for correct spelling permit evaluation of the full range of objectives in spelling instruction. Folders of pupils' written expression are kept to determine their progress in the application of spelling and handwriting skills. Handwriting scales are available in chart form to facilitate rating of pupils' work. Using such charts in addition to standard handwriting models enables children to evaluate their progress as their skills improve.

In order to assure evaluation of the full range of appropriate objectives, teachers may utilize objectives in courses of study or other classifications of objectives as guidelines. Examples of the use of certain taxonomies of educational objectives (Bloom, 1956; Krathwohl, Bloom, & Masia, 1964) in the evaluation of learning in the language arts include the following:

Cognitive Domain

> *Knowledge level*: **Knowledge of the structure of language, including vocabulary development, knowledge of grammatical structure, knowledge of spelling "rules," spelling of specific words, and knowledge of forms for functional writing may be evaluated by means of objective tests. Knowledge of appropriate forms of written expression and of accurate grapheme forms may be evaluated through tests and observation of pupil work. Check lists are used to guide such evaluation as well as the evaluation of pupils' knowledge of rules for effective speaking and attentive listening.**

> *Comprehension level*: **Pupils' abilities to abstract generalizations about language structure from sets of particular examples may be evaluated by means of standardized and teacher-made tests and observation of children's written work and oral expression. Ability to derive appropriate rules for listening, speaking, and written expression may be determined on the basis of charts developed by the pupils.**

> *Application level*: **Skill in the use of language knowledge and comprehension is manifested in the pupil's application of**

knowledge to new communication tasks and situations. In all areas of the language arts program, skill in application is evaluated by observation of pupils' written work, listening habits, and oral expression. The teacher uses check lists and rating scales to guide this observation and may evaluate individual progress by means of anecdotal records.

Analysis level: Pupils' abilities to analyze statements, to determine relevancy and irrelevancy in information or arguments, and to think and listen critically may be evaluated by means of check lists, rating scales, and anecdotal records of pupil behavior. Analysis skills involved in outlining, note-taking, and other forms of functional writing are evaluated by observation of the child's written work. Analysis in creative writing is utilized by the pupil in self-evaluation. This skill is evaluated through teacher observation.

Synthesis level: The child's abilities to produce unique and appropriate efforts in written and oral expression are evaluated by means of direct observation of his work in accordance with guidelines and standards which may be developed cooperatively by pupils and teacher.

Affective Domain

Receiving level: The child's willingness to listen to others and his ability to listen or read with selective attention may be evaluated by teacher observation guided by check lists of appropriate pupil behavior.

Responding level: The child's willingness to respond orally and in writing and the level of his satisfaction in such response may be evaluated through observation of his behavior and the fluency apparent in his expressive efforts.

Valuing level: Evidence of the child's value preferences may be found through observation of his behavior, and can be noted by the teacher in anecdotal records in order to evaluate progress over a period of time. In grammar, usage, spelling, and handwriting instruction, the teacher will note the child's acceptance of agreed-upon standards, his preference for alternative standards, and his commitment to various standards as manifested in his adherence to such standards in all areas of his language work. Values related to the child's acceptance of the rights of others to differing opinions, his appreciation of the contributions made by others to class activities, and his interest in the written and oral expression of other children are similarly noted by means of teacher observation, anecdotal records, and attitude or interest questionnaires.

EVALUATION OF THE PROGRAM

Adequacy and effectiveness of the instructional program may be evaluated according to such criteria as the following:

Foundations

Do the aspects of the language arts program reflect the utilization of current recommendations in linguistics and language education?

Is the language program developed in accord with the needs, interests, experiences, and activities of children?

Structure

Are the content and methods proposed in the program consistent with present knowledge of the structure and operation of the English language and the interrelationships of the language arts?

Objectives

Are objectives clearly defined in relation to:

Knowledge of language structure and acquisition of communication skills?

Development of positive attitudes toward language learning?

A focus on a carefully limited selection of standards appropriate and attainable for each grade level?

Complete program

Does the language program include experiences that stimulate children's thinking, develop observation skills, encourage imagination, and provoke a desire for communication and expression?

Is emphasis placed upon the development and practice of oral language skills?

Does the program provide specific instruction to meet language needs in other subject areas?

Is provision made for day-long application of language skills?

Is instruction in all the language skills organized into a sequential developmental program from grade to grade?

Teaching strategies

Is skill instruction provided in a pattern that includes readiness experience, clear direction, meaningful application, and maintenance of skills already learned?

Are skills taught from a positive approach, with correct forms presented as a means for habit formation?

Is the teacher encouraged to function as a model for correct intonation, appropriate usage, and other language skills?

Are children taught to develop understandings through an inductive approach?

Does the program provide for individual differences in children's interests, abilities, and levels of achievement by means of flexible grouping within or between classes, differentiated regular, enrichment, and remedial activities, and a variety of instructional materials?

Is provision made for appropriate utilization of multisensory instructional media?

Pupil evaluation

Is continuous evaluation an integral part of instruction?

Are children encouraged to develop skills of constructive self-evaluation?

Is evaluation individualized, with diagnostic analyses made of each child's strengths and weaknesses?

Program evaluation

Does the program incorporate utilization of school library and public library facilities?

Does the program provide for continuous evaluation of textbooks and use of alternative textbooks?

Are parents made aware of the objectives and content of the language program?

Teacher preparation

Are teachers provided with opportunities for in-service education that will keep them cognizant of innovations in instructional techniques and up-to-date on linguistic insights into the nature of language and the language learning of children?

Are teachers directly involved in the planning and continual evaluation of the language program?

REFERENCES

Anderson, Verna D., et al. *Readings in the language arts.* New York: Macmillan, 1964. Selections on oral and written language, grammar and usage, reading, children's literature, and foreign language in the elementary school.

Bloom, Benjamin S. (Ed.) *The taxonomy of educational objectives: cognitive domain.* New York: McKay, 1956. Classification of objectives and examples of test items.

Bryant, Margaret M. *Current American usage.* New York: Funk & Wagnalls, 1962. Important variations of usage in six geographic regions and at three "cultural" levels; useful for an understanding of variations in acceptable usage throughout the United States.

Burns, Paul C., & Lowe, Alberta L. *The language arts in childhood education.* Chicago: Rand McNally, 1966. Emphasizes "guided discovery" methods of instruction.

Buros, Oscar K. *The sixth mental measurements yearbook.* Highland Park, N.J.: Gryphon Press, 1965. Information on language achievement tests published between 1959 and 1964; reviews of earlier tests in preceding volumes.

California. State Advisory Committee for an English Framework. *Preliminary reports.* Sacramento: State Department of Education, 1966. Suggestions for a K-12 program of instruction.

Commission on English. *Freedom and discipline in English.* New York: College Entrance Examination Board, 1965. A review of the structure of English. Chapter on "Language" gives attention to language learning in the early years.

Dawkins, John. Linguistics in the elementary grades, *Elem. English,* November, 1965, **42**, 762–768, 786. Suggestions for inductive development of linguistic principles as an inquiry approach to language learning for elementary pupils.

Dawson, Mildred A., Zollinger, Marian, & Elwell, Ardell. *Guiding language learning.* (2d ed.) New York: Harcourt, Brace, 1963. Principles and practices of the elementary language arts program.

Francis, W. Nelson. *The English language: an introduction.* New York: Norton, 1965. A reference for the structure of English.

Gleason, H. A., Jr. *Linguistics and English grammar.* New York: Holt, 1965. Evaluations of traditional, structural, and transformational-generative grammar.

Green, Harry A., & Petty, Walter T. *Developing language skills in the elementary schools.* (2d ed.) Boston: Allyn and Bacon, 1963. Principles and techniques of instruction.

Hall, Robert A., Jr. *Introductory linguistics.* Philadelphia: Chilton, 1964. A detailed explanation of linguistics as language description. Also deals with linguistic change, uses of linguistics, and the relation of linguistics to other disciplines.

Hanna, Paul R., and Hanna, Jean S. Applications of linguistics and psychological cues to the spelling course of study, *Elem. English,* November, 1965, **42**, 753–759. Suggestions for the use of linguistic principles in determining the scope and sequence of the spelling program.

Hogan, Robert F. "English," *New curriculum developments.* Washington, D.C.: Association for Supervision and Curriculum Development, 1965. Review of new developments and bibliography of curriculum and other projects.

Jacobs, Roderick A. A short introduction to transformational grammar, *Education,* November, 1965, **86**, 138–141. A concise, useful outline for teachers and curriculum workers.

Krathwohl, David R., Bloom, Benjamin S., & Masia, Bertram S. *Taxonomy of educational objectives: affective domain.* New York: McKay, 1964. Classification of objectives and sample test items in the area of attitude and value development.

Lamb, Pose. (Ed.) *Guiding children's language learning.* Dubuque, Iowa: Wm. C. Brown, 1967. Chapters on various aspects of oral and written language and related teaching techniques.

Lefevre, Carl A. A concise structural grammar, *Education*, November, 1965, **86**, 131–137. A brief, useful outline for teachers and curriculum workers.

Loban, Walter D. *The language of elementary school children.* Champaign, Ill.: National Council of Teachers of English, Research Report No. 1, 1963. Report of a study of language patterns in children's speech.

Los Angeles City Schools. *Course of study for elementary schools.* Los Angeles: Board of Education, 1964. Outlines for a K-6 program in language arts.

National Council of Teachers of English. *Summary progress report of English curriculum study and demonstration centers.* Champaign, Ill.: The Council, 1966. Report on activities of Project English Centers and special interest programs.

National Council of Teachers of English. *Curriculum projects in English.* Champaign, Ill.: The Council, 1966. A report on 172 projects in 35 states.

Nebraska Curriculum Development Center. *A curriculum for English: introduction to the elementary school program: K-6.* Lincoln, Nebr.: University of Nebraska, 1963. Mimeographed. Proposals for a K-6 program, with emphasis on literature, and a description of units prepared by the Center.

New York State. *K-12 English syllabus revision project: reading section, part* 1. Albany, N.Y.: State Education Department, 1964. Experimental materials constituting the first part of proposals for K-12 curriculum in reading, listening and speaking, language, composition, and literature.

Phenix, Philip H. *Realms of meaning.* New York: McGraw-Hill, 1964. A philosophy of curriculum development. Chapter 5 discusses the structure of language.

Ponder, Eddie G. Understanding the language of the culturally disadvantaged child, *Elem. English*, November, 1965, **42**, 769–774, 797. Introductory discussion of language patterns of several disadvantaged groups and related questions of language instruction.

Pooley, Robert C. *Teaching English grammar.* New York: Appleton-Century-Crofts, 1957. Useful background reference on grammar. Chapters 9 and 10 outline principles and techniques of elementary school language instruction.

Roberts, Paul. *Roberts English series: a linguistic program.* New York: Harcourt, Brace, 1966. Teacher's editions of textbooks for grades 3 through 6 outline lessons on language, literature, and composition with emphasis on written language.

Russell, David H. *Language and thinking.* Middletown, Conn.: Department of School Services and Publications, Curriculum Letter No. 61, Wesleyan University, 1965. Brief, useful discussion of the interrelationship of language and thinking. Includes a bibliography for further reference.

Sapir, Edward. *Language.* New York: Harcourt, Brace, 1921. A classic reference for the structure of language.

Squire, James R. The teaching of writing and composition in today's schools, *Elem. English*, January, 1964, **41**, 3–8. Suggestions for the development of skills in written expression.

Strickland, Ruth G. *The contribution of structural linguistics to the teaching of reading, writing, and grammar in the elementary school.* Bulletin of the School of Education, Vol. 40. Bloomington, Ind.: Indiana University,

1964. Discussion of linguistic principles applied to elementary language instruction.

CURRENT PROJECTS IN WHICH ELEMENTARY SCHOOL MATERIALS ARE BEING DEVELOPED

An Articulated Program in Composition (K-13). c/o Paul A. Olson, University of Nebraska, Lincoln, Nebr.

A Sequential English Language Arts Curriculum in Linguistics, Logic, Semantics, Rhetoric, Composition, and Literary Analysis and Criticism for Grades K-12. c/o Robert C. Pooley, University of Wisconsin, Madison, Wis.

ESPITE MANY DIFFERENCES in details, definitions of reading agree that it is a process, a *thinking* process. Russell (Russell and Fea, 1963, p. 868) succinctly describes the reading process as consisting of two major aspects: identifying the sound symbol and obtaining meaning from the recognized symbol. The process is more fully identified as composed of four overlapping stages: sensation, perception, comprehension, utilization (Russell, 1961, p. 99).

Several sources offer expanded definitions which incorporate these aspects (New York City, 1963; Robinson, 1965; Russell, 1961; San Diego, 1961; Smith and Dechant, 1961; Strang, 1961; Tinker and McCullough, 1962). Reading is viewed as a sequence from symbol recognition to ensuing stimulation of comprehension to resulting change in the reader's thought or behavior, as shown in Chart 4–1.

Reading, according to these views, begins with an "unlearned" response, the visual and mental sensation of graphic symbols. The reader then proceeds to a learned response, association of graphic symbols with specific sounds, an aspect of the reading process often characterized as the "decoding" of graphic symbols into speech.

The oral, or primary, form of language thus decoded serves to stimulate, in the mind of the reader, recall of meanings already possessed, association of ideas or information with known meanings or the reader's experience, or the interpretation and construction of new meanings based on the reader's manipulation of prior concepts and experiences. This comprehension of the *meaning* of the decoded sounds may be a literal understanding, or it may extend to higher thought processes and the reader's reaction to what is read in terms of critical analysis, creative interpretation, emotional response, and aesthetic appreciation.

These responses by the reader to the material he reads lead to modifications in thought or behavior which are manifested in his personal and social growth.

In recent years, linguistic scholars have turned their attention to the teaching of reading. With reference to the discipline of linguistics, learning to read is often defined as the development of skill in decoding graphic symbols. The subsequent aspects, comprehension and utilization, are viewed as indeed descriptive of the child's experience with reading. However, the skills involved are considered primarily thinking skills, which,

Chart 4–1.   Reading: From symbol recognition to behavior.

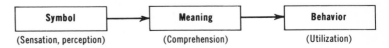

applicable as they are to written language, are equally well developed and applied to sources of information other than graphic language symbols. Since they are not unique to reading, they are excluded from the definition (Bloomfield & Barnhart, 1961; Fries, 1963). Other linguists extend their definition of reading to include comprehension of what is read in meaningful thought units—phrases or sentences—rather than mere word meanings (Carroll, 1964; Diack, 1960; Lefevre, 1964; Soffietti, 1955).

Recent programs of reading instruction reflect the acceptance by many school systems of the fuller definition of the reading process (Chart 4–1, above). Linguistic definitions of reading are not in conflict with broader definitions, because they parallel the initial aspects of the reading process. Most programs utilize an eclectic approach to reading instruction and, therefore, may effectively utilize the contributions of linguists in the development of reading skills.

READING AND THE OTHER LANGUAGE ARTS

The interrelationships of the four language arts have been indicated in the previous chapter, but some aspects of the interrelationships bear restatement in this context.

The primary form of language is manifested in oral language. Written language is man's attempt to record oral language and is, therefore, a secondary, and differing, form. Reading material is speech recorded in graphic symbols, in the organizational patterns of language's written form. There is some evidence that there is a positive relationship between close correspondence of written language patterns to familiar oral patterns and the child's comprehension of such written material (Ruddell, 1965; Strickland, 1962).

Oral language is also the primary form encountered in the child's experience. He comes to school at the age of five or six with an extensive speaking vocabulary, an even more extensive listening vocabulary, a good command of language structure, and some fluency in the use of oral language. The sound symbol that is the spoken word is in itself an abstract representation of reality. The graphic symbol represents a further level of abstraction. Graphic symbols can have little meaning for the child unless there is a concrete or vivid referent for the meaning in his experience and fund of concepts. Therefore, concept development must proceed concurrently with reading instruction throughout the elementary grades.

When the child's familiar oral patterns differ considerably from standard forms, his problems with meaning go beyond concepts to difficulties with the structures of idea units such as phrases and sentence patterns.

Fluency with oral patterns of standard English must be developed before the child finds written material meaningful.

The relationship of reading and writing offers another avenue to the child's grasp of meaning. As a prereader, he observes his teacher recording his own, or his classmates', speech in graphic symbols. As he learns to reproduce these symbols himself, concurrent with beginning reading instruction, his understanding of the relationship of oral and written language is reinforced, along with his skill in reading.

FOUNDATION DISCIPLINES

The disciplines underlying the four language arts have been outlined in the previous chapter. As each language art is considered separately, the contributions of these disciplines vary. In the area of reading, linguistics and comparative literature play a major role in providing understanding of the structure of language, the conventional forms into which written language is organized, and the modes of inquiry which develop reading skill and comprehension. Psychology and neurology contribute to an understanding of the aspects of the reading process, modes of learning, and causes of reading disability. Sociology provides insights into content, format, needs, and tastes in contemporary literature and other written language forms.

Concepts and Concept Clusters

Reading activities

silent	critical	recreational
oral	creative	functional
	retentive	

Meaning

(determinants)	(levels)	
culture	literal	definitions
experience	connotative	connotations
concepts	symbolic	concepts

(units)	
grapheme	phrase
morpheme	clause
word	sentence
tagmeme	paragraph

Reading readiness

mental age	experiential background
language fluency	visual discrimination
motivation	auditory acuity

Forms of written language organization

(sentences)	(larger forms)	
statement	story	novel
question	essay	poem
command	report	play

Prose

fiction	narrative	myth
nonfiction	description	folktale
biography	dialogue	legend
autobiography		allegory

Poetry

stanza	meter	lyric	sonnet
verse	stress	epic	couplet
refrain	rhythm	narrative	limerick

Drama

comedy	lines	introduction
tragedy	scenes	turning point
epic	acts	climax
genre		resolution

Literary analysis

(character)	(plot)
function in plot	sequence
motivation for actions	setting
emotions, perceptions	pace

(style)		
alliteration	simile	imagery
onomatopoeia	metaphor	symbolism
euphony	hyperbole	allusion

Use of books

table of contents	chapters	index
list of illustrations	sections	appendix
preface	footnotes	bibliography
	glossary	

Oral reading

projection	cadence	enunciation
modulation	pace	pronunciation
intonation	phrasing	accent

Generalizations

Generalizations from the foundation disciplines previously outlined for the other language arts are also applicable to reading. Other relevant generalizations include the following:

> **Reading material is oral language recorded in graphic form.**
> **Reading is a tool through which knowledge becomes accessible, a learning tool basic to all areas of the curriculum.**
> **Changes in societal conditions affect people's needs for various reading skills.**
> **The culture in which an individual lives and his particular experiences are major determinants of language meaning for that individual.**
> **The act of reading is a complex process involving many overlapping levels and modes of thinking.**
> **Learning to read is a developmental task; developmental reading is a process of sequential extension of the needs and abilities of each child to interpret graphic symbols.**
> **Learning to read is a highly individualized experience and is most effectively accomplished by appropriate differentiation in instruction.**

STRUCTURES IN READING INSTRUCTION

Reading instruction in the elementary school evolves from three structural bases: the structure of the reading process, the structure of language, and the structure of the instructional program. (Diagrams of structures of reading and of language are found in Charts 4–1 and 3–2, respectively.) The relationship of these structures may be interpreted as indicated in Chart 4–2.

The decoding aspect of the reading process involves the association of sound symbols with graphic symbols in units of graphemes, morphemes, syllables, or words. This association is brought about through instruction in the use of such word-analysis techniques as configuration, phonetic analysis, structural analysis, and use of context to determine appropriate words.

Word analysis involves the use of visual discrimination of letter and word forms, observing, comparing, associating, recalling, identifying, and making inferences. In addition to these modes of thinking and inquiry, phonetic analysis utilizes auditory discrimination, imitating sounds, selecting, classifying, and generalizing about single graphemes, letter combina-

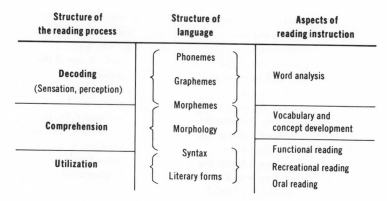

Structure of the reading process	Structure of language	Aspects of reading instruction
Decoding (Sensation, perception)	Phonemes / Graphemes	Word analysis
Comprehension	Morphemes / Morphology	Vocabulary and concept development
Utilization	Syntax / Literary forms	Functional reading / Recreational reading / Oral reading

Chart 4–2. *Relationships among reading, language, and instruction.*

tions, and syllables. Structural analysis utilizes selecting, classifying, and generalizing about the morphemes, or meaning units, of words. Use of context clues involves questioning and utilizes the meaning conveyed by words and by word-order patterns.

Generalizations in phonetic and structural analysis are the "rules" of specific grapheme-phoneme correspondence and the meanings of morphemes, roots, affixes, and inflectional changes in words. Instructional programs provide for the introduction of these generalizations in a sequence based jointly upon inherent complexity of the generalization and its degree of applicability to the child's language needs at a particular level. Although there is some variation in suggested sequences, many courses of study utilize the following sequence from the preprimer to third-reader level.

PP initial consonants
   recognition of
     rhyming words
   plural nouns ending
     in s
   verb forms ending
     in s

P ending consonants
   capital and lowercase
     letters
   digraphs wh, th, ch
   root words (verbs)
   ed ending on verbs
   possessive 's

1 medial consonants
   digraphs wh, th,
     ch, ck, sh
   consonant blends
   rhyming endings
   long vowel sounds,
     final e rule
   verb endings ed,
     s, ing
   compound words

2 short vowel sounds	3 three-letter blends
double vowels	silent letters; kn,
diphthongs	gh, wr
contractions	variant vowel sounds
soft and hard sounds	syllabication
of c and g	plural ies
similar sounds; x/cks	changing f to ves
doubling consonants	suffixes y, ly, er, en,
before adding ing	ful, est, less, self
dropping final e	prefixes a, be, un
before adding ing	voiced s and z
changing y to i before	hyphenated words
adding es plural	

Comprehension and utilization are overlapping aspects of the reading process. Acquiring understanding and utilizing or applying understanding are interacting, not sequential, processes.

Vocabulary and concept development takes place during learning of oral language, prior to, and then concurrent with, reading instruction. Analyses of the structural meaning units or morphemes, the morphological classifications, and the etymological derivations of words in their graphic form are techniques utilized in reading instruction to enhance and extend vocabulary and concept development.

Study of syntax develops meaning in larger thought units: word-sequence patterns of phrases, clauses, sentences. Study of the structure of various forms of organization of written language, such as the essay, letter, poem, flow chart, or an entire book, also develops an understanding of the content of these forms as well as skill in their use.

The term *functional reading* designates those aspects of the reading program which provide for development of comprehension and utilization skills in areas of study, reference materials, and reading in the subject fields. *Recreational reading* designates aspects of the program which provide for the development of comprehension in areas of personal interest and literature, skills of utilization of interest and literary materials, and development of appreciations and taste in selection and enjoyment of reading matter.

Vocabulary and concept development, comprehension, and development of utilization skills in the areas of functional and recreational reading—all utilize the following general modes of thinking or inquiry:

observing	identifying	abstracting	evaluating
perceiving	associating	generalizing	imagining
recalling	comparing	inferring	integrating
discriminating	classifying	hypothesizing	synthesizing
selecting	organizing	analyzing	interpreting

	R	PP	P	1	2	3	4	5	6
WORD-RECOGNITION SKILLS									
Word meanings									
Context clues		×	×	×	×	×	×	×	×
Understanding definitions		×	×	×	×	×	×	×	×
Using phonetic analysis		×	×	×	×	×	×	×	×
Recognizing root words				×	×	×	×	×	×
Recognizing contractions and compound words					×	×	×	×	×
Using prefixes, suffixes						×	×	×	×
Using syllabication						×	×	×	×
Dictionary									
Diacritical marks					×	×	×	×	×
Using guide words and pronunciation key						×	×	×	×
Checking meanings						×	×	×	×
Accent marks, syllabication							×	×	×
COMPREHENSION SKILLS									
Finding main idea									
In picture series	×								
Recalling, discussing idea		×	×	×	×	×	×	×	×
Finding for outline, summary							×	×	×
Key sentences in paragraphs							×	×	×
Sequence									
In picture series	×								
Arranging sentence sequence		×	×	×	×	×			
Retelling story in sequence		×	×	×	×	×		×	×
Outlining sequence						×	×	×	×
Finding details									
To answer questions		×	×	×	×	×	×	×	×
To follow directions		×	×	×	×	×	×	×	×
To support main ideas							×	×	×
Creative and critical reading									
Drawing conclusions, predicting outcomes, inferring	×	×	×	×	×	×	×	×	×
Recognizing cause and effect		×	×	×	×	×	×	×	×
Making comparisons		×	×	×	×	×	×	×	×
Distinguishing between									
Fact and fancy	×	×	×	×	×	×	×	×	×
Relevancy and irrelevancy		×	×	×	×	×	×	×	×
Similarities and differences				×	×	×	×	×	×
Relating story to personal experiences	×	×	×	×	×	×	×	×	×
Appreciating imagery and literary style		×	×	×	×	×	×	×	×
Interpreting attitudes and feelings		×	×	×	×	×	×	×	×
Analyzing and using varying literary forms					×	×	×	×	×
Interpreting author's style and point of view							×	×	×

Chart 4–3.   Sequence of development of basic reading skills.

	R	PP	P	1	2	3	4	5	6
UTILIZATION SKILLS									
Locating information									
Using maps, charts, diagrams	×	×	×	×	×	×	×	×	×
Using titles in lesson	×	×	×	×	×	×	×	×	×
Using table of contents		×	×	×	×	×	×	×	×
Using alphabetical order		×	×	×	×	×	×	×	×
Skimming for information				×	×	×	×	×	×
Composing, selecting titles					×	×	×	×	×
Using index, encyclopedia, card catalogue							×	×	×
Using information									
Classifying pictures	×								
Classifying words, sentences		×	×	×	×	×	×	×	×
Classifying longer forms					×	×	×	×	×
Reading to follow directions		×	×	×	×	×	×	×	×
Classifying events, information				×	×	×	×	×	×
Summarizing					×	×	×	×	×
Outlining						×	×	×	×
Taking notes							×	×	×

Chart 4–3. Sequence of development of basic reading skills (continued).

Examples of specific utilizations of these various modes may be seen in Chart 4–3, which represents the sequential development of decoding, comprehension, and utilization skills from the reading-readiness stage through the level of the sixth reader, as suggested in several recent courses of study. (These *textbook* levels do not necessarily coincide with grade levels.)

Oral reading involves the translation of written language into speech through oral expression techniques derived from the discipline of rhetoric. Inquiry modes utilized in oral reading include use of graphic punctuation marks as clues for meaning, intonation, pitch, and stress and use of diacritical and accent marks for appropriate word pronunciation.

The structure of the instructional program consists of three interwoven aspects: goals, curricular framework, and instructional techniques. Goals are set forth in broad statements of objectives and are reflected in curricular activities. The curricular framework is defined along its vertical dimension by sequential stages of reading skill development, and across its horizontal dimension, at every grade level, by the categories or aspects of the reading program. Teaching strategies, materials of instruction, and methods of evaluation complete the structure of the reading program. These aspects will be outlined in greater detail in the remainder of this chapter.

OBJECTIVES OF INSTRUCTION

The objectives of reading instruction expressed in courses of study and professional publications tend to cluster about three major goals: acquisition of word-recognition skills; development of comprehension, reference, and thinking skills; and inculcation of interest and good taste in reading. The first goal is essential and consumes much time in beginning reading instruction; it is viewed as basic to the achievement of the other goals, which receive greater attention in statements of objectives. Greater emphasis is being given to the development of critical and creative responses by the child to the material he reads and to his utilization of the ideas and information he encounters. Examples of recently stated objectives include enabling the child to:

> **Develop word-attack skills leading to independence in reading**
> **Read silently with efficiency and satisfactory speed**
> **Read effectively for differing purposes, adapting his rate of reading to specific purposes**
> **Acquire an increasing vocabulary**
> **Read orally with skillful expression**
> **Learn to locate information, select and evaluate a variety of reference materials, and organize information derived from these sources**
> **Understand and interpret the materials read by thinking critically and creatively about what he has read, organizing ideas, inferring implicit meanings, evaluating conclusions, and applying ideas to daily life**
> **Develop the attitude that reading is thinking**
> **Acquire the motivation for permanent interest in functional and recreational reading**
> **Become familiar with various literary forms and styles**
> **Develop refined literary tastes and appreciations**
> **Advance his social and personal development by presenting ideas and developing attitudes associated with good character and citizenship**
> **Acquire an appreciation of the ways in which reading can enrich life, widen experience, and enhance an understanding of the world in which he lives**

DEVELOPMENTAL STAGES IN READING INSTRUCTION

Learning to read, to grow in reading skills, is recognized as a sequential and developmental process (NSSE, 1961). The sequence of developmental

PROVIDENCE
COLLEGE
LIBRARY

stages in reading growth is based upon the structure of English, the child's language abilities, experience, and mental maturity, patterns of learning, and the child's developmental tasks.

While it is considered valid to apply a defined sequence to *all* learners, the particular pace of learning and ultimate achievement of individuals will vary according to the differences of learners and of instructional techniques. Because of differences in pace of learning and the fact that reading growth proceeds only when the sequential stages are developed without shortcuts or omissions, many school systems have given up the practice of setting skill expectations for each grade level. Instead, courses of study provide outlines of developmental stages of reading growth which do not coincide with grade levels. Reading skill expectations are indicated for each developmental stage. The child meets these expectations in accordance with his uninterrupted progress through these stages, without regard to his grade-level designation.

Some outlines of developmental stages are broadly stated, such as the following example (California, 1957):

I. Prereading stage

During this stage, the child is engaged in a program of experiences designed to enhance his oral language development to a level equal to or greater than the level of materials for beginning reading. Experiences are also provided to broaden his references for concept development and comprehension. The child is trained in auditory and visual discrimination, listens to, tells, and discusses stories, and learns basic work and study habits. Further experiences are provided to develop his mental, physical, emotional, and social readiness for reading.

II. Initial reading stage

The child at this stage gains practice in following left-right sequence, in dictating stories based on current experiences which are recorded on charts for rereading, and in recognizing from about fifty to over one hundred words by sight. He begins to use picture, context, and configuration clues to recognize words, and then goes on to beginning instruction in phonetic and structural analysis techniques. He learns to use and handle books, acquires the understanding that reading yields information, and begins to develop skills in finding main ideas, anticipating outcomes, making inferences, finding details, and noting sequence.

III. Stage of rapid progress

During this stage, the child extends his use of a variety of word-recognition techniques and begins to use the dictionary for word meaning, spelling, and pronunciation. He extends his vocabulary and comprehension skills, he reads with understanding a greater variety of materials, and he begins to read independently for information and pleasure.

IV. Stage of extended reading experience and rapidly increasing reading efficiency
At this level, the child has greater facility in reading, uses word-recognition techniques automatically, and is almost completely independent in reading. He reads with understanding in the subject areas, extends his dictionary and reference-use skills, uses the library independently, and begins to use reading as a tool in problem solving.

V. Stage of refinement in reading abilities, attitudes, and tastes
The child at this stage has acquired independence in locating and utilizing a variety of materials, is aware of varied purposes for reading, and has developed skills of critical evaluation of material read. His reading interests are extended, and his literary tastes refined. This refinement process actually begins with initial reading instruction and proceeds into adult life.

Some school systems utilize outlines of developmental stages which include references to levels of basal textbooks appropriately used at each stage. Englewood, New Jersey (1963), and New York City (1964) utilize outlines similar to the following example. Both courses of study provide charts indicating, for each stage, evidence of pupil readiness, word-recognition standards, and appropriate comprehension and work-study skills.

Basal texts	*Stages of reading growth*
	A. Reading readiness: identical to the prereading stage of the previous outline; oral language activities.
PP, 1–1, 1–2	**B.** Initial instructional level: coincides with initial reading stage of previous outline.
1–2, 2–1, 2–2	**C.** Initial independent level: a transitional stage between levels *B* and *D*, during which the child gains skill in word-recognition techniques, follows written directions independently, shows increased enjoyment of rhyming sounds and repetitive phrases, shows increasing interest in reading a variety of materials, and voluntarily selects books for his own use.

2–2, 3–1, 3–2   *D.* Late primary level: the child is now growing rapidly in reading skills and is reading more widely on his own. His vocabulary increases in complexity and he adds syllabication to his increased fluency in use of word-attack skills. He begins to grasp thought by phrases, develops a steady, rhythmic progress along the line of print in silent and oral reading, and begins to develop skills in content-area reading.

3–2, 4, 5   *E.* Early intermediate level: the child extends his reading skills, rate, and comprehension. He needs careful, systematic instruction to equip him with skills in comprehending and utilizing more complex reference and content-area materials. He displays interest in things and events beyond his immediate experience and environment and extends his reading interests through use of varied materials. He develops a variety of new purposes for wider functional and recreational reading and uses reading in problem solving. He is ready for reading experiences that stimulate intuitive insight and emphasize dimensions of comprehension related to feelings and appreciations.

5, 6, 7   *F.* Late intermediate level: the child is becoming interested in figurative language, connotations and shades of meaning, and technical uses of words. He begins to recognize components of authors' styles, purposes, and attitudes. He is ready for guidance in literary appreciation and in the application of interpretive skills and critical thinking. He begins to apply principles or generalizations to new learnings, works independently with varied source materials, and evidences interest in a wider range of functional and recreational reading.

6, 7, 8, 9   *G.* Secondary level: at this level, the child refines his interpretive and evaluative skills, grasps implied ideas, and begins to evaluate an author's background, qualifications, purposes, and the quality and value of his work. He has established habits of reading regularly for pleasure and information and is discriminating in selection of reading material. He withholds judgment in the absence of sufficient data, questions the validity

and realiability of information sources, and evidences more perceptive interpretation of what he reads as he approaches adult levels of reading skill.

Most recent courses of study provide guidelines for specific activities and instruction in the kindergarten program designed to develop reading readiness. A few school systems are exploring the advisability of beginning formal reading instruction in kindergarten.

THE COMPLETE READING PROGRAM

The developmental stages of reading growth represent the vertical axis of the elementary reading program. Along its horizontal axis, the program is defined by aspects which run as strands through all stages or levels. These aspects may be outlined on the basis of reading materials or, more frequently, in terms of areas of reading activities. When the former outline is used, activities are centered around, and skills developed in connection with, the use of specific materials. Examples of such organization in recent courses of study (San Diego, 1961; Pasadena, 1961) are outlined in Chart 4–4.

The first program provides specified textbook series for areas I and II, with a variety of trade books and library works utilized in area III, and subject-matter materials, reference sources, maps, diagrams, newspapers, and magazines utilized in area IV. The second program is provided with a choice of two basal series for area I, several basal and supplementary series for use in area II, one specific textbook series for area III, and one specific textbook series for area IV.

When reading activities and skill areas are used to define the program, a greater variety of materials is utilized in connection with each activity. Many recent courses of study follow this approach. In some courses of

Chart 4–4. **Programs organized around reading materials.**

I Basic text reading	I Basal text program
II Supplementary text reading	II Supplementary reader program
III Personal interest reading	III Literature program
IV Reading in content fields, reference and news reading	IV Moral and spiritual values program

study, the areas listed below are grouped into three or four categories; in others they appear individually, but may be worded differently. However, provision is made in recent courses of study for all the following areas:

1. **Vocabulary and concept development**
2. **Word-analysis techniques**
3. **Comprehension skills**
4. **Oral reading**
5. **Reference and study skills**
6. **Reading in subject areas**
7. **Independent recreational reading**
8. **Appreciation of poetry and literature**
9. **Development of positive attitudes, interests, and good taste in reading**

TEACHING STRATEGIES

Vocabulary and Concept Development

Extensive vocabulary and concept development is essential to all areas of the curriculum and all aspects of the child's mental growth. Because meanings and concepts are expressed most commonly through the medium of verbal symbols, curricular efforts to promote vocabulary and concept development in the early grades are carried on primarily through language arts activities. The child's grasp of meaning is based largely upon his background of experience. The provision of further appropriate experiences, direct and concrete, vicarious and abstract, is an important part of the elementary curriculum. In addition, teachers encourage oral expression to develop language fluency, to introduce new words inductively after experience has provided understanding, and to enable children to apply new words and concepts. As the child progresses through the grades, there is a shift in emphasis from direct experience to more abstract analysis in terms of language itself. Verbal context is used to provide meaning through definitions, examples, restatements, modifiers, and position in word-order sequence. Roots, affixes, synonyms, antonyms, and homonyms are analyzed and compared in the middle elementary grades. In the upper grades, children explore word connotations and figurative language in order to enrich understandings, and they encounter special or technical meanings and complex concepts in subject areas. While occasions arise for specific lessons in vocabulary and concept development, learnings are acquired in all areas of the curriculum throughout the school day as well as outside the school.

Word-analysis Techniques

Word analysis involves the decoding of phoneme-grapheme correspondence and the recognition of words, the first aspect of the reading process. Most reading experts agree that no single word-recognition technique is adequate for all situations because of the phonetic irregularities of English and the differences in individual learning styles. The several techniques are usually introduced in the following sequence: sight vocabulary, configuration, picture clues, context, phonetic analysis, structural analysis, and use of the dictionary. All these techniques are introduced in the primary grades, during levels corresponding to II and C of the developmental stages outlined above, and are utilized in varying degrees by children at succeeding levels of reading growth.

Many educators recommend that children be taught to recognize some words in their entirety as a first step in learning to read. The graphic pattern of the whole word thus becomes the symbol corresponding to the total sound symbols of the spoken word. Each word is unique; there is no generalization of phoneme-grapheme correspondence from one word to another. The intent of this recommendation is twofold: (1) to provide about fifty to one hundred words, recognized by the child, which can be used as examples for the development of phonetic and structural analysis skills, and (2) to give the child practice in reading whole sentences with understanding sooner than would be possible on the basis of phonetic analysis. The child thus comes to understand reading as a process of deriving meaning, not merely sounds, from graphic symbols. Selection of words for the child's sight vocabulary is largely at each teacher's discretion. Words are usually chosen on the basis of their use in curricular activities, the special interests of the class, high frequency of use in the children's oral vocabulary, and appearance in preprimers and primers to be used by the class.

Some linguistic scholars oppose this approach and instead recommend that reading instruction begin with the learning of the alphabet, grapheme-phoneme correspondences of initial consonant sounds, and the introduction of phonetically regular short-vowel one-syllable words and phonograms. Other linguists maintain that this procedure limits the child's derivation of *meaning* from graphic symbols. They recommend that structural or functional words and some words of high frequency of use in the child's oral vocabulary be introduced as sight words concurrent with instruction in phonetic and structural analysis principles consistent with linguistic principles of the structure of English.

When sight words are used, children are taught to recall and recognize them by means of configuration, picture, and context clues. These techniques involve analysis of length, height, letter shapes, and overall configuration of a printed word; observing and interpreting pictorial illustrations; making inferences beyond the literal content of illustrations; and grasping word meaning on the basis of a word's position in a sentence and the meaning of the total context.

Phonetic analysis is the identification of sounds in printed words. Instruction in this skill, phonics, is the application of phonetic principles to reading and spelling instruction. There is general agreement in most courses of study on the sequence in which principles of phonetic analysis are introduced.

1. **Phoneme-grapheme correspondence of initial consonant sounds**
2. **Consonant digraphs: ch, sh, wh, th, ck, ph**
3. **Consonant blends: bl, br, cl, dr, str, etc.**
4. **Short vowel sounds in single syllables, phonograms**
5. **Final e rule for long vowel sounds**
6. **Vowel digraphs: au, ai, ay, ee, ie, oa, oe**
7. **Diphthongs, blended vowels: oi, oy, ow, ou**
8. **Variant vowel sounds, vowels followed by r, w, ll**
9. **Sound of soft c and g**
10. **Silent letters in consonant combinations: kn, ght, mb, lm, lk, gh, wr, gn, ps**

These phonetic principles are not presented to the child for memorization and deductive application. Instead, he learns to understand a principle by acquiring it inductively as a result of examination, comparison, and observation of a number of examples which follow that principle. The following concept formation strategy may be used:

1. **Children are presented with several examples of words following the same principle.**
2. **They listen to examples in oral form, observe the graphic symbols, and note similarities, common elements, or differences in the examples.**
3. **They express, discuss, and compare their observations. This leads them to express the principle or generalization in their own words.**
4. **They apply their understanding by finding additional examples and testing exceptions to the rule.**
5. **They use their understanding of the principle as a word-recognition technique.**

While phonetic analysis deals with graphic representations of sound, structural analysis deals with visual observation and word meaning, as children identify the parts of a word which form meaningful units. Words may be grouped into three structural categories: root words with inflectional changes, root words with affixes, and compound words. In addition, polysyllabic words may be separated into their syllabic construction, with phonetic analysis techniques applied to separate syllables. Each specific inflectional change and each use of an affix constitutes a structural analysis principle. There are numerous generalizations regarding syllabication, as well. A few examples are listed below:

> *I.* *Root words with inflectional changes*
>   *A.* **Endings: ed, ing, s, es, est, er, 's**
>   *B.* **Internal changes: man/men, run/ran**
>
> *II.* *Root words with affixes*
>   *A.* **Definitions of roots: duc = lead, graph = write**
>   *B.* **Definitions of prefixes: anti = against, ex = out of, from**
>   *C.* **Definitions of suffixes: —ant = being, one who, —ic = like, made of, —less = without**
>
> *III.* *Compound words*
>   *A.* **Two root words combined: chalkboard, maybe, merry-go-round**
>   *B.* **Contractions: can't = cannot, he'd = he had, he would**
>
> *IV.* *Syllabication*
>   *A.* **There are as many syllables in a word as there are sounded vowels.**
>   *B.* **When a consonant occurs between two vowels, the first syllable is usually open and has a long vowel sound (o-bey, ba-by).**

Many structural analysis principles may be derived inductively. As in the case of phonetic analysis, children should not be expected to understand a principle unless they use a sufficient number of words following the principle and are ready to encounter many more.

Children learn to use the dictionary to check spelling and syllabication, learn word meanings, investigate word derivations, discover synonyms, antonyms, or variant meanings, and determine proper pronunciation. They approach the dictionary in the earliest grades after training in alphabetical order. As they explore various dictionaries, they may be guided to discover such generalizations as the extension of alphabetizing beyond the initial letter of a word, the letters marking the dictionary into thirds or quarters for convenient reference, and the meanings of accent marks, diacritical marks, and the international phonetic alphabet.

Other important approaches to the teaching of beginning reading deal with the problems of word recognition in differing ways. One approach (Gattegno, 1962) uses letters in forty-seven different colors and shades in order to identify that number of phonemes in the English language. The color used for a phoneme is constant, regardless of the varying spellings of the sound. After children have learned to associate sounds and colors, they are taught to write and read familiar materials in black and white.

Another attempt to overcome the difficulties posed by irregularities of spelling is the Diacritical Marking System (Fry, 1964) which, like the words-in-color system, uses traditional spelling but supplements it with dia-critical marks to indicate sounds of vowels, and some digraphs and single consonants.

A third approach receiving wide attention employs the Pitman Initial Teaching Alphabet (i/t/a). This augmented alphabet supplies forty-four symbols for a one-to-one correspondence with the distinctive phonemes of English (Downing, 1961; Pitman, 1961). Children are taught to recog-nize the sound-symbol relationships, which, unlike the spelling of words in traditional orthography (TO) remain constant. When the child has reached a level of independence in reading corresponding to the third-reader level, he begins a transition to traditional orthography. Proponents of the pro-gram state that most children taught to read with i/t/a make the transition at the end of the first grade. Because of the regularity of grapheme-phoneme correspondence, teachers using i/t/a have found that the first- and second-grade pupils are more fluent and prolific in their independent written expression than are pupils who learn to read through traditional orthogra-phy.

The i/t/a program was instituted in England in 1961. Tryouts in the United States began in 1963. Enthusiasm for the program is expressed by many teachers who have used it. They claim that it enables children to learn to read easily, that the children proceed more quickly to higher levels of reading than those using TO, and that the transition to TO is easily ac-complished. The claims for the effectiveness of i/t/a may seem to be more dramatic than those on behalf of other programs because of the unfamiliar element involved—the new sound symbols. Proponents of the i/t/a program have been challenged to support their claims through well-designed com-parative studies and longitudinal research. Much controversy surrounds existing reports of research and evaluation of i/t/a programs. Debates about the validity of this research and evaluation have been published and discussed in professional journals (Barrett, 1965; Gillooly, 1966; Mazurk-iewicz, 1965; Mazurkiewicz & Dolmatch, 1966). It is clear that children *are* able to learn to read using i/t/a, but important questions remain. What is the relationship between the same child's reading ability in i/t/a and in TO? What problems do children encounter in making the transition to TO? Is this transition more difficult for some types of learners? Once the transition is made, what are the comparable reading skill levels of children who have and have not used i/t/a? Are there differences in the reading skills

Chart 4–5. Initial Teaching Alphabet.

of the two groups when the children have reached the upper elementary grades?

Some programmed materials, based on linguistic approaches to reading, are beginning to be used for initial reading instruction in many school systems. Early tryouts have indicated success for this approach as well as for those outlined above. Longitudinal and comparative research and evaluation are needed to determine the effectiveness of each approach for different types of learners.

Comprehension Skills

Reading comprehension may be defined as *thinking* stimulated by the printed word symbols (New York State, 1963, p. 40). Comprehension skills may be considered in terms of three categories related to thinking qualities: literal comprehension, critical comprehension, and appreciative comprehension. "Interpretive" comprehension is a term applied to either of the last two categories, since both involve interpretation. These are not mutually exclusive categories; literal comprehension is basic to other levels, and a child may utilize all three levels with any given reading material, depending upon his purposes in reading.

Literal comprehension involves the following skills:

1. Understanding the main idea of paragraphs, stories, and other forms of written language
2. Noting details, finding relevant details to answer questions, support viewpoints, or contribute to other comprehension skills
3. Following sequences and predicting outcomes of stories and descriptions
4. Following directions, which involves sequence and details

Critical comprehension involves:

5. Critical evaluation; noting relevancy and irrelevancy, distinguishing between fact and opinion, comparing, evaluating the authenticity of a source of information, determining veracity or bias of materials that are read, evaluating author's viewpoint, purpose, style, and qualifications
6. Seeing implied relationships and hidden meanings; sensing cause-effect relationships
7. Interpreting and explaining; summarizing, organizing, synthesizing ideas or information
8. Drawing conclusions, deriving generalizations, and making inferences on the basis of what is read

Appreciative comprehension involves:

9. Noting elements of style in writing
10. Obtaining sensory impressions from descriptive writing
11. Sensing mood, feeling, and atmosphere created by elements of writing style
12. Identifying with characters; understanding motivation and relationships in story or narrative

13. **Sensing humor, satire, nonsense, and exaggeration and understanding their purpose in what is read**
14. **Relating ideas and feelings to personal experience**

Critical reading is the application of critical comprehension skills; creative reading is the application of appreciative comprehension skills. Beginning readers must devote much attention to grappling with literal comprehension skills during initial stages of their instruction. But the effective teacher will begin development of critical and appreciative comprehension skills suitable to the level of the child's mental maturity and the nature of his reading materials concurrently with skills at the literal level. Early training in critical reading is necessary to meet current objectives of education, which place a high value on the child's ability to think.

Continuing development of comprehension skills is brought about by means of a variety of approaches, each of which is a combination of specific types of media and instructional procedures.

Individualized reading is a term applied to procedures which may vary but which have the following characteristics in common: (1) availability in the classroom of numerous trade books, library books, magazines, and other materials in a wide range of reading levels and topics; (2) the teacher's observation, encouragement and guidance of self-selection of books by pupils; (3) children's progression from one book to another at their own pace; (4) development and evaluation of comprehension primarily through individual pupil-teacher conferences.

Basal textbook series are being developed with vocabulary and sentence structure based upon the suggestions and direct participation of linguists. Concomitant attempts are being made to write primary-grade stories in the manner of children's natural speech patterns. There is a trend toward inclusion of excerpts of works of children's literature in order to improve literary quality and acquaint the child with the best of classic and recent poems, stories, and essays. Several recent basal series include multiethnic content, stories of integrated groups of people in urban settings. The purpose of these books is to overcome the difficulties in comprehension that the disadvantaged urban child may encounter when he must read stories unrelated to his sociocultural environment.

A third type of program is based on the assumption that children can more easily read material that they have written. The "experience" program in the primary grades usually begins with provision for enriching curricular and co-curricular experiences of the pupils. Children are then guided to record their personal and group experiences in their own words. These records constitute the children's major reading material, but discussion and related activities lead to reading of related commercial materials.

A similar program for slow readers in the upper elementary grades utilizes creative writing and retelling stories to a greater extent than it does personal experience. It is referred to as the "multimedia approach" because it uses films, records, dramatizations, and other media to stimulate intensive discussion of topics of interest, to generate creative ideas, or to present a story to be retold in the pupils' own words. The resultant reports, discussion summaries, or stories are duplicated and read by the group or class. The experience and multimedia approaches actually go beyond reading instruction; they are strategies for the simultaneous development of skills in all the language arts.

Oral Reading

In some classrooms, oral reading is a major activity of the reading program, but may be very sterile if the teacher is unaware of the uses of oral reading and confines it to round-robin recitations without question or comment. Reading educators today recommend oral reading because of its value as an expressive activity and as an adjunct to development of reading and thinking skills.

During early instruction, oral reading is used by the teacher to evaluate the child's association of sounds and graphic symbols. At all reading levels, the teacher listens as the child reads in order to determine his ability to see and comprehend words in idea units of meaningful phrases. Direct instruction in the oral reading skills of eye span and vocal phrasing help the child to read silently in idea units.

Oral reading serves to enhance reading and thinking skills when children select a passage to read aloud in order to answer questions, share information, prove a point, interpret meaning through oral expression, share favorite passages, highlight colorful writing, or entertain others. Children should be helped to formulate standards for oral expression as well as for the listening skills that constitute appropriate responses to the purposes for oral reading.

One of the systems of language structure that provides signals for meaning is intonation: pitch, stress, juncture, and pauses. Children need to learn, as they are learning graphemes formed by letters, that the punctuation graphemes also correspond to sounds and to durations of silence between sounds and that these sounds and silences convey meaning.

Reference and Study Skills

Reference and study skills applicable to all areas of the elementary curriculum may be considered under the categories of locating and utilizing information.

Location of information involves acquisition of knowledge about relevant information sources and knowledge of the organization of information within these sources. Young children begin to become familiar with the resources of school, public, and special libraries when they visit a library to hear stories and look at books. When they are allowed to borrow books, they begin to need skills in locating and caring for them. At about the third-grade level children begin to use the card catalogue and indexes. As needs arise at every reading level, teachers introduce pupils to such relevant materials as dictionaries, encyclopedias, almanacs, directories, atlases, periodicals, and newspapers. Each of these sources has its own structure or organization, and pupils need appropriate instruction in such skills as alphabetizing, defining topical references in encyclopedias, utilizing the various organizational parts of a book, and using the different sections and features of a newspaper.

Utilization of information involves the reading of special materials and the recording and organization of acquired ideas or information. Different types of source materials utilize different syntax and specialized vocabularies. An encyclopedia article usually has a noun or noun phrase as its title, presents a primarily factual narrative, and utilizes appropriate abbreviations. A newspaper article utilizes a special syntax in its title, which sometimes includes unique abbreviations, spellings, or specially coined words, and presents a narrative that is selectively (and not always completely) factual. In addition to needing instruction regarding language structure in different source materials, the child needs to learn to adapt his rate of reading to his purpose and to the content and level of difficulty of the material he reads.

Reading materials include much information that is best conveyed in ways other than verbal description. Illustrations in fiction, nonfiction, and textbooks often complement or augment verbal descriptions. The child needs training in relating, analyzing, and utilizing this pictorial material, which offers both literal and implied information. Cartoons and schematic drawings convey meaning less directly; the child needs instruction in recognition of symbols and comprehension of symbolism. Charts, graphs, tables, time lines, and diagrams use verbal and quantitative symbols in conjunction with pictorial symbols, such as arrows, lines, boxes, circles, grids. Maps and globes use a variety of quantitative, verbal, and pictorial symbols that unlock both literal and implied understandings.

Language skills in locating, recording, and organizing information from reference sources include skimming to find details, for general understanding, and for preliminary appraisal of materials, collecting, classifying, outlining, note-taking, synthesizing, and summarizing.

All the reference and study skills outlined above must be taught directly; teachers cannot assume that even the most independent readers will be able to acquire all these skills incidentally. Instruction is most effective when it is provided in response to specific learning needs, carried on with appropriate materials for every child, and followed by meaningful practice and application.

All the graphic reference sources cited above, both verbal and pictorial, provide information needed by the child in all areas of the curriculum and in the pursuit of co-curricular interests. When any of these skills are taught in connection with a particular subject area, the teacher should be sure that students note the application of the skill to other curricular areas as well.

Reading in Subject Areas

All the reading comprehension skills and reference-study skills previously cited are applied to reading in the subject areas. Beyond this common ground of reference sources, reading skills, and study skills, each subject differs in the nature of its textbooks and related materials. Social studies, science, and arithmetic textbooks differ considerably in format, sequence of content, style, and syntax and in the use of specialized or technical vocabulary. Applicable thinking skills vary in emphasis from one subject area to another.

Social studies textbooks seem, at first glance, to resemble reading books, but the resemblance is superficial. Stories are read and forgotten as unrelated stories are encountered, but important facts, significant concepts, and major generalizations acquired during earlier readings must be available for recall as the child progresses through the social studies textbook. Sentences are longer and more complex, more information is packed into each sentence, and each paragraph may deal with several complex and imprecise concepts. Both factual and opinionated material may be included, leading to a need for skill in distinguishing fact, opinion, and bias. Reproductions or facsimiles of documents may be included in the text; each of these requires specific comprehension and utilization skills. Unlike other subject areas, social studies courses may have several textbooks, requiring skill in making comparisons of sources and applying other critical comprehension skills. The child will also need to skim for information, locate relevant details, relate main and subordinate ideas, note cause-effect relationships, relate what he reads to his own experiences, be alert to propaganda devices, classify, attain concepts, draw conclusions, formulate generalizations, and make inferences.

Many of these skills also apply to reading in science textbooks. In addition, textbooks and materials in both areas utilize illustrations and diagrams which are essential to understanding. Unlike the social studies book, the science textbook may have several self-contained sections or units, with less book-long continuity of concepts. Like arithmetic, science employs a highly technical vocabulary, involves precise concepts, and requires the reading of various measurement devices. The child needs skill in following a sequence or cluster of relevant details, locating information for problem solving, interpreting cause-effect relationships and correlations, reading for precise information, following directions for research and experiments, and identifying classification patterns.

Arithmetic textbooks have a unique sequence of organization. Topics such as numeration, measurement, subtraction, or multiplication are not dealt with as units, but are developed sequentially throughout the book. The child spends a page or two on one topic, goes on to another, and picks up the next step in the first topic after several other topics have intervened. (Of course, teachers may alter the sequence in their instruction if they deem it necessary.) The child needs to read at a pace that will ensure accuracy of understanding and grasp of all details. He will have to retain facts, concepts, and generalizations related to each topic. The information he encounters is given in quantitative and pictorial symbols which he must translate into words, phrases, or sentences, such as $6 + 4 = 10$ or $50 \div x = 2$ (x). Symbols such as U, ( ), $\neq$, must be translated into words which have meaning at a conceptual level. Verbal statements of quantitative problems have unique syntactical structures that call for specific skills in determining questions, selecting relevant information, and choosing appropriate processes. In addition, as he is reading, the child often needs to form visual images of what he reads.

Readings in the areas of art and music are similar to those in social studies and science, in that special terms are used, processes are described, directions are given, and historical or biographical narratives are read.

Because materials and content differ, transfer of common skills from one subject to another should not be assumed to be automatic. Skill instruction should be provided for each subject area, often within the reading program, and then followed up with application and reinforcement in subsequent subject-area lessons.

Literature

The school is often the child's major contact with various forms of literature. This encounter should be designed to provide him with opportunities for enjoyment and creativity; with an extension of his experiences, interests, vocabulary, and understanding; and with an enrichment, through related literature, of learnings in all subjects areas.

As the child is introduced to poetry, stories, trade books, plays, and the creative written expression in his own classroom, he learns not merely to recognize, but to use, the different structural forms and elements of literature. He also encounters recurring literary themes and discovers man's use of literary forms to express human feelings and ideas through all ages of recorded history.

A strategy for literary analysis (outlined for secondary instruction but applicable to the elementary curriculum) provides a framework for questions dealing with the comparatively objective analysis of the formal structure of the work and the more subjective or divergent consideration of its value (Commission on English, 1966, p. 58). The framework for classroom questions may be restated in terms suitable to any grade level. The parenthetical notations indicate the level of the questions in each category in terms of the taxonomies of cognitive and affective objectives (Bloom, 1956; Krathwohl, Bloom, & Masia, 1964).

I. Questions about the text itself
    A. Questions of form (knowledge, analysis)
        1. What is its kind?
        2. What are its parts?
        3. How are the parts related?
    B. Questions of rhetoric (knowledge)
        1. Who is speaking?
        2. What is the occasion?
        3. Who is the audience?
    C. Questions of meaning (comprehension)
        1. What meaning has each word in its particular context?
        2. What do the diction and grammar of the text tell about its purpose?
        3. What is the paraphrasable content of the work, its "statement"?
        4. What intention is apparent, and how is it made apparent?
        5. What part of meaning is sacrificed by paraphrase— by substitution of words other than those used by the author?

II. Questions about the value of the text
    A. Questions about personal response (responding, valuing)
    B. Questions about the excellence of the text (evaluation)

Using a guideline such as this, the classroom teacher may determine the relative emphasis to be given to questions of structure and value, the sequence of questions to be discussed, the particular works that may be compared, and any other modifications that suit the specific text and grade level. The teacher may present a guideline for discussion as a conceptual invention upon which pupils may expand, or particularly in the upper elementary grades, the pupils may be guided, through comparative examination of several works, to develop their own inquiry tools. Examples of concept clusters derived from this framework include (1) form: type, component parts, relationship of parts; (2) rhetorical aspects: speaker, occasion, audience; (3) meaning: words in context, meaning in syntactic structure, theme, message, intention.

Another strategy is provided by a curriculum project which organizes instruction in language and composition around the direct study of literature in grades 1-12 (Nebraska, 1963). The Nebraska program is designed to identify the concepts and generalizations which describe the classifications, structures, and themes of literary works and to develop these understandings at increasingly complex levels through the grades. The spiral development of the curriculum carries forward nine classification strands from first to sixth grade: folktales, fanciful stories, animal stories, adventure stories, myths, fables, stories of other lands and people, historical fiction, and biography. The concepts developed in these grades are intended to provide a basis for the study of more formal, analytical units in junior and senior high school: units on the epic, tragedy, the idea of a play, and so on.

The overall strategy of the project is the presentation of selected works, in oral or written form, as sources of enjoyment to be discussed informally and to which children may respond in creative ways. Although each unit contains a literary analysis for the teacher's background, the children are not expected to analyze the works in adult terms. Rather, the stories are intended to provide a fund of examples upon which children may draw for inductive discovery of patterns and classifications.

A basic strategy for presentation of a specific work involves the following procedures:

> *Preparation*: **The teacher familiarizes herself with the story, poem, or book and any relevant background information. If she plans to read aloud or recite, she practices in order to convey style, mood, meaning. If a pupil is to present the work, he too should be adequately prepared.**

> *Response*: **Pupils express their responses in oral and written form. Although they do not engage in formal analysis, they may outline sequences with pictures or act out a story. Such responses add activities at the levels of application and synthesis, in contrast to the analytical strategy outlined previously.**

> *Composition*: **The form, patterns, or theme of the work may be used as a model or stimulus for the pupils' own written or oral compositions. As an aid to concept formation, visual models or pictures are utilized—symbolic figures and objects which represent thematic elements such as the monster, the hero, the secure home, rather than the characters of a specific work.**

Additional readings: The teacher guides each child in the selection of related readings appropriate to his individual requirements.

Evaluation: Evaluation of each child's written or oral responses is individualized and positive. Attention is given to one or two important areas of improvement, without correction of every detail. This is not to say that some errors are ignored; rather, some change is made in the composition, while other corrections are made in the form of separate activities or language lessons.

Effective teachers provide a classroom atmosphere conducive to the enjoyment of literature. Materials are made available which represent a broad range of reading levels and content as well as a variety of sources and forms. All the language arts come into play as children listen to poems and stories read aloud, recite or dramatize what they hear or read, and discuss what they have heard, read, enacted, and written. They utilize different literary forms in their creative written expression, and, of course, they are provided with time to read.

Professional publications and recent courses of study recommend an emphasis on enjoyment and stimulation of children's creative power by providing a relaxed atmosphere in which children are free to respond in divergent ways. Overanalysis of form and meaning is not encouraged. Instead, children should be guided to discover elements of form and to express their own interpretations of meaning. Although the literature studied carefully by the entire class may be, in a sense, prescribed in order to contribute to the sequential development of specific concepts, an important goal of literature experiences in the classroom is the development of the child's independence in reading as he is given the opportunity for self-selection of materials and thoughtful, individualized appraisal of what he reads. Recreational reading provides the child with opportunities to apply his reading skills to areas of his own interests and permits a greater degree of individualization of learning.

GUIDELINES FOR THE TEACHER

Many guidelines have been explicitly stated and implied in the preceding section. Additional guidelines found in curriculum outlines and professional publications include the following suggestions:

Utilize a variety of approaches to reading instruction.   No single method has been shown to be the best solution to the full range of reading problems in any school system or even within one class. Select the techniques and materials best suited to the varying needs of different groups or of individual learners.

Use flexible grouping. Organize children in different groups for specific skill instruction, common interests, or special activities. Provide opportunities for children to work in groups that cut across reading levels. Evaluate progress continuously, and regroup children whenever their needs change.

Provide a variety of reading materials in the classroom. Try to obtain materials on diverse topics, and at reading levels below, at, and a year or two above the range of the pupils' reading levels. Encourage children to cross grade or reading levels in their use of these materials.

Recognize individual differences and involve every child in every lesson. Encourage the participation of each pupil and ask questions that are geared to specific kinds and levels of comprehension.

EVALUATION OF PUPIL PROGRESS

Reading involves much more than a unitary skill. Indeed, the term "reading" applies to a broad complex of behaviors including, among others, word-recognition skills, comprehension, reference, and thinking skills, tastes, attitudes, and interests. Acquisition of this complex of behaviors is a highly individualized process and varies both in rate and level of attainment among children in the same grade or age group. Therefore, evaluation of pupil progress in reading must extend to all aspects of reading instruction and must be individualized. These two characteristics of pupil evaluation are found in recently published courses of study. Although specific programs and instructional techniques vary, the following guidelines (Artley, 1965) are applicable to all programs of reading instruction.

Evaluation of the individual pupil's reading achievement should be made in relation to his capacity for achievement. This guideline involves such determinations as the following:

1. How does the individual's current reading achievement compare with measures of his intelligence?
2. How does his performance compare with that of other children of the same age?
3. What level of material is he able to read independently, at what level does he require instructional help, and at what level does he reach the point of reading frustration?
4. What is the rate and consistency of his progress in all areas of reading behavior?

Questions 1 and 2 are assessed by means of a variety of techniques. Standardized achievement tests given early in the school year provide one measurement scale, but such tests are too limited in scope to be suitable as the sole form of measurement. Further dimensions of achievement and ability are gained by means of diagnostic tests and the use of cumulative records of a child's reading experiences. Forms for such records are provided in many school systems as new reading programs are implemented.

Question 3 refers to the child's independent reading level, defined as the level at which he recognizes 99 per cent of the words and comprehends at least 90 per cent of what he reads; the level at which he profits from instruction, defined as recognition of 95 per cent of the words and about 75 per cent comprehension; and the frustration level, defined as 70 per cent word recognition and about 50 per cent comprehension (Betts, 1957). This question, as well as the first two questions, is determined by means of individualized informal textbook tests (for which directions are provided in recent courses of study), teacher-made tests, and observation of the child's reading performance in a broad range of classroom activities. This type of observation, guided by check lists, also enables the teacher to assess question 4.

Evaluation of pupil progress must be continuous. More effective instruction is possible when evaluation of pupils' difficulties and achievement levels is continuous and is thoroughly integrated with individualized instruction.

Self-evaluation should be encouraged. Because learning to read is an individualized process, the pupil gains independence in learning when he is taught, through teacher-pupil conferences or class discussions resulting in cooperatively prepared criteria, to recognize and evaluate his own difficulties and accomplishments.

Evaluation must be directly related to all the objectives of the instructional program and should assess the pupil's growth both in and through reading. The classroom teacher may accomplish this by enumerating the objectives of the reading program, such as those discussed in this chapter, and determining appropriate evaluative instruments and techniques for each objective. If the stated objectives are limited, taxonomies of objectives may be used, as in the examples that follow (Bloom, 1956; Krathwohl et al., 1964).

Cognitive Domain

> *Knowledge level*: Basic language knowledge, concept and vocabulary development, knowledge of word-recognition techniques, and knowledge of criteria or procedures for oral reading, study skills, and reading in subject areas. These and other examples of language knowledge may be evaluated by means of standardized and teacher-made tests, observation of pupil performance, and workbook assignments.

Comprehension level: Literal and critical comprehension as described on page 112, above. The specific skills therein outlined may be evaluated by means of teacher-made tests, both formal and informal, oral questions and classroom discussions, informal textbook tests, teacher-pupil conferences to discuss pupils' records of individualized reading, workbook activities, pupil reports, and anecdotal records to evaluate growth in comprehension skills.

Application level: The child's use of his word knowledge, word-recognition skills, comprehension skills, study skills, and oral reading skills in his encounters with new reading materials in the developmental program, in subject-area reading, and in recreational reading. Teacher observation of the child's performance in varieties of reading situations is an appropriate technique and may be structured by means of check lists, rating scales, skills inventories, and anecdotal records. Informal classroom questions, teacher-pupil conferences, workbook assignments, and children's reports add to the dimensions of evaluation at the level of application.

Analysis level: The child's application of critical thinking to his reading experiences, involving skills of critical comprehension as outlined on page 112, above. Analytical skills may be evaluated by means of teacher-made tests, reports by pupils, and teacher-pupil conferences.

Synthesis level: The child's creative interpretation of reading content and his utilization of his readings in the formulation of his own thinking or creative expression. Skills of appreciative comprehension, outlined on page 112, fall within this level and may be evaluated by teacher observation, check lists, rating scales, anecdotal records, pupil compositions and reports, classroom discussions, and teacher-pupil conferences.

Evaluation level: In reading instruction, skills at the levels of comprehension, analysis, and synthesis, developed from the earliest grades, are utilized in combination by children in the upper elementary reading levels as more highly developed skills of evaluation of the content, purposes, and literary techniques of reading materials. Such evaluative skills may be observed and rated in a similar manner to the related skills at other levels.

Affective Domain

Receiving level: At the reading-readiness stage, the child's attention to what is read to him and his attentiveness and interest in beginning reading instruction. An effective evaluative technique is teacher observation, guided by check lists, rating scales, anecdotal records, and cumulative record cards.

Responding level: Evidence of the child's interest and satisfaction in reading. In addition to the techniques utilized at the receiving level, evaluation at both the responding and valuing levels may be conducted by means of pupil records of individual reading, reports and compositions, classroom discussion, questionnaires, and pupils' responses to incomplete projective statements.

Valuing level: Evidences of the child's regard for reading, his valuing of reading activities, development of scope and depth of interests in reading, valuing of critical appraisal of reading material, care of books, use of libraries, and further reading at home. In addition to techniques outlined above, attitudes and values may be evaluated in teacher-parent conferences.

Organizing level: The child's development of sets of values, criteria, attitudes, and tastes in regard to reading. Pupil-teacher conferences, class discussion, and pupils' reports provide evaluative information at this level.

Characterization level: The child's assimilation of reading experiences into his total growth and development; his use of reading to extend his experiences and enhance his understanding of the world in which he lives. This level of behavior transcends identifiable subject lines and requires assessment techniques relevant to the child's total outlook and behavior, primarily through anecdotal records and case study procedures.

Reporting Procedures

Reporting procedures found in recently published courses of study evidence recognition of the trends toward provision of evaluation for a broad range of objectives and individualization of evaluation. Unitary ratings such as satisfactory, improvement needed, excellent, poor, and percentage or letter grades for a single category called "Reading" have been replaced by broader check lists. An example of a reporting form drawn from a recent program (Englewood, 1963) provides for an indication of the child's reading level, which may differ from his grade level. On this form, reading is divided, for purposes of evaluation, into three aspects: the child's recognition of new words and knowledge of their meaning, his understanding of what he reads, and his growth in study skills related to reading. Each of these aspects may be rated as "commendable," "satisfactory," or "needs improvement." In addition, the teacher indicates whether the child is reading "as well as can be expected of him" or whether he is capable of doing better work in reading.

Other examples of reporting forms used in recent programs include additional aspects and more qualitative ratings. An example is the form used for upper elementary grades in Joplin schools (Joplin Unified School District, 1962). This form lists the categories of oral reading, silent reading, word skills, and recreational and supplementary reading. Each of these categories is provided with six or seven statements; more than one statement may be checked in each category as it applies to individual pupils. Examples of these statements include: "Reads with ease and fluency," "Has shown considerable improvement," "Needs more training in projecting voice and in expression," "Not consistent—works well some days, is careless on others."

EVALUATION OF THE INSTRUCTIONAL PROGRAM

Continuous evaluation of the instructional program is nowhere more essential than in the area of reading. The individualized nature and complexity of the process of learning to read calls for continual teacher evaluation of a broad range of materials and familiarity with varieties of instructional techniques, as well as constant appraisal of the activities and aspects of the whole reading program, in order to achieve and maintain a program of instruction that is effective for all pupils. Guidelines for evaluation of the program include the following:

Foundations
Does the instructional program take into account current thinking in linguistics regarding language structure and language learning?

Is the program sequentially organized on the basis of developmental stages rather than grade levels?

Structure
Are the structural elements of the reading process recognized in provisions for instruction?

Are learning experiences and materials consistent with current views of language structure and the interrelationships of all the language arts?

Objectives
Do the objectives of the program place importance upon development of positive attitudes and lifelong interest in reading, as well as skill development?

Is provision clearly made for the development of critical and creative thinking skills?

Are appropriate objectives specifically defined for each particular stage in the sequential developmental program?

Are objectives geared to the needs of each child? Is provision made for background and enrichment experiences as these are required to develop the language learnings of disadvantaged pupils?

Complete program

Does the scope of the program include development of all the skills the child needs now and in preparation for adult reading experiences? Does it meet individual needs?

Is the program balanced to include learning activities in the areas of functional reading, independent recreational reading, reference and news reading, and reading in the subject fields?

Is the program sequentially planned in the light of knowledge about children's learning abilities and interests at each developmental level?

Is there clear articulation in the continuity of the reading program from elementary to secondary schools?

Are adequate supplies of instructional materials provided? Are these materials consistent with current thinking on language structure and effective language learning procedures?

Teaching strategies

Are teachers encouraged to select the instructional procedures best suited to the learning needs of the individual pupil?

Are all of the child's reading activities purposeful and meaningful for him?

Do learning experiences in reading stimulate thinking?

Does instruction meet individual needs by means of flexible grouping within or between classes and by utilization of differentiated remedial, regular, and enrichment activities?

Is provision made for utilization of a variety of appropriate multisensory instructional materials?

Pupil evaluation

Is provision made for measurement of the child's progress in all phases of reading and in all aspects of the reading program?

Is continuous evaluation provided as an integral part of reading instruction?

Are children helped to develop skills of constructive and reponsible self-evaluation?

Is evaluation individualized in the light of the particular learner's needs, language background, and level of reading development?

Are diagnostic analyses made of each individual's strengths and weaknesses in reading skills?

Are varieties of appropriate techniques used to evaluate both cognitive and affective objectives of reading instruction?

Program evaluation

Is continuous evaluation made of instructional techniques, scope, and sequence of the reading program?

Are textbooks and other instructional media continually evaluated and revised as needed? Are alternative textbooks and materials made available? Are new materials thoughtfully evaluated before they are adopted?

Teacher preparation

Is provision made for in-service training to enable teachers to increase competency and become familiar with new techniques and instructional media?

Do reading specialists provide assistance and guidance in the teacher's planning for classroom instruction?

Do reading specialists provide supplementary extra-classroom instruction as required to meet the needs of various pupils?

Are teachers directly involved in the planning and continual evaluation of the total reading program?

REFERENCES

Arbuthnot, May Hill. *Children and books.* (rev. ed.) Chicago: Scott, Foresman, 1957. A standard reference on children's literature, with annotated bibliography of selected books for children.

Artley, A. Sterl. Evaluation of reading, *Instructor*, March, 1965, **74**, 89, 110. Outline of evaluation techniques.

Austin, Mary C., & Morrison, Coleman. *The first R: the Harvard report on reading in elementary schools.* New York: Macmillan, 1963. Recommendations for reading instruction based on a nationwide survey of programs.

Barrett, Thomas C. i/t/a: a step forward or sideways? *Educ. Leadership*, March, 1965, **22**, 394–397. Questions and suggestions regarding effectiveness of evaluations of i/t/a.

Betts, Emmett A. *Foundations of reading instruction.* New York: American Book, 1957. Evaluation guidelines which continue to be utilized.

Bloom, Benjamin S. (Ed.) *The taxonomy of educational objectives: cognitive domain.* New York: McKay, 1956. Classification of objectives and examples of test items.

Bloomfield, Leonard, & Barnhart, Clarence L. *Let's read: a linguistic approach.* Detroit: Wayne State University Press, 1961. Guidelines and lessons for beginning reading instruction.

Bond, Guy L., & Wagner, Eva Bond. *Teaching the child to read.* (4th ed.) New York: Macmillan, 1966. Classroom procedures for reading instruction.

Buros, Oscar K. *The sixth mental measurements yearbook.* Highland Park, N.J.: Gryphon Press, 1965. Information on tests of reading achievement and reading readiness published between 1959 and 1964; reviews of earlier tests in preceding volumes.

California. *The elementary school program in California.* Sacramento: State Department of Education, Bulletin 26, No. 2, 1957. Description of developmental stages in learning to read.

Carroll, John B. The analysis of reading instruction: perspectives from psychology and linguistics. *Theories of learning and instruction.* Sixty-third Yearbook, Part I, National Society for the Study of Education. Chicago: University of Chicago Press, 1964. A linguistic scholar's discussion of the nature of reading and the reading process.

Commission on English. *Freedom and discipline in English.* New York: College Entrance Examination Board, 1965. A review of the structure of English, with useful guidelines in the structure of literary analysis.

Cutts, Warren G. (Ed.) *Teaching young children to read.* Washington, D.C.: U.S. Office of Education, 1964. Review of reading practices since 1900 and report of current practices in elementary schools.

DeBoer, John J., & Dallmann, Martha. *The teaching of reading.* (rev. ed.) New York: Holt, 1964. Principles and practices of reading instruction.

Diack, Hunter. *Reading and the psychology of perception.* Nottingham, England: Peter Skinner, 1960. Discussion of a linguistic approach to the reading process.

Downing, John A. *The augmented roman alphabet: a new two-stage method to help children to learn to read.* London: University of London Institute of Education, 1961. Description of the i/t/a program.

Educ. Leadership, March, 1965, **22**, 373–452. Entire issue devoted to reading instruction.

Englewood. *Course of study in reading.* Englewood, N.J.: Board of Education, 1963. Elementary reading program.

Figurel, A. Allen. (Ed.) *Changing concepts of reading instruction.* Englewood, N.J. *Scholastic* Magazines, 1961. Report of the conference proceedings of the International Reading Association.

Fries, Charles C. *Linguistics and reading.* New York: Holt, 1963. A linguistic scholar's discussion of the reading process.

Fry, Edward. A diacritical marking system for beginning reading instruction, *Elementary English*, May, 1964, **41**, 526–529. Outline of a suggested system to facilitate initial reading instruction.

Gattegno, Caleb. *Background and principles: words in color.* Chicago: Encyclopaedia Britannica, Inc., 1962. Description of a suggested system for beginning reading instruction.

Gillooly, William B. The promise of i.t.a. is a delusion: yes! *Phi Delta Kappan*, June, 1966, **47**, 545–550, 552–553. Criticism of research and evaluation on the use of the i/t/a in the United States.

Gunderson, Doris V. *Research in reading readiness.* Washington, D.C.: U.S. Office of Education, 1964. Review of research conducted on readiness for reading instruction.

Instructor, March, 1965, **74**, 55–110. Special supplement on reading instruction.

Joplin Unified School District. *Curriculum in reading.* Joplin, Mo.: Board of Education, 1962. K-6 reading program.

Kerfoot, James F. (Ed.) *First grade programs.* Newark: International Reading Association, 1965. New emphases in beginning reading instruction.

Krathwohl, David R., Bloom, Benjamin S., & Masia, Bertram S. *Taxonomy of educational objectives: affective domain.* New York: McKay, 1964. A classification of objectives and sample test items in the area of attitude and value development.

Lee, Dorris M., & Allen, R. V. *Learning to read through experience.* (2d ed.) New York: Appleton-Century-Crofts, 1963. Description of reading instruction based on children's own experiences and written expression.

Lefevre, Carl A. *Linguistics and the teaching of reading.* New York: McGraw-Hill, 1964. A linguistic scholar's approach to reading instruction.

McKee, Paul. *Reading, a program of instruction for the elementary school.* Boston: Houghton Mifflin, 1966. Detailed suggestions for teaching all phases of reading; selected bibliography on research.

Mackintosh, Helen K. (Ed.) *Current approaches to teaching reading.* Washington, D.C.: Department of Elementary-Kindergarten-Nursery Education, NEA, 1965. Brief summaries of eight approaches to reading instruction.

Mazurkiewicz, Albert J. The initial teaching alphabet for reading? Yes! *Educ. Leadership*, March, 1965, **22**, 390–393, 437–438. Description of i/t/a program and results of research studies.

Mazurkiewicz, Albert J., & Dolmatch, Theodore B. The promise of i.t.a. is a delusion: no! *Phi Delta Kappan*, June, 1966, **47**, 550–552. Reply to critique by W. B. Gillooly in same issue.

National Society for the Study of Education. *Development in and through reading.* Sixtieth Yearbook, Part I. Chicago: University of Chicago Press, 1961. Discussions of the nature of the reading process and instruction in the elementary school.

Nebraska Curriculum Development Center. *A curriculum for English: introduction to the elementary school program: K-6.* Lincoln, Nebr.: University of Nebraska, 1963. Mimeographed. Outline and procedures for the study of literature in the elementary grades.

New York City. *Sequential levels of reading growth.* New York: Board of Education, Division of Elementary Schools, 1963. Description of developmental stages in the process of learning to read.

New York City. *A practical guide to individualized reading.* New York: Board of Education, Bureau of Educational Research, 1964. Principles and procedures for implementation of an individualized reading program in the elementary classroom.

New York State. *The teaching of reading.* Albany: State Education Department, Bureau of Elementary Curriculum Development, 1963. Concise overview of principles and techniques in all aspects of the elementary school reading program.

Pasadena. *Course of study: reading.* Pasadena, Calif.: Board of Education, 1961. K-6 reading program.

Phenix, Philip H. *Realms of meaning.* New York: McGraw-Hill, 1964. A philosophy of curriculum development. Chapter 5 discusses structure of language; chap. 15 outlines structure in literature.

Pitman, I. J. Learning to read: an experiment, *J. roy. Soc. Arts*, February, 1961, **109**, 149–180. London: G. Bell. Outline of the i/t/a program.

Read. Teach. March, 1965, **18**, 420–500. Special issue on teaching reading to the culturally disadvantaged child.

Robinson, Helen M. Teaching reading today, *Instructor*, March, 1965, **74**, 56, 65. Definitions and outline of emerging practices in reading.

Ruddell, Robert B. The effect of oral and written patterns of language structure on reading comprehension, *Read. Teach.*, January, 1965, **18**, 270–275. Report of research on the relationship of reading comprehension to the degree of similarity between children's oral language and reading material.

Russell, David H. *Children learn to read.* Boston: Ginn, 1961. Principles and procedures in elementary reading instruction.

Russell, David H., & Fea, Henry. Research on teaching reading. *Handbook of research on teaching.* Chicago: Rand McNally, 1963. Review of research on reading instruction procedures.

San Diego Unified School District. *Course of study in reading.* San Diego, Calif.: Board of Education, 1961. K-6 program in reading.

Smith, Henry P., & Dechant, Emerald. *Psychology in teaching reading.* Englewood Cliffs, N.J.: Prentice-Hall, 1961. Analysis of the reading process.

Soffietti, James P. Why children fail to read: a linguistic analysis, *Harvard Educ. Rev.*, Spring, 1955, **25**, 63–84. Analysis of learning and instruction in beginning reading by a linguistic scholar.

Stern, Catherine, & Gould, Toni. *Children discover reading: an introduction to structural reading.* New York: Random House, 1965. Description of an approach to reading instruction.

Strang, Ruth McCullough, Constance M., & Traxler, Arthur E. *The improvement of reading.* (4th ed.) New York: McGraw-Hill, 1967. Guidelines for elementary reading instruction.

Strickland, Ruth G. *The language of elementary school children: its relationship to the language of reading textbooks and the quality of reading of selected children.* Bulletin of the School of Education, Vol. 38. Bloomington, Ind.: Indiana University, 1962. Discussion of use of children's language patterns in reading material.

Strickland, Ruth G. *The contribution of structural linguistics to the teaching of reading, writing, and grammar in the elementary school.* Bulletin of the School of Education, Vol. 40. Bloomington, Ind.: Indiana University, 1964.

Tinker, Miles A., & McCullough, Constance M. *Teaching elementary reading.* (2d ed.) New York: Appleton-Century-Crofts, 1962. Principles and practices of reading instruction, with bibliographies of references and reading tests.

FOREIGN LANGUAGE INSTRUCTION in elementary schools (FLES) has grown tremendously during the past two decades. Although some elementary schools still do not provide instruction in foreign languages, the trend is clearly toward systematic instruction for children before they leave grade 6. California requires that instruction in a foreign language begin not later than grade 6, many schools begin instruction in grade 4 or 5, and a few begin in the primary grades. There is increasing agreement that FLES should be a basic part of the curriculum.

A variety of reasons may be cited for providing instruction in foreign language in elementary schools. A key factor has been recognition of the educational value of foreign language instruction. The typical American's lack of facility in a second language has been highly publicized and the need to provide instruction has been stressed by many groups. Increased interest in foreign language instruction has led parents, civic leaders, and foreign language associations to bring pressure to bear on boards of education to offer FLES. Large grants have been made by governmental and independent agencies to develop instructional programs and materials and to make studies of second-language learning. The outcome has been the extension of FLES throughout the country. Any elementary school which is not offering foreign language instruction is clearly out of step with a significant development in American education.

The fact that foreign language instruction for children is not new in this country should be recognized. French and German were taught as early as 1749 in Philadelphia, and Spanish was added in 1766. During the 1850s, German was taught in Chicago, Milwaukee, and other Midwestern cities owing to the influx of Germans. Other communities taught Scandinavian or Balkan languages, depending on the country of origin of immigrants. Classes were usually held in parochial schools or religious summer schools; a main objective was to keep the "old culture" alive by having children learn their parents' native language. With the advent of World War I the teaching of foreign languages at all levels was greatly reduced, and German in particular nearly disappeared from the curriculum.

The oldest of the current public elementary programs in foreign language instruction was initiated in Cleveland in 1921 to teach French to able children in grades 1 through 6. A few other cities initiated programs of instruction during the 1920s and 1930s. National needs for greater language facility were accentuated by World War II. Attention focused on improvement of collegiate and secondary teaching procedures, and interest extended to explorations of the introduction of foreign language in the elementary school. Rapid growth since 1952 has resulted in a curriculum revolution without parallel in elementary education. A major change has been the shift from traditional instruction through reading and translation to emphasis upon speaking and communication.

Although the terms "foreign language" and "second language" are often used, the language studied may actually be a third or fourth language for the learner. In addition, current professional study of language instruction includes the teaching of English to the non-English speaker. Therefore the term "target language" is frequently utilized in professional literature to refer to instruction in any language other than that which is native to the learner.

FOUNDATION DISCIPLINES

Many of the basic disciplines that undergird instruction in the language arts, as noted in the preceding chapters, also constitute the foundations of instruction in foreign languages. The impact of linguistics has been great in terms of providing insights into the nature of language and contrastive features of the target languages. The linguist's concept of language as primarily oral communication undergirds the audio-lingual approach, which is used in newly developed instructional programs. Linguists have identified structural elements of language and have suggested appropriate learning techniques, such as pattern practice, based on these elements. Branches of linguistic science have also contributed to foreign language learning. Contrastive linguistics compares the structure of two languages and points up differences which constitute difficulties in learning the second language. Historical linguistics contributes an understanding of the interrelationships of languages and of peoples of various language groups. Linguistic geography provides an understanding of relationships among languages, dialect patterns, cultures, and locations.

From anthropology and other social sciences has been drawn information about the culture in which the target language is used, about the cultural content the language conveys, and about the functions of the language and its dialects and accents in that culture. Studies of the art, music, literature, and history of different countries contribute materials and information that can be used to enrich foreign language instruction. From psycholinguistics and studies of language learning have been drawn guidelines for improving instruction. Information useful in demonstrating how difficult sounds are made has been drawn from studies of the human vocal mechanism. From communication engineering have come improved ways of taping, televising, and presenting models of speaking the target language. The many high-quality programs currently available for use in elementary schools reflect the impact of studies that have been made in these and related disciplines (Birkmaier, 1963; Lado, 1964b).

Concept Clusters and Generalizations

The examples below, taken from references listed at the end of this chapter, are illustrative of concept clusters and generalizations from linguistics that are important in foreign language instruction and helpful in understanding the rationale underlying such instruction (Lado, 1964b). These concept clusters are stressed by experts in target-language teaching:

Structure in target languages: phonemes, permitted phoneme sequences, tonemes (contrastive pitch units), intonation, morphemes, patterns of word formation, word sequences, and syntax

Pronunciation: consonants, vowels, intonation, stress, rhythm, junctures and their sequences; syllable patterns, sound clusters, phrase patterns

Elementary meaning units (EMU): culturally rooted meanings, including words, semantic distinctions, idioms, idiomatic expressions, proverbs

Learning language units and patterns: expression, content, association; trace, habit, facility

Language variation: regional, cultural, social, historical; idiolect, dialect, level of usage

Writing form: alphabetic, syllabic, logographic

Target-language teaching stages: mimicry-memorization, conscious choice, pattern practice, free selection

Vocabulary levels: basic patterns and word pronunciation, communication in widely used areas of the language, technical and literary communication

Teaching vocabulary: hear the word, pronounce it, grasp the meaning, use it in sentences, reinforce through practice

Some examples of generalizations are as follows:

Language is an integral part of culture, and it is used to express various aspects of culture.

Each language has its own system of phrase and sentence patterns, consonants, vowels, intonation, and stress. For example, English has nine simple vowel phonemes, French has fifteen, and Spanish has five.

Marked differences may be noted from region to region in the language spoken by people in many countries.

All languages change over time; changes in writing tend to lag behind changes in speaking.

Speaking and listening are fundamental processes in learning a second language. Reading and writing are parallel processes that require a thorough grounding in listening and speaking.

Language learning involves the acquiring of facility for hearing and speaking each of the following in appropriate sequences: phonemes, words, phrases, and sentences.

The sentence is the smallest unit of full expression.

Language usage or dialects within a region may vary according to social levels.

OBJECTIVES OF TARGET-LANGUAGE STUDY

A large number of purposes for providing instruction in a foreign language in the elementary school curriculum may be found in the literature. The following are frequently cited:

To begin the early development of the ability to use a target language proficiently in understanding, speaking, reading, and writing; to develop the ability to understand the speech, writings, and literary works of native users of the language in terms of the target language and culture

To provide for continuity of language study beginning in the elementary school and continuing through the secondary school

To develop an insight into, and an appreciation of, other languages, cultures, and people, and to understand the role of language in a culture

To develop children's ability to communicate with others in a bilingual area

To develop skill in reading and writing the target language on the basis of more direct comprehension without use of conscious translation

To provide opportunities for comparative language study and to stimulate interest in the origin of words and the similarities between a target language and the child's native language

To extend interests for leisure-time activities and to develop a background for educational and career activities

To enrich the curriculum and to provide learning opportunities for gifted children

Purposes related to an understanding of other people and other cultures are important in social studies, art, music, literature, and other areas of the curriculum as well as in foreign language study. In fact, until the child develops a fairly high level of proficiency in the language, he will learn more about others through the medium of his native language. Therefore, the cultural-understanding objectives of the language program are developed by experiences in other subject areas.

Related to these purposes is the claim that study of the second language in bilingual communities contributes to the development of respect for the national heritage and culture of the minority group and raises the social status of that group in the community. While this may be true, it can be argued that similar results might be achieved by singling out the group and giving it recognition in other ways. The point here is simply that the development of attitudes is a complex process, and it is doubtful that language study per se in the elementary school will do the job, although it should contribute as much as possible to such a worthy purpose.

A COMPLETE PROGRAM

The complete foreign language program in today's elementary school includes thoroughly integrated learnings of both language and culture. The instructional program includes use of the target language in classroom instruction, direct practice of target-language patterns without parallel translations, cultural information built into practice patterns and dialogues, use of films and televised lessons to provide pronunciation models and cultural understandings, opportunities for use of the language in oral communication, tapes used in classroom or language laboratory to provide models, practice, and self-evaluation, and use of written materials produced in the target culture in later stages of language learning. Within this framework, sequences and grade placement of learnings may vary as seen in the examples in the following section.

SEQUENCES OF INSTRUCTION

Although there is widespread agreement that the audio-lingual approach should be used, there are some differences in the sequences of instruction currently provided in elementary schools. A few programs begin with informal instruction in the early grades. Some begin with systematic instruction in grade 3 or 4, while others delay systematic instruction until grade 5 or 6. Some give little or no attention to reading, writing, and grammatical aspects of language whereas others include them as a part of the instructional program.

In general, most programs stress speaking and listening during the first year or more of systematic instruction. It is recognized that reading and writing should be based on material that has been learned audio-lingually.

In those programs in which grammatical aspects of the target language are considered, instruction is rooted in material that has been used to develop listening and speaking competence. In short, the thinking strategies and instructional guidelines reported later in this chapter are generally followed in most programs.

The following examples of developmental programs of instruction are illustrative of current practices. The first example begins with informal instruction in kindergarten and is closely related to conditions and situations in the immediate environment and to the social sciences education program. The other examples are illustrative of systematic programs of instruction that begin in the elementary school and serve as a base for instruction in secondary school.

A Developmental Program Beginning in Kindergarten

The following example is adapted from the Los Angeles City Course of Study (1964) in which conversational Spanish is begun in kindergarten and is taught by teachers who are competent in Spanish. Daily experiences are provided and the learning of Spanish is related to other class activities. The major purposes of the program are to develop an oral fluency within limited content, an appreciation of the contributions of Spanish-American culture to the culture of the Southwest, an understanding of Spanish-speaking neighbors in the community and across the border, and a feeling of acceptance and pride on the part of Spanish-speaking children in school. Grade emphases are:

Kindergarten
Learning greetings, expressions such as "thank you," simple songs, how to give one's name and to talk about pets, toys, and common objects

Grade 1
Continuing the above and learning sentences and phrases related to members of the family, friends, and animals

Asking and answering simple questions about the family, identifying pictures and objects, engaging in dramatic play, playing guessing games, learning simple poems and songs

Grade 2
Learning sentences and phrases related to the study of the farm and market, colors, foods, numerals from 1 to 10, descriptions of farm animals, guessing games, action games, and simple dialogues

Asking and answering questions, using pictures to convey meaning, participating in guessing games and dramatic play, responding to directions, and singing songs

Grade 3

Providing for practice of earlier learnings and introduction of new sentences and phrases related to the study of explorers, missions, and early Los Angeles, numerals from 11 to 15, community workers

Learning rhymes and songs, creating original stories, engaging in dramatic skits, playing vocabulary and number games, planning dialogues related to school activities, learning the names of objects in the classroom, learning sentences and phrases related to the park and zoo, asking and answering questions

Grade 4

Learning phrases and sentences in the study of early and modern California

Learning numerals 16 to 20, appropriate songs, days of the week, names of clothing, foods, dishes, and silverware, and simple dialogues

Grade 5

Learning phrases related to months, dates, seasons, telling time, numerals 21 to 100, weather, parts of the body, geographical features

Asking and answering questions about holidays, birthdays, areas of the United States where Spanish is spoken

Learning the verbs to wash, to comb, to speak, to write, to read, to arrive

Presenting information on name, address, age, number of brothers and sisters, occupation of parents

Grade 6

Learning words and phrases related to rooms of the house, furniture, meals, class roll call, a trip to Mexico, a Mexican market, countries of Central and South America, cities of South America

Providing for discussion of topics related to the study of Mexico and Central and South America

Providing systematic instruction in accordance with state requirements

A Systematic Program Beginning in Grade 3

The French program in the University Elementary School in Chicago is designed to provide systematic instruction beginning in grade 3 and continuing through secondary school (Dunkel & Pillet, 1962). Audio-lingual skills are stressed in the early part of the program, reading is added during the second year, and selected aspects of grammar are included. Approach, time allotments, vocabulary load, and other features of the program are as follows:

> *Grade 3*: audio-lingual approach; fifteen minutes daily; emphasis on activities at home and school; around 380 words included in the program; emphasis on home and school activities, clothing, food, expressions of courtesy, colors, numbers, parts of body; verbs in present tense, first person singular, and second person plural
>
> *Grade 4*: audio-lingual approach; twenty minutes daily; around 350 words on topics begun in grade 3 and on such new units as animals and geography; verbs in present tense, all persons; introduction to reading by means of scripts for playlets after aural-oral practice
>
> *Grade 5*: audio-lingual approach plus oral reading and reading comprehension; twenty-five minutes daily, four days a week; reading practice continued after aural-oral drill on reading material; around 380 words on shopping, dishes, furniture, and other new topics; some homework assigned; students grouped in terms of achievement; systematic attention to verb forms; *passé composé* introduced
>
> *Grade 6*: increased attention to reading; twenty-five minutes daily, four days a week; reader used as source of material for conversation and for oral reading and reading comprehension; about 1,000 new words in reader; introduction of future and imperfect tenses; homework assigned regularly
>
> *Grade 7*: transition to standard secondary school approach; fifty minutes a day, two days a week; use of standard grammar; conversation and reading continued

A Systematic Program Beginning in Grade 4

The New York City program, beginning in grade 4, is an optional area of the curriculum in which students may take French, Spanish, Italian, or Hebrew (New York, 1965). The program is offered as part of a sequence that continues through secondary school. By the end of grade 6 students are expected to understand a native speaker in conversation related to children's experiences, to speak in conversation, and to read and write material that has been learned audio-lingually. Cultural understanding, a favorable attitude toward language study, and identification of talented language students are viewed as additional outcomes. Reading-readiness activities and simple writing activities are begun in grade 4. It is recommended that systematic reading instruction be provided in the middle of grade 5. Grammatical structures are taught through pattern practice in which analogies are discovered and generalizations are made. The following sequence of grammatical items for the Spanish program is illustrative of the requirements in each grade (New York, 1963).

> *Grade 4*: **definite, indefinite, and plural adjectives; gender and number of nouns; agreement and possessive form of adjectives (*mi, tu, su, nuestra*), first conjugation of verbs, irregular verbs (*ser, estar, ir, hacer, ver, poner, tener*), first person singular, familiar and polite forms in second person, third person singular; numerals from 1 to 20; time on the hour and half hour; *de* in possessive form and contractions (*del*); days of the week; use of *tener* (*tener hambre*); use of *hacer* (weather)**

> *Grade 5*: **review of above; contraction of *a* (*al*); adjective position; numerals 20 to 100, dates and arithmetical expressions; *decir* in various forms**

> *Grade 6*: **review of the above; possessive adjectives; first conjugation and irregular verbs in present tense for all persons singular and plural in negative, affirmative, and interrogative form**

Guidelines for teaching the reading and writing of audio-lingually learned material are as follows:

> 1. **For reading, the teacher distributes material, reads it while the children listen, reads it while the children follow line by line, reads a phrase and has the children repeat it in chorus, reads a sentence and has the children repeat in chorus, reads a sentence and has an individual child repeat it.**
> 2. **For writing, the teacher reads a selection while the children listen, reads it again with pauses between phrases and clarification of punctuation, so the children can write, reads it again with repetition of punctuation in the target language while the children check their copy and correct errors. Provision is also made for other exercises such as completion and multiple choice.**

TEACHING STRATEGIES

Use of the audio-lingual approach is increasing throughout the country. Because it is a closer approximation to the natural mode of learning a language, it is considered the most effective means of teaching a target language. The audio-lingual approach is based on the assumptions that language is first of all a means of oral communication, that hearing and speaking a language precede reading and writing, that language learning is a matter of acquiring a new habitual speech pattern rather than memorizing a body of facts, and that exclusive use of the target language in instruction increases learning because it increases the child's need and motivation for communication.

The teacher and students use the target language from the very beginning of instruction. Listening to a good model, mimicry and memorization, and practice on basic speech patterns until they become habitual are strategies that are emphasized. A typical sequence of lessons includes recognition, imitation, repetition, variation, and selection, as shown in the examples in the next section. Audio-lingual strategies enable students to learn the language, not *about* the language, by *using* it in conversing, responding, questioning, singing, playing games, and practicing a variety of exercises.

Related aspects of culture included in up-to-date instructional materials provide a meaningful context for language learning. Songs, stories, poems, pictures, films, slides, and filmstrips are used to extend understanding of terms and concepts. Notes to the teacher in textbooks and teaching manuals include informational material on customs, foods, travel, holidays, recreation, family life, schools, and other topics that may be used to enrich and enliven dialogues, practice exercises, and discussion. In addition, relevant cultural content may be presented through related social studies units.

Specific Techniques

The following examples taken from a teaching guide are illustrative of specific techniques that are used in the audio-lingual approach (California, 1964). Each unit in the guide begins with a dialogue and is followed by listening and speaking activities. After the teacher reads the English dialogue so that children will understand the meaning, a recording of the dialogue in the target language is played at least five times while the students listen. Oral practice follows listening and each sentence in the dialogue is mastered before proceeding to the next. The recording is played as needed to ensure correct response. Varied activities are provided, as shown in the following sequence, which includes lessons for several days of study.

1. **Students look at pictures as the teacher reads the dialogue in English.**

2. **The teacher plays the dialogue as the children listen.**
   Buenas tardes.   *Buenas tardes, señor.*
   ¿Cómo te llamas, joven?   *Me llamo Pablo.*   **Etc.**

3. **Repetition drill is provided by having boys repeat:**
   ¿Cómo te llamas?   *Me llamo Juan.*
   ¿Cómo te llamas?   *Me llamo Diego.*   *Etc.*

4. **Repetition drill is provided by having girls repeat:**
   ¿Cómo te llamas?   *Me llamo Elena.*
   ¿Cómo te llamas?   *Me llamo Anna.*   *Etc.*

5. **Substitution drill is provided by having boys answer:**
   ¿Cómo te llamas? Pedro.   *Me llamo Pedro.*
   ¿Cómo te llamas? Alberto.   *Me llamo Alberto.*   *Etc.*

6. **Substitution drill is provided by having girls answer:**
   ¿Cómo te llamas? Anna.   *Me llamo Anna.*   *Etc.*

7. **The teacher plays a song while the children listen.**

8. **The children sing the song line by line.**

9. **A series of drills is provided to clinch what has been taught.**

10. **A comprehension exercise is provided to evaluate learning. For example, students select the best answer as they listen:**
    La muchacha se llama.   A. Juan   B. Pedro   C. Anna
    La respuesta correcta es C.   *Etc.*

An analysis of what has been taught is presented at the end of each unit. For example, in the preceding unit attention was given to the following:

Grammar: *llamarse.*

Patterns: *¿Cómo te llamas?*   *Me llamo* _____.

Idioms: *Buenas tardes.*

Sounds: *ll, j.*

Vocabulary: *buenas tardes, señor, me llamo, se llama, Anna, etc.*

Variety in Activities

A wide variety of practice activities may be noted as instructional materials are examined. The following examples drawn from several different units are illustrative of the main types currently used:

Identification: **Students watch pictures as they listen.**
   Aquí está la escuela.   *Aquí está la maestra.*   *Etc.*

Repetition: **Students repeat sentences used in preceding exercises.**
   Aquí está la escuela.   *Aquí está la maestra.*   *Etc.*

Question and answer: **Students answer questions.**
   ¿Dónde está la escuela?   *La escuela está aquí.*   *Etc.*

Transformation: Students change the sentence.
Juan busca el libro.   **Juan no busca el libro.** *Etc.*

Comprehension: Students select the correct response.
La escuela es grande. La escuela no es grande. *Etc.*

Substitution: Students substitute key words in the sentence.
Juan está bien.   **Anna está bien.**
Yo estoy bien.   **Juan y yo están bien.** *Etc.*

Contrast: Students repeat different forms.
Aquí está la escuela.   **Aquí están las escuelas.** *Etc.*

Replacement: Students repeat various forms in basic patterns.
Yo busco mi cuaderno.   **Ella busca mi cuaderno.** *Etc.*

Double substitution: Students substitute two forms in basic patterns.
Yo busco el libro.   **Pablo busca el cuaderno.** *Etc.*

Directed dialogue: Students use a pattern in a chain drill or in response to the teacher.
Presenten Juan a Anna.   **Anna, te presento a Juan.** *Etc.*

Rejoinder: Students respond to a sentence.
Tengo hambre.   **Bueno, aquí hay pan.** *Etc.*

Addition: Students expand a basic sentence.
Tengo un libro.   **Tengo un libro grande.**
Tengo un libro grande de historia. *Etc.*

Synthesis: Students combine two simple sentences into a single more complex pattern.
Anna está enfirma.   **Sé porqué.**
Sé porqué Anna está enfirma.   **Etc.**

Word Clusters

Many pattern practice exercises include word clusters that facilitate learning. These clusters are familiar to children in their native language and tend to be learned readily in the target language. For example, the cluster that includes the furniture in the living room is:

La sala: el sofá, el sillón, la televisión, la lámpara, . . .

An illustrative pattern practice that includes the cluster is conducted by having students answer the question "What is this?" as the teacher points to pictures:

¿Que es esto?   **Es el sofá.**
¿Que es esto?   **Es el sillón.**
¿Que es esto?   **Es la lámpara.**
¿Que es esto?   **Es la televisión.**

After identification of each item and mastery of the vocabulary, additional practice may be given as follows:

¿Dónde está el sofá?	*El sofá está en la sala.*
¿Dónde está el sillón?	*El sillón está en la sala.*
¿Dónde está la televisión?	*La televisión está en la sala.*
¿Dónde está la lámpara?	

After completion of such exercises as these, children may generalize as follows: *El sofá, el sillón, la televisión y lámpara están en la sala.* Similarly, after appropriate practice they may group other terms together as the teacher asks:

¿Que están en la recámara?
La cama, el tocador, y el ropero están en la recámara.
¿Que están en la casa?
La sala, el comedor, la recomára, el baño, y la cocina están en la casa.

Relationships between Units

Lessons and units should be planned so that there is a logical development of language power. This may be accomplished by arranging lessons in a logical sequence and by including material taught earlier in succeeding units. The following excerpts show how lessons and units are related in one program (Eriksson, Forest, & Mulhauser, 1964, pp. 33, 35):

Unit A: Les couleurs. In this unit and the following one, attention is given to colors, agreement and placement of adjectives, and single verb form. Notice the carry-through from step to step of selected terms and the ways in which repetition is built into the sequence.

Step 1. Presentation of three basic colors:
Voilà le *drapeau américain.*
Le drapeau américain est *rouge, blanc,* et *bleu.*
  (The teacher points to each color as he says it.)
De quelle couleur est le dapeau américain?
  (The answer is given first, the question is asked, then the answer is taught.)
Voilà le drapeau *français.*
Le drapeau français est bleu, blanc, et rouge.
De quelle couleur est le drapeau français?

Step 2. Review and presentation of additional colors:
Le papier est *vert.*
Le papier est *jaune.*

Le papier est *marron.*
Le papier est *noir.*
> (Each time, the teacher points to a piece of paper of the color he is naming. He may continue with any number of colors on subsequent days, but two or three new ones will suffice at a time.)

Step 3. Drill:
Touche le papier noir.
Montre le papier jaune.
Où est le papier vert?
Est-ce bleu? Oui, c'est bleu.
Non, ce n'est pas bleu. C'est rouge.

Step 4. Game activity:
Jeu de devinette, oui et non. A pupil leaves the room, the class chooses an object and the pupil must guess what has been chosen. Example:
Pupil: Est-ce le papier noir?
Class: Non, ce n'est pas le papier noir.
Pupil: Est-ce le crayon vert?
Class: Oui, c'est le crayon vert.

Several succeeding lessons provide for practice and review of the colors and contrast feminine and masculine forms.

Unit B: New adjectives and verbs. In this unit two new adjectives, a verb (*montrer*), and several nouns are emphasized. Ideas presented earlier on the imperative form are used, and the second and third persons singular of widely used verbs are introduced. Notice how the material taught in the preceding unit is applied in new contexts.

Step 1. Presentation:
Montre le gros chien.
Je montre le gros chien.
Oui, tu montres le gros chien.
Tout le monde: *Il* montre le gros chien.
Donne-moi le gros chien s'il te plaît.
Voici le gros chien.
Montre le *petit* chien.
Je montre le petit chien.
Oui, tu montres le petit chien.
Tout le monde: *Elle* montre le petit chien.
Mets le petit chien sur la table.
Je mets le petit chien sur la table.

Step 2. Drill:
De quelle couleur est la petite balle?
La petite balle est blanche.

> Mets la *petite balle blanche* sur la chaise.
> Je mets la petite balle blanche sur la chaise.
> Donne-moi la petite gomme verte.
> Voici la petite gomme verte.

This unit is followed by others in which review and practice are provided as new material is introduced.

Cultural Understanding

Since language is a key aspect of culture, students inevitably learn a great deal about other cultures as they study languages. To assure positive outcomes, the teacher should serve as a model of linguistic aspects of the culture. The native speaker of a language speaks naturally, with the pronunciation, intonation, and rhythm that are essential to encourage language growth and provide subtle cultural insights. Common gestures, exclamations, and mannerisms are a natural part of the native speaker's expression. If the teacher is not a native speaker, films and television programs should be used to show natural expression. Throughout the instructional program, cultural understandings can be developed through authentic and natural presentation of a model of the target language.

Direct attention should be given to various aspects of culture that add meaning to the terms, phrases, and dialogues being taught. Meaning is lost if students do not understand the cultural context in which an utterance is made. For example, visual materials may be used to distinguish the French *pharmacie* from the typical American drugstore and to develop accurate and realistic perceptions of foods, clothes, and other items. If this is not done students may think that what they are studying in other cultures is exactly the same as in their own.

Special comments by the teacher help to develop understanding of a foreign culture. In a recent guide, notes are included for use in class discussion (California, 1964). These notes present a variety of information ranging from the type of work done by city and farm workers to activities in village markets and at festivals. The notes are especially helpful in giving background to terms, phrases, and sentences used in the different units of the course. When these guides are supplemented by visual materials and realia, students can develop cultural understandings that are directly related to their classwork.

A variety of other materials and activities contribute to cultural understanding. Poems and stories, especially when learned in the target language, games and folk dances, art and music activities, resource visitors from the community, and study trips in the community—all can be used to enliven instruction and extend learning.

The classroom itself can be arranged to create an atmosphere that is conducive to cultural understanding. Posters, maps, and pictures may be displayed and discussed. Collections of coins, stamps, and other items can be shared. Newspaper clippings and magazine cutouts can be posted. A calendar can be kept to announce exhibits, radio and television programs, and special events. Materials should be changed from time to time to reflect the content of the instructional program.

Perhaps a word of caution is needed at this point. Since the primary purpose of foreign language instruction is to develop listening and speaking competence, and later reading and writing competence, language instruction should not be turned into a social studies course. As pointed out in a teacher's guide (New York, 1965), geography, history, art, literature, and so on are best handled in other areas of the curriculum. If there is curricular latitude, units of study in other subjects may be planned to contribute to cultural understanding in the language program. But care should be taken to keep other areas of the curriculum in balance and to clarify relationships between various courses of study.

INSTRUCTIONAL MEDIA

Effective instruction in a foreign language calls for a variety of resources in addition to textbook materials. The teacher may work with a total system of materials provided in a publisher's language program, or he may use a variety of quite diverse materials.

Packaged instructional systems, designed for teachers who are not language specialists may be centered on filmed or taped lessons. Teachers with greater language proficiency may utilize a coordinated set of materials. Examples of these systems are indicated in Chart 5–1. (See p. 148.)

A variety of additional materials, many of which were mentioned above, may be used to enhance language learning. Realia, such as authentic clothing, artifacts, coins, and special collections of objects, should be made available for children to handle and examine so that they may associate terms with real objects and gain insight into material aspects of the culture. Specific objects may be used to stimulate discussion and practice. Films provide a simulation of experience that brings the target culture "to life" in the classroom and provides models for pronunciation, intonation, and typical gestures used to convey meaning. Films, filmstrips, and slides may also be used to stimulate language practice, particularly when the classroom teacher is able to prepare an accompanying tape appropriate to the level of the class. Commercial films, television and radio programs, and museum exhibits may enrich the program by highlighting aspects of the culture or providing specific information; the value of such activities is greater if

Filmed instruction	Taped instruction	Classroom teacher
1. Filmed lesson shown on television or in classroom; about fifteen minutes	1. Taped lesson to introduce learnings; about ten to twenty minutes	1. Classroom teacher is speech model; may use pictures on flash cards
2. Teacher's guide gives background information and follow-up for film lesson	2. Teacher's guide has script of tape and follow-up suggestions	2. Teacher's guide with complete lessons and practice exercises
3. Pupil Activity Book has pictures, no words; guides oral practice	3. Pupil Book with pictures, no words, to guide oral practice	3. Pupil Book with pictures similar to those used by teacher
4. Disk records for use in follow-up lessons, and disks for take-home practice	4. Disk records for pupil use at home and disk of songs in target language	4. Disk records for language model and practice, used in classroom
5. Teacher-preparation films and records for in-service use	5. Display charts, pictures, or movable figures to illustrate taped lesson and follow-up practice	5. Disk records of songs in target language
6. Testing materials provided in program	6. Testing materials provided in program	6. Tests prepared by classroom teacher

Chart 5–1. **Examples of foreign language instructional systems.**

children are prepared beforehand and if the experiences are followed up in the classroom.

Pictures and photographs displayed on charts or bulletin boards, duplicated, or found in books can provide information on many aspects of life in the target culture. Posters and travel brochures highlight interesting geographic and cultural features. All these materials can be effectively used to stimulate dialogues or provide a focus for oral drill if they are displayed at the time they are most relevant to what is taught and if displays are changed as needed. Maps may be on permanent display for continual cultural reference as well as oral practice based on locations, distances, travel, or geographic descriptions.

As children reach levels of instruction where reading becomes an important activity, school libraries may be able to provide authentic newspapers and examples of children's periodicals and literature. These may be coordinated with a lesson or read by individual pupils. Relevant current and special events should be noted to provide ongoing contact and up-to-date information about the target culture, to stimulate interest in the language, and to provide a focus for language practice.

Disks and tapes may be used to provide language models by a variety of native speakers, to narrate stories in the target language, to teach songs, and to provide variety in pattern practice. Tapes may be effectively used in teacher appraisal and pupil self-evaluation of pronunciation and comprehension. Tapes may also be used to provide group or individualized language practice for children in the upper elementary grades if language laboratory facilities and competent instructors are available.

GUIDELINES FOR THE TEACHER

In addition to the suggestions included in the preceding sections, the following guiding principles are frequently recommended in FLES instructional guides and courses of study:

Use an audio-lingual approach in which the child hears an excellent model of language and repeats what he hears. The teacher who serves as a language model should face the children when speaking so that lip movements, facial expressions, and gestures may be observed. In the beginning stages the class should participate in choral responses. If mistakes are made, the teacher should give the correct form and then go on. Prompting may be used as needed, but lengthy grammatical explanations are not helpful to beginners. Use individual responses after the group has been prepared for them and can use them to stimulate learning.

Use complete expressions in the target language. As a general rule, comprehension is facilitated when new material is introduced in complete sentences rather than in isolated words. Ask the children questions that call for complete answers, rather than yes or no answers. For example, instead of asking, "Do you have a book?" ask, "What do you have?" or "What kind of a book do you have?" Encourage pupils to answer in complete sentences.

Use the target language throughout the lesson. The teacher may find it necessary to make a few introductory remarks in English, but instruction should be carried on in the target language, with English used only during a brief question-answer period, if needed, at the end of the lesson. Continual translation into English hinders the acquisition of the new habitual speech behavior that constitutes understanding and expression in the target language. As vocabulary is developed, use the language in giving directions, everyday greetings, games, songs, dramatizations, expressing simple courtesies, folk stories, poems, identifying pictures and objects, conversation, and other appropriate activities.

Use a conversational approach to introduce new words and structural patterns. Use of conversation or model dialogues provides a more natural setting for the language. Children should carefully mimic, practice, and memorize the patterns represented in the dialogues. Teach patterns through *practice*, rather than talking *about* the grammatical principles of the language. Base the teaching of structural elements of the language on the child's background of experience in listening and speaking. For example, after *using* masculine and feminine gender in different situations, the child can focus on the rules that govern the use of articles and endings. Thus in Spanish the child learns how to apply *el* and *la* after he has experienced them in different activities.

Teach the language within the atmosphere of the culture. Language is a cultural pattern, and cultural information and forms of expression should be woven into model dialogues and pattern practice. Art objects, literature, and films can be used to develop appreciations for the target culture. Realia, pictures, and other materials can be used to transform the classroom, for a while at least, into a "little extra-territorial segment" of the target country (California, 1964).

Utilize a variety of appropriate materials. Use materials that are suitable to the children's language level and contain information related to objects and situations with which they are familiar, related aspects of the target culture, or units of study developed in the language program. Use available recordings, tapes, films, and television programs if they are appropriate to the needs of the class. Although these are not a substitute for a good teacher, they are helpful in teaching specific expressions, utilizing native speakers, enriching the program, and extending children's learning. Children should be encouraged to use these resources on their own. Use pictures, study prints, objects, and pantomime to introduce words and phrases and to provide a focus for practice. If necessary, give a very brief description first in English, then adhere to the target language throughout the subsequent use of the materials.

Use the rote method of the music program to teach songs in the target language. Begin with a very brief explanation of the song in English. Then, using the target language, sing it all the way through for the class. Follow this by teaching each phrase, first the words alone, and then the words with the melody. Make sure that the children pronounce each phrase clearly and correctly. Rhymes and poems may also be taught by the rote method.

Plan each lesson in detail. Plan ahead. Vary activities to keep interest and attention high. Provide some activities that allow the pupils to move around. Give the children opportunities to use their skills in a variety of different situations. Try to acquire appropriate instructional materials and be sure all needed materials are available.

Use grouping procedures, varied instructional materials, diagnostic tests and appropriate practice, and other techniques for individualizing instruction. Recognize individual differences, and encourage each child to achieve the highest level of proficiency of which he is capable.

Provide for continuous teacher appraisal and pupil self-evaluation of all language-learning skills. Use a tape recorder to evaluate progress in speaking. Help children to use tapes and tests to identify their strengths and weaknesses and to plan work that will lead to improvement.

CURRENT PROBLEMS AND RELATED PRACTICES

In their foreign language programs, school systems must face up to a number of critical problems. The following are of current importance:

Staffing. Qualified teachers are needed so that children will have a good model to follow in learning accurate pronunciation and inflection. With such a model children can learn to speak a foreign language naturally and fluently. The vocal flexibility of children is such that they do not have the difficulties typical of most adults. However, if the teacher is not a native or near-native speaker of the language, the children will develop speech habits that later will have to be remedied. In some elementary schools, it has been possible to use high school teachers of foreign languages by freeing them from the teaching of nonlanguage courses. In others, special teachers have been employed. Teaching by means of recordings and television has been successful in some school systems, but such an approach should not be viewed as a substitute for a qualified classroom teacher. Teachers are needed who fully understand the audio-lingual approach and are acquainted with methods and instructional materials appropriate for use with children.

Selection of pupils. In some school systems foreign language instruction is open only to gifted students who are selected on the basis of such criteria as mental ability, achievement in language arts, and interest in learning a foreign language. In others, classes are arranged for children whose parents request that they be enrolled. In still others, all children have an opportunity to participate in the program. Some individuals argue that since foreign languages are elective in the high school, they should be elective in the elementary school. In the opinion of the writers all children should have opportunities to receive instruction provided that staffing needs can be met, instructional materials can be supplied, and the program can be individualized so that gifted children move ahead rapidly, methods and materials are varied as needed, and each child gains something worthwhile from the program. In short, if a second language is to be taught the same care should be given to planning instruction as is given in other subjects, and the benefits of the program should be available to all children.

Selection of languages. The languages most widely taught in the elementary school in order of frequency are Spanish, French, and German. Scandinavian and other languages are taught in some communities where there are groups of individuals interested in them. In deciding which languages to teach, school systems use such criteria as interests and wishes of parents, availability of teachers, opportunity to use the languages in the community, proximity to groups that speak the languages, and opportunity for continuing study. Nearness to a group that speaks a foreign language and opportunities for children to use the language studied are important considerations that should be used to advantage in the instructional program. The more the children can use a language, the more fluent they will become. This is one reason why children in Europe make rapid progress in learning a second language. Such criteria as cultural value, prestige, and ease of learning are sometimes used as criteria, but they have little or no validity. Children seem to learn any of the modern languages with comparative ease when an audio-lingual approach is used. Cultural value and prestige depend upon personal values that can be met by planning for instruction in those languages of greatest interest in a given community. Objectively speaking, no one language has cultural superiority over another. As far as use throughout the world is concerned Spanish is spoken by around 150 million people, French by 75 million to 90 million, and German by over 100 million. Future possibilities of traveling abroad are sometimes mentioned as a reason for studying German, French, Spanish, and the Scandinavian languages. It seems that, except for English, there is no one best language for all children. Local conditions will, in large part, determine the foreign language to be taught. Thus Spanish in the Southwest, French in Louisiana and in the Northeast near the Canadian border, and German and Scandinavian languages in the Midwest will continue to be popular languages in the elementary school. In addition, personal preferences of parents will continue to play a large part in selecting languages to be taught.

Grades in which instruction is begun. Instruction in many school systems is begun in the middle grades after children have developed basic reading, speaking, writing, and listening skills in English. However, in some places instruction has been started earlier with success. Grade level does not appear to be so important as other factors, such as the nature of the program, availability of teachers, and continuity of the program after it has been initiated. There is much to be said for a program that is begun in the primary grades, provided that basic instruction in English is not neglected. Whatever the grade, every effort should be made to plan a coordinated program on through the secondary school so that offerings at each level are closely related.

Finding a place in the schedule. The typical program is taught in periods varying from fifteen to thirty minutes, with an average of sixty to seventy-five minutes or slightly more per week. Programs have been offered before and after school, in a separate period on regular school time, and as part of instruction in other subjects. An ideal arrangement seems to be systematic instruction in a separate period coupled with use of the language in other subjects. Some individuals believe that the school day might well be extended, not just to take care of foreign language instruction, but to meet other educational needs that are of increasing importance at the present time. Until this is done, time for foreign language study will have to come from other subjects in the program or be offered before or after school.

EVALUATION OF INSTRUCTIONAL OUTCOMES

Direct observation of students' performance is a primary mode of evaluation of cognitive and affective outcomes of foreign language instruction. As teachers listen to children's responses, they can make immediate judgments regarding growth in listening and speaking competence. Continuing evaluation is thus an integral part of the instructional program as teachers use daily observations to appraise progress.

Cognitive Domain

In addition to daily observation, specific testing may be conducted to assess growth in listening, speaking, reading, and writing ability. Although primary attention is given to listening and speaking ability in the elementary school, test exercises are provided in reading and writing when instruction extends to those skills. The following test items are illustrative of those in current use in assessing cognitive outcomes.

Knowledge level. A major part of language learning falls within this category: memorization of phoneme-grapheme correspondence; memorization of words, phrases, elementary meaning units, and sentence patterns; acquisition of knowledge about the target culture. Examples of test items for cultural understandings and various language skills are as follows:

> *Listening ability*
> 1. **Students follow commands and carry out instructions given in the target language, ranging from "Please open the door" to "Go to the chalkboard, take a piece of chalk, and write the numeral 5."**
> 2. **Students mark pictures on duplicated sheets that show objects named or action described by the teacher or played on tape.**

Speaking

The student repeats (mimics) what is heard, and his response may be rated on a numerical scale as superior, satisfactory, or unsatisfactory.

Reading

Students mark the best response among multiple choices to questions based on a selection they can read or such questions as *"La recamara esta en la* _____," followed by *A. escuela B. casa C. estación.*

Writing

Students copy words, phrases, sentences, or selections as dictated by the teacher or played on tape.

Culture

Students select the correct response in multiple-choice or true-false questions about cultural information, such as "The Langue d'oc dialect is spoken in parts of_____." *A.* Normandie, Bretagne *B.* Southeastern provinces *C.* Alsace-Lorraine *D.* Le Pays Basque.

Comprehension level. Another major aspect of language learning is the ability to understand communications in another language, with or without direct translation.

Listening

Students listen to a paragraph or story and mark the best answers to questions spoken by the teacher or played on tape.

Speaking

Students respond orally in the target language to questions posed by the teacher, or they respond to pictures or objects by telling what is shown.

Reading and writing

Students write words, phrases, or sentences in response to questions posed by the teacher or read by the children.

Culture

Students demonstrate an understanding of important features, characteristics, or values of the target culture by drawing their own "travel posters" for a trip to the target country.

Application level. This category of cognitive outcomes includes use of listening, speaking, reading, and writing abilities in activities other than instructional drill and practice.

Speaking

The students' oral responses are appraised on a rating scale in terms of pronunciation, intonation, rhythm, and fluency.

Listening and speaking

Students are rated for adequacy of response in dialogues and conversation with the teacher or with other students.

Reading

Students respond to questions designed to determine their comprehension and literary evaluation of selections they read.

Writing

Students write brief compositions on selected topics related to specific lessons or units of study.

Culture

Students collect books, pictures, objects, and other materials that provide cultural information and classify them for display in appropriate settings or describe and discuss the materials with the rest of the class.

Analysis level. This category includes the analysis of elements of language and an understanding of the relationships of these elements.

Speaking and listening

Students respond with the correct form to questions calling for use of appropriate inflectional changes in nouns and adjectives or changes in the conjugation or tense of verbs.

Reading and writing

Students arrange scrambled sentences in proper sequence or write brief critiques of selections they have read.

Synthesis level. At this level, children in the elementary school may use the target language with the teacher or among themselves for communication other than that based directly on specific lessons.

Speaking and listening

Students compose and enact skits, dialogues, puppet shows, etc., entirely in the target language. The teacher observes skills in use of the language.

Writing

Students use the target language in creative written expression or in functional writing activities initiated by the students, apart from classroom instruction. The teacher appraises the students' use of vocabulary and idiomatic expressions.

Evaluation level. Children engage in self-appraisal of their language skills and evaluate the accuracy of informational materials dealing with the target culture.

> **Speaking**
> Students listen to tape recordings of their own speech and note accuracy of pronunciation in comparison with correct models.
>
> **Reading**
> Students respond to questions about the literary qualities or authenticity of selections read.
>
> **Writing**
> Students compare their written responses or brief compositions with accurate models, noting and correcting errors or revising their work.
>
> **Culture**
> Students compare sources of information with regard to date of publication, intent of writers or producers, and other criteria.

Affective Domain

Outcomes in the affective domain are also significant in foreign language instruction. Teacher observation of pupil behavior, guided by rating scales and check lists or noted in anecdotal records, is the primary means of evaluation. Questionnaires and inventories of attitudes and interests are also useful evaluative tools.

Receiving level. Awareness and appreciation of cultural patterns of different groups and attentiveness in language learning. Sample questions on inventories might include items of identification similar to those used at the knowledge level, except that affective items refer to the child's immediate awareness without reliance on extensive memory of previous learnings.

Responding level. The child evidences satisfaction in foreign language learning, shows interest in the target culture, and engages in voluntary classroom and study activities related to language learning. Sample questions may be of the completion type, such as "Learning a different language is———," or they may employ a scale, such as "often, sometimes, never." A question of the latter type might be, "Do you ever use French in conversations outside the classroom?"

Valuing level. The child accepts, or indicates a preference for, a value, such as a continued desire to develop skill in using the target language and a sense of empathy or kinship with people of other nations and ethnic backgrounds. Attitude questionnaires may use statements requiring selection of a response in a range, such as "agree, uncertain, disagree." For example: "All Mexicans are lazy," "Influences of Hispanic culture can be found in many areas of life in the United States," or "I would enjoy being able to speak a different language."

Organization level. The child recognizes and appreciates the viewpoints and values of his own as well as the target culture, particularly as these are conveyed in conventions of the language. Completion questions such as the following may be used: "We are learning to speak Spanish because ———," "Bastille Day is not exactly the same as our Independence Day because ———."

EVALUATION OF THE FOREIGN LANGUAGE PROGRAM

The following criteria are examples of those which may be used in evaluating programs of foreign language instruction in elementary schools.

Foundations

Are learning activities and content organization based on knowledge drawn from the linguistic disciplines?

Are learning activities based on an understanding of foreign language learning as the acquisition of new habitual speech behavior?

Structure

Are content organization and language practice consistent with the structural characteristics of the target language?

Are structural patterns presented in a manner that makes them clear to the child?

Is pattern practice used to strengthen language habits?

Inquiry

Do children learn to understand language patterns by generalizing from examples they have used and practiced?

Objectives

Are objectives clearly defined in regard to acquisition of listening, speaking, reading, writing, and comprehension skills?

Is emphasis placed upon language understandings in terms appropriate to the target culture, rather than in terms of English "equivalents"?

Are objectives stated in regard to development of positive attitudes and interests in language learning and appreciation for the target culture?

Complete program

Is the program designed to lead into appropriate language programs in secondary schools?

Does the program include both language learning and the development of understandings about the target culture?

Does the program emphasize listening and speaking skills and afford the children opportunities for application of newly acquired aural-oral skills?

Teaching strategies

Do children learn to comprehend and use the spoken language to some level of proficiency before they begin to use the language in written form?

Are reading and writing activities based on language patterns used in the children's oral communication?

Are appropriate speech models presented to the children by the teacher and in the form of tapes by a variety of native speakers?

Are pattern practice drills utilized to provide maximum opportunities for pupil response and language use in each lesson?

Do children use only the target language throughout the lesson for maximum practice and development of comprehension without direct translation?

Are a variety of multisensory materials provided to facilitate and enrich learning experiences?

Evaluation

Is continuous evaluation called for as an integral part of instruction?

Are children taught skills of self-evaluation?

Are evaluative criteria realistic in terms of individual differences and stages of language learning?

Teacher education

Are in-service activities provided to enable teachers to develop their own language skills as well as proficiency in language teaching?

Are specialists available to assist teachers in planning, instructional techniques, and selection of materials?

Program evaluation

Is provisión made for ongoing evaluation and revision of the program in the light of emerging contributions from related disciplines and newly developed language programs and materials?

REFERENCES

Birkmaier, Emma. Foreign languages. *Using current curriculum developments.* Washington, D.C.: Association for Supervision and Curriculum Development, 1963. Review of new developments; detailed bibliography of available instructional materials.

Birkmaier, Emma. Foreign languages. *New curriculum developments.* Washington, D.C.: Association for Supervision and Curriculum Development, 1965. Updated review of developments; additions to bibliography.

Bishop, G. R. (Ed.) *Culture in language learning.* New Brunswick, N.J.: Rutgers University, 1960. Reports of a conference on culture in language learning.

Bloom, Benjamin S. (Ed.) *The taxonomy of educational objectives: cognitive domain.* New York: McKay, 1956. Sample objectives and test items.

Brooks, Nelson. *Language and language learning: theory and practice.* (2d ed.) New York: Harcourt, Brace, 1964. Principles and techniques for promoting language learning.

California. *French: listening, speaking, reading, writing.* Bulletin 31, No. 4. Sacramento: California State Department of Education, 1962. Outlines four sequential phases of foreign language learning in patterns beginning at different grade levels.

California. *Guide to the teaching of Spanish: grade six.* (experimental ed.) Sacramento: State Department of Education, 1964. Specific suggestions for beginning instruction.

Childers, J. Wesley. *Foreign language teaching.* New York: The Center for Applied Research in Education, Inc., 1964. Brief history and recent developments in foreign language instruction, from FLES to college level.

Dunkel, Harold B., & Pillet, Roger A. *French in the elementary school.* Chicago: University of Chicago Press, 1962. Guidelines for planning and providing a systematic program of instruction.

Eriksson, Marguerite, Forest, Ilse, & Mulhauser, Ruth. *Foreign languages in the elementary school.* Englewood Cliffs, N.J.: Prentice-Hall, 1964. Specific techniques of teaching; sample lessons included.

Finocchiaro, Mary. *Teaching children foreign languages.* New York: McGraw-Hill, 1964. Principles and techniques to use in elementary schools.

Keesee, Elizabeth. *Modern foreign languages in the elementary school.* Washington, D.C.: U.S. Office of Education, 1960. Illustrative teaching techniques for various phases of instruction.

Keesee, Elizabeth. *References on foreign languages in the elementary school.* Washington, D.C.: U.S. Office of Education, 1963. A bibliography of available resources.

Krathwohl, David R., Bloom, Benjamin S., & Masia, Bertram B. *Taxonomy of educational objectives: affective domain.* New York: McKay, 1964. Sample objectives and test items.

Lado, Robert. *Language testing: the construction and use of foreign language tests*. New York: McGraw-Hill, 1964. (a) Principles and techniques of test construction.

Lado, Robert. *Language teaching*. New York: McGraw-Hill, 1964. (b) Theory and practice of teaching based on linguistics.

Los Angeles City Schools. *Course of study for elementary schools*. Los Angeles: Board of Education, 1964. Outlines for a K-6 program.

New York City. *Italian in the elementary schools*. New York: Board of Education, 1965. Specific techniques of instruction; bulletins available for other languages.

New York City. *Spanish in the elementary schools*. New York: Board of Education, 1963. Outline of program and techniques of instruction.

Parlons Français: teacher's guide. Boston: Heath deRochemont Corp. Not dated. Outlines teaching strategies used in a program of instruction in French for the elementary school.

Phenix, Philip H. *Realms of meaning*. New York: McGraw-Hill, 1964. A philosophy of curriculum development. Chapter 5 discusses the structure of language.

Rivers, Wilga M. *The psychologist and the foreign language teacher*. Chicago: University of Chicago Press, 1964. Use of psychology in foreign language teaching.

Valdman, Albert. (Ed.) *Trends in language teaching*. New York: McGraw-Hill, 1965. Review of developments in language instruction at all levels, including articles on FLES, new instructional media, and teaching of socio-cultural contexts of target languages.

Chapter Six

MATHEMATICS EDUCATION

MATHEMATICS IS COMPOSED of quantitative concepts and generalizations, their properties and relationships, and modes of logical reasoning that have widespread applicability. Like man's verbal language, mathematics consists of arbitrary symbolic forms with rules of construction and interpretation. It is organized into logical systems that enable man to think about, utilize, and communicate quantitative ideas and the relationships among them with a high degree of precision.

While mathematics may be viewed as principally a study of structure and a logical application of human reason, it is also a body of knowledge and information. The content of mathematics is the product of its deductive, postulational method and is particularly useful in the physical and social sciences as well as directly relevant to most avenues of human endeavor. While this content is neither absolute nor incontrovertible, it does provide the substance of mathematical thinking. Thus, today's mathematics is concerned with the study of structure, the creation of systems of ideas, the pursuit of generalization through reason and logic, and the systematic abstraction of content. It is a part of the realm of symbolics (Phenix, 1964).

In recognition of these characteristics, curriculum planners have transformed the *arithmetic* program into a program of elementary school *mathematics*. The change of designation gives recognition to the changes in content and approach which have characterized the reform of this curriculum area. The program for children is part of a continuum of mathematics which extends from early number identification to complex abstraction. Furthermore, the term "mathematics" gives support to the view that the separation of material into various compartments, such as grade levels, or into particular specializations, such as algebra, fractions, and percentages, should be done only for instructional convenience. The modern elementary school mathematics program accents the relationships among mathematical ideas and promotes the continuous development of mathematical thinking.

FOUNDATION DISCIPLINES

Because of its unique derivation and special characteristics, pure mathematics may be viewed as a foundation discipline in its own right, dependent only upon the discipline of logic. Applied mathematics, however, rests upon most of the natural and social sciences because it is a precise medium of expression in these sciences. New elementary school programs and modern programs at more advanced educational levels have a distinct theoretical or pure mathematics bias. Applications, particularly those related to science, are given minimal attention. While there is some evidence that applied mathematics is receiving increased consideration in recent program formulations, theoretical mathematics with its base in logic is the foundation of the modern school program. Psychology and philosophy are used as sources of ideas for adapting mathematics to the elementary school program. The following sections show how key ideas from foundation disciplines are incorporated in modern mathematics instruction.

Concept Clusters

Clearly apparent in current materials of instruction are concept clusters drawn from mathematics. The following are indicative of the scope of the conceptual structure of new programs of instruction.

> *Numbers*: counting or natural, zero, whole, integers, cardinal, ordinal, positive, negative, fractions, prime, composite, rational, irrational, real
>
> *Sets*: collection, members or elements, notation, number property, counting, one-to-one correspondence, matching or equivalent, serial ordering, proper, improper, finite, infinite, empty or null, subset, operation, intersection, union, disjoint, Venn diagrams
>
> *Hindu-Arabic system*: position as functionary, place value, base, additive property, symbols as placeholders, compounding, powers, exponents
>
> *Operations*: primary, inverse, addition, multiplication, subtraction, division, synthesizing, analyzing, comparing, binary properties, counting
>
> *Axiomatic properties*: set closure, commutation, association, distribution, identity, inverse, zero
>
> *Fractional numbers*: comparison, ratio, the geometric continuum, dense characteristic, equivalence, numerator, denominator, ordered pairs, positional expressions (decimal fractions), per cent, equality
>
> *Measurement*: units, dimensions, arbitrary units, standard units, calibration, scale, precision, accuracy, error, relative error, approximate numbers, absolute error
>
> *Symbolism*: mathematical sentences, variables, equations, formulas, graphing, set nomenclature, expression of relationship, functions, identities
>
> *Geometry*: point, line, line segment, plane and space figures, ray, arc, end point, angle, vertex, sides, intersection and union of sets of points, open and closed figures, interior, exterior, polygons, congruence, bisect, perpendicular, parallel
>
> *Mathematical reasoning*: estimation, approximation, inference, induction, deduction, problem solving, generalization, proof, symbols, definitions, undefined forms, sentences, identities

> *Primitive number theory*: factors, multiples, primes, composites, least common multiple, greatest common factor, tests for divisibility, relations
>
> *Relations*: pairing, ordered pairs, ratio, per cent, plane of number lines, mapping pairs on a plane, cartesian system, graphing, slope, intercept, interpolation, extrapolation, equations for straight lines, functional relationships, equivalence relations

Within the above major clusters are many smaller clusters of subconcepts. For example, *place value* includes concepts of grouping, the decimal characteristic, notation, nondecimal bases; *subtraction* includes concepts of taking groups apart, comparing groups, compensation, equal additions, decomposition, complements; and *prism* includes concepts of faces, edges, and vertex. Subconcepts within these smaller clusters are developed and brought together with others to form major clusters which are in turn organized into logical systems. Ideally, the treating of relationships among concepts leads to the formulation of generalizations.

Generalizations

The following are illustrative of generalizations from mathematics which are incorporated in programs of instruction:

> **Sets and set operations provide a basis upon which mathematical knowledge may be built.**
>
> **Number is a property of sets that is expressed through mathematical forms and symbols.**
>
> **Operations may be defined on sets; other operations may be defined on numbers.**
>
> **Number systems may be isolated and studied.**
>
> **Number systems may be classified according to the existence of various properties.**
>
> **Operations may be defined on pairs of elements from particular sets of numbers.**
>
> **The sum or product of an addition or multiplication is unaffected by the order of the elements under these operations.**
>
> **The manner of grouping elements has no effect upon results in addition and multiplication.**
>
> **Zero is the identity element for addition because the addition of zero to any number results in that number.**
>
> **An inverse element relates to another in such manner that the identity is produced under a particular operation.**
>
> **Operations may be viewed as having an inverse relationship to one another; addition undoes subtraction; multiplication undoes division; and vice versa.**
>
> **Mathematical sentences may express equalities or inequalities; they may be true or false.**

> Throughout his history, man has invented notation systems and measurement systems to meet his needs.

EXAMPLES OF STRUCTURE

Structure in Mathematics and Elementary Mathematics

The structure of a mathematical system may be viewed as consisting of primitive and derived terms, properties in the form of axioms and postulates, chains of logical reasoning, and resulting theorems or conclusions. Chart 6–1 shows the relationships between the structure of mathematics systems and the structure of elementary mathematics.

Chart 6–1. *Elements in the structure of elementary mathematics and mathematics systems.*

Symbols	Structure of elementary mathematics	Structure of mathematics systems
$\{\}\ \phi$	Set Definitive collections and classes	Set
$.02\ \ 5/10\ \ \pi\ \ 3^2$ $\sqrt{4}\ \ ''\ \ °\ \ \$\ \ \measuredangle$ $XI\ \ 10\ \ \Delta\ \ mph$	Number Property of sets Number systems Notation systems Measurement units	Elements
$\cup \cap\ \&\ =\ +\ -$ $\div\ \times\ :\ \neq\ <$ $>\ \sqrt{\ }\ (\ )\ \approx$	Relations, operations	Rules of combination
$\infty\ \ \ 1,0\ \ \ x,\ y$ $1/5\ \ \ l \times w$ $b^2\ \ \longmapsto\ \ \square$	Terms Space Volume Prime Inverse Variable, etc.	Defined terms
$a + (b + c) =$ $(a + b) + c$ $a + b = b + a$ $ab = ba$	Closure, distribution, association, commutation	Postulates
$\longleftrightarrow\ \ \ \longrightarrow$ $/\ \ \therefore\ \ \sim\ \ P$ $Q\ \supset\ \wedge$ $[(\,)]\ \ \vee$	Generalization, proof, problem solving	Logical reasoning
Combinations of the above symbols	Conclusions	Theorems

(Right margin annotations: "Undefined terms" and "Basis of system" brace the first three rows; "Total system" brackets the whole; "Basis of system" extends through the Postulates row.)

Structure of the Number System

Primary attention is given in the elementary school mathematics program to sets of numbers within the real number system. Most of the program is concerned with the set of whole numbers. The structure of the real number system and the place of other numbers in this system are shown in Chart 6–2.

Beginning with the natural numbers, zero is added to form the set of whole numbers. This subset, together with those numbers defined by any pair of whole numbers under subtraction, make up the set of integers. The integers plus other numbers defined by any pair of whole numbers (except 0) under division (actually of the ratio form a/b where $b =$ a natural number) make up the rational numbers. The real number system is composed of the rational numbers and the irrational numbers (those represented by nonrepeating decimal fractions such as $\sqrt{2}$).

The systematic characteristics of selected sets of numbers are studied in the elementary school with primary attention given to operations and properties. Given the two fundamental operations, addition and multiplication, the remaining two operations of subtraction and division are derived as operational inverses. The properties given attention are closure, commutation, association, distribution, identity, and inverse. Table 6–1 includes these axiomatic properties with reference to the core of elementary school mathematics, the set of whole numbers. (See p. 168.)

Modes of Inquiry

Mathematicians construct a mathematical system and extend its conclusions, primarily by means of deductive reasoning and inference, proceed-

Chart 6–2.   Structure of the real number system.

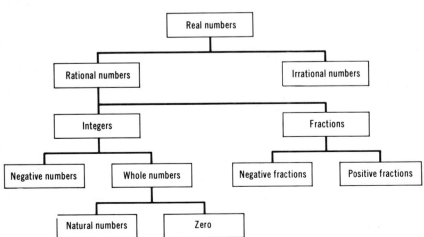

ing from basic premises to postulates to conclusions through inferential ("if-then") reasoning. These conclusions may serve as premises in a further chain of deductive inference.

Analytic techniques identified as basic mathematical procedures (Spencer & Brydegaard, 1966, pp. 11–15) include identification, comparison, and measurement. Identification involves differentiating a part from the whole. Comparison involves discernment of characteristics, such as shape, direction, or amount, and comparison of referent and relatum. Measurement introduces comparison with a given referent and leads to quantifying of identified elements or characteristics. As these basic procedures are developed to increasing levels of refinement, they lead to higher levels of mathematical thought, which include analysis of constancy, variability, and relations, study of the direction of variation mapped on a continuum, the interpretation of functional relationships, and the involvement of deductive reasoning.

The student of elementary mathematics does not begin his study with the mode of inquiry used in the construction of systems. He may approach deductive reasoning in the manner outlined above. He also may utilize deductive inference in his application of inductively derived understandings and generalizations to new mathematical situations. But he begins to build his understanding of mathematical structure by means of inductive reasoning. This inductive procedure involves the student in gathering factual data, identifying particular instances and characteristics, matching and comparing, classifying, exploring for patterns and relationships, and asking questions which guide his analysis of experiences and observations and enable him to discover general conclusions.

The learner goes from inductively derived conclusions to the application of these conclusions to new mathematical problems. He utilizes problem-solving techniques in the analysis of new situations and deductively infers the appropriate principles and procedures required. He further confirms his understanding by verifying his conclusions by such means of probable inference as measurement, analogy, enumeration of all cases, or pragmatic effectiveness. He may learn to prove his deductive inferences according to logical patterns of thinking. For example, the common problem form: $\frac{2}{3}x = 10$, $x = \Box$ may be generalized: If $\frac{2}{3}x = 10$, then $\frac{1}{3}x = \frac{1}{2} \times 10$. $x = \frac{3}{1} \times \frac{1}{2} \times 10 = 15$. Therefore, $\frac{2}{3}(15) = 10$.

DEVELOPMENTAL COGNITIVE STAGES AND MATHEMATICS INSTRUCTION

In the area of reading and language arts skill development, the concept of readiness is clearly defined in terms of the child's growth and physiological

TABLE 6-1. Axiomatic Properties with Respect to Operations in the Set of Whole Numbers

Properties	*Operations*			
	Addition	*Subtraction*	*Multiplication*	*Division*
Closure	The whole numbers are closed under addition $0+2=2; 3+4=7$	The whole numbers are not closed under subtraction $5-5=\Box; 5-7=\triangle$ $\Box$ and $\triangle$ are not members of the set of whole numbers	The whole numbers are closed under multiplication $3\times0=0; 5\times4=20$	The whole numbers are not closed under division $3\div4=\Box; 7\div2=\triangle$ $\Box$ and $\triangle$ are not members of the set of whole numbers
Commutation	Addition is commutative in the set of whole numbers $3+5=8; 5+3=8$ $\therefore 3+5=5+3$	Subtraction is not commutative in the set of whole numbers $4-2=2; 2-4\neq2$	Multiplication is commutative in the set of whole numbers $3\times6=18; 6\times3=18$ $\therefore 3\times6=6\times3$	Division is not commutative in the set of whole numbers $6\div3=2; 3\div6\neq2$
Association	Addition is associative in the set of whole numbers $(2+3)+7=5+7=12$ $2+(3+7)=2+10=12$ $(2+3)+7=2+(3+7)$	Subtraction is not associative in the set of whole numbers $(8-2)-4=6-4=2$ $8-(2-4)=8-(-2)\neq2$	Multiplication is associative in the set of whole numbers $(3\times6)\times4=18\times4=72$ $3\times(6\times4)=3\times24=72$ $\therefore (3\times6)\times4=3\times(6\times4)$	Division is not associative in the set of whole numbers $(16\div4)\div2=4\div2=2$ $16\div(4\div2)=16\div2\neq2$
Distribution	Addition is not distributive over other operations in the set of whole numbers $3+(2\times4)=3+8=11$ $(3+2)\times(3+4)=5\times7\neq11$	Subtraction is not distributive over other operations in the set of whole numbers $7-(2\times3)=7-6=1$ $(7-2)\times(7-3)=5\times4\neq1$	Multiplication is distributive over addition and subtraction (where applicable) in the set of whole numbers $3\times(4+2)=3\times6=18$	Division is not distributive over other operations in the set of whole numbers $12\div(4+2)=12\div6=2$ $(12\div4)+(12\div2)=$ $3+6\neq2$

	Addition	Subtraction	Multiplication	Division
Distribution	or $3+(6-2)=3+4=7$ $(3+6)-(3+2)=9-5\neq7$	or $7-(5+1)=7-6=1$ $(7-5)+(7-1)=2+6\neq1$	$(3\times4)+(3\times2)=12+6=18$ $\therefore 3\times(4+2)=$ $(3\times4)+(3\times2)$ $3\times(6-2)=3\times4=12$ $(3\times6)-(3\times2)=18-6=12$ $\therefore 3\times(6-2)=$ $(3\times6)-(3\times2)$	$12\div(6-3)=12\div3=4$ $(12\div6)-(12\div3)=$ $2-4\neq4$ although in special cases (right-hand property) $(8\div4)\div4=12\div4=3$ $(8\div4)+(4\div4)=2+1=3$ $\therefore (8\div4)\div4=$ $(8\div4)+(4\div4)$ or $(12-4)\div4=8\div4=2$ $(12\div4)-(4\div4)=3-1=2$ $\therefore (12\div4)-(4\div4)=$ $(12\div4)\div4=$
Identity	Addition has the identity element 0 in the set of whole numbers $5+0=5; 0+3=3$	Subtraction has no identity element in the set of whole numbers while $2-0=2; 0-3\neq3$	Multiplication has the identity element 1 in the set of whole numbers $3\times1=3; 1\times6=6$	Division has no identity element in the set of whole numbers $5\div1=5; 1\div4\neq4$
Inverse	Addition has no additive inverse element within the set of whole numbers Addition and subtraction may be regarded as inverse operations $3+5=8$	Subtraction has no inverse element within the set of whole numbers Subtraction and addition may be regarded as inverse operations $8-5=3$	Multiplication has no multiplicative inverse element within the set of whole numbers Multiplication and division may be regarded as inverse operations $5\times4=20$	Division has no inverse element within the set of whole numbers Division and multiplication may be regarded as inverse operations $20\div4=5$

development, intellectual development, and experiential background. The idea of readiness for mathematical learning is not so clearly defined. Physical characteristics of the learner are not so significant in mathematical learning as in development of language skills, but intellectual and experiential factors may be identified and classroom activities suggested.

In regard to the child's experiential background, there is no clear identification of a level of quantitative knowledge that would constitute "readiness" for elementary mathematics learning nor any clear set of criteria that distinguish the ready from the unready learner. The concept of number-mindedness is sometimes used to describe the child's awareness of some of the social uses of number. As part of his daily life throughout his preschool years the growing child encounters number and quantity in varying situations. He associates number with his age, the size of his family, a collection of toys, money that he handles. Number names denote his birthday, weight, and the time of day. Children come to the kindergarten and grade 1 with varying backgrounds and levels of number-mindedness. Classroom activities in the nursery school and the earliest elementary grades provide the child with a wealth of experiences with number. Recent courses of study provide explicit directions to teachers for provision of such experiences. They include direct instruction in the kindergarten on rational and rote counting, sets and simple number analysis, concepts of natural numbers and simple fractions, recognition of coins and geometric shapes, time divisions of the day, use of the calendar, and rudimentary measurement activities. Thus, experiential readiness for mathematical learning is not a fixed condition, but rather the earliest phases of the sequential development of mathematical concepts. Because number experiences at each grade level provide a basis for conceptual growth at higher levels, experiential readiness may be regarded as a continuing aspect of classroom mathematical activities.

Research studies which were carried out in the 1920s and 1930s in attempts to determine appropriate mental ages at which children can comprehend specific concepts and processes have proved inadequate as indicators of readiness or developmental levels, because their findings were based upon children's arithmetic achievement under existing programs and instructional techniques. Two considerations have since tended to modify the notion that mental age is a significant factor in mathematical readiness: the nature and logical sequence of currently recommended elementary mathematics programs and the identification of stages of the child's intellectual development toward increasingly more abstract levels of thought.

In regard to the latter consideration, the findings of Piaget (1952) indicate that the child's intellectual development proceeds through distinct stages, with differing intellectual processes playing major roles at each stage. According to this description, the child of five and six, typical ages for kindergarten and grade 1, is in the preoperational stage. His thinking is centered about himself and his direct experiences and is geared to manipulate the world through action, rather than mediation of experience. An important consideration for mathematical reasoning is the tendency for the child at this stage to lack the concept of reversibility or conservation of quantity—a concept which may underlie arithmetic operations.

At about the age of seven, the child begins to exhibit characteristics of the stage of concrete operations in his thinking. At this stage, he has acquired the concept of reversibility. Concrete operations of objects and symbols are internalized to some extent as the child engages in problem solving rather than direct action. The concrete operational stage roughly encompasses the seventh, eighth, ninth, and tenth years or grades 2, 3, 4, and 5 of the elementary school sequence.

When the child is eleven, his thinking becomes more characteristic of the stage of formal operations, in which he is able to operate on hypothetical propositions and deal with abstract concepts, principles, and processes. The child achieves this stage in grade 6. This relationship of chronological age and stage of intellectual development is descriptive of the child in the broad range of "average" intelligence. While it is hypothesized that all normal children will proceed through these stages, it is understood that they will do so at differing rates.

With respect to mathematics there is apparently no *general* readiness. Rather, learning readiness must be related to specific mathematical tasks. Stages of instruction are suggested for development of concepts and processes based upon the idea that learning proceeds most effectively when introductory concrete experiences are provided prior to abstract considerations. This instructional pattern proceeds through three levels. The new concept or process is introduced in the context of a functional everyday experience or in terms of a concrete problem. Real or concrete objects are utilized in the exploration of concept or process at this level. A transition is then made to the semisymbolic or graphic level, in which concrete objects are replaced first by nonrepresentational manipulative materials and then by pictures of objects or nonrepresentational forms. The learner utilizes these semisymbolic materials and pictures as he thinks a problem through mathematically. After this experience, he proceeds to the abstract level, using numerals and operational symbols, algorithms, principles, and generalizations. In the earliest grades, in accordance with the child's mode of thinking, much concrete experience precedes attainment of an abstract level for any particular conceptualization. As he progresses through the middle and upper elementary grades, the child is increasingly able to move more rapidly from limited concrete experience and semisymbolic activities to completely abstract representations and is able to acquire understandings through a proportionately greater experience at more abstract levels of mathematical reasoning.

OBJECTIVES OF INSTRUCTION

At the turn of the century, objectives of mathematics instruction in the elementary school centered upon the development of computational skill. In the 1920s and 1930s, goals shifted to a focus on practical application and everyday mathematical usage. These objectives have not been cast aside in current practice, but they have been placed in a more balanced perspective. Educational scholars today are cognizant of cultural and technological changes which have created needs for greater understanding of mathematics concepts and reasoning on the part of an increasing proportion of the population. In addition, the future is expected to bring new and changing requirements for mathematics skills. Many educators and mathematicians suggest that needs for current understanding as well as for future learnings are most effectively met when the pupil is able to perceive and understand structure in mathematics: concepts, relationships, principles, and modes of mathematical reasoning. Recent courses of study tend to give attention to three major, interrelated goals: understanding of mathematical structure and patterns, computational skill, and use of logical reasoning in abstract and practical problem-solving activities.

The following statements represent a summary of objectives stated in recent courses of study and professional publications. Instruction in elementary mathematics is intended:

> **To help the child to understand number concepts, structure of number systems, relationships, principles, and operations, and to enable him to formulate generalizations about patterns and structure in mathematics**
>
> **To develop computational skill which encompasses (1) facility with number facts and (2) an understanding of the principles of operations and the positional system, with particular insight into computational algorithms**
>
> **To teach the child to think in quantitative terms and to utilize mathematical concepts and principles in his development of clear, precise mathematical reasoning**
>
> **To give the child an appreciation of how man has evolved systems and instruments of measurement to meet his needs and to develop the child's understanding of the meaning and process of measurement**
>
> **To help the child to appreciate mathematics as part of his cultural heritage and to develop an understanding of mathe-**

matics as a language which enables man to express and record quantitative ideas

To develop in the child an appreciation and enjoyment of mathematics and an interest in its practical and theoretical aspects; to extend to him the opportunity to learn as much mathematics as his capacity and interest will permit

Basic objectives such as these are defined behaviorally or operationally in order to facilitate planning and evaluation. For example, the objective "to develop mathematical understanding" may be defined as including such behaviors as:

Recognizes and uses the set of counting numbers: 1, 2, 3, . . .

Shows that 107 includes 107 ones, or 10 tens and 7 ones, or 1 hundred and 7 ones

Explains what is done as regrouping is carried out in addition

Detailed listings of behavioral objectives may be found in textbooks for teachers (for example, see Marks, Purdy, & Kinney, 1965, pp. 33–37).

A COMPLETE PROGRAM

The scope and sequence of currently recommended elementary mathematics programs are constructed on the basis of the following assumptions:

The elementary mathematics program is a single, monolithic structure of mathematical concepts which are interrelated at every grade level.

These concepts must be developed sequentially over a period of time, in a spiral program that treats each topic at intervals in increasingly complex forms.

These concepts are most effectively learned if they are presented in a suitable form, in accordance with the pupil's modes of thinking, from the child's earliest school experiences.

Previously held assumptions about inherent difficulties of mathematical topics, and rigid grade-level assignments based on these assumptions, are being challenged today by the results produced by curriculum planners trying out new programs at varying grade levels. Use of the materials and programs of curriculum projects such as the School Mathematics Study Group (SMSG), Greater Cleveland, Madison Project, Minnemath, and others leads to the suggestion that children may be able to learn complex concepts earlier than previously considered possible and that simple geometric concepts and algebra in the form of number sentences may be easier for the primary grade child than are some "traditional" aspects of the program. In short, scholars in education and mathematics now suggest that all mathematics topics may be introduced in an appropriately simple form in the earliest grades and that adherence to a rigid grade-placement sequence is not necessary. In kindergarten and grade 1 the child may engage in manipulation of concrete objects that will provide the experiential basis for mathematical ideas that are developed in semisymbolic and abstract terms in the later grades. He may deal with forms of concepts and basic mathematical ideas that will serve him in his later mathematics.

Questions may be raised about the grade placement of topics in new programs. If it is shown that children *can* learn something at an earlier grade, does this necessarily imply that they *should*? What modifications in methodology affect the ease with which concepts or processes may be learned at early grade levels? What significance do children find in topics introduced in the early grades? For many curriculum planners today, however, the question appears to be not *when* to begin a given topic, but rather *how* to begin it and how to pace development of the topic through the grades.

There is much agreement on topics of importance, although organization and relative emphasis on topics differ considerably among courses of study. Most programs provide for the introduction of some basic topics in appropriately simple forms in kindergarten or grade 1, with a subsequent treatment of the topics at higher grade levels. An example of this approach is found in the identification of thirty-two mathematics generalizations and suggestions for their appropriate development at different grade levels in the Twenty-fourth Yearbook of the National Council of Teachers of Mathematics (1959, pp. 480–498). These generalizations or basic mathematical ideas are drawn from topics designated as number and operations, relations and functions, proof, measurement and approximation, probability, statistics, language and symbolism, and mathematical modes of thought. Another outline of topics suggests that number systems, geometry, measurement, and application are basic elementary mathematics strands which must be augmented by attention to the topics of sets, functions, logic, and mathematical sentences (California, 1963). These and other representative professional publications and courses of study indicate that the following topics are considered important areas for instruction in the elementary grades. In the process of instruction, topics listed as concepts and procedures are developed in relation to those listed as major areas.

Recent courses of study outline their programs in varying combinations of these topics as shown in Chart 6–3.

The structure of mathematics systems is conveyed through the medium of the topics of the elementary mathematics program. The following outline indicates this relationship of structure to organization of instruction.

Major areas	Concepts and symbolic representation	Procedures
Number and numeration	Set	Approximation
Operations, functions, relations	Vocabulary	Estimation
	Symbols	Generalization
	Graphs and tables	Proof or verification
Laws governing operations	Number lines	Application
	Mathematical sentences	Problem solving
Measurement		Logical deduction
Geometry		
Probability		

Set: use of nomenclature and set operations, such as intersection, union, cartesian product, to integrate concepts in all instructional areas

Elements:
1. Number, number systems, notational schemes
2. Measurement units (degrees, seconds, etc.)

Rules of combination: operations, relationships
1. One-to-one correspondence, counting, and basic operations using number lines, number sentences, graphs

Chart 6–3.   The structure of selected mathematics curricula.

Greater Cleveland, 1964	Philadelphia, 1963	Palo Alto, 1964
Exploration and discovery	Study of number	Sets
Systems of numbers and numerals	Number system	Number and numeration
Sets	Set operations	Mathematical sentences
Mathematical sentences	Laws	Graphs
Measurement	Use of number	Nonmetric geometry
Functions	Money	Measurement
Geometry	Fractions	Mathematical systems
Statistics	Measurement	Special topics
Logic	Graphs, charts	
	Geometric figures	
	Vocabulary	
	Problem solving	
	Supplementary practices	

Idaho, 1965	Minnesota, 1964	SMSG, 1964
Number, numeration, computation	Sets	Number systems
Sets	Geometry	Properties and operations
Measurement	Measurement	Geometry
Geometric forms	Ratio and proportion	Measurement
		Applications

2. **Ratio, proportion, measurement, operations, arrays, functions**
3. **Geometric relationships**

Defined terms: introduced in all topics

Postulates: derived during the course of instruction on various
operations, functions, and relationships

Logical reasoning: developed in connection with all topics

SEQUENCE OF TOPICS

The following outline indicates the general grade-level sequence of instruction representative of recent courses of study. Dots indicate periods of readiness, cross marks indicate instruction and development, and dashes indicate levels of reinforcement or mastery.

	K	1	2	3	4	5	6
Set and set operations							
Equal sets, subsets, empty sets, union, separation	. x x	x x x	x x x	– – –	– – –	– – –	– – –
Notation, symbols, terminology	.	. x x	x x –	– – –	– – –	– – –	– – –
Finite and infinite sets				. . .	x x x	x x x	– – –
Number and numeration							
Cardinal numbers as properties of sets	. . x	x x x	x – –	– – –	– – –	– – –	– – –
Ordinal numbers	. .	. . x	x x x	x – –	– – –	– – –	– – –
Recognition and reproduction of collections	. . x	x x x	x x x	x – –	– – –	– – –	– – –
Frames, numerals	. . .	. x x	x x x	x x x	x x x	x x x	x x x
Use of number line		. . x	x x x	x x x	x x x	x x x	x x x
Concept of 10 and 100	.	. . x	x x x	– – –	– – –	– – –	– – –
Uses of zero	.	. . x	x x x	x x –	– – –	– – –	– – –
Understanding millions				. . x	x x x	x x x	x x x
Roman numerals				. . x	x x x	x x x	x x x
Place value		. . x	x x x	x x x	x x x	x x x	x – –
Nondecimal bases						. . x	x x x
Positive and negative integers					. . .	. x x	x x x
Approximate numbers					. . .	. x x	x x x
Exponential notation						. .	. x x
Fractions: 1/2	. . x	x x x	x x –	– – –	– – –	– – –	– – –
1/3, 1/4	. .	. x x	x x x	x x x	– – –	– – –	– – –
1/5, 1/6, 1/8		. .	. . .	x x x	x x x	– – –	– – –
Decimal fractions notation				. .	. . x	x x x	x x x
Operations							
One-to-one correspondence	. . x	x x x	x x x	– – –	– – –	– – –	– – –
Rote and rational counting	. . x	x x x	– – –	– – –	– – –	– – –	– – –
Counting by 2s, 5s, 10s, etc.		. .	. x x	x x x	– – –	– – –	– – –
Addition	. . .	. x x	x x x	x x x	x x x	x x x	x – –
Subtraction	. . .	. x x	x x x	x x x	x x x	x x x	x – –
Multiplication	.	. . .	. x x	x x x	x x x	x x x	x x x

	K	1	2	3	4	5	6
Division	·	· · ·	· × ×	× × ×	× × ×	× × ×	× × ×
Generalization of properties of operations	·	· · ·	× × ×	× × ×	× × ×	× × ×	× × ×
Number sentences			· · ×	× × ×	× × ×	× × ×	× × ×
Operations upon rational numbers					· · ×	× × ×	× × ×
Relations							
Comparison vocabulary and symbols	· · ·	· × ×	× × ×	× × ×	× × ×	× × ×	× × ×
Use of graphs	·	· · ×	× × ×	× × ×	× × ×	× × ×	× × ×
Use of scale drawings				·	· · ·	× × ×	× × ×
Ratio					· · ·	· × ×	× × ×
Per cent						· · ·	× × ×
Measurement							
Time of day, use of calendar	· · ×	× × ×	× × ×	× × ×	× × ×	— — —	— — —
Measurement: temperature, weight, volume, linear	· · ×	× × ×	× × ×	× × ×	× × ×	× × ×	× × ×
Standard units	·	· · ×	× × ×	× × ×	× × ×	× × ×	× — —
Monetary units	·	· × ×	× × ×	× × ×	× — —	— — —	— — —
Surface and volume measurement				·	· · ×	× × ×	× × ×
Estimation, error interval					· · ·	× × ×	× × ×
Geometry							
Recognition of two-dimensional shapes	· · ×	× × ×	× × ×	× × ×	× × ×	× × ×	× × ×
Understanding points, lines, planes	· ·	· · ·	· × ×	× × ×	× × ×	× × ×	× × ×
Recognition of solid figures	·	· · ·	· × ×	× × ×	× × ×	× × ×	× × ×
Rays, angles, properties of circles		·	· · ·	· × ×	× × ×	× × ×	× × ×
Perimeter, area, volume				· · ·	· × ×	× × ×	× × ×
Proof or Verification:							
Using experience, concrete materials	· · ·	· × ×	× × ×	× — —	— — —	— — —	— — —
Using counting, number line		· × ×	× × ×	× × ×	— — —	— — —	— — —
Using inverse operations			· ·	· × ×	× × ×	× × ×	× — —
Using estimation	·	· · ·		· × ×	× × ×	× × ×	× × —
Using alternative procedures				· ·	· · ×	× × ×	× × ×
Using logical reasoning				· ·	· · ·	× × ×	× × ×

SPECIAL FEATURES OF NEW CURRICULUM PROJECTS IN ELEMENTARY MATHEMATICS

Since the late 1950s, scholars in mathematics and education have worked together on the development of instructional programs in elementary mathematics. Although these curriculum projects vary in approach and treatment, they deal basically with the same material. Three of the major projects, SMSG, Greater Cleveland, and Minnemath, provide complete programs for the elementary grades. Other projects have concentrated upon particular grades or particular aspects of a total program. For example, all the Madison Project materials are suitable for elementary school grades beginning with grade 2, but they are intended as a supplement to existing courses of study. The former University of Illinois Project directed by David Page and the Stanford University Project of Patrick Suppes provide specific units on selected topics.

There are numerous differences among the projects, but they have many objectives and characteristics in common. A major purpose shared by all projects is the exploration of mathematical content appropriate to various grade levels or types of learners, including classroom trial of curricula, materials, and instructional techniques. Other objectives shared by these projects include the following:

> **To provide teachers with more effective approaches to elementary mathematics instruction**
>
> **To help children develop insight into mathematical structure**
>
> **To teach children to think and reason according to mathematical modes of inquiry**
>
> **To stimulate children's interest and pleasure in mathematics**
>
> **To broaden the curriculum beyond the fundamental algorithms and limited "social arithmetic" problems**
>
> **To develop creative thinking and flexibility with mathematical ideas**
>
> **To develop effective computational skill**
>
> **To provide a sequential and spiral program of concept development**
>
> **To introduce important mathematical concepts in a suitable form at early grade levels**

In addition to these objectives, the Illinois and Madison Projects emphasize the discovery of algebraic properties and generalizations through abstract representations. The Minnemath program is designed to provide a geometric model for various systems of numbers, with emphasis upon the organization of the real number system. Concrete visualization of mathematics is stressed because of its value in improving learning.

Many similar topics and instructional techniques are developed in the six projects listed above. Before these are outlined, some differences might be noted. Most of the programs are prepared for specific grade levels, but the Madison and Illinois materials are planned for use, with appropriate modifications of pace and method, at varying grade levels. While all projects emphasize structure, they differ on the relative importance of various concepts. SMSG and the Stanford materials place heavy emphasis upon sets and set operations in accordance with the view that mathematics may be integrated through such concepts. Planners of other projects subscribe to the idea that set concepts should be introduced but that they are not the only means through which ideas of number and operations may be understood. The Minnemath and Madison materials give much attention to teacher preparation through films, demonstrations, and in-service courses. While all projects recommend the use of various manipulative materials, only Minnemath and Greater Cleveland have produced specific materials for use with project units.

Relationships of curriculum project topics to the complete elementary mathematics program may be outlined as follows.

Sets. The concept of set is introduced in all projects. Suppes, in the Stanford Project, has developed units on sets, set operations, and numbers for kindergarten through grade 6. SMSG and Minnemath include recurring units on sets, while Greater Cleveland and the Madison Project incorporate set nomenclature throughout the program.

Number. The Stanford Project presents number as a property of sets. In addition to providing units on the whole number system and systems of numeration, SMSG, Greater Cleveland, Madison Project, and Minnemath provide units which extend number concepts to negative integers, exponents, and roots. The Madison Project introduces vectors and matrices in upper elementary grades, while Minnemath introduces irrational numbers on the number line in earlier grades.

Operations and laws governing operations. Number lines are utilized in most projects to develop number concepts and to permit visualization of operations. The Illinois Project gives particular attention to number line enrichment games as a medium for building understanding of the number continuum. Number sentences also are used extensively in the projects, usually with frames in the shape of squares, triangles, or circles. Sentences using two variables are also used.

Properties of the various operations are presented after the learner has gained facility with the basic facts. The Illinois and Madison Projects present these properties in mathematical sentences as identities. These identities provide a pattern for the property which is applied through substitution of numbers for frames.

Functions and relations. Number sequences, factoring, inequalities, ratio, ordered pairs, and coordinates are topics included in the Madison, SMSG, and Greater Cleveland programs. Minnemath uses the number line and cartesian plane as structural components of the program, and primitive ideas of analytic geometry are dealt with, beginning in the early elementary grades.

Mathematical reasoning. Whereas development of mathematical reasoning is an integral part of all project materials, the projects also focus on specific reasoning techniques. SMSG introduces organization and description of data in grade 4. Greater Cleveland provides units on simple informal proof for grades 5 and 6. The Illinois Project stresses explanation and intuitive proof of numerical solutions and provides exercises in estimation as an important skill in mathematical reasoning. The Madison

Project includes material from logic, including mathematical implication, truth tables, programming, and mathematical induction, primarily for grades 5 and 6. A complete course in mathematical logic for the upper grades has been developed by the Stanford project. Minnemath attempts to integrate mathematics and science. It emphasizes acquisition of knowledge through observation, classification, measurement, generalization, prediction, and the testing of predictions.

Geometry. SMSG gives much attention to informal geometry, with units on such topics as sets of points, congruence, and sets and circles. Greater Cleveland introduces geometric forms and properties in the elementary grades, while the Stanford Project develops geometric ideas through geometric constructions stressing the use of protractors, compasses, and rulers in grades 1, 2, and 3. The Madison Project presents concepts from Euclidean and vector geometry. Minnemath develops geometric understandings in grade 1 through a topological study of shapes, based upon the experiments and findings of Piaget.

Measurement. Measurement is given some attention in most projects, but its development is minimized because of the emphasis upon theoretical rather than applied mathematics.

Statistics. The Madison Project includes an upper-grade unit on concepts of descriptive statistics.

Aids to Curriculum Planning

The six projects discussed above offer several contributions to curriculum planning:

> *Lowering of grade placement*: **Experimentation with project materials has indicated that many mathematical topics formerly reserved for later introduction may be successfully treated in early elementary school grades.**

> *Balance of subject matter*: **The projects provide content designed to broaden the child's foundations in elementary mathematics by means of the logical integration of mathematical topics.**

> *Discovery encouraged*: **Project materials include guidance for teachers in the use of techniques that will encourage children to raise questions, work with specific cases to arrive at generalizations, and discover patterns in mathematical fields.**

> *Mathematical reasoning developed*: **Project programs organize content with a view to the child's acquisition of understanding and application of modes of mathematical thought.**

> *Teacher education*: Pre-service and practicing teachers may find bases for curriculum planning in guidebooks, films, demonstrations, and in-service courses prepared by some of the projects.

School systems may adopt complete project programs or incorporate separate units into existing curricula in order to supplement courses of study or provide needed learning materials.

PROPOSED TOPICS

There has been considerable speculation about the limits of the current revolution in elementary mathematics. How far should it extend? How rapidly should elementary programs be changed? Only very tentative answers have been given to questions such as these. One group has proposed consideration of such advanced topics as the following (Educational Services Incorporated, 1963):

> *Kindergarten-3*: nondecimal bases, negative integers, cartesian coordinates, neighborhood of a point, decimals by change of scale, additive slide rule, division with fractional answers, inverse with respect to operations, graphs of linear functions, additive property of area, geometric transformations, the group property, idea of set and function, and estimating orders of magnitude

> *Grades 4-6*: Archimedean property, nested intervals, mensuration formulas, conic sections, cartesian coordinates in three dimensions, polar coordinates, symmetry of sophisticated figures, scale models, indirect measurement, vectors, statics and linear kinematics, truth tables for logical connectives, axioms and theorems of real numbers, inference, flow charting, truth sets, infinite sequences, logarithm function, trigonometric functions, partial and linear orderings, stabilization through swamping, modular arithmetic, finite fields, isomorphism, elementary Diophantine problems, and integral exponents

The contrast between the proposed program and the yet to be achieved modern program is sufficient to prompt serious reflection on the objectives of school mathematics. The proposed program would have to be accompanied by a major shift in objectives if it were to be implemented, since it includes mathematics that is generally regarded as beyond the range of "arithmetic and computational literacy" to be developed in general education.

TEACHING STRATEGIES

Although inductive approaches have been emphasized in current projects, some attention has been given to deductive approaches. All projects have stressed the importance of discovery. In addition, special attention has been given to the relating of mathematical ideas so that students gain insight into mathematics as a cohesive system of logical thinking. General models have been developed to serve as flexible guides for the planning of teaching strategies.

Inductive and Deductive Discovery

A key idea in new teaching strategies is that of discovery. In a sense, discovery methods follow two paths, which may be called deductive and inductive. In deductive discovery, the child is urged to perceive relationships and patterns in particular constructions which permit him to generalize and supply missing parts of a construction. While no formal imposition of logical methods is made, the child's success is related generally to his scheme of logical analysis. Examples of this kind of activity are found in abundance in materials prepared by Wirtz, Botel, Beberman, and Sawyer (1962). Numerical data are presented in tabular or graphic form, and children are led to observe the relationship between the entries in the table or the configuration of the graph and some independent phenomenon. Then the child must, on the basis of his analysis, supply the parts of the table or graph that have been omitted. The accuracy of his entries provides an immediate evaluation of the extent to which his observation of number patterns has been complete. An example is the following from the material for the fifth grade. The rules are:

> 1. **Multiply each number in the shaded row by the number at the top of each column. Add the products. This sum must be the same as the number in the box on the left.**
> 2. **Fill in the unshaded row with numbers, following 1, so that the sum of these numbers is as small as possible.**

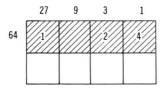

The perceptive child may generalize the properties of our positional system using a base of three and gain experience with the regrouping necessary to develop a base three numeral in its final form.

Inductive discovery depends upon the child's creation of mathematical ideas that build upon one another and proceed to some generalizations. "Guided discovery" is a more accurate expression because of the remote likelihood that children will simply create systems of new mathematical ideas without assistance from the teacher. Guided discovery may be illustrated by one of the "intermediate invention activities" prepared by Page (1962). Working with lattices, children are encouraged to develop an array for familiar numerals, within which certain definitions relating to operations may be defined. Within an arrangement approximating the 10 × 10 array with which children are familiar, values are assigned according to a place of origin and displacement from the origin. For example, the child may develop a scheme where 13 → → means with 13 as an origin, progress two entries to the right. The value of the expression is 15. Eventually the scheme may be developed so that the child sees → and ← or ↑ → and ∠ as inverses. He may develop equations such as 13 → ↑ = 36 ∠ ← or he may merely observe that the order of appearance of the same arrows does not affect the value represented. In any event, the emphasis upon detection of patterns or generalizations and upon the development of skill in observation and analysis is the same as with the deductive mode. In this case the child operates without a preexisting model of generalization.

In both deductive and inductive modes children are participating in a study of mathematics through means that depart significantly from the mechanical computational mode still prominent in too many classrooms. They are more likely to enjoy their study and they are infinitely more susceptible to learning and appreciating the logical nature of mathematics.

Discovering Generalizations

The aspect of guiding the discovery of generalizations is clearly revealed in the following activity abstracted from many possibilities included in materials developed by the Madison Project. A common teaching strategy employed by this project is to have the learner critically examine what has been done by imaginary children elsewhere. For example, Ruth's and Jerry's lists of identities are given as follows:

Ruth's list	*Jerry's list*
$3 \times \square = \square \times 3$	$\square \times (\triangle + 3) = (\square \times \triangle) + (\square \times 3)$
$4 \times \square = \square \times 4$	$\square \times (\triangle + 5) = (\square \times \triangle) + (\square \times 5)$
$1960 \times \square = \square \times 1960$	$\square \times (\triangle + 2) = (\square \times \triangle) + (\square \times 2)$
$1,000,000 \times \square = \square \times 1,000,000$	

Then the child is asked whether he can shorten the lists or whether he can contribute to some organization of a list. The hope is that the general identities for commutation with respect to multiplication and for distribution of multiplication over addition will be developed.

Discovery, when associated with material that has no direct role in the systematic program, has been called "exploration" (Educational Services Incorporated, 1963). It is recommended as a device to develop intuition and sophistication. Examples of opportunities recommended as suitable for exploration are: (1) How can you characterize a finite set without specifying the number of members? (2) Observe the Pythagorean triples (3, 4, 5), (5, 12, 13), (8, 15, 17), (7, 24, 25). How would you generate them? How is this problem related to algebraic identities? How is it related to circles in the plane?

Related Ideas

Although all projects have not provided the same opportunity for the child's discovery of important ideas, all have been supportive of the principle that teaching should emphasize a cluster of related mathematical ideas rather than treat concepts in isolation. While the instructional strategy may be mainly expository, it prompts a kind of learning that is based upon something other than rote recall. For example, SMSG has the following activity in grade 3: Mary has 4 hot dogs and Judy has 7 buns. How many more buns are there than hot dogs? The children are to solve the problem through previously acquired concepts related to sets. They consider the number property of sets through pairing members of the sets, consider equivalence, use subsets in the analytic procedures, and develop an equation for their observations. It is not sufficient to remember merely that 7 minus 4 equals 3. A similar reference to set concepts is seen in the activities of sets and numbers developed by the Stanford Project. This project emphasizes set ideas and nomenclature in the development of understanding of the arithmetic operations. In the second grade the following transition is expected:

$$N \{a \ b \ c \ d\} - N \{h\} = 3$$
$$4 - 1 = 3$$

Operations upon numbers should be seen as evolving from operations upon sets (with characteristic differences clarified). Unique among the curriculum development groups, Minnemath has explored the strategy of introducing mathematical ideas through simple stories. The following paragraph taken from the experimental first-grade material will illustrate this teaching approach. The written material is accompanied by illustrations that provide some help with difficult reading passages.

> This is the book Miss Green gave to Dick. He used his library card so he could take the book home to read it. Mother and Dick walked home fast. They wanted to read Dick's book. "I will read my book to you, Mother, while you are working," said Dick. He opened the book and this is what he read: Long, long ago people measured things with their feet. But all feet were not the same size. This made trouble. Some feet were longer. Some feet were shorter. Long ago an inch was as wide as a man's thumb. But not all thumbs were the same size, just as all feet were not the same size. This made trouble, too. In 1400, King Edward II of England made a law. It said, "An inch is equal to three grains of barley laid end to end." It was hard to measure with grains of barley. Once a king of England said a yard would always be the distance between his nose and the thumb of his hand when he stretched out his arm. But all arms were not as long as the king's arm. Or maybe they were longer. This made trouble, too. As time went on, more people wanted to buy and sell things. Sometimes the people they wanted to buy or sell from lived far away. They had to decide how to measure things. So they had many meetings. In the United States, the people of George Washington's day gave Congress the right to say what size all weights and measures should be. After a long time, the National Bureau of Standards was set up in our capital, Washington, D.C. Anyone who wants to ask questions about measurement can write to the men who work there. Today people use many ways to measure things. They use the measure that is best for them. But now people agree on the standards of measure. This makes it easier to buy and sell goods. Now people can buy and sell things without quarreling. Aren't you glad?

A Model for Teaching Strategies

Current teaching guides usually include a model for planning lessons on different topics in the elementary mathematics program. An example is given in Chart 6–4 (Marks et al., 1965, p. 59). (See p. 186.) Notice that a sequence of steps is outlined and that purposes, activities, and materials are illustrated for each step. As is typical of such models, this one begins with preparation, moves to exploration and discovery, provides for abstraction and organization, includes the fixing of skills, and concludes with application. This model has applications to other subjects as well as to mathematics.

STEP	PURPOSE	ACTIVITIES	MATERIALS
1. Preparation	To provide readiness: both subject matter—including prerequisite skills, vocabulary, and concepts—and interest	A checkup–formal or informal–on prerequisite skills and vocabulary	Tests, if necessary, teacher-made or commercial. Models, real objects, and other learning aids as necessary
2. Exploration and discovery	To lead the pupil to develop the concept (or operation) as a solution to a problem situation	Presentation of a stimulating problem situation requiring improvisation of the process, concept (or operation) as a means of solution.	Learning aids as needed to provide the setting. Materials as required for manipulation in exploratory activities
3. Abstraction and organization	To develop an understanding of the nature of the operation (or concept) and the interrelationship with other operations	Development of generalizations about the operation (or concept) and its interrelationships to others	Textbooks and semisymbolic manipulative materials
4. Fixing skills	To make manipulation of the operation automatic and to provide overlearning to assure retention	Memorization of facts, organization and memorization of tables, repetitive practice with the operation	Textbooks, practice materials, tests
5. Application	To promote transfer of training by developing ability to recognize the typical situation calling for use of the operation (or concept)	Experience in application to a variety of situations, with emphasis on identifying the appropriate situations	Life and simulated problem situations, models, visual aids, textbooks, bulletin boards

Chart 6–4.   Flow chart of the learning sequence.

GUIDELINES FOR THE TEACHER

Objectives of recently developed elementary mathematics programs are most effectively attained when teachers provide opportunities for children to acquire as much learning as possible through discovery approaches. Although there are times when the teacher must show, demonstrate, tell, and explain, the major part of the child's learning experience should consist of opportunities to explore mathematical situations, make observations, compare, classify, discern patterns, perceive relationships, discover meanings, inductively derive generalizations, and deductively apply these generalizations to new mathematical situations.

In order to develop mathematical thinking skills, pupils should be encouraged to reason through to solutions on their own. Allowing children to explore different ways of arriving at an answer helps them to develop genuine understanding before they are guided to selection of a specific algorithm or technique. Thinking is further developed when children are taught to estimate solutions. Creative aspects of mathematical thinking are enhanced when the classroom atmosphere is conducive to expression of guesses and conjectures, when children are free to explore, experiment, and even make mistakes that may be constructively analyzed.

Mathematical judgment and reasoning may be developed when the child is encouraged to explain his computational procedures and find ways to prove his solutions. He should be encouraged to extend his reasoning skills by forming hypotheses or deductive inferences which he applies in appropriate new situations. Application is a necessary aspect in the complete development of understanding of concepts, principles, and operational techniques. As each concept or process is developed, time should be allotted for practice which does not involve the use of paper and pencil. This technique provides an effective means of practicing and applying mathematical reasoning.

Active participation by the learner promotes more effective learning. Such participation may be achieved through the discovery approaches outlined in the suggestions above. It is further implemented through the consistent use of realia and manipulative materials which offer the child a direct sense encounter with mathematical ideas.

Understanding is most thoroughly developed by means of a variety of experiences involving the learner's active mental participation. After understanding is attained, the child may refine his skills and achieve habituation through practice and drill with varied materials. However, such drill defeats the purposes of learning if it precedes adequate comprehension or if it is applied to concepts which involve analytic procedures rather than routine manipulative skills.

Effective learning is continuous and developmental. Discovery of relationships is developed in order to provide for understanding which may be transferred to new situations. Spiral development of concepts promotes retention of understanding.

Individual differences in rates and modes of learning may be met by suiting instruction to the level of the learner, regardless of his grade level. Individualization involves provision of successful learning experiences at every stage of concept and skill development, concrete experiences and opportunities for varying explorations of problems, and motivation through introduction of problems in settings that are meaningful to the child. Varieties of materials and instructional aids should be utilized in order to clarify meanings and elicit thoughtful responses from the learner. Children should be grouped in accordance with specific instructional purposes and should be regrouped as needs arise for skill development, further understanding, or extension of mathematical interests.

Problem-solving experiences provide opportunities for meaningful applications of learnings in all areas of the elementary mathematics curriculum. Children can develop greater skill in problem solving if they are provided with a model for analyzing problems rather than a piecemeal, nonmathematical technique such as the use of somewhat ambiguous "word clues." An example of such a model may include the following steps:

1. **Read (or listen to) the entire problem.**
2. **Determine the problem: what the reader is asked to find.**
3. **Identify the facts that are given.**
4. **Determine the relationships between these facts.**
5. **Determine the nature of the task to be undertaken and select the appropriate operation for the task.**
6. **Utilize concrete materials or drawings, if needed, to visualize the problem.**
7. **Select the proper algorithm.**
8. **Estimate the answer.**
9. **Compute and solve the problem.**
10. **Compare the solution with the estimated answer, and check the solution.**
11. **Reanalyze the problem if the solution is incorrect.**

EVALUATION OF OUTCOMES OF INSTRUCTION

The definitive nature of mathematics has lent itself over the years to precise objective evaluation of facts. It has been possible to measure the student's facility with mathematical material or the effectiveness of an arithmetic program through either pure computational exercises or "word" problems. The evaluation of learning has been, in its simplest terms, the percentage of problems to which correct responses have been assigned. Though such appraisals were regarded as adequate in the past (when in truth they were not), there is general agreement on their insufficiency today. They fail to give proper recognition to the new dimensions of the modern program, even though they continue to play a role in the total evaluation program.

Increased attention is being given to evaluation schemes which measure the entire field of conceptual outcomes while also treating some aspects of

MEANS OF SECURING INFORMATION FOR EVALUATION

Objectives	Observation	Instrument
Vocabulary	Ability to express ideas and use the technical terms correctly	Vocabulary test
Interest	Immediate: Does the pupil manifest a desire to pursue the topic? General: As defined on check list	Check list
Meanings Principles	Ability to apply principles that he has learned	Test on understanding basic to addition with fractions
Application of the concept of addition to fractional numbers	Verification of the properties for the set of fractional numbers under addition	
Skills In the operations	As demonstrated in classwork, during supervised study, and in written assignments	Computational tests
Verbal problems	Ability to analyze and solve problems during class discussions and in written assignments	Problem tests
Generalizations Identification of addition situations with fractions	Ability to state in class why addition applies to a given situation	Later: Tests on ability to differentiate addition from subtraction
Application of what is learned to life situations	Ability to handle concepts and operations in new situations during class discussions	Later: Test on ability
Illustration and use of the properties for the set of fractional numbers under addition	Ability to explain and use the properties in algorithms	Class discussion and test on generalizations

Chart 6–5. Plan of evaluation.

instruction beyond the cognitive domain. Such evaluation dictates not only the development of a vast array of new and different objective tests but also the creation of appraisal tools which may be neither objective nor tests. As interest continues in the development of evaluation which is properly adapted to the goals of newer programs, there is likely to be an evolution of evaluation procedures and techniques which parallels the evolution of the "modern" elementary school mathematics program.

A comprehensive plan of evaluation includes the use of direct observation and a variety of instruments to assess the attainment of objectives. Shown in Chart 6–5 is a plan of evaluation as conceived by three specialists in mathematics education (Marks, et al., 1965, p. 437).

A broad plan of evaluation involves a variety of individuals in addition to the teacher. Much greater attention is being given the child's self-evaluation, and many new programs have built-in self-evaluation guides and suggestions. Cooperative evaluations involving groups or teams of teachers or supervisory personnel have offered promise. Various new techniques have been tried, with some notable success. In the cognitive domain, manipulative performance tests, nonverbal logicomathematics tasks, discovery tests of the "What's my rule?" variety, and process-oriented diagnostic instruments have attracted attention. In the affective domain such tools as recorded discussions, nondirected interest surveys, recreational time-usage logs, surveys, reports of unassigned reading, and informal attitude probes often reveal much information about the impact of mathematics instruction. In general, diversity of tools and techniques is felt to be superior to the characteristically narrow computational measures. The comprehensive program should be concerned not only with changes in the facts, concepts, and generalizations which have been acquired, but also with the growth in basic performance and problem-solving skills, the sophistication manifested in inquiry models, the changes in attitudes and interests, and the growth in transfer ability.

Using Taxonomies of Objectives

The taxonomies of educational objectives may be used to plan questions and items for use in assessing both cognitive and affective outcomes of instruction (Bloom, 1956; Krathwohl, Bloom, & Masia, 1964). An example of a question and a test item is given in the following outline which includes each level of the cognitive and affective taxonomy.

Cognitive Domain

Knowledge level: **Who can define and give an example of the associative property? Put an X by the one of the following expressions which represents the associative property.**
___$4 + 0 = 4 = 0 + 4$
___$(3 + 2) + 4 = 3 + (2 + 4)$
___$(4 + 2) \times 6 = (4 \times 6) + (2 \times 6)$
___$16 + 9 + 11 = 11 + 16 + 9$

Comprehension level: **Does the commutative property deal with manner of grouping elements, order of elements, or size of elements? Express the commutative property in equation form.**

Application level: **If Gordy has more bottle caps than Sally, and Sally has more bottle caps than Susie, who has more bottle caps, Gordy or Susie?**
Use the transitive property to put the Jones children in proper order with respect to their ages.

Analysis level: If $3 \times (2 \times 5) = 30$
and $(3 \times 2) \times 5 = 30$
then $3 \times (2 \times 5) = ?$

Analyze the line graph and predict the coordinates for its extension.

Synthesis level: How many ways are there to divide common fractions? See if you can find a way that no one else uses.
Devise a plan to show the relationship between the number of even prime numbers and odd prime numbers.

Evaluation level: Is the solution to problem *A* correct? Is it the best one for solving the problem?
Check the steps which were followed in bisecting angle *B* to see if they were the best steps we could use.

Affective Domain

Receiving level: Did everyone contribute some good ideas to our discussion of multiplying fractions? Give two cases where if we had not listened to someone's idea our understanding of multiplying fractions would not be so complete.

Responding level: Which way of dividing whole numbers do you like best? Make an outline of the good features of your choice.

Valuing level: How does arithmetic help people to live better lives? Name a few jobs that cannot be done if we do not know arithmetic.

Organization level: What are the advantages of thinking how new mathematics ideas fit with important ideas we already know?
Some children do not like our new mathematics. Give some reasons for their feeling and suggest ways to help them increase their interest in this subject.

EVALUATION OF THE INSTRUCTIONAL PROGRAM

Evaluation of the instructional program may be made in terms of each of the major topics presented in this chapter. The following questions are illustrative of criteria to use in assessing various dimensions of a modern mathematics program:

Foundation disciplines
Is the program based on a logical integration of selected mathematical topics and the methodology of logic?

Is the program geared to children's developmental stages of logical and quantitative thinking?

Structure

Is the structure of the real number system outlined in a way that shows how various topics are related?

Are concepts, concept clusters, and generalizations clearly identified in relation to each topic?

Are topics organized sequentially to provide for the development of insight into mathematics as a field of knowledge?

Inquiry

Is the logical, postulational approach of mathematicians emphasized?

Are both inductive and deductive approaches included?

Objectives

Are objectives defined in terms of outcomes that are consistent with new emphases in modern mathematics instruction?

Is attention given to both cognitive and affective objectives?

Complete program

Are strands or key topics used to define a balanced program of instruction?

Are mathematical examples chosen which have transfer value and which highlight relationships?

Teaching strategies

Are both inductive and deductive approaches used in a way that promotes individual thinking, creativeness, and logical analysis and synthesis?

Are general models for teaching used flexibly to meet individual differences and to present different mathematical topics?

Are mechanical modes and memorization embedded in meaning and used only to fix skills?

Evaluation

Is there a comprehensive plan of assessment for evaluating all aspects of instruction?

Are the roles of the teacher, consultants, and others defined in so far as evaluation is concerned?

Is self-evaluation by students given systematic attention?

Teacher education

Are provisions made for deepening teachers' understanding of mathematical ideas?

Are consultants available to teachers as questions and problems arise?

Program revision

Is the program updated as new approaches and materials become available?

Is the program revised in ways that will facilitate learning now and in later years as students progress to higher levels?

REFERENCES

Bloom, Benjamin S. (Ed.) *Taxonomy of educational objectives: cognitive domain.* New York: McKay, 1956. A classification of educational objectives into a hierarchy of complexity.

Buros, Oscar K. *The sixth mental measurements yearbook.* Highland Park, N.J.: Gryphon Press, 1965. Reviews of mathematics achievement tests published between 1959 and 1964.

California. Summary of the report of the advisory committee on mathematics to the California state curriculum commission, *Bull. Calif. dep. educ.*, Vol. 33, No. 6 (December, 1963). A report emphasizing the strands which should be woven into a modern school mathematics program.

Courant, R., & Robbins, H. *What is mathematics?* (4th ed.) Fair Lawn, N.J.: Oxford, 1961. A thorough treatment of the discipline of mathematics, with emphasis upon its fundamental components.

Dienes, Z. P. *An experimental study of mathematics learning.* London: Hutchinson, 1963. Deals with a research on the developmental stages through which mathematical learning proceeds from early sense encounters to symbolization and interpretation.

Educational Services Incorporated. *Goals for school mathematics.* Boston: Houghton Mifflin, 1963. A report of the Cambridge Conference on School Mathematics; recommendations for an emerging mathematics program for the schools.

Fehr, Howard F., & Hill, Thomas J. *Contemporary mathematics for elementary teachers.* Boston: Heath, 1966. A textbook on foundations of arithmetic and geometry for teachers of elementary mathematics.

Fehr, Howard F., & Phillips, Jo McKeeby. *The teaching of mathematics in the elementary school.* Reading, Mass: Addison-Wesley, 1967. An up-to-date treatment of the adaptation of the modern mathematics program to the elementary school classroom.

Ford, G. W., & Pugno, L. *The structure of knowledge and the curriculum.* Chicago: Rand McNally, 1964. Pp. 50–70. Discusses the important conceptual centers of mathematics with some illustrations of content and new developments.

Inlow, Gail M. *The emergent in curriculum.* New York: Wiley, 1966. A humanistic theory of curriculum development with emphasis upon placing the disciplines of knowledge in perspective.

King, A. R., Jr., & Brownell, J. A. *The curriculum and the disciplines of knowledge.* New York: Wiley, 1966. Develops a theory of curriculum which focuses upon the disciplines of knowledge and treats inquiry, organization, and purpose.

Kovach, Ladis D. *Introduction to modern elementary mathematics.* San Francisco: Holden-Day, 1966. Topics of sets, real number system, geometry, and number theory, with each topic covered in three sequential chapters increasing in complexity.

Krathwohl, David R., Bloom, Benjamin S., & Masia, Bertram S. *Taxonomy of educational objectives: affective domain.* New York: McKay, 1964. A classification of objectives according to degree of internalization.

Lovell, K. *The growth of basic mathematical and scientific concepts in children.* New York: Philosophical Library, 1961. A psychological work for teachers on children's concept formation, including discussion of the author's replication and analysis of some of Piaget's work with children.

Marks, J. L., Purdy, C. R., & Kinney, L. B. *Teaching elementary school mathematics for understanding.* (2d ed.) New York: McGraw-Hill, 1965. One of the better volumes on instructional method and organization for the elementary school mathematics teacher.

Morrisett, L. N., & Vinsonhaler, J. (Eds.) Mathematical learning. *Monogr. Soc. Res. Child Develpm.*, Vol. 30, No. 1. Chicago: University of Chicago Press, 1965. A summary of a conference devoted to the exploration of mathematical learning from the point of view of the learning theorist and the mathematician.

National Council of Teachers of Mathematics. *The growth of mathematical ideas: grades K-12.* Twenty-fourth Yearbook. Washington, D.C., 1959. A treatment of the basic mathematical understandings, the theoretical bases for mathematical learning and the pedagogical approaches which should characterize the mathematics curriculum.

National Council of Teachers of Mathematics. *Instruction in arithmetic.* Twenty-fifth Yearbook. Washington, D.C., 1960. An overview of the modern arithmetic with special emphasis upon topics of interest to the practicing teacher.

National Council of Teachers of Mathematics. *Topics in mathematics for elementary school teachers.* Twenty-ninth Yearbook. Washington, D.C., 1964. A presentation for elementary school teachers on the content of eight fundamental topics of modern mathematics.

Page, David A. *Maneuvers on lattices.* University of Illinois Arithmetic Project, 1962.

Phenix, Philip H. *Realms of meaning.* New York: McGraw Hill, 1964, Chapter 6 deals with the classification of mathematics as a discipline of symbolics and the analysis of its fundamental components.

Phi Delta Kappa. *Education and the structure of knowledge.* Chicago: Rand McNally, 1964. Pp. 148–187. A treatment of the structure of physical knowledge as a heuristic blueprint; discussion of this point of view.

Piaget, J. *The child's conception of number.* New York: Humanities Press, 1952. The observations of the renowned psychologist-logician on children's patterned development of number knowledge.

Sanders, N. M. *Classroom questions: what kinds?* New York: Harper, 1966. Questions on the various levels of the taxonomy of educational objectives. Deals with social studies but can be used as models for questions in other subject areas.

Scott, L. F. *Trends in elementary school mathematics.* Chicago: Rand McNally, 1966. A perspective on the modern elementary school mathematics curriculum placed on a developmental continuum.

Spencer, P. L., & Brydegaard, M. *Building mathematical competence in the elementary school.* New York: Holt, 1966. A survey of the development of children's mathematical ideas with special attention to inferential reasoning.

Ward M., & Hardgrove, C. E. *Modern elementary mathematics.* Reading, Mass.: Addison-Wesley, 1964. One of the better volumes treating the content of modern elementary mathematics.

Wirtz, Robert W., Botel, Morton, Beberman, Max, & Sawyer, W. W. *Math workshop teacher's guide.* Chicago: Encyclopaedia Britannica, Inc., 1962.

MAJOR ELEMENTARY SCHOOL MATHEMATICS PROJECTS

Computer-based Mathematics Instruction. c/o Prof. Patrick Suppes, Ventura Hall, Stanford University, Stanford, Calif.

Greater Cleveland Mathematics Project. c/o Research Council of Greater Cleveland, Cleveland, Ohio.

The Madison Project of Syracuse University and Webster College. c/o Prof. Robert B. Davis, Webster College, St. Louis, Mo. 63119.

Minnesota Mathematics and Science Teaching Project. c/o Prof. Paul C. Rosenbloom, 2d floor TSCE, University of Minnesota, Minneapolis, Minn. 55455.

School Mathematics Study Group. c/o Prof. E. G. Begle, S.M.S.G., Cedar Hall, Stanford University, Stanford, Calif.

University of Illinois Arithmetic Project. (Now associated with Educational Services Incorporated) Watertown, Mass.

ELEMENTARY SCHOOL SCIENCE PROJECTS WHICH HAVE CONTRIBUTED ELEMENTARY SCHOOL MATHEMATICS MATERIALS

Study of a Quantitative Approach in Elementary School Science. c/o Prof. Clifford E. Swartz, Department of Physics, State University of New York, Stony Brook, N.Y.

University of California Elementary School Science Project. c/o Prof. Lloyd Scott, Department of Education, University of California, Berkeley, Calif.

Chapter Seven

SCIENCE EDUCATION

THE NATURAL SCIENCES are focused on the study of phenomena in the natural world. Nonliving phenomena are studied through such physical sciences as physics and chemistry. Living phenomena are studied through such life sciences as botany, zoology, and physiology. Within the physical sciences are special groupings of disciplines, such as the earth sciences, which include geology and meteorology. Within the life sciences are interdisciplines or specializations that cut across disciplines, such as biochemistry and biology. In these and the many other disciplines in the broad domain of science a central goal is to increase man's understanding of the natural world.

Scholarly study in the natural sciences epitomizes man's objective and empirical search for understanding of the world and the universe. Free and open inquiry, precise definition of terms, formulation of testable hypotheses, objective collection of data, replication of findings, public review of findings, theory building, and a continuing search for better explanations are key features of scientific inquiry. Explanation, understanding, and prediction are central outcomes that may be presented in deductive, probabilistic, functional, or genetic models (Nagel, 1961). Because of the objective and empirical nature of scientific study, the natural sciences are classified in the realm of empirics (Phenix, 1964).

Since the natural sciences have been the fountainhead for the unparalleled technological revolution of the past few decades, they have drawn much interest and attention. There has been concern not only that the natural sciences be given a role in the school curriculum that is commensurate with their contributions to the advance of civilization but also that the approach to scientific study in the schools reflect the nature of scientific study as practiced by the professional scientist. The concern has been especially evident within the past ten years, reflecting a maturing awareness of prevailing conditions and an urgency which appears to stem, in part, from the technological competition between the advanced nations.

FOUNDATION DISCIPLINES

While contemporary instructional materials for elementary school science education reflect the tendency to focus upon unifying characteristics of the sciences, there has been a parallel emphasis upon depth study in particular science areas. The basic disciplines of physics, chemistry, zoology, and botany have received most attention, although some of the specializations that lend themselves to interdisciplinary treatment have served as centers for curriculum formulations. For example, segments of astronomy, meteorology, ecology, physiology, and embryology have been found to be fruitful for scientific study which includes depth, yet may draw more freely from a broad range of scientific knowledge.

Science is strongly dependent upon the discipline of mathematics. The descriptions of the world which are provided by the sciences, particularly the physical sciences, are communicated through mathematics. In one sense, mathematics may be seen as the language of science. It is through physical measurements and mathematical formulations that the observations and descriptions of the world may be universally recognized and accepted. Likewise, it is from such measurements and formulations that generalizations, laws, and theories are synthesized. Without mathematics, science as we know it would not have developed.

The development of science programs for elementary schools involves not only the basic sciences and mathematics, but also the disciplines of psychology and logic. The work of Piaget (Ripple & Rockcastle, 1964) has been reviewed, and the stages of development presented in the preceding chapter on mathematics education have been considered by some science educators. In addition, analyses have been made of sequences of instruction in selected processes of science (AAAS, 1965). From these foundation disciplines have been drawn a variety of conceptual and process structures as shown in the sections that follow.

Concept Clusters

Key concepts from foundation disciplines have long been stressed in science education. Both old and new concepts have been incorporated in materials of instruction in recent years. The following are illustrative of key concepts and related subconcepts in current materials:

> *Simple machines:* **lever, pulley, wheel and axle, inclined plane, wedge**
>
> *Functions of machines:* **multiply force, multiply speed, change direction of force**
>
> *States of matter:* **solid, liquid, gas**
>
> *Energy:* **solar, nuclear, electrical, magnetic, mechanical, light, heat**
>
> *Light:* **sources, behavior, refraction, reflection, waves, particles, paths, speed**
>
> *Reactions:* **chemical, physical, nuclear**
>
> *Chemical change:* **burning, rusting, decay, growth**

Living things: growth, adaptation, life cycles, reproduction, structure, functions, interrelationships of plants and animals

Cell structure: nucleus, cytoplasm, cell membrane

Systems: nervous, muscular, skeletal, respiratory, circulatory, digestive, excretory

Photosynthesis: light energy + water + carbon dioxide → sugar + oxygen

Heredity: genes, chromosomes, DNA

Classification of rocks: metamorphic, sedimentary, igneous

Solar system: sun, planets, related bodies, orbit, satellite, gravitation

Key concepts such as those listed above are embedded in learning experiences, used to guide inquiry, and used to organize instructional materials. They also serve as the basis for making generalizations.

Generalizations

Generalizations from foundation disciplines are used extensively as structural components of the science education curriculum. The following examples are taken from current instructional materials:

Simple machines make work easier and faster by overcoming inertia, gravity, and friction.

When matter changes from one state to another, the total amount of matter remains unchanged.

Energy must be put into a system in order to get energy out of the system.

All life is dependent on energy from the sun.

Light may be refracted or bent as it passes through certain materials at different speeds.

Nuclear reactions produce the radiant energy in the sun and other stars.

Chemical change involves change in the composition of substances.

Chemical and physical changes involving the transformation of energy are going on constantly.

Living things are adapted by structure and function to their environment.

The cell is the fundamental unit of structure of living things.

The systems of the human body are interrelated.

Green plants use energy from sunlight to produce food through the process of photosynthesis.

Living things are the products of their heredity and environment.

The rocks of the earth's crust may be classified into three basic groups according to the way in which they were formed.

Modes of Inquiry

The modern science curriculum emphasizes inductive modes of inquiry. Contrasted to the curriculum of a few years ago, which treated science as dogma, the change is marked and radical. In a large sense, the difference stems from one's view of the nature of science. In oversimplified terms, if science is regarded as an accumulation of facts about our world, then it is defensible to design curricula with the goal of creating the most efficient scheme for teaching these facts. On the other hand, if science is regarded as a process for acquiring knowledge about the world, curricula must be designed to bring the learner into a direct encounter with this process. Of course, in practice the distinction is not so clearly marked. The substance of inductive inquiry must be data; data and concepts are essential ingredients in inquiry. However, they are not the totality of science; processes of inquiry must be included.

In today's elementary school science program, according to Brandwein (1965, p. 29), "Inquiry is a mix of human activity in search of meaning." It thus involves the student, no less than the teacher, in an active process. Teacher recitation and student absorption are seen to be antithetical to the modes of inquiry given support in modern curricula.

Schwab and Brandwein (1962) defined two modes of inquiry which interact in scientific investigation. The first is called "stable enquiry"; this mode assumes the validity of certain principles and treats phenomena related to the principles. The second mode, "fluid enquiry," brings into question the principles themselves. In this mode the inquirer is involved with what is lacking in the principles as bases for explaining observed phenomena. The inquirer employs invention and trial of new conceptions which may serve as principles for explaining a wider range of phenomena. In the elementary school it is expected that most of the inquiry opportunities for children will be of the "stable" variety. In essence, elementary school science education is seen as a prime vehicle for bringing into the total curriculum fertile opportunities for the direct interaction of the child's mind and his world.

Among the many available lists which attempt to characterize scientific inquiry, the one presented by the National Society for the Study of Education has received wide attention (1947). Major items in this list are sensing significant problems, defining problem situations, studying a situation for all facts and clues bearing upon a problem, making the best tentative explanation or hypothesis, selecting the most likely hypothesis, testing the hypothesis, accepting tentatively or rejecting the hypothesis and testing other hypotheses, and drawing conclusions.

Such lists are not held in high regard by many scientists who are apt to be more impressed with brief and simple descriptions of the inquirer's perspective than with science procedures. Outlines of characteristics of the scientific attitude appear to enjoy higher regard among scientists involved in elementary school science curriculum formulation. For example, an attitude characterized by a conviction of universal cause and effect relations, sensitive curiosity, habit of delayed response, habit of weighing evidence,

Chart 7–1. Schema of the scientist's way.

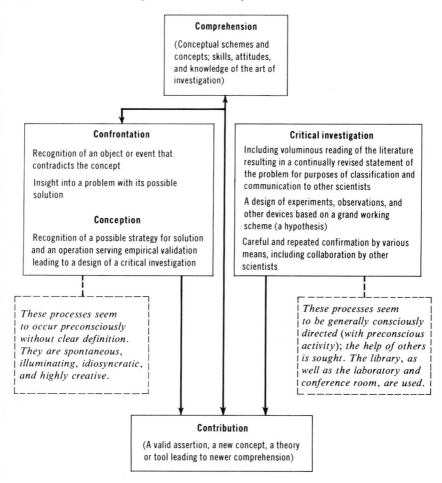

and respect for other viewpoints and evidence describes a scientific approach from the scientist's view.

According to Brandwein (1965), emphasis should be given to the art of scientific investigation. The so-called "steps of scientific study" are a gross oversimplification of the way in which scientists work. The creative, idiosyncratic, and intuitive aspects of inquiry are overlooked and the complexity of the scientist's task is not reflected in statements that outline the steps of scientific inquiry. As an alternative, Brandwein (1965, p. 23) proposes the "schema of the scientist's way" shown in Chart 7–1.

OBJECTIVES OF INSTRUCTION

The reform movement in science education has been characterized by a shift in emphasis rather than by a drastic restatement of the purposes of science education. In the past, emphasis was placed on technological applications of science and on the content of science. Currently, emphasis is given to the study of science qua science, and content and process are intertwined. A central goal is to develop scientific literacy based on the direct study of the natural world. Systematic descriptions and explanations of natural phenomena are desired outcomes. If the concepts and generalizations developed in the instructional program are related to technological development, then their social significance well may be considered. However, it is argued that instruction should not be centered on social significance as a point of departure. Rather, the focus should be on science and "sciencing" so that students will move progressively toward the attainment of such objectives as the following:

> **Scientific literacy based on a functional understanding of scientific concepts and methods of inquiry**
>
> **Increased competence in examining, analyzing, and understanding the world and a desire to continue to develop this competence**
>
> **Understandings and appreciations of both the products and processes of science**
>
> **Enhanced competence in evaluating and applying knowledge obtained through scientific modes of inquiry**
>
> **Insight into science as a creative enterprise in which continual discovery of new knowledge is emphasized**
>
> **Such attitudes and appreciations as thoughtful skepticism, suspended judgment, intellectual honesty and curiosity, respect for empirical inquiry, and appreciation of the contributions of scientists to our cultural heritage**
>
> **Ability to apply scientific modes of inquiry to other intellectual pursuits where their use is appropriate**

> Improved skill in making judgments and in discriminating among values through the use of processes of rational inquiry
>
> Ability to observe, understand, and deal with the natural environment
>
> Insight into the interrelationships of science and other areas of human experience
>
> Interests in science which may carry over into leisure-time activities

Broad objectives such as those listed above need to be stated behaviorally if they are to be used in planning and evaluating instruction. This may be done by specifying the operations or behaviors related to an objective as shown in the following examples:

> *Observing.* The student who is developing competence in observing:
>
> Identifies objects and changes in objects
>
> Distinguishes one type of object from another
>
> States how objects are alike and similar
>
> Identifies changes in temperature, color, and shape when a liquid changes to a solid
>
> Uses comparative terms to state changes in the weather
>
> Identifies objects in a group which can be used for a particular purpose
>
> *Inferring.* The student who is developing competence in predicting:
>
> Distinguishes an inference from an observation
>
> Gathers adequate information on which to base inference
>
> States reasons for making an inference
>
> Recognizes that more than one inference may be made from some observations
>
> Uses an inference to explain an event
>
> Shows or tells how an inference may be changed by further observation
>
> Uses further observation to test an inference

Additional examples of objectives stated in terms of behaviors or operations may be found in references at the end of the chapter (AAAS, 1965; Bloom, 1956; Krathwohl, Bloom, & Masia, 1964).

A COMPLETE PROGRAM

A complete program of science education designed to achieve the foregoing objectives may be viewed in a variety of ways. First, it may be viewed in terms of content and processes drawn from such foundation disciplines as physics, chemistry, astronomy, biology, physiology, and geology. Or it may be viewed in terms of interrelated areas of science, such as living things, matter and energy, the earth, and the universe. A third way to view a complete program is in terms of themes or strands that are emphasized throughout the program—variety and pattern, continuity and change, and interaction and interdependence. Completeness also may be viewed in terms of processes, such as classification, observation, measurement, inference, and prediction. Still another way is in terms of broad conceptual schemes drawn from the natural sciences; for example, energy may be transformed but it cannot be created or destroyed.

There is merit to all the foregoing views. And all of them may be found as bases for designing the overall instructional program. In some programs a combination, such as areas of science and basic themes, may be used. In others, emphasis may be given to processes of science. Specific examples are given in the following section.

STRUCTURE OF THE CURRICULUM

Structures noted in new teaching guides and in current projects range from conceptual schemes stated on a high level of generality to concept clusters and processes of science stated in specific and detailed terms. The overall structure of science education programs is usually stated in terms of generalizations that include key concepts believed to be of fundamental importance. The structure of units and courses is usually defined in terms of more specific or limited principles and concepts. The following examples are illustrative.

Structure in Terms of Conceptual Schemes and Process

One group has proposed a list of conceptual schemes (generalizations) and basic processes of science to serve as guides for overall planning (National Science Teachers Association, 1964). Both the products of science (concepts and principles) and processes of science (methods of inquiry) are included. Notice in the following that key concepts from the physical sciences are highlighted.

CONCEPTUAL SCHEMES

All matter is composed of units called fundamental particles; under certain conditions these particles can be transformed into energy and vice versa.

Matter exists in the form of units which can be classified into
hierarchies of organizational levels.

The behavior of matter in the universe can be described on a
statistical basis.

Units of matter interact. The bases of all ordinary interactions
are electromagnetic, gravitational, and nuclear forces.

All interacting units of matter tend toward equilibrium states
in which the energy content (enthalpy) is a minimum and
the energy distribution (entropy) is most random. While
the process of attaining equilibrium is going on, energy
transformations or matter transformations or matter-energy
transformations occur. Nevertheless, the sum of energy and
matter in the universe remains constant. One of the forms of
energy is the motion of units of matter. Such motion is
responsible for heat and temperature and for the states of
matter: solid, liquid, and gaseous.

All matter exists in time and space and, since interactions occur
among its units, matter is subject in some degree to changes
with time. Such changes may occur at various rates and in
various patterns.

MAJOR ITEMS IN THE PROCESS OF SCIENCE

Science proceeds on the assumption, based on centuries of experience, that the universe is not capricious.

Scientific knowledge is based on observations of samples of
matter that are accessible to public investigation in contrast
to purely private inspection.

Science proceeds in a piecemeal manner, even though it also
aims at achieving a systematic and comprehensive understanding of various sectors or aspects of nature.

Science is not, and will probably never be, a finished enterprise,
and there remains very much more to be discovered about how
things in the universe behave and how they are interrelated.

Measurement is an important feature of most branches of
modern science because the formulation and the establish-
ment of laws are facilitated through the development of
quantitative distinctions.

Each of the above is elaborated to indicate specific concepts that should
be developed in both physical and life science units of study. For example,
the generalization "Matter exists in the form of units which can be classified into hierarchies of organizational levels" is discussed in terms of the
following concept clusters:

Hierarchies of organization: particles, atoms, molecules and ions,
aggregates of molecules and ions (sand, mountains, oceans),

heavenly bodies, solar systems, galaxies, galactic aggregates, universe

Hierarchies in the biological world: particles, atoms, molecules and ions, macromolecules (nucleic acids, proteins), organelles (chromosomes), cells, tissues, organs, organ systems, organisms, populations

Populations: species, genera, families, orders, classes, phyla, kingdoms; living in communities, biomes, biospheres

The above examples are illustrative of how key concepts from physical sciences are being utilized in the biological sciences. Thus the unity of science is stressed not only at the level of broad generalizations but also in the development and relating of specific concepts.

Structure in Terms of Themes and Generalizations

One course of study that attempts to show the relationships between major themes and generalizations has outlined a structure of science (Santa Clara County, 1964), reproduced on pages 208–209. The teaching guide contains lower-order generalizations related to each of the major themes and higher-order generalizations. The lower-order generalizations are stated on three levels of instruction as shown in the following examples which are related to the second theme—energy:

Primary: **Energy is the ability to do work.**

Intermediate: **Energy may be classified as potential or stored energy and as kinetic or energy of motion.**

Upper: **Work is force exerted over a distance.**

Structure in Terms of Strands and Areas of Content

A statewide committee has proposed four basic strands as broad themes that run through the science education program (California, 1964). It is suggested that content be selected from four major areas of science and used to design units of study in which concepts and generalizations related to the four strands are brought to higher levels of development from year to year. The strands and areas of content may be illustrated by clustering a sampling of concepts related to each of them as follows:

STRANDS OF SCIENCE

Variety and pattern: likenesses and differences occurring among living and nonliving things; variety of functions, sizes, shapes,

A STRUCTURE OF SCIENCE

Major themes	*and*	*Major generalizations*

Matter

1. All objects are made of matter and although this matter can be altered or transformed, sometimes into energy, it cannot be created or destroyed.

  1.1. Matter is any substance that occupies space and has weight.
  1.2. Matter has several physical states—(solid, liquid, or gas) determined by the degree of molecular activity.
  1.3. Matter is considered over a wide spectrum of sizes from sub-atomic particles to the immensely large phenomena such as galaxies and universes.
  1.4. Matter may be living or non-living.

Energy

2. All activity living or non-living involves energy. This energy can change form, but it cannot be created or be destroyed.

  2.1. Energy is the ability for doing work. (Anything that "happens" requires energy.)
  2.2. Energy is derived primarily from four sources: gravity, electricity, magnetism, and nuclear activity.
  2.3. Some convenient designations for available energy are: heat, sound, light, electrical, chemical, atomic, and muscular energy.
  2.4. Energy can be changed from one form to another.

and structures in objects; similarity in patterns to permit classification; common metabolic functions in living things; differences between plants and animals

Continuity and change: continual change in living and nonliving things; exchange of matter and transfer of energy; cyclic and noncyclic change; patterns of continuity and constancy; individuality of living organisms

Interaction and interdependence: occurrence among living and nonliving things; interactions due to relationships in time, position, and energy; plants' use of radiant energy to convert materials from air, soil, and water into compounds for growth functions

Major themes	*and*	*Major generalizations*

Interaction

3. There is a continuous interaction of energy and matter (or of materials), both living and non-living.

- 3.1. Energy is involved in all interaction of non-living matter.
- 3.2. Gravity affects the position and movement of molecular, terrestrial and celestial objects.
- 3.3. Living organisms are dependent directly or indirectly on solar (nuclear) energy.
- 3.4. Living organisms require certain environmental conditions to exist, and these environmental factors usually limit the abundance and distribution of the organism.

Change

4. Most materials of the universe and of the organisms found on the earth experience aging, changing or evolving processes.

- 4.1. The surface of the earth is continually changing.
- 4.2. Prehistoric organisms and earth strata give evidence of an evolutionary change.
- 4.3. There is evidence of continuity and change in the development of living organisms.
- 4.4. Our celestial universe seems to be constantly changing.
- 4.5. A state of balance or equilibrium occurs between any two opposing forces or influences.

Evolutionary development: changes over long periods of time in galaxies, planetary systems, and development of life; interaction with the environment; continuity through heredity; evolution of plants and animals

AREAS OF CONTENT

Living things: plants and animals; relationships among living things; growth and change; classification by function and structure; cells and chemicals

The earth: rock, soil, water, air; movement in space; geological changes; interaction of air, water, and other materials; energy from the sun

> *The universe*: vastness in time and space; objects in outer
> space; cycles of celestial phenomena; relationships among
> objects in outer space; continuing evolutionary development
>
> *Matter and energy*: matter as occupying space and having
> weight; energy as ability to do work or change the composi-
> tion of matter; sun as source of energy; materials made of
> natural elements; energy involved in change

Generalizations suggested for primary, intermediate, and upper grade
levels for each area of content give specific direction to program planning.
For example:

> *Primary*: Animals change with the seasons.
>
> *Intermediate*: Animals vary in the way they adapt to seasonal
> change.
>
> *Upper*: Animals control their environment, adjust to it, move,
> or perish.

Structure in Terms of Processes

In a new program called *Science: A Process Approach* (AAAS, 1965),
processes of investigation have been identified and defined in detail. Each
process is believed to be a basic intellectual activity of scientists that can
be used in studying content from different scientific disciplines. The processes are used as guidelines for constructing sequences of instruction that
begin with simple operations and move to increasingly more complex ones.
Terminal behavior is specified for each process, and the sequence of tasks
that should be completed to develop the terminal behavior is outlined in detail by means of task analysis (Gagné, 1965).

The proponents of the process approach point out that the content approach usually leads to an overemphasis on information, requires too
much time and effort, and may fail to develop relationships among concepts.
They argue that, instead of being structured around such concepts as force
and energy, the program should be built around processes such as observation and measurement, which can be applied to force, energy, and a host
of other concepts. They also reject the creativity approach because creativity is not believed to be a generalizable and unitary trait that can be
trained as such. Rather, the advocates of the process approach argue that
students become creative in specific ways. Thus they emphasize creativity
in using the basic processes of science. They believe that the process
approach is a good middle ground between the content and creativity approaches, drawing content from the disciplines to use as processes are de-

veloped and nurturing the creative use of each process in ongoing units of study.

Two sets of processes have been outlined. The first includes eight processes that are introduced in the early grades and continued in later grades. The second set includes six integrated processes that are introduced in the middle grades and continued in later grades. Each process is briefly summarized and illustrated in the following sections.

Processes Introduced in Early Grades

Classification. The desired terminal behavior is competence in making multistage classifications which others can use to identify members of a collection. Experiences are suggested for classifying objects according to such properties as smoothness, texture, color, and special characteristics. Single-stage classifications are followed by two-stage and multistage classifications, as shown in the following illustrative sequence: Name objects in a collection of shells or leaves; name several properties, i.e., color, texture, shape; make and explain a single-stage classification; make a two-stage (or more) classification; use a color code to classify the objects; make a multistage classification.

Inference. The desired terminal behaviors include competence in drawing more than one inference from a set of data, demonstrating that inferences can be tested by further observation, and demonstrating that an inference can be tested by applying known tests of the properties of objects under study. Special attention is given to distinguishing between observations and inferences and between the observer and what is observed. The following sequence is illustrative: Use the concept "evaporation" to explain how water is lost by plants; demonstrate a way to measure the water used by a plant; infer and demonstrate that water drawn through plants is transferred to the atmosphere; show that an inference may be tested by additional observations.

Communication. The desired terminal behavior is competence in describing an experiment so that an individual who has not seen it can carry it out. Experiences in identifying and naming objects are followed by graphing and describing measured changes as shown in the following example: Identify and name events that can be quantified, such as five bounces of a ball; make a column in a bar graph to represent the frequency of an event; distinguish events shown in a graph; make a bar graph; describe measured changes in speed, temperature, and other properties; make a prediction on the basis of recorded measures; make a graph to show the prediction; describe an experiment so that others might do it.

Measurement. Desired terminal behaviors include competence in making representations of the direction of forces, in showing ways to measure the magnitude and direction of variation in an illusion, and in explaining that differences exist in perceptions of the dimensions (length, weight, area, volume, rate of evaporation, rate of change) of the physical world. The following sequence is illustrative: Distinguish objects by using such terms as heavier and lighter; identify relative weight by lifting; use a balance to distinguish heavier from lighter objects; show differences in weight by means of a spring; use standard units of weight; explain effects of gravitation and inertia; measure the weight of various objects; describe differences in weight; identify, state, and demonstrate differences in perception of weight.

Numbers.   The desired terminal behavior is competence in naming rational numbers "greater than one as a product of ten and a rational number between one and ten." The intention is to develop those number concepts needed to handle the other processes. The following sequence is illustrative: Identify sets and their members; name sets with most and fewest members; identify and name the ordinal relationship between two or more counting numbers; label the position of a number on a number line; show the position of positive and negative integers on a number line; find the sum of two numbers on a number line; use sentences to give the sum of two natural numbers; show how to find the product of two natural numbers; name natural numbers in exponential form using base ten.

Observation.   The desired terminal behavior is competence in "describing a series of observations from one individual to another." Attention is given to both oral and written descriptions of such items as length, area, volume, and temperature. The hierarchy begins with identifying and naming activities and moves to the describing of relationships between variables as shown in the following example: Identify and name colors, textures, relative sizes, and other properties of objects; distinguish differences in temperature; read temperature on a thermometer; identify and name factors in weather, such as temperature and precipitation; identify possible causes of change, such as heat, wind, and air pressure; show the effect of causes of change on an object such as a balloon; distinguish between adequate and inadequate descriptions of observations; describe selected items so that others can identify it; identify and name the components of a system; identify and name the main parts of a plant; describe plant growth over a period of time; describe the relationships between two variables.

Space/Time.   The desired terminal behaviors include competence in ordering objects according to position or rate of change and in stating the rate of change or the position of an object. Concepts of shapes, space, time intervals, and distance are given attention as shown in the following example: Identify and name cones, cylinders, triangles, squares, and other two- and three-dimensional shapes; identify and name right angles; distinguish size of angles; identify and name angular and compass directions of change in position; show how distance and other factors are related to the observer's position; distinguish between speed and time of arrival of an object; state speed of objects; use a rule to find speed of an object; order objects in terms of speed.

Prediction. The desired terminal behavior is competence in conducting experiments to test predictions of relationships between two measurable quantities. Various tasks are included, such as plotting data, making and interpreting graphs, and observing from different vantage points. The following example is illustrative of a sequence that involves graphs: Analyze a graph to determine the pattern of relationships (increasing, decreasing, stable); use a graph to predict water loss from plants; make predictions from a series of observations; recognize the value of making predictions from several observations; demonstrate the truth or falsity of predictions by means of graphs; conduct an experiment to test predictions.

Integrated Processes Introduced in Grades 4 through 6

Six integrated processes that build upon those introduced in the early grades are used to design learning experiences in the middle grades. The six processes may be briefly illustrated as follows:

Formulating hypotheses: stating a hypothesis regarding causes of a phenomenon or the relationship between two variables

Making operational definitions: defining terms so that another person can identify specified agents in terms of operations (or behaviors)

Controlling and manipulating variables: arranging conditions to observe by deliberately controlling and manipulating objects in an experiment

Experimenting: planning, conducting, and communicating experiments in which the problem is clarified, hypotheses are stated, observations are made, and conclusions are drawn

Model formulation: building simple models to account for phenomena in order to give students a feeling for the scientific approach

Interpreting data: getting the most out of data without overgeneralizing, drawing conclusions supportable by the data, and considering alternative explanations

Each of the above processes is developed in the context of exercises which utilize content from various domains of science. The content is selected from four broad areas: the universe, the structure and properties of matter, the conservation and transformation of energy, and the interaction between living things and the environment. An example of an exercise designed to develop processes is presented later in the section on "Teaching Strategies."

Structure in Units of Study

Many good examples of the structuring of concepts may be found in units of instruction. In fact, it is in actual unit plans that structure becomes most meaningful in the sense of showing how ideas are related. Notice in the following examples that some of the components of structure presented earlier may be identified.

What Am I? A Unit on Human Physiology

Basic concepts from human physiology are included in a four-part sequence for school children (Elementary School Science Project, University of California) designed to provide opportunities for students to discover answers to the question, "What Am I?" The underlying structure consists of four major concepts related to qualities of life or what it means to be alive: reproduction, growth, response to the environment, and metabolism. The plan is to provide a sequence of studies that begins with "How I Began" and "How I Move" in the early grades, presents "How I Know" in third or fourth grade, and concludes with "How I Keep Alive" in grade 5 or 6.

Each of the units is structured in terms of key concepts around which are clustered related concepts. The following examples have been prepared to show the conceptual structure of the unit "How I Move," which is divided into two parts:

> *Nature and function of muscles*: muscle contraction; types of muscle tissue; other body tissues; how muscles receive food and give off waste products; voluntary and involuntary muscle action; function of the nervous system in muscle action

> *Nature and function of the skeletal system*: the skeleton as a framework; function of the skeleton in body movement, in determining shape of the body and in protecting vital organs; need for calcium compounds

Within each of the above one may find specific concept clusters that are used to plan learning experiences. The following examples show concepts that are linked together in specific teaching plans:

> *Muscles and movement*: contraction, pairs of muscles and more complex groups of muscles, tone; facial expressions, movement of food, control of body openings, movement of blood
>
> *Alimentary system*: mouth, esophagus, gall bladder, stomach, large intestine, small intestine, anus
>
> *Muscle and other tissues*: skeletal or striated, visceral or smooth, cardiac; tendons—connect muscle to bone; ligaments—connect bone to bone
>
> *The skeleton and body movement*: bending places called joints; gliding joint in ankle and wrist; ball-and-socket joint in hip and shoulder; hinge joints in elbows, fingers, knees, and lower jaw; gliding or disk joint between movable vertebrae
>
> *The skeleton and protection of vital organs*: brain—skull; heart and lungs—rib cage, breastbone, spinal column; liver—rib cage; kidneys—some protection by lower ribs and spinal column

Units on Objects, Systems, Subsystems, and Interaction

The units on objects, systems, subsystems, and interaction are part of the program under development in the Science Curriculum Improvement Study (Karplus & Thier, 1967). The central purpose of the project is to develop scientific literacy. Special attention is given to the provision of direct learning experiences in which students investigate the interaction of objects in systems and subsystems. The units are designed to provide new and unusual experiences and to develop or reinforce concepts children can use to interpret the experiences. A guiding principle is to provide concrete instances or operations in which scientific concepts are invented and used as a basis for assimilating new experiences. In each unit, attention is given to concepts believed to be of importance throughout the broad field of science. The following clusters have been abstracted to illustrate concepts that make up the structure of the units:

> *Material objects*: material, object, property, serial ordering; shape, size, color, texture; classifying objects; living and nonliving objects; plants and animals
>
> *Systems*: a grouping of objects treated as a unit; defining, selecting, inventing, recording, and representing systems

> *Subsystems*: an entity that is part of a larger system; mixtures, liquids, solids, solutions; melting, evaporation, condensation
>
> *Interaction*: pattern of behavior, cause-effect relations; identification of objects in a system, experimentation, observation of changes, evidence of interaction; interaction at a distance; interaction in chemical, thermal, magnetic, and electrical systems

Units in the ESS Project

The Elementary Science Study Project has been set up to explore various approaches to the teaching of science in elementary schools (ESI, 1965). A sequential program is not planned. Rather, units dealing with a variety of topics are being prepared to provide opportunities for students to "participate in honest science in a meaningful way." The major aim of the project is to guide students to examine, analyze, and understand the world about them in a way that promotes their desire to do so. Experimentation is stressed, and students are encouraged to express findings in their own words. Basic threads or processes of science are defined to include inquiry, evidence, instrumentation, measurement, classification, and deduction. The following have been abstracted from selected units to illustrate concepts that are included.

> *Growing seeds*: what a seed is; inside a seed; planting; sprouting; pods; observing and graphing growth
>
> *Kitchen physics*: some properties of liquids; the beading effect; heaping and drops; measuring "heaviness" and "grabbiness"; making a tensiometer; the skinlike effect; absorption and evaporation; rise of liquids
>
> *Gases and airs*: air as a real substance; expansion and contraction; burning; interaction of wet steel wool and air; the active part of air; controls in experimentation; temperature and pressure control
>
> *Small things*: using a microscope; measuring the size of specimens; cellular structure; animal and plant cells; epithelial cells; paramecia; protozoa; amoebas; euglena; crystals; yeast cells

Units on Astronomy

Materials on astronomy for students in grades 5 through 8 have been prepared by the project staff at the University of Illinois (Elementary School Science Project, 1965). Astronomy is a good choice because it is interdisciplinary, interesting to children, and included in most programs of instruction. The materials are presented in six illustrated booklets which are structured around such fundamental principles and concepts as using angles and baselines to measure distance, the parallax effect, intensity of light in relation to distance, seasonal constellations, the solar system, Kepler's and Newton's laws, gravitation, models of light, the light spectrum, measuring the speed of light, and the Doppler effect. An analysis of the materials reveals that many concept clusters from mathematics, geophysics, and physics have been included. The following examples are abstracted from the first four booklets:

1. CHARTING THE UNIVERSE

Measuring distance: linear measures; use of degrees, angles, and baseline to determine distance; astronomical unit (sun-earth distance); diameter of the earth's orbit as a baseline; parallax effect; brightness of light in relation to distance; light-year

The universe: the solar system; galaxies; the Milky Way

2. THE UNIVERSE IN MOTION

Measuring the sun's position: time, bearing, length, angle

Mapping the sky: North Polar constellation; autumn, winter, spring, and summer constellations; South Polar constellations

The solar system: Ptolemy's model; Copernicus' model; Kepler's laws of planetary motion; orbits; speeds of planets

3. GRAVITATION

Forces and motion: friction, matter, inertia, mass; curved motion; backward force, forward force, net force; acceleration and mass; gravity and acceleration; velocity; law of gravitation; Newton's laws of motion

Planets: gravitation; planetary masses; orbital periods; discovery of outermost planets

Stars and galaxies: gravitation; star masses; center of mass; luminosity; the Milky Way; galaxies; clusters of galaxies

4. THE MESSAGE OF STARLIGHT

Studying stars and light: telescopes—refractor (system of lenses), reflector (system of mirrors); spectroscope—spectrum (band of color)

Models of light: particle model—stream of fast-moving particles; wave model—wave length, trough, crest; diffraction; inter-ference

Electromagnetic spectrum: Gamma rays, x-ray, ultra-violet, visible light, infra-red, radio waves

T A B L E 7 – 1 . Emphasis on Science Topics in Grades K–6
(Los Angeles City Schools, 1964)

Areas of science and related topics	Grades						
	K	1	2	3	4	5	6
Living things:							
Relationships among living things	x	x	x				
Plant life	x	x	x				
Animal life	x	x	x				
Animal and plant diversity				x		x	x
Growth and development				x	x	x	x
Structures and functions				x	x	x	x
Interrelationships of plants and animals				x	x	x	x
Matter and energy:							
Nature of matter and energy	x	x	x	x	x	x	x
Mechanical energy	x	x	x		x	x	
Magnetic energy	x	x					
Electrical and magnetic energy			x	x	x	x	x
Sound energy	x	x	x	x	x		x
Light and heat energy		x	x	x		x	
Physical and chemical change			x	x		x	x
Solar energy							x
Nuclear energy							x
The earth:							
Structure and changes	x	x		x		x	
Atmosphere and weather	x	x	x		x	x	x
Seasons and climate		x	x		x	x	x
Oceanography				x		x	x
The universe:							
Earth-moon-sun relationships	x	x	x	x	x	x	x
Interstellar space			x			x	x
Solar system					x		x

SEQUENCE OF INSTRUCTION

The diversity in sequences of instruction in science programs is convincing evidence that no single pattern has general acceptability. Most programs are organized in terms of a topical sequence of one kind or another. Departures from the traditional topical sequence may be noted in current projects as shown below. When limited science topics do not serve as a basis for sequencing the program, the processes of science or pervasive scientific ideas appear as popular choices. Regardless of the basis chosen it may be noted that, in general, more abstract or complex study areas are reserved for the higher grades. However, distinctions as to placement in the program are often made with regard to depth of study rather than to acceptance or rejection of a particular study topic. That is, almost any topic may be studied to some depth at any grade level. Deeper penetration and higher-order abstractions are not expected or introduced until the pupil's maturity and experiential background are appropriate.

A Topical Sequence

In most areas of study one may find the sequence of instruction outlined in terms of areas of science and selected topics, an approach that has been used for many years. An example is given in Table 7–1 (Los Angeles, 1964). Notice the emphasis given to certain topics at nearly all levels of instruction, e.g., nature of matter and energy, atmosphere and weather, and earth-sun-moon relationship. Some topics, such as plant and animal life, are stressed in early grades, whereas others, such as solar and nuclear energy, are placed late in the program.

Hierarchies of Processes

Sequences have been outlined for each of the processes of science included in the AAAS project (1965). Each sequence begins with first-level behaviors at the bottom and moves to terminal behavior as shown in the example of classifying presented in Chart 7–2. (See p. 220.) An advantage of arranging such hierarchies is that a student's vertical position can be determined, and instruction can be planned to provide for ongoing growth to higher levels (Gagné, 1965). The attainment of behaviors on each higher level depends on development of the behaviors listed at the preceding level. The teacher should keep two key questions in mind as instruction is planned: Has the student attained the behavior specified at a given level? What experiences should be provided to move to the next level? The teaching guides are arranged to provide learning exercises in a sequence that will enable the

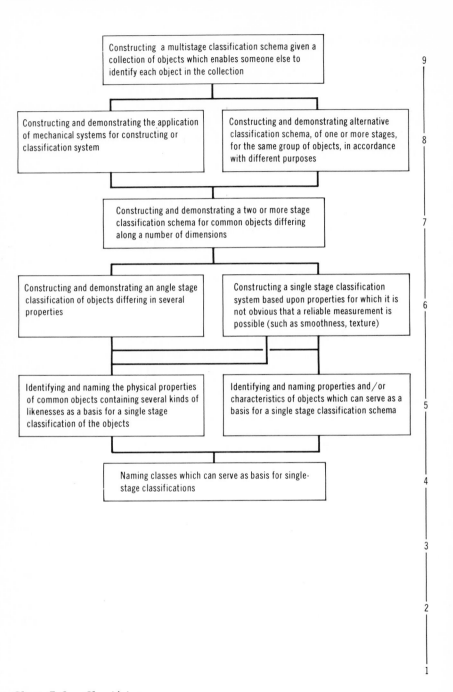

Chart 7–2.   Classifying.

child to move to increasingly higher levels. Also provided are exercises that extend learning horizontally to encompass all the behaviors specified at each level.

Sequence may also be viewed in terms of the relative emphasis given to processes of science in kindergarten through grade 6 (AAAS, 1965). Table 7–2 shows the number of exercises related to each process and is arranged to show grade-level emphasis. Notice that six of the processes are introduced in kindergarten, two in grade 2, and the remainder in grade 4. Notice also the early emphasis on observing and the relatively small amount of attention given to formulating models and to experimenting late in the program.

Pervasive Scientific Ideas

The scope and sequence of the program being developed by the staff of the Science Curriculum Improvement Study are patterned in terms of pervasive ideas as shown in Chart 7–3 (Karplus & Thier, 1967). (See p. 222.) The two implicit main strands in the sequence are the physical sciences and the life sciences. Lines connecting the unit titles show interrelationships. The unit on variation and measurement at level 1 is designed to develop concepts that will be used and extended throughout the program; similarly the study of phenomena interaction, systems, and classification is expected to

TABLE 7–2. Number of Exercises on Processes in Grades K–6 (AAAS, 1965)

Processes	K	1	2	3	4	5	6	Total
Observing	10	5	3	4				22
Space/Time relations	6	6	3	3		1		19
Classifying	3	3	2	3	2			13
Using numbers	2	3	4	3	3	2		17
Communicating	1	4	3	4	1			13
Measuring	2	5	6	2	3			18
Inferring			3	4	2			9
Predicting			2	3	1	1		7
Defining operationally					2	3	4	9
Controlling variables					7	5	3	15
Interpreting data					3	11	5	19
Formulating hypotheses					1	3	3	7
Formulating models					1	1	6	8
Experimenting					1	1	6	8

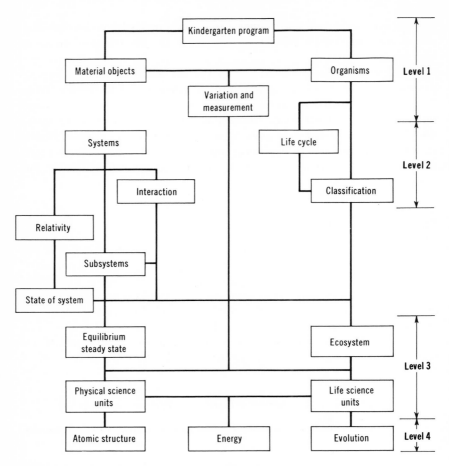

Chart 7–3.   Scope and sequence of the SCIS curriculum.

be applied broadly to the study of other topics. Another important feature of the program is an adaptation of the stages of cognitive development. The *levels* at the right correspond roughly to Piaget's stages of intellectual development: 1—transition from preoperational to concrete thought; 2—concrete operations; 3—transition to formal operations; and 4—formal operations.

TEACHING STRATEGIES

Examples of teaching strategies that are directly linked to modes of inquiry may be found in new science instructional materials. Discovery through firsthand experience is universally emphasized and expository approaches are universally condemned. Intensive efforts have been put forth to devise strategies that are fully consistent with the spirit and the methods of science as practiced by scientists.

The primary role of the teacher is to arrange conditions so that children themselves can engage in inquiry. The teacher takes a nonexpository stance, raising questions, arranging materials, and making suggestions that promote inquiry on the part of children. Although no set patterns of problem solving or scientific inquiry are strictly followed, definite guidelines are provided, as shown in the following examples drawn from various instructional materials.

Exploration, Invention, Discovery

The teaching strategy employed in units from the Science Curriculum Improvement Study (Karplus & Thier, 1967) may be summarized in three steps as (1) preliminary exploration to introduce a new experience, (2) invention of concepts to interpret the experience, and (3) discovery or application of the concepts in new situations. Before a new concept is introduced children are provided opportunities to explore familiar objects in a way that creates a problem they cannot handle adequately. This is followed by the teacher's introduction of a concept that may be used to interpret the experience. The concept is introduced through concrete instances or operations as presented in a demonstration, reading material, or a film. The verbal label of the concept is given so that children may use it to communicate with others. The discovery phase follows as children use the concept to observe, analyze, and interpret new experiences. The key principle is that discoveries in the realm of science can be made only if the concept is clearly in mind.

The three phases of exploration, invention, and discovery may be illustrated by the following examples drawn from the unit on systems:

> *Exploration:* **In the first lessons in the unit children select objects, such as a battery, wire, paper clips, string, and scissors and paper, and use them in an experiment. Each child records the objects that were selected and used. Children make arrangements of parquetry blocks and record the blocks in the arrangements.**
>
> *Invention:* **In the next set of lessons the teacher uses blocks to demonstrate a system and the word "system" is used to describe it. Other systems are demonstrated and the term "system" is used to describe them and is written on the chalkboard. Children are asked to identify objects in each system.**

> *Discovery:* In the remaining lessons children use the systems concept to observe and analyze other systems. Objects are arranged and used in a system; records are made of each system; and objects in pictured systems are identified and discussed. Systems in the classroom, such as bookshelves, scissors and paper, and the clock, are discovered and discussed. Systems are drawn and records are made of objects in them. Systems are isolated from their environment and discussed. The concept is extended by identifying and discussing systems found out of school, such as cars, toys, and sports equipment.

A Strategy for Teaching Processes of Science

Complete and detailed lesson plans are presented in the teacher's guides of *Science: A Process Approach* (AAAS, 1965). Each lesson plan contains sections in which objectives, rationale, vocabulary, and materials are outlined to facilitate preparation by the teacher. Next is presented the recommended teaching strategy under the following headings: originating the problem, instructional procedures, generalizing experience (as appropriate), and appraisal. The following summary of a lesson plan entitled "Observing Animals" is illustrative:

> *Objectives:* To distinguish one animal from another by using one's senses; to state similarities and differences; to make a grouping of animals.
>
> *Rationale:* This exercise provides opportunities to observe and group animals. The importance of careful observation is stressed. Grouping is related to the development of classification skills.
>
> *Vocabulary:* Names of animals used.
>
> *Materials:* Three groups of animals, such as cat, rabbit, hamster; turtle, goldfish; parakeet, duckling.
>
> *Originating the problem:* Have three animals in front of the children and ask: Which one do you know most about? What do you know about this one? How did you find out about it?
>
> *Instructional procedure:* Hold an animal so that children can observe its teeth, feet, and ears. Have them feel and smell it. Do the same with the other two. Ask: Which two are most alike? How are they different? Use the same procedure on following days with three different animals.

Generalizing experience: Show pictures of common animals and have children group them. Ask for reasons for placing them in a particular group.

Appraisal: Ask children to describe an animal they have not yet studied (such as a snail). Their descriptions should contain information obtained from two or more senses.

A Strategy for Experimentation

Opportunities for students to carry out experiments are provided in connection with a variety of topics and problems in new science education programs. The following example drawn from the Elementary School Science Project (ESI, 1965) shows how exploration of equipment, demonstration of use of equipment by the teacher, experimentation and tabulation of data by students, discussion of findings conducted by the teacher, and formulation of conclusions flow in a sequence designed to spark thinking and discovering on the part of students. The purpose of the experiment is to find out how the size of the opening in bottle caps is related to the time needed to empty a bottle of water. The students work in pairs. Suggested procedures are:

1. Distribute bottles and caps to the students and permit exploration of them so that they will learn to fill and empty the bottles and will notice the different sizes of the openings in the caps.
2. Demonstrate the filling and emptying of the bottles. Ask the students to predict how size of opening will affect the time it takes to empty a bottle. Ask the students to suggest procedures that may be used to find out.
3. Have each team of two students proceed with the experiment, keeping time records for each one (in metronome ticks so that students can observe the experiment).
4. Discuss the findings of different teams. Have the class explore reasons why minor differences in findings were noted (errors in counting, errors in writing, etc.).
5. Consider conclusions that may be made regarding the time needed to empty a bottle in relation to the size of opening.

This experiment is followed by others designed to explore the properties of liquids. Similar procedures are suggested for each experiment. Emphasis is given to observing, questioning, predicting, designing experiments to test predictions, and collecting and analyzing data. Rigid steps of procedure are not suggested. Rather, students wrestle with questions and propose answers on their own level. The teacher's role is to help students conduct their own experiments. The main elements in the strategy are arranging time for exploration and manipulation of equipment, demonstrating to clarify use of equipment, and questioning to sharpen predictions and collection and analysis of data. Students raise questions, plan procedures, conduct the experiment, make their own observations, and draw their own conclusions.

A Field-test Strategy for Corroborating Findings

After children have made a series of observations it is often desirable to provide an activity or experiment which will unify subjective findings and reinforce major scientific goals. The experiments which serve to unify and corroborate findings are necessarily direct and often more prescriptive than the flexible and open development of experiments identified with children's fact finding. An example of such an activity may be found in the University of California Elementary School Science Project Unit "Animal Coloration: An Introduction to Natural Selection" (Elementary School Science Project, 1966).

After the children have studied animal coloration through a carefully designed series of subjective experiences, it is expected that they are aware that (1) the color blending of an animal and its background reduces the conspicuousness of the animal, and (2) concealing coloration bears a relationship to survival in a predatory environment. The development of an experiment to unify and substantiate the bases for this awareness is a part of a suggested strategy for the lesson which includes the following recommended procedures:

1. **Discussion and summary of previous experiences**
2. **Preparation for the experiment**
3. **Conduct of the experiment**
4. **Recording the data**
5. **Discussion of results**
6. **Recording of results**
7. **Discussion of experimentation involving animals**
8. **Revisiting the experimental site (to confirm experimental results)**

The particular experiment chosen is a good model for the adaptation of the experimental mode to the group enterprise. It is titled "The Caterpillar Search" and involves all children in the imaginative role of birds preying upon caterpillars. Each child (bird) has a "crop" into which caterpillars are placed and later counted. The "caterpillars" are half-toothpicks, some with concealing coloration and some with contrasting coloration. For example, if a lawn is available 500 half-toothpicks are colored green to match the lawn and 500 are uncolored. The experiment is conducted by having the children (birds) search for the toothpicks (caterpillars) for a given short period (one to two minutes). The caterpillars are placed in receptacles (crops), which are emptied upon return to the classroom. Graphs are constructed which show the distribution of "eaten" camouflaged and uncamouflaged "caterpillars." The result of the experiment is a convincing demonstration of the role of adaptive coloration in animal survival. It reinforces the earlier subjective observations and corroborates the summary results of these observations. It also provides a model of experimentation which may be generalized for individual scientific inquiry. Significantly, the experiment provides a field-study experience in the life sciences, which enriches the study in a manner not possible within the confines of a school building.

Strategies for Demonstrations

Demonstrations may be conducted for a variety of purposes ranging from showing how to use equipment to performing an experiment. Strategies vary in terms of the immediate purpose and the point of view of the teacher. For example, if the purpose is to test a specific concept or principle and the teacher believes that it is wise to use a straightforward approach, then direct instruction may be provided in a preplanned sequence. On the other hand, if the purpose is to perform an experiment and the teacher wishes to involve the students to a maximum degree, then a more flexible and open approach may be used so that students can raise questions, suggest hypotheses, and engage in other phases of the learning experience. The difference in the approaches may be characterized by referring to one as a *telling* demonstration and the other as a *questing* demonstration (Gega, 1966, pp. 34–37). The following examples are illustrative of each approach.

Telling demonstrations. The straightforward teaching of the cause of night and day might proceed as follows in a telling demonstration:

1. **A globe and a light bulb are placed on a table in the front of the classroom in which the shades are drawn.**
2. **The students are asked to observe carefully in order to find out about (discover) the cause of night and day.**
3. **The place where the students live may be shown by the teacher or indicated by a student.**
4. **The lighted bulb is held at a distance from the globe which makes it possible for the students to see the light and dark hemispheres. The students are asked to tell where it is day and night.**
5. **The globe is turned slowly and the students are asked to observe the change from day to night.**

6. Students are asked to make a conclusion regarding the cause of day and night. Further demonstration may be provided as needed.

Questing demonstrations. Here the strategy is designed to involve students more actively in the learning experience. For example, if the purpose is to guide students to discover the cause of night and day, using the same materials as noted above, the steps of procedure might be as follows:

1. The teacher introduces the problem by a discussion of the question: Why do we have night and day?
2. The students suggest possible reasons or causes.
3. The teacher asks for suggestions regarding ways in which the globe and light bulb might be used to show the cause of day and night.
4. The students' proposals are considered and tried out. For example, one student may rotate the globe while another holds the lighted bulb. In another demonstration, a student may hold the globe while another walks around it with the lighted bulb.
5. The different demonstrations are discussed and students attempt to bring concepts learned earlier to bear upon the question: Which demonstration is the better explanation?
6. Students are asked to generalize about the cause of night and day or to search for further information if they are unable to do so.

The trend is clearly toward the use of questing demonstrations in new science education materials. However, there are times when telling demonstrations are suggested, particularly in teaching the use of equipment, in clarifying a concept or principle, in posing a problem, and in clinching an idea that is to be used in subsequent activities. In all demonstrations, whether telling or questing, it is recommended that plans be made ahead of time in light of objectives, equipment be checked to make sure it works, a trial run be conducted, pacing be keyed to capabilities of the students, students be involved to the extent that is feasible in light of objectives, and motivation for further study be obtained even if the demonstration does not materialize according to the plan.

A Generalized Strategy

A generalized model for planning a lesson that is related to a generalized model of the scientist's art of investigation has been proposed (Brandwein,

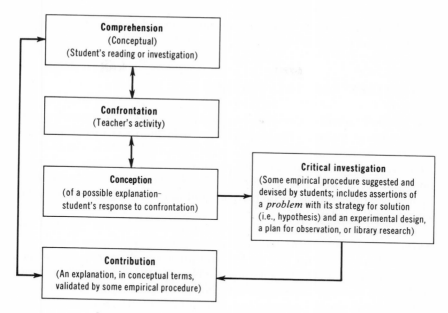

Chart 7–4. *Schema of a generalized lesson plan for the science teacher.*

1965). Chart 7–4 shows the key elements in the model. Notice the arrows that show the relationships among different dimensions of the model. This model should be compared with Chart 7–1 presented in the section on "Modes of Inquiry." The view is taken that both the scientist and the student begin an investigation with a background of comprehension that includes concepts, skills, and attitudes. Even though there may be great differences between the scientist and the student, it is with his own background of understanding that each must begin. Confrontation is the next part of model; it includes recognition of an object or event that does not square with conceptions held by the individual and may include insight into a way to solve the problem. In the teaching model, it is the role of the teacher to devise ways to confront students with an object or event in need of explanation. After confrontation there is a process of conception in which the scientist recognizes a possible strategy for investigating the problem and possible means of empirical validation. For the student the stage of conception may be a possible explanation of the problem. Critical investigation follows conception and may include reading, experimentation, a plan for observation, or other techniques on the part of either the scientist or the student. Finally, the stage of contribution is reached in which the scientist may confirm a hypothesis, develop a new concept or theory, or propose a new tool for studying a given problem. For the stu-

dent, the contribution may be an explanation rooted in concepts and vali-
dated by some empirical procedure.

GUIDELINES FOR THE TEACHER

The primary role of the teacher in science education is to guide inquiry
on the part of students. The strategies noted in the preceding section are
illustrative of how this role may be carried out. The inductive approach in
which students are confronted with problems, discrepant events, and questions and use a variety of techniques to handle them has a dominant place
in new programs of instruction. Basic guidelines for the teacher may be
summarized as follows:

*Intertwine content and processes as appropriate to further in-
quiry.* Both are essential to inquiry and both are a part of science.
Data and concepts must be coupled with processes of science as students
investigate the variety of topics and problems in science education. Help
students to discover that experiments, field studies, observation, and other
techniques call for the creative use of information and concepts and that
sound generalizations are based on verified data. Conversely, help students
discover that facts and concepts take on dynamic meaning when embedded in processes of investigation.

Use models of inquiry and problem solving flexibly. Models
that include such phases of inquiry as encountering problems, raising
questions, formulating hypotheses, gathering and verifying data, interpreting data, and drawing conclusions should be viewed as general guidelines to inquiry, not as steps to be followed routinely. The creative and
intuitive flashes of insight that occur in inquiry are highly personal and
cannot be ordered in a series of steps. On the other hand, there is a place
for consideration of the inquiry process to be sure that no important
phase is neglected. A flexible approach makes it possible to spark creativity
by drawing useful ideas from a model. Thinking should not be restricted
by slavishly following a model.

*Keep attention focused on key concepts, conceptual schemes,
and generalizations around which content can be organized.* The
vast storehouse of content in the natural sciences makes it imperative that
a critical selection of "organizers" be made. Students need concepts and
principles to organize their ideas about the natural world. Helping students
to cluster subconcepts around key concepts is a means of assuring steady
growth toward the comprehension of the big ideas, the principles, the
generalizations that have greatest value. Introducing concepts at the pro-
pitious moment when students need them to sharpen and organize thinking
is a part of the art of teaching that may be improved by drawing sug-

gestions from guides, diagnosing individual progress, and using strategies as shown in the preceding section. Premature pressure on students to generalize should be avoided. Generalizations must be based on adequate data and a clear grasp of the concepts that are used to make them. Each child develops his own generalizations and the process of generalizing is aided by a planned sequence of instruction. Clues as to when to focus on generalizing can be obtained from students themselves as they interpret data, share ideas in discussion, and consider needs for further information.

Gear the instructional program to the capabilities of the students. Encourage individual enterprise and provide group activities that spark contributions from each student. Provide opportunities for students to suggest and carry out different approaches to investigation of problems. Avoid the imposition of abstract terminology, adultlike record keeping, and other activities that smack of an artificial view of science. A guiding principle is to maximize each student's opportunity to investigate questions and problems to the best of his ability in a sequence of experiences that lead to continuing growth.

Formulate questions and make comments that promote active inquiry on the part of students. Questions and comments should stimulate a continuing search for better answers rather than "the right answer." Such questions as, What do you think? How can we find out? What techniques should we use to gather data? What materials do we need? Which idea is most useful? How can we test the value of these ideas? How can we improve the statement of the problem? How can this be clarified? are illustrative of those which keep responsibility for inquiry on the shoulders of students. Similarly, comments such as the following help to promote inquiry: Explain it in your own words. Describe it as you saw it. Tell us what your idea is. Show us how it should be used. A guiding principle is to be supportive of each student but neutral with reference to his ideas (Suchman, 1966).

Provide for the use of a variety of techniques to investigate questions and problems. Experiments are useful when certain variables must be controlled. Direct observation of events is useful when plants, animals, or other objects are studied in a natural habitat. Field studies are useful to gather data on phenomena in the local area. Library research is useful in gathering background information on a host of topics. Interviews are useful in gathering specific data on a variety of questions. These and other data-gathering techniques such as reading, studying collections, seeing exhibits, using audio-visual materials, and seeing demonstrations should be selected and used as appropriate. The notion that scientists "just experiment" should be dispelled; they use whatever technique is appropriate in a given situation. Students should grow in their ability to do the same.

Provide opportunities for the direct consideration of processes of inquiry. Students can grow in their understanding of inquiry processes if at appropriate times the teacher will provide for discussion and evaluation sessions in which questions such as the following are considered (Suchman, 1966): What are theories? Where do we get them? How are they used? What other means can we use to gather data? What does it mean to know something? How do we know that water freezes? How can we make decisions about causes? How can data be used to explain something? How can theories be used to explain something? What are scientific laws? How do we get them? What is the difference between data and laws?

Arrange for the use of a variety of instructional media as needed to investigate questions and problems. A guiding question is: What equipment and materials are essential in this situation? The answer will vary in terms of objectives, techniques of inquiry to be used, capabilities of students, and available instructional materials. Science kits, prepackaged units, film loops and other audio-visual materials, textbooks and library materials for reference, resource persons to interview, materials for experiments and demonstrations, and possible study trips in the community should be considered. The selection of materials for a given situation should be arranged for students' use so that investigation on their part is maximized. Students themselves should have a hand in selecting materials needed to handle a given topic or problem. After all, equipment and materials are a part of the inquiry process, and the desired outcome is growth in the ability to handle all aspects of inquiry.

Maintain a classroom atmosphere that is consistent with the spirit characteristic of scientific approaches to knowing. Attitudes and values are an important part of the scientific enterprise. Of key importance are longing to know and understand, questioning of all things, searching for data and their meaning, seeking verification, respecting logical operations, considering premises, and considering consequences (Educational Policies Commission, 1966). By studying in a classroom in which values such as these are paramount, students will grow in affective as well as cognitive dimensions of scientific literacy.

EVALUATION OF OUTCOMES OF INSTRUCTION

The evaluation of learning outcomes in elementary school science is beset with difficulties similar to those found in other curriculum areas. The factual material of science lends itself to the group written test, and factual knowledge remains an accepted product of successful instruction. However, many dimensions of the modern program are not adequately appraised by the fact-oriented group written test. Some attempts have been made to provide group tests biased toward the appraisal of approach and process, but little success has been noted. At the high school level, some success has been achieved with the use of group written tests which do not call for outlines of fact but rather present new and unfamiliar situations for analysis. In this test situation, knowledge of science material and familiarity with the processes of science are purportedly revealed as the tester seeks for understanding of the unfamiliar situation.

In newer elementary school programs, recognition is given the fact that if the objectives of instruction are placed in behavioral terms, the evaluations of learning must have a major behavioral component. Such behavior may be observed or appraised in a hierarchy of learning stages or steps. It also may be differentiated into tasks which relate to scientific procedures such as naming, recognizing, identifying, classifying, distinguishing, describing, and ordering. Above all it must be observable in children's work in science.

The range of evaluation has been extended through the use of self-evaluation guides for children's use, behavioral check lists to be completed by children, attitude and interest surveys, informal surveys of time allocations and other devices. Some characteristic approaches to evaluation in elementary school may be noted in the examples which follow.

Completion of Tasks

Direct assessment of instructional outcomes may be obtained by having students complete tasks that require application of what has been included in teaching episodes. Tasks for use in assessing process outcomes have been outlined in detail in a current project (AAAS, 1965). Two examples are:

Classification. Have students place the following into groups according to any scheme they choose: several plastic knives, forks, and spoons of differing sizes and assorted colors. Note the basis for classification on the chalkboard: size, color, set, such as knife, fork, and spoon, or multiple basis, such as a set of the same size and color. Ask if they can think of other ways to group them (all knives, all knives of same color, all knives of same color and size, etc.). Record the different suggestions that are made.

Predicting. Divide the class into two equal groups and have the students in each group list their three favorite flavors of ice cream. Have the students summarize the information obtained from one group and make a bar graph of the findings. Ask individuals in the class to make predictions of what will be found when the second group's list is summarized. List predictions on the chalkboard. Summarize and graph the second group's listings and compare findings with predictions. Have different children tell how they made their predictions.

Using Check Lists

A variety of outcomes may be assessed by using check lists which include statements or questions designed to focus attention on specific behaviors. Chart 7–5 is illustrative.

Chart 7–5. Check lists for assessment of instructional outcomes.

Making predictions	**Making classifcations**	**Measuring length**
__ Collects and organizes data	__ Classifies by single item such as color or length	__ Uses comparative measures such as longer and shorter
__ Makes a graph of data	__ Classifies by two items such as color and length or color and use	__ Identifies equal and unequal lengths
__ States how prediction may be tested	__ Classifies by several items such as color, use, and size	__ Compares objects with an arbitrary standard
__ Changes prediction on basis of new data	__ Changes classification as purpose changes	__ Uses standard measures such as inches and feet
		__ Uses metric units such as centimeter and meter

Using the concept cluster "types of rock"	**Understanding the concept cluster "body systems"**
__ Recognizes properties of metamorphic rocks	Describes the structure and explains the function of
__ Recognizes properties of sedimentary rocks	__ Nervous system __ Muscular system
__ Recognizes properties of igneous rocks	__ Skeletal system __ Circulatory system
__ Classifies different rocks into one of the above groups	__ Digestive system __ Excretory system
	__ Differentiates among muscle, skin, and nerve tissue
	__ Knows functions of the heart, liver, and other organs of the body system

APPRAISING INTEREST IN DIFFERENT TOPICS

Rating	Topics						
	A	B	C	D	E	F	G
__ Intense interest							
__ Active interest							
__ Some interest							
__ Little interest							
__ No interest							

Using the Taxonomies of Objectives

Appraising instructional outcomes in science may be structured and systematized through use of taxonomies of educational objectives. Classroom questions and performance tasks may be patterned to the various levels of the taxonomies to provide a comprehensive evaluation program. The following examples include a question and an item for each level in the cognitive and affective domains (Bloom, 1956; Krathwohl et al., 1964).

Cognitive Domain

Knowledge level: What is Newton's third law?
Put a circle around that chemical expression in the following list which represents carbon dioxide: H_2O, $CaCO_3$, CO_2, HCO_3, H_2O_2.

Comprehension level: What concepts should be clustered together in the key concept "life cycle"? Underline each of the following that is a part of the life cycle. . . .

Application level: Why did Ann fall out of the front of the wagon when the wagon hit the board and stopped?
Write O before each statement that is an observation. Write I before each statement that is an inference.
———There are drops of water on the steps.
———It must have rained last night.
———There is water on the lawn.
———Dew formed on the surface of uncovered objects.
———Someone may have watered the yard this morning.

Analysis level: Why did crystals develop when solution A was evaporated, whereas the evaporation of solution B produced no crystals?
List all the reasons you can for explaining why the polar bear is white.

Synthesis level: How can we test the hypotheses that have been proposed?
From our many experiments with growing plants make a summary chart showing those things which are necessary in order for plants to grow.

Evaluation level: Is our explanation for the behavior of mercury correct? Are there other possible explanations?
List the strengths and the weaknesses of our experiment on evaporation of water.

Affective Domain

Receiving level: Were we careful to consider everyone's ideas in designing our experiment?

Let us design an experiment that will bring together the ideas of committee A and committee B.

Responding level: Which experiment can we do in the classroom? List on a sheet of paper any suggestions you may have for committee A to make their experiment as effective as possible.

Valuing level: Why is science important to all people in our world today?

Tell why we must be careful to gather all the information we can before we draw conclusions.

Organization level: What is a scientist?

Suggest some things we should do in all our learning even though we discovered them in our science class.

EVALUATION OF THE INSTRUCTIONAL PROGRAM

Information gleaned from assessment of students' learning should be used along with criteria such as the following to evaluate the instructional program:

Foundations

Is the program rooted in up-to-date material drawn from the physical and life sciences?

Is the primary focus on basic science as opposed to technology?

Is relevant material drawn from mathematics as needed to give precision to the communication of scientific ideas?

Is knowledge of child development and learning used to facilitate instruction?

Structure

Is the conceptual structure clearly outlined in terms of concepts, conceptual schemes, and generalizations?

Are processes of science clearly outlined and directly related to the conceptual structure?

Are the conceptual and process structures embedded in units of study?

Inquiry

Are models of inquiry identified and used flexibly in instruction?

Are specific techniques of inquiry such as experimentation and field study incorporated in units of study?

Objectives

Are content or substantive outcomes defined behaviorally?
Are process or inquiry outcomes defined behaviorally?
Are underlying attitudes or values defined behaviorally?

A complete program

Is the program balanced in terms of the overall sequence?
Is the program balanced in terms of content and process?
Is the program balanced in terms of areas of science?

Teaching strategies

Is emphasis given to strategies that promote active inquiry and discovery on the part of students?
Are teaching strategies consistent with the styles of thought and ways of inquiring used by scientists?
Are various techniques and instructional media selected and used in consonance with objectives, capabilities of students, and characteristics of the teaching-learning situation?

Evaluation

Is evaluation an integral and continuing part of instruction?
Are devices and items designed on various levels of complexity to assess all outcomes of instruction?
Is emphasis given to self-evaluation on the part of students?

Teacher education

Is continuing growth of teachers in the content and processes of science provided?
Is attention given to new developments in current projects?
Are teachers involved in trying out new approaches?
Is consultant service available to teachers?

Continuing revision

Is ongoing revision under way with attention to new ideas from science and new developments from current projects?
Are teachers participating in the development of new approaches?

REFERENCES

AAAS, Commission on Science Education. *Science: a process approach.* (3d experimental ed.) Washington, D.C.: American Association for the Advancement of Science, 1965. Hierarchies of processes charted in *An evaluation model and its applications*; suggestions for teaching exercises designed to develop processes of science in fourteen booklets; background information in *Commentary for teachers.*

Blackwood, Paul E. Science. *New curriculum developments.* Washington, D.C.: Association for Supervision and Curriculum Development, National Education Association, 1965. A review of new developments in current science education projects.

Blackwood, Paul E. *Science teaching in the elementary schools.* Washington, D.C.: U.S. Office of Education, OE–29059, 1965. Survey of objectives, teaching patterns, and other aspects of science teaching.

Bloom, Benjamin S. (Ed.) *Taxonomy of educational objectives: cognitive domain.* New York: McKay, 1956. Sample behavioral statements and test items arranged on six levels of complexity.

Blough, Glen O., & Schwartz, Julius. *Science for elementary teachers.* (3d ed.) New York: Holt, 1964. Suggestions for teaching four basic areas of science.

Brandwein, Paul F. *Substance, structure, and style in the teaching of science.* New York: Harcourt, Brace, 1965. Essay on structure, art of investigation, and art of teaching.

Buros, Oscar K. *The sixth mental measurements yearbook.* Highland Park, N.J.: Gryphon Press, 1965. Reviews of science achievement tests published between 1959 and 1964.

California. *Science curriculum development in the elementary school.* Sacramento: State Department of Education, 1964. Information on strands and generalizations in selected areas of science in chap. 4.

Carin, Arthur, & Sund, Robert B. *Teaching science through discovery.* Columbus, Ohio: Charles E. Merrill Books, Inc., 1964. Methods, materials, and lesson plans.

Educational Policies Commission. *Education and the spirit of science.* Washington, D.C.: National Education, 1966. Values of rational inquiry.

Gagné, Robert M. *The conditions of learning.* New York: Holt, 1965. Analysis of eight types of learning with suggestions for guiding each type.

Gega, Peter C. *Science in elementary education.* New York: Wiley, 1966. Principles and specific techniques for teaching science in elementary school.

Hone, Elizabeth, Joseph, Alexander, & Victor, Edward. *A sourcebook for elementary science.* New York: Harcourt, Brace, 1962. Detailed suggestions for specific learning activities.

Jacobson, Willard L., & Tannenbaum, Harold E. *Modern elementary-school science: a recommended sequence.* New York: Teachers College, Columbia University, 1961. A recommended scope and sequence.

Kambly, Paul E., & Suttle, John E. *Teaching elementary-school science.* New York: Ronald, 1963. Methods, resource units, and source materials.

Karplus, Robert, & Thier, Herbert D. *The science curriculum improvement study.* Chicago: Rand McNally, 1967. Discussion of theory, procedures, and instructional materials in the Science Curriculum Improvement Study.

Krathwohl, David R., Bloom, Benjamin S., & Masia, Bertram B. *Taxonomy of educational objectives: affective domain.* New York: McKay, 1964. Sample behavioral statements and test items arranged according to degree of internalization.

Lewis, June E., & Potter, Irene C. *The teaching of science in the elementary school.* Englewood Cliffs, N.J.: Prentice-Hall, 1961. Content and activities arranged by topics and questions.

Lockard, J. David. *Report of the International Clearinghouse on science and mathematics 1966.* College Park, Md.: Science Teaching Center, University of Maryland, 1966. Concise reviews of new projects in the United States and foreign countries.

Los Angeles City Schools. *Course of study for elementary schools.* Los Angeles: Board of Education, 1964. An outline of topics by grades under living things, matter and energy, the earth, and the universe.

Lovell, K. *The growth of mathematical and scientific concepts in children.* New York: Philosophical Library, 1962. Replications and discussions of many of Piaget's studies on children's learning of scientific concepts.

Nagel, Ernest. *The structure of science.* New York: Harcourt, Brace, 1961. Discussion of types of scientific explanation by a philosopher.

National Science Teachers Association. *Theory into action in science curriculum development.* Washington, D.C.: National Education Association, 1964. Theory of science education, conceptual and process components of structure, and suggestions for developing the curriculum.

National Society for the Study of Education. *A program for science teachers.* Thirty-first Yearbook, Part I. 1932; *Science education in American schools.* Forty-sixth Yearbook, Part I. 1947; *Rethinking science education.* Fifty-ninth Yearbook, Part I. 1960. Chicago: University of Chicago Press. Yearbooks devoted to surveys of thought and practice related to science education in the schools.

Navarra, John, & Zafforoni, Joseph. *Science today for the elementary school teacher.* New York: Harper, 1960. A general source for elementary science teaching.

Phenix, Philip H. *Realms of meaning.* New York: McGraw-Hill, 1964. A philosophy of curriculum development. Chapters 8 and 9 discuss structure and meaning in physical science and biology.

Ripple, Richard E., & Rockcastle, Verne N. (Eds.) *Piaget rediscovered.* Ithaca, N.Y.: School of Education, Cornell University, 1964. A report on the Piaget conferences at Cornell and the University of California, Berkeley.

Santa Clara County. *Science teachers' guide, grades K-8.* San Jose: County Board of Education, 1964. Concepts and generalizations for elementary school science.

Schwab, Joseph J., & Brandwein, Paul. *The teaching of science.* Cambridge, Mass.: Harvard, 1962. Essays on inquiry and various aspects of science teaching.

Suchman, J. Richard. *Developing inquiry.* Chicago: Science Research Associates, 1966. Principles and techniques for developing inquiry.

Tannenbaum, Harold, Stillman, Nathan, & Piltz, Albert, *Science education for elementary school teachers.* (2d ed.) Boston: Allyn and Bacon, 1965. A treatment of content and pedagogy of elementary science.

Victor, Edward. *Science for the elementary school.* New York: Macmillan, 1965. Outlines of content, methods, and activities.

Zafforoni, Joseph. *New developments in elementary-school science.* Washington, D.C.: National Science Teachers Association, National Education Association, 1963. A survey of new programs in elementary science teaching.

CURRENT PROJECTS

American Association for the Advancement of Science. 1515 Massachusetts Avenue, N.W., Washington 5, D.C.

Elementary School Science. c/o Educational Services Incorporated, 108 Water Street, Watertown, Mass.

Elementary School Science and Curriculum Study Project. c/o Department of Physics, Cornell University, Ithaca, N.Y.

Elementary School Science Project. c/o Department of Education, University of California, Berkeley 4, Calif.

Elementary School Science Project. c/o Department of Education, University of Illinois, Urbana, Ill.

Elementary Science Project. c/o Minnesota National Laboratory, Minnesota State Department of Education, St. Paul, Minn.

Science Curriculum Improvement Study. c/o Department of Physics, University of California, Berkeley 4, Calif.

Science Manpower Project. c/o Teachers College, Columbia University, New York 27, N.Y.

Chapter Eight

SOCIAL SCIENCES EDUCATION

THE SOCIAL SCIENCES are focused on the study of man in society—human behavior in groups, changes in human relationships, the nature of the human condition. Both quantitative and qualitative approaches are used to study man in society. Some studies are highly scientific and objective, whereas others are highly humanistic and subjective. Empirical modes of inquiry in which data are gathered and used to test hypotheses are valued along with philosophical modes in which logical analysis of issues and problems is dominant. High premium is placed on analytic studies which can be used to explain and predict behavior in groups. One can also find much descriptive and prescriptive material that is based on systematic investigation of human relationships. Probably no other broad domain of knowledge is characterized by so much diversity as the social sciences.

Yet there is a good deal of unity among the social sciences. For example, unity may be found in the emphasis on the study of man in society, as noted above. Unity also may be noted in the common emphasis on styles of thought that are marked by free and open inquiry, thoughtful skepticism, analytical procedures, care in generalizing, open review of findings, testing of hypotheses, and other characteristics of scholarly study. Further unity may be discerned in the use of concepts such as culture, socioeconomic status, social change, and decision making in many of the social sciences. Similarly, scholars in many different disciplines use techniques of inquiry such as case studies, interviewing, observation, and historical methods.

The social sciences as a division of knowledge include a variety of disciplines, ranging from economics and sociology to cybernetics and general systems theory. Such disciplines may be classified in the realm of empirics (Phenix, 1964) because of the empirical, theoretical, and generally scientific modes of inquiry that are employed. History, a key subject in social sciences education, is a synoptic discipline (Phenix, 1964) that is classified as a social science by a few individuals and as a humanity by most. Content from art, literature, and philosophy—humanistic disciplines —also can be found in the social sciences and in the instructional program. Thus we find in the social sciences, and in social sciences education, a variety of material from nearly all the realms of meaning discussed by Phenix even though a predominant part may be drawn from the realm of empirics or synoptics. However, the trend is clearly to emphasize certain disciplines in social sciences education as shown in the following section.

FOUNDATION DISCIPLINES

Six disciplines are used as the primary foundation of the social sciences program of instruction in current projects and teaching guides: geography, history, economics, political science, sociology, and anthropology. Also employed as sources of data for curriculum planning are psychology and philosophy. (For a detailed discussion of each discipline, see Michaelis & Johnston, 1965; Muessig & Rogers, 1965.)

Economics is well advanced as a specialized policy science and there is widespread acceptance of many key concepts and the rational methods of analysis that can be applied to economic problems. Some branches or aspects of psychology, sociology, and anthropology are clearly scientific in emphasis (e.g., experimental psychology, group behavior, and physical anthropology), while others are speculative, humanistic, and philosophical in emphasis (e.g., aspects of clinical psychology, cultural anthropology, and social theory). Geography cuts across the physical and social sciences, draws concepts from other disciplines to describe and analyze regions, relies heavily on scientific methods, and is a powerful integrator of content in a spatial context. History cuts across the social sciences and humanities, draws concepts from other disciplines to describe and analyze particular events, relies heavily on critical analysis of sources, and is a powerful integrator of content in a time context. Political science is a specialized policy science that draws many concepts from other disciplines to describe and analyze political power and government.

Three highly integrative disciplines are human geography, history, and anthropology; all draw material together to give a rather complete view of the region, period, or society under study. The other disciplines have a more specialized focus, although some sociologists do integrate material from other disciplines, and some economists and political scientists are concerned about relationships to other disciplines.

Concept Clusters and Generalizations

Because social sciences education is based on a large number of disciplines, a variety of concept clusters and generalizations may be found in the instructional program. In the past, many have been drawn from geography, history, and political science. Currently, many are drawn from economics and the behavioral sciences, especially anthropology and sociology. The examples listed below have been taken from current projects and new teaching guides. Others may be found in the references listed at the end of this chapter.

The following concept clusters are widely used in units of study based on a single discipline as well as those based on several disciplines.

Resources: **people, animal life, vegetation, minerals, soils, water**

Settlement patterns: **isolated, village, town, suburb, city, metropolis, megalopolis**

State history: Indians, explorers, settlers, first towns, transportation, communication, business, schools, government, industry, agriculture, labor, recreation

Factors of production: land, labor, capital, management, government

Economic processes: production, exchange, distribution, consumption

Processes of government: legislative, executive, judicial

Civil liberties: freedom of thought, speech, worship, petition, association

Some culture universals: language, marriage, child training, religion, funeral rites, property, art, moral code, toolmaking

Basic institutions: family, education, economics, religion, government

Social roles: leadership, followership, aggression, submission

Individual differences: appearance, tastes, habits, attitudes, beliefs, abilities, learning

Judging: clarifying what is to be judged, defining criteria for judging, applying the criteria, making the judgment, comparing judgments

The following generalizations are illustrative of those used as main ideas to organize units of study and sought as outcomes of the instructional program. Notice that each example includes the key concept of one of the clusters cited above.

How people use the resources in their environment is largely determined by their culture.

There has been a shift from isolated rural settlement patterns to concentrated urban patterns.

Factors of production need to be considered in deciding what to produce.

Civil liberties are a basic part of the American way of life.

There are universal aspects of culture that may be found in all societies.

Social institutions provide the means for realizing group values.

Individuals assume different roles in the groups to which they belong.

The process of making judgments involves the examination of a situation in terms of criteria.

Other concept clusters and generalizations may be noted in the sections that follow. Notice especially those included in the next section in which examples are given of the structure of K-12 programs of instruction.

EXAMPLES OF STRUCTURE

Structure is defined in a variety of ways in current social sciences education programs. Definitions of structure need to be considered in terms of the substantive units—concepts, generalizations, themes—used in planning the overall K-12 program and in devising courses and units within the overall program. First attention is given to the overall program. This is followed by examples related to courses and units of study.

Structure of K-12 Programs

The substantive structure of K-12 programs is usually defined in two ways. The first and most widely used approach is based on generalizations; the second is based on concepts. Whichever approach is used, however, one can be sure to find both concepts and generalizations in units of instruction because they are inextricably interrelated. And in the process of instruction in both types of program, students discover, develop, and extend concepts, using them to formulate and test generalizations.

Generalizations. Fundamental generalizations have been identified in history and the social sciences in three recently developed programs (California, 1962; New York City, 1965; Wisconsin, 1964). In this approach, the assistance of scholars is obtained in identifying those generalizations which are believed to be basic in each discipline and which should be developed to higher levels of understanding as students progress through the program. The generalizations serve as strands that run through the program and are guides to the selection of content and learning experiences. Each generalization contains key concepts as shown in the following examples taken from three different programs.

> *California*
> **Soil, water, solar energy, and air are the natural resources most indispensable to man.**
> **Man constantly seeks to satisfy his needs for food, clothing, and shelter and his other wants; in so doing, he attempts to adapt, shape, utilize, and exploit the earth.**
> **Interdependence has been a constant and important factor in human relationships.**

New York City
> Societies develop economic systems in order to allocate limited resources.
> Governments exist to make rules for group living.
> Governments have grown more complex in response to changing needs and conditions.

Wisconsin
> Citizenship involves active participation in the process of governing.
> Human beings are in part a product of their culture.
> Every group tends to develop various social processes and institutions to give order and stability to relationships among people.

A general practice is to embed generalizations, or subgeneralizations, in units of study at different levels. The intent is to develop increasing depth and breadth of understanding as students progress through the program and encounter the generalizations in a spiral plan of development. For example, interdependence as a constant factor in human relationships may be first considered in studies of homes, schools, and communities. Understanding is extended in later studies of the state, nation, and other lands. Attention is customarily given to interdependence in economic and political contexts as well as in historical and geographical contexts (for examples, see Michaelis, 1966).

Concepts. The use of concepts to define the structure of the social sciences program differs from the generalizations approach primarily in emphasis. Attention is given to key concepts that are of critical importance in guiding inquiry and study. Each concept is defined, and related generalizations may be identified either in the statement of concepts or in related teaching guides.

Social Studies Curriculum Center, Syracuse. The concepts approach may be illustrated by considering examples taken from a publication of a current project (Price, Hickman, & Smith, 1965). Thirty-four concepts have been defined in three categories as follows:

> *Substantive concepts:* sovereignty of the nation-state, conflict, industrialization-urbanization, secularization, compromise and adjustment, comparative advantage, power, morality and choice, scarcity, input and output, saving, modified market economy, habitat and its significance, culture, institution, social control, social change, interaction
>
> *Value concepts:* dignity of man, empathy, loyalty, government by consent of the governed, freedom and equality

> *Concepts of method*: historical method, geographical approach, causation, techniques and aspects of method—observation, classification and measurement, analysis and synthesis, questions and answers, objectivity, skepticism, interpretation, evaluation, evidence

Curriculum planners may use the concepts as appropriate in planning units and courses at all levels of instruction. For example, social change is relevant to studies of local, state, national, and international problems. The many factors producing social change can be considered along with processes of change such as invention, innovation, and diffusion. Generalizations can be formulated to fit different situations; e.g., change is more rapid in industrialized societies than in preliterate societies.

Geography.   The concepts approach has been used by the Curriculum Committee of the National Council for Geographic Education (Hill, 1962). Nine concepts were identified; they are summarized below in the form of concept clusters to show selected dimensions of each concept.

> *Globalism*: sphericity, grid system, earth-sun relationships, rotation, revolution, inclination and parallelism of axis
>
> *Round earth on flat paper*: projections, directions, relief, symbols, scale
>
> *The life layer*: lithosphere, hydrosphere, atmosphere, fundamental elements—soil, air, water
>
> *Areal distinctions, differences, likenesses*: differences in people and environments from place to place, areal variations and interactions, arrangements and associations of things in selected areas
>
> *The region*: technique of regionalizing, identifying meaningful aggregations in space, using criteria to define regions, scale, physical, economic, political, rural, urban, and other aspects of regions
>
> *Resources culturally defined*: culture as prime determinant of how man uses resources, technology, change, human resources
>
> *Man the chooser*: opportunities and restraints confronted by people in different regions, decision making, political, economic, social, and physical environmental impactors
>
> *Spatial interaction*: connections and movements within and between regions, communication, transportation, circulation of goods, men, and ideas.
>
> *Perpetual transformation*: changes due to occupance of an area, natural forces, stage of development

These concepts may be used singly or in combination as units and courses are planned. For example, regions occupied by American Indians may be defined and considered in terms of how resources were used by the Indians and later by groups with a different culture. The role of culture in determining resource use can be illumined as attention is given to food, shelter, clothing, work, and other aspects of daily life. The concepts are deepened and extended as they are put to use in studying other areas which have been occupied by diverse cultures, e.g., Latin America, the Middle East, and Africa.

Structure of Disciplines

A model for outlining the structure of a discipline has been devised by Senesh (Morrissett, 1966), who is preparing materials for a K-12 program. The model consists of basic principles or generalizations and a flow chart which shows relationships among them. Chart 8–1 shows the relationships among several principles drawn from economics:

> **The conflict between unlimited wants and limited resources is an economic problem faced by all individuals and countries.**
> **Division of labor increases productivity; labor may be divided geographically, occupationally, and technologically.**
> **Interdependence results from division of labor and leads to trading, which is facilitated by money and transportation.**
> **Societies develop allocating mechanisms that determine what to produce, how much to produce, methods of production, and levels of production and employment.**
> **The market is the major allocating mechanism in our society. Broad social goals which influence economic decisions are growth, stability, security, freedom, and justice.**

The model has been used to prepare materials for the primary grades. Similar models have been developed for anthropology, geography, political science, and sociology (Senesh, 1966). Such models should prove to be quite helpful to curriculum builders because of their simplicity and their inclusion of fundamental ideas in chart form to show relationships.

Structure in Units and Courses

Success in curriculum planning probably depends as much on the skill with which structure is incorporated in units and courses as on any of the other factors that must be considered. Excellent examples of how this may be done are appearing in current project materials. A guiding principle appears to be to identify one or more concept clusters or a set of related main ideas and to build instruction around them.

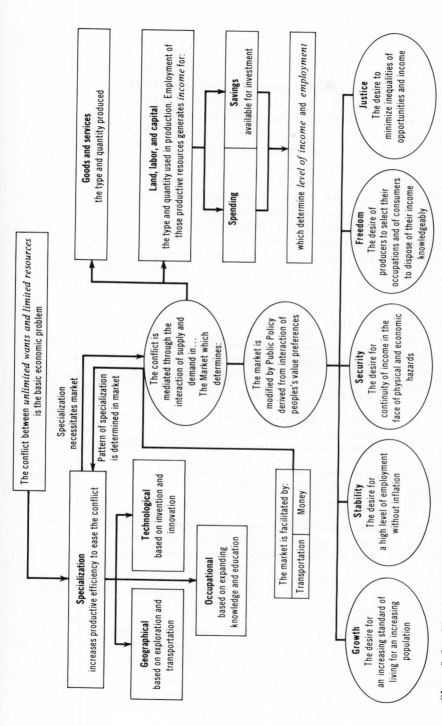

Chart 8–1. The fundamental idea relationships of economic knowledge.

The conflict between *unlimited wants and limited resources* is the basic economic problem

Specialization necessitates market

Pattern of specialization is determined in market

Specialization increases productive efficiency to ease the conflict

Geographical based on exploration and transportation

Technological based on invention and innovation

Occupational based on expanding knowledge and education

The conflict is mediated through the interaction of supply and demand in.... The Market which determines:

The market is modified by Public Policy derived from interaction of peoples's value preferences

The market is facilitated by:

| Transportation | Money |

Goods and services the type and quantity produced

Land, labor, and capital the type and quantity used in production. Employment of those productive resources generates *income* for:

Spending

Savings available for investment

which determine *level of income and employment*

Growth The desire for an increasing standard of living for an increasing population

Stability The desire for a high level of employment without inflation

Security The desire for continuity of income in the face of physical and economic hazards

Freedom The desire of producers to select their occupations and of consumers to dispose of their income knowlegeably

Justice The desire to minimize inequalities of opportunities and income

Structure in this instance is somewhat different from the overall structure of the program. Selected aspects of the overall structure may be used, or the units may be constructed independently without attention to an overall structure. Independent planning of units has occurred in both the social sciences and the science education programs. Ideally, it seems that greatest teaching and learning benefits are possible when unit and course structures are seen as a part of the overall structure. Nevertheless, some units and courses have been developed independently and they contain good examples of what may well be called microstructures because they deal with a small delimited part of the total program.

Man: A course of study. In an experimental course being tried out in grade 5, structure is defined in terms of three questions and five great humanizing forces (Bruner, 1966). The three questions are intended to guide study throughout the course. The humanizing forces are viewed as interrelated sets of ideas. Each force may be viewed as a major concept around which related concepts and themes can be organized as shown in the following excerpts.

QUESTIONS

What is human about human beings? How did they get that way? How can they be made more so?

HUMANIZING FORCES

Language: acquisition, contrastive features, signs and symbols, advantages of a voice-ear system, type and order, phonemes as building blocks, syntax, language and thought

Tool making: the program guiding use of tools, tools as amplifiers of human capacities, substitution of tools, tools and evolution

Social organization: changing structure of society, roles, reciprocity and exchange, family, extended family, kinship, contrast to social organization of higher primates

Child rearing: dominance of sentiment due to long childhood, mastery of skill for its own sake, childhood as shaper of the man

World view: urge to explain and represent the world, myth, art, legend, use of symbols, hunting-gathering societies

Special attention is given to contrast, hypothesizing, gaming, and stimulating self-consciousness in each unit of instruction. For example, contrasts between modern and early man, hypotheses related to hunting, language games, and getting students to consciously consider ways of inquiring are included in the course. An attempt is made to get students to use concepts as models for guiding study, a practice that has been stressed for some time in economic education.

Economics in grades 4–5.   In a project designed to prepare students' materials, structure is delimited to a consideration of the economic processes of consumption and production and the relationships between them (Rader, 1964). Key concepts are developed in eleven units as follows:

> *Grade 4:* How Americans obtain goods and services
> 1. Scarcity—universal problem (unlimited wants and limited resources)
> 2. Wants—priority of human wants, their characteristics, why all wants cannot be satisfied, why choices must be made
> 3. Work—relationships among wants, work, and money
> 4. Money—our system of exchange, functions of money
> 5. Consumption and savings—importance of consumer choices, why people save
> 6. Summary—relationships among wants, work, money, and consumption and savings
>
> *Grade 5:* How Americans produce and obtain goods and services
> 7. How Americans obtain goods and services—production of goods and services, marketing of goods
> 8. Overview—way in which Americans produce goods and services and market goods
> 9. Production—why people organize business, what is needed for production, how labor, materials, and equipment are combined in production
> 10. Marketing—relationship of production, marketing, and consumption
> 11. Summary—how wants, work, money, consumption and savings, production and marketing are related

In each unit specific attention is given to the development of concepts and the formulation of generalizations. For example, in the study of money, opportunities are provided for students to ground themselves on the meaning of money, money as payment for work, exchange of money for goods and services, and the functions of money. A key generalization is that people earn money by working and exchange it for goods and services. Relationships among wants, work, money, and consumption of goods and services are considered. The summary units provide opportunities for students to structure the ideas that have been taught and to discover relationships among them.

A structure for studying a region. Increased interest has been shown in recent years in patterns or models that may be used in regional or area studies. The current emphasis on culture regions has sharpened this interest. The example that follows has been adapted from several recently prepared outlines to show concepts and concept clusters that may be used to guide study of a particular region and to make comparative studies of two or more regions.

THE SETTING—PHYSICAL FEATURES

Location: latitude and longitude, relative—site, situation, in relation to other places, time and distance from own location

Spatial features: area (size), shape, length and width, boundaries—natural and political

Major landforms: plains, hills, plateaus, mountains; pattern of distribution

Water features: underground waters, rivers, lakes, seas, oceans, bays, straits, coastlines and shorelines

Climate: temperature—range, average, growing season; precipitation—average, seasonal amounts, causative factors

Resource base: soils, water, vegetation, animal life, minerals

THE PEOPLE—HUMAN ACTIVITIES

Population: number, growth rate, origins, migrations, racial characteristics, distribution, settlement patterns, areas of concentration, central city, other key cities

Economic activities: agriculture, industries, trade, transportation, communication, relation to other areas

Political processes: ideological base, political processes, form of government, decision making, administrative units, relations with other nations

Sociocultural features: links to other cultures; dominant social values; social control; social stratification—classes, castes, minorities, rigidity-fluidity; social institutions—the family, education, religion; social and cultural change; language; art; music; architecture; health and sanitation; other features

Key problems and future plans: economic development, population growth, health, standard of living, nationalism, social and political tensions, relations with other nations, urbanization, others

An outline such as this can be used flexibly as a model to study a variety of regions, ranging from local areas to international groupings of nations. Topics of greatest importance can be highlighted as a given area is studied. Relationships among topics can be emphasized and topics can be combined as desired to show links between them, e.g., problems and future plans can be made a part of preceding topics, economic and political activities can be intertwined, etc. Beginning with a few selected topics in early grades, others can be added in subsequent grades to round out regional studies.

OBJECTIVES OF INSTRUCTION

Increased emphasis on the disciplines as foundations for planning the social sciences curriculum has brought changes in statements of the objectives of instruction. One change has been to indicate more specific outcomes of social sciences education rather than broad general goals which are sought in the total educational program. A second change may be noted in the emphasis on conceptual and inquiry outcomes that are directly related to foundation disciplines. A third change may be noted in the emphasis on contributions that a solid grounding in concepts and methods of inquiry can make to citizenship education as opposed to approaches based on citizenship activities in which foundational concepts may be neglected. In short, objectives of instruction are clearly focused on intellectual outcomes, as shown in the following statements which have been summarized from current projects and recently prepared programs. One may get a feeling for the flavor of recently stated objectives from the two summaries that are given. The first is a statement of objectives that appear to be common to many programs (Michaelis, 1965). The second contains abbreviated statements of objectives adapted from a sampling of current projects.

Objectives Common to Many Programs

To develop understanding of key concepts, generalizations, and themes in a form that gives a sense of structure to history and the social sciences

To develop competence in using methods of inquiry that are drawn from the disciplines and are most useful in lifelong learning

To develop the basic skills needed to use conceptual systems and modes of inquiry in studying social sciences materials

To develop attitudes of objectivity, thoughtful skepticism, regard for evidence, open-mindedness, and respect for differing viewpoints

To develop favorable attitudes toward and appreciations of history and the social sciences as fields of inquiry

Objectives of Selected Programs

In the Greater Cleveland program (1965) attention is given to the intellectual capabilities, attitudes, and behavior patterns needed to function in a free democratic society, including:

> **Understanding of concepts from the disciplines, our culture and its relation to other cultures, and interdependence among individuals and groups**
>
> **Development of skills which facilitate learning, growth in critical thinking, and willingness to act consistently with the decisions reached**
>
> **Recognition of the importance of group action and the carrying out of related responsibilities**
>
> **Appreciation of our nation "extending the blessings of earned responsibility and freedom under law to other nations"**
>
> **Respect for other individuals and groups, their rights, views, and achievements**
>
> **Self-direction with self-understanding and concern for the welfare of others**

In the program of Educational Services Incorporated (1965) attention is given to the development of intellectual powers, key ideas and principles, and attitudinal outcomes, including:

> **Development of intellectual powers, such as mastery of self, disciplined taste, confidence in one's mental capabilities, respect for the power of thought**
>
> **Competence in the processes of generalizing, valuing, inquiring, and discovering and development of capacities and further appetite for learning**
>
> **Introduction of conceptual tools as such, insight into key ideas and principles, development of the student's ability to deal with modern conditions**
>
> **A view of history as a discipline which depends on and illustrates generalizations about human behavior**
>
> **Understanding of aspects of our heritage that have lasting significance and of forces that give shape to contemporary life**

In the materials for grade 4 (Bailey & Rice, 1965), specific objectives for anthropological studies are given, including:

> **Insight into how anthropologists study people**
>
> **Understanding of the culture concept**
>
> **Insight into cultural universals and variations**
>
> **How people learn cultural traits (enculturation) and how cultures change and grow (cultural dynamics)**

In a teaching guide on Japan (Michaelis, 1967), contributions to the objectives of social sciences education are outlined, including:

> **Understanding of the geography, history, and culture of Japan, deeper insight into our own culture through comparative study of another, and recognition of interconnections among countries**
>
> **Competence in using such techniques of inquiry as content analysis, photo and map interpretation, and making cross-cultural comparisons**
>
> **Skill in questioning, hypothesizing, organizing data, and making generalizations**
>
> **Favorable attitudes toward and appreciations of different ways of living**
>
> **A grasp of general concepts and methods that can be used to study other cultures**

A COMPLETE PROGRAM

Two considerations are dominant in designing a complete program of instruction in social sciences education. The first is to view balance or completeness of the program in a K-12 context rather than in the context of separate elementary and secondary programs. The second is to check completeness in terms of the attention given to the foundation disciplines in units and courses. When these two are used together it is possible to design a program that has the following characteristics:

> **The themes and units suggested for different grades in the overall program include both the past and present, representative culture regions ranging from local to international, and key economic, political, and social conditions and problems.**
>
> **Concepts, generalizations, and themes are selected from all the foundation disciplines and used as appropriate in units and courses, with a spiral development from level to level.**
>
> **In some units and courses special attention is given to each discipline so that students can develop deeper insights into the conceptual structure and the methods of inquiry that are used.**
>
> **Opportunities are provided for students to use multidisciplinary approaches, for example, in area studies, in order to gain a more complete or cohesive view of a culture or region than they would obtain if a separate-discipline approach were used.**

In summary, a complete program includes content and methods of inquiry from all the foundation disciplines and provides opportunity for both separate-discipline and multidiscipline approaches, whichever is more appropriate in a given context. Examples of recently designed programs which illustrate completeness in the sense described above are given in the following pages.

SEQUENCES OF TOPICS AND UNITS

Organization of the social sciences instructional program has been affected in a number of ways by recent developments. The program in the early grades is being extended to include topics and units far beyond the immediate environment, e.g., families and communities around the world. Some programs for the middle grades include area studies, case studies, and aspects of history formerly included in later grades. Some programs in secondary schools include comparative political systems, world cultures, and capstone courses in which individual social sciences are studied in depth.

Table 8–1 contains an abstract of topics and units in four different programs and is illustrative of recent developments. (See p. 258.) Special attention should be given to several features of these programs. All of them draw material from history and the social sciences and appear to use both multidiscipline and single-discipline approaches. Economics and the behavioral sciences appear to receive greater attention than in the past. Planning across grades is evident in the two-year blocks on families, communities, culture regions, and Eastern and Western civilizations. Planning across several grades is evident in the strands represented by area studies and historical units at several levels. In addition to balance in terms of foundation disciplines, balance may be noted in the treatment of countries in both the East and the West.

TEACHING STRATEGIES

The current emphasis on inquiry in the instructional program is reflected in social sciences education in several ways. Permeating many new programs is an emphasis on discovery through active inquiry. Discovery through inquiry is provided in the use of various inquiry models and specific techniques of inquiry. A promising development is to guide inquiry by means of questions that are formulated on increasing levels of complexity. In addition, attention is given to strategies that are useful in attaining such objectives as developing an understanding of main ideas, developing key concepts, and developing basic skills. The following examples are illustrative of these new developments.

Inquiry Models

Various aspects of problem solving continue to be emphasized in discussions of teaching strategies based on inquiry models. For example, Bruner (1966) has recently discussed such aspects as defining the overall problem, formulating and testing hypotheses, and comparing the results of tests with some criterion. Accompanying these are such processes as problem finding, formulating questions, gathering and verifying data, organizing and interpreting data, and formulating conclusions. Notice how these and other aspects of problem solving are included in the models that follow.

A social science model. This model is widely used with minor variations in a number of current projects and curricula (Michaelis, 1963):

> **Finding and defining problems or issues**
> **Formulating hypotheses or questions to guide inquiry**
> **Gathering, evaluating, and organizing data**
> **Using data to test hypotheses and answer questions**
> **Formulating and checking conclusions**

A problems model. Similar in several respects is the following model that gives attention to action based on the conclusion or decision that has been made (McCutcheon, 1963):

> **Be aware of the existence of the problem.**
> **Define the problem specifically.**
> **Consider plans for studying the problem and taking action.**
> **Gather, organize, and interpret data.**
> **Formulate and test the conclusion or decision.**
> **Take action consistent with the conclusion or decision.**

An economics model. This model may be used to analyze economic and other problems in which choices must be made in light of various alternatives (National Task Force, 1961):

> **Define the problem, considering facts and issues and "where we are in relation to where we want to go."**
> **Clarify goals and place them in order of priority.**
> **Consider alternative ways of achieving goals.**
> **Analyze consequences of various alternatives, choosing the most effective.**

A history and social science model. The following simple four-step model has been used in a current project as a "mode of inquiry used by historians and social scientists" (Fenton & Good, 1965):

> **Developing hypotheses**
> **Asking the proper questions**

TABLE 8–1. Topics in Recently Developed Social Sciences Education Programs

Grade	New York City	New York State	Greater Cleveland	Minnesota Project
K	The Child in Home & School: Home, Family, & School in Other Cultures; Beginning Globe Study; Patriotism	Local Studies: Family & School, Social, Economic, & Political Organization; Geography; Patriotism	School, Family, Neighborhood; Globe Study; Children in Other Lands; The Five Senses in Thinking/Learning	Earth, Home of Man: Varied Resources, Many Peoples, Changes Made by Man, Our Global Earth
1	Changing Communities, How We Live Together; Families, Workers, Different Communities, Patriotism	Local Studies: Family & School Long Ago & Today; Villages, Cities & Farms Today; Geography; Patriotism	My School, How We Learn about Our World & Country; Great Americans, Explorers, Discoverers; Village in Japan	Families around the World: Chippewas, Hopi Family, Quechua of Peru, Family in Japan
2	How People Live & Work around the World: Community Organization; Communication & Transportation; Meeting Needs; Patriotism	Community Studies: Social, Economic, & Political Organization; Geography; Patriotism	Varied Communities: Own, Static & Dynamic Communities; Different Communities in the United States	Families around the World: Boston, 18th Century, Soviet in Moscow, Kibbutz in Israel, Hausa in Africa
3	How Man Lived in Other Times & Cultures: Desert, Plains, Forest, Mountains, Marine; Primitive & Developed; Early Urban Cultures	Community Studies: Desert, Northern Forest, Tropical Rain Forest, Mountain, Prairie Farming; Patriotism	Anglo-America: Geography, Exploration, Colonization, through Industrialization; Metropolitan America, Cleveland	Communities around the World: Own, Rural & Urban, Frontier Mining Town, Manus in New Guinea, Paris
4	American People & Leaders: How the U.S. Began & Grew, Discovery, Exploration to the Present	American People & Leaders: Discoverers & Explorers, Great Leaders in Government, Industry, etc.; Science, Rights; Patriotism	Story of Agriculture; Story of Industry; India: A Society in Transition (Area Study)	Communities around the World: (Economic Systems) Our Own, Soviet, Trobriand Islanders, Village in India
5	Western World, Geographic & Economic Studies: U.S., Canada, Latin America, & Europe	Major Culture Regions: Western Hemisphere; Geographic & Historical Introduction; U.S. Stressed; Canada & Latin America	Human Adventure: Ancient & Medieval Civilizations; The Middle East (Area Study)	Regional Studies: Case Studies of Cities in 4–5 Time Periods in U.S. and Latin America; Independent Study of Region in Africa
6	The Western World, Historical & Cultural Beginnings & Development; Geography, History, Government, Search for Freedom, Contributions	Major Culture Regions: Middle East, Western Europe, Eastern Europe; History, Geography, Social, Economic, & Political Aspects	Human Adventure: Early Modern History to Enlightenment, Later Modern to 1918; Latin America (Area Study)	Foundation of American Society: Indian America, Colonization, Revolution, through Reconstruction

7	American History; Colonial Times to Present; Geographic & Political Settings; Development of Democratic Government & Society; Movement of People	Our Cultural Heritage: The Americas, Pre-Columbian through Colonial; New York State from Early Period to Megalopolis; Local & State Government	Intermediate Geography; Area Study of Africa; Human Adventure—Our Contemporary World; The Far East—China & Japan; Geography of North America	Man & Culture: Biological Bases of Behavior; How We Become Human; The Family (An Institution); The School (Another Institution); Minority-group Problems
8	Urban Growth, Challenges of a Changing Society: Here and Abroad; New York City Area & State; Federal-State Relations	United States History: The New Nation, National Period, Jackson, Division and Reunion, Economic Growth, World Power; U.S. Government	American History: To 1790, 1790–1865; 1865–1918; Since 1918; Exploration, Colonization through Present Period	Our Political System: Need for Government & Law; Political Parties & Elections; Legislative; Executive; Judicial; Intergovernmental Relations; Local Decision Making (Case Studies)
9	Eastern Civilization, Regional Studies: Middle East, Africa–North, South of Sahara, India, China, Japan, USSR–Linking East & West	Asian & African Culture Studies: World Cultures Today; Africa; India & Pakistan; China; Japan; Southeast Asia	Comparative Economic & Political Systems; Parallel Study in Geography & Anthropology; Research & Problems Unit	Our Economic System & Socioeconomic Problems; Economic Ideas Related to Topics & Problems; Role of Government & Political Process
10	Western Civilization, History & Culture: Europe from Renaissance to National States; Industrialization, Democracy, Nationalism, East-West Relations, War, 20th Century, Problems	Modern World History: Europe—Heritage, Emergence; Rise of Democracy; Industrialism, Nationalism; Colonialism; Conflicting Ideologies & 20th Century Conflict; Europe in Mid-20th Century	International Politics & Economics; Review of History of Civilization; Philosophy and Religion I; Research & Problems Unit	American History: Colonial Age; Republican Age, Democratic Age; Civil War, Reconstruction, Modern America: Industrialization, U.S. as World Power
11	American History (American Studies): Government, Foreign Policy, Selected Institutions, Optional Topics	American History (Studies): The People; Government & Politics; Economic Life; World Affairs; American Civilization in Perspective	Economics & Sociology; History of Civilization; Philosophy and Religion II; Research & Problems Unit	Area Studies: Western Europe, USSR, China, India; Multidisciplinary; Cultural Values; Relations to U.S.
12	First Term: Economics; Second Term: One course: Problems; Advanced Placement Course; Behavioral Sciences; Geography; Asian, African, or Latin Am. Studies; Metropolitan Studies	Specialized Courses: Economics, Government; Others —Asian, African, Latin Am. Studies; Anthropology, Psychology, Sociology; Great Issues; Middle East, Advanced Placement Courses	American Government, Special Reference to Supreme Court Decisions; Research & Problems Unit (e.g., Power Politics, Revolutions, Race Relations, Pressure Groups, Education, etc.)	Value Conflicts & Policy Decisions: Security & Freedom; Underdeveloped Countries; Racial Discrimination; Economic Growth in U.S.; South Africa; War & Peace; What Is the Good Life?

> **Uncovering the relevant data**
> **Validating, modifying, or rejecting the original hypothesis**

Models such as these are helpful if used as flexible guides to inquiry; they should not be viewed as rigid, step-by-step procedures. They are general plans for guiding inquiry that should be modified to fit problems and issues under study. They are also helpful in putting specific methods of inquiry listed in the next section into a meaningful pattern.

Specific Techniques of Inquiry

Involved in the inquiry models presented above are specific techniques of inquiry that are used to gather, process, and organize data. These techniques are drawn from the disciplines and used in ways that are consistent with their use by historians and social scientists. In considering specific techniques, one must rememher that questions or hypotheses should be formulated prior to data gathering and that each technique should be an integral part of the inquiry process. The following may be found in new projects and curricula:

Analyzing source materials	Simulating decision-making
Doing field studies	processes
Examining artifacts	Role playing
Using autobiographies	Interpreting maps and
and diaries	photographs
Interviewing specialists	Interpreting graphs, tables,
Making case studies	charts
Observing political and	Interpreting models made by
other activities	others
Taking polls on issues	Making and analyzing
Using questionnaires	recordings
Keeping logs and diaries	Making maps, charts, graphs
Analyzing models	Making models

A strategy for developing competence in using techniques of inquiry. Direct attention should be given to the development of the competencies needed to use the techniques of inquiry listed above. Detailed suggestions are included in the references at the end of this chapter. The following example is indicative of the basic considerations that are important in using any specific technique of inquiry:

> 1. **Be sure that the problem is clear and that questions or hypotheses are in mind to guide the collection of data.**
> 2. **Plan in detail the steps of procedure that are to be followed as the technique is used. For example, one group used the following procedure to carry out interviews: (*a*) Introduce**

yourself. (*b*) Tell the purpose of the interview. (*c*) Ask questions in order. (*d*) Give the other person time to answer. (*e*) Take notes on hard points. (*f*) Ask questions on special points. (*g*) Express thanks when finished (Michaelis, 1963).

3. Organize the information in relation to the questions or hypotheses. Evaluate use of the technique, noting strengths and weaknesses.

4. Note needs for additional information, gathering and organizing it to fill the gaps.

5. Make and test conclusions, noting and assessing the contributions of each technique that was used. Consider ways in which the use of each technique can be improved and situations in which each is most useful.

Inquiry Guided by Questions on Varying Levels of Complexity

Inquiry is guided in many new projects and curricula through skillful questioning on the part of the teacher. The essence of this strategy is to use questions in a sequence that raises thinking, study, and discussion to higher and higher levels. Bloom's *Taxonomy of Educational Objectives: Cognitive Domain* (1956) may be used as a guide to formulate questions that range from the knowledge level to the evaluation level (Sanders, 1960). Questions are devised on each level and fitted into unit and lesson plans in a sequence that provides for the intake and comprehension of ideas and moves to the application and evaluation of ideas, as shown in the following example:

Knowledge level: What does fiord mean? How can we find out about the importance of fiords in Norway?

Comprehension level: Can you tell in your own words why fiords are important in Norway? How can we organize the information on fiords to show their importance? How are they used by seamen?

Application level: How can we use maps to show the use of fiords in shipping? What changes may come in the use of fiords as air transport increases?

Analysis level: What key ideas on fiords are presented in this report? What difficulties and problems arise in using fiords for shipping?

Synthesis level: How can we show on a mural (or in a report) the importance of fiords in Norway? What conclusions can be made about the economic values of fiords?

Evaluation level: What correct ideas about fiords are in this film? How can our reports be improved?

Similar questions may be devised on other topics and problems. The principle to keep in mind is that questions should be on increasing levels of complexity. A common pitfall is to use questions on the knowledge level only, failing to move to higher levels. Yet it should be recognized that higher levels cannot be reached if students do not know basic facts or do not comprehend key concepts. By starting with questions on the first two levels, teachers can proceed to higher levels at a pace that is consistent with capabilities of students in the class. Preplanning of questions on all levels is a safeguard that can be used to guide inquiry in the most profitable directions.

A Strategy for Inductive Development of Main Ideas

Widely used in several recently developed programs is a strategy for leading students to develop a grasp of main ideas (Michaelis, 1966). A sequence is planned that builds upon students' backgrounds of understanding and moves to higher levels of conceptualization and generalization. Each unit is built around several main ideas that include key concepts (Taba & Hills, 1965). The students are guided toward the development of a main idea through a sequence of learning experiences that begins with *openers* in which students recall related ideas, clarify the problem, and lay a foundation for subsequent activities. Next, *developmental* learning experiences are provided, leading to the development of the main idea. Third, *concluding* experiences are provided for relating and interpreting what has been learned and for formulating generalizations. The following summary is illustrative:

> *Main idea*: **Land, labor, and capital are needed to produce goods.**
>
> *Opener*: **Ask, "What does a person need to run a dairy farm?" List responses and have children group those which go together (e.g., tools and equipment, workers, land).**
>
> *Development*: **Show filmstrips on dairy farms, gathering ideas on the work of the dairy farmer, materials used, etc.**
> **Visit a dairy farm to gather additional information.**
> **Read stories and interpret photographs to find more data on: How is milk produced?**
> **Provide a variety of other experiences related to the main idea.**
>
> *Conclusion*: **Plan and complete an illustrated story about what is needed to run a dairy farm.**
> **Identify and discuss what might be needed on any farm.**
> **Arrange picture displays under such a heading as, To Produce Goods Farmers Need These. . . .**

Included in the main idea approach is specific attention to such cognitive processes as conceptualizing, interpreting, inferring, and generalizing. Concept attainment is promoted through questions and discussion that help students discriminate common elements and group related items together. Inferring, interpreting, and generalizing are facilitated by having students contrast, compare, and relate ideas. Predictions, explanations, and conclusions may be drawn as ideas are contrasted, compared, and interpreted.

A Concept Development Strategy

A somewhat different teaching strategy may be noted in approaches in which emphasis is given to concept building. Direct instruction is provided to develop understanding of selected concepts; generalizations are formulated as the concepts are grasped and brought together in meaningful statements. For example, in a recently developed economics program (Senesh, 1964) specific purposes are outlined for each lesson. Recordings, stories, films, and other materials are used to build meaning of the concepts. Activities are provided by means of which the concepts can be reinforced, put to use, and discovered in new contexts. The following summary of one lesson is illustrative:

> *Purposes*: **To develop an understanding of division of labor and how dividing the work improves output, promotes specialization, and increases interdependence.**
>
> *Development of concepts*: **Play the recording of "Pelle's New Suit" as children look at pictures showing wool shearing, the making of yarn and cloth, and the tailoring of Pelle's suit.**
> **Ask: Why couldn't Pelle make the suit? What did each worker do? Was each one good at his job? How did they depend on one another? How did Pelle and his grandmother divide the work?**
> **Discuss dividing the work at home, e.g., jobs of mother, father, children.**
> **Carry out an experiment in which several individual children do a job while a like number of other children do the same job on an assembly line (e.g., assembling and stapling dittoed picture sets, making paper clothes, or making cookies). Keep a record of the output of each group. Discuss why the assembly-line group produced more, how each child did one special job, and how they depended on one another.**
> **Discuss specialization and interdependence in the home, school, and neighborhood.**
> **Summarize and conclude by having the group discuss pictures that show division of labor. Make a list of special jobs of**

workers in home, school, and neighborhood, and point out how interdependence is increased.

A Skill-development Strategy

The full range of basic skills may be found in recently developed programs. Two major tasks are (1) to adapt skills developed in language arts and arithmetic, and (2) to develop map-reading and other skills that are within the domain of social sciences education (Carpenter, 1963). The example that follows illustrates strategies that may be used to develop basic skills. Notice that key concepts, a fundamental aspect of skill development in social sciences education, are a part of the example.

Reading to find concept clusters. Skill in reading to find concept clusters is related to such key skills of comprehension as reading to find the main idea and other pertinent details. Opportunities to find and use concept clusters is important because of the many ways students can use the clusters to gather and organize data, to make comparisons, and to analyze material. The following example is related to a study of South America in which comparisons are made with North America; it may be generalized to other areas.

> *Purpose:* To find the concept cluster "major landforms" and to use it in comparing land features of North and South America.
>
> *Procedures:*
> Ask: What are the main landforms of our country? Can you recall them from your study of the United States? Which of these are also found in Canada? In Mexico?
> List responses on the chalkboard. Include all responses, such as valleys, hills, cliffs, and others, even though some of them are not major landforms.
> After the list is made, ask the class to indicate the responses they think are major landforms. Use their suggestions as hypotheses to guide reading.
> Have the class check reading materials to find major landforms (hills, plains, plateaus, mountains) in South America. Discuss the difference between major and minor landforms. Compare major landforms of North and South America.

GUIDELINES FOR THE TEACHER

The teacher has an inquiry-oriented role to play in new programs of social sciences education. The strategies noted above are illustrative of key aspects of the teacher's role. To be sure, teaching styles vary greatly and most teachers employ a combination of strategies and approaches ranging from inductive and discovery methods to straightforward development of key concepts and main ideas. In spite of variations in style and use of various strategies, the following guidelines appear to be in the forefront in new projects and curricula.

Plan and use teaching strategies that are consistent with the modes of inquiry used in history and the social sciences. For example, economists and other scholars typically associate rather precise meanings with concepts, and the meanings may vary widely from popular usage. Historians and geographers may organize data into various periods and regions. Sociologists, anthropologists, and economists tend to use concepts and concept clusters as organizing centers. Historians tend to deal primarily with themes and generalizations related to particular events, while social scientists deal primarily with generalizations that cut across societies and cultures.

Provide opportunities for students to use models and techniques of inquiry drawn from the disciplines. Help students grow in the ability to select models and techniques that are most useful in different situations. Although primary attention may be given to critical reading and analysis of source materials, provide for the study of pictorial, graphic, and other resources. Go beyond the analysis of content as prepared by others and presented in textbooks, films, and other media to original content production based on interviews, direct observation of activities, field trips, simulation, and other techniques.

Use questions formulated on varying levels of complexity to guide inquiry. Bear in mind that questions are needed on the knowledge and comprehension level to assure adequate foundations of understanding. Proceed to higher levels in a sequence and at a pace that suits the capabilities of students in the class. Help students learn to formulate questions on varying levels of complexity so that they will become increasingly independent learners.

Keep attention focused on concepts, themes, and main ideas around which content can be organized. Avoid fact gathering and isolated learning of unrelated details. Guide students to organize and classify information within periods or regions or around themes and concepts. Modes of organizing data employed by historians and social scientists should be used consistently to help students develop an ever-growing understanding of the structure of key concepts and ideas in history and the social sciences.

Give special attention to concept clusters as guides to study and original inquiry. Use them to organize information, make comparisons, and formulate generalizations. For example, the cluster "major landforms: plains, hills, plateaus, and mountains" can be used to formulate questions, gather data, compare countries, and make generalizations as the United

States, India, China, Japan, and other countries are studied. The cluster "factors in production: land, labor, capital, and entrepreneurship (know-how)" may be used as economic problems are studied in the community, state, nation, and other lands. Students themselves should discover concept clusters and link them to others in cognitive maps that are a part of their grasp of the underlying structure of the social sciences.

Develop the basic study skills that are essential to a high level of mastery of methods of inquiry. Basic skills of importance in social sciences education and in other subjects include locating, organizing, and evaluating information, reading, listening, observing, communicating in oral and written form, interpreting pictures, charts, graphs, and tables, and working with others. Skills which should be developed in social sciences education include reading social sciences material, applying thinking processes to social issues and problems, interpreting maps and globes, and understanding time and chronology. The foregoing skills are put to many uses as methods of inquiry are employed in the social sciences and in history.

Select instructional resources in relation to concepts, themes, and main ideas to be developed and individual differences among students. Use textbooks to give an overview, to place depth studies in a broad context, and to summarize key ideas. Select source materials to illustrate pertinent points and to provide opportunities for students to gain experience in analyzing and interpreting original resources. Select audio-visual materials for their content value as well as their aesthetic value. For example, a realistic portrayal of a street scene may be more informative than an artistically executed landscape. Make extensive use of library materials in both group and individual study activities. Provide guides to readings and have students locate additional materials in relation to selected themes, concepts, and main ideas. Use instructional media, including original source materials, at the time they will contribute maximally to the development of particular points under study. Be constructively critical of instructional materials and provide opportunities for students to discover strengths and limitations of different materials.

EVALUATION OF OUTCOMES OF INSTRUCTION

Promising developments in evaluation include the use of basic principles and techniques in innovative ways, the use of a mix of subjective-informal and objective-formal techniques, systematic use of taxonomies of objectives, and appraisal of the program of instruction in terms of criteria as well as assessments of students' learning. Increased attention is being given to the appraisal of conceptual outcomes and processes of inquiry. Direct observation of students in discussion and other activities continues to be a primary means of gathering evaluative data. Evaluation is being made an integral part of instruction in new project materials. Self-evaluation on an individual and group basis is an important part of the inquiry and discovery approach that should begin with initial exploration of problems and hypotheses and extend through the formulation and checking of conclusions.

Critical need continues to exist for the development of instruments that can be used to systematically appraise basic outcomes associated with the study of history and the social sciences. This need has been met in part by the inclusion of evaluative questions and/or items in teaching guides and students' materials (Michaelis, 1965).

In the sections that follow attention is focused on (1) basic principles and techniques that may be used throughout the instructional program, (2) taxonomies that may be used to improve evaluation, and (3) criteria for evaluating the instructional program. The end-of-chapter references contain additional suggestions on ways of meeting common problems that arise in evaluating outcomes of instruction.

Basic Principles and Techniques

Several fundamental principles are useful as guidelines for evaluating outcomes of social sciences education (Michaelis, 1963). Evaluation should be planned as an integral and continuing part of instruction, beginning with initial planning and continuing through unit and course assessments. Of critical importance is the keeping of purposes of instruction in sharp focus during all phases of evaluation. Cooperative evaluation involving teachers, curriculum specialists, and experts from the disciplines is characteristic of many programs. Self-evaluation by students themselves is important in relation to concept attainment, use of modes and techniques of inquiry, development of skills, and changes in attitudes and values.

A variety of techniques and devices may be used to assess outcomes of instruction. It is useful to view techniques in two broad categories, as follows:

> *Subjective-informal*: **observation, discussion, group interviews, individual interviews, logs, diaries, charts, check lists, rating sheets, anecdotal records, examination of students' work**

> *Objective-formal*: **standardized tests, teacher-made tests, student-made tests, raing scales, attitude inventories**

A mix of subjective-informal and objective-formal techniques is typically used to assess basic purposes. A primary reason for using such a mix is that many outcomes are best appraised by a combination of devices ranging from observation of behavior to testing. Included in the following summary are specific techniques related to each of the major purposes of social sciences education.

> *Information, concepts, generalizations*: tests, samples of work, check lists, observation of use in various situations, interviews
>
> *Models and techniques of inquiry*: discussion, samples of work, charts showing inquiry models, interviews
>
> *Basic skills*: tests, samples of work, observation of use in various situations, check lists, discussion
>
> *Values and attitudes*: discussion, observation of behavior, inventories, rating devices, anecdotal records

Techniques such as those listed above can be improved by using taxonomies of objectives as shown in the following section.

Using the Taxonomies to Improve Evaluation

The taxonomies of educational objectives (Bloom, 1956; Krathwohl, Bloom, & Masia, 1964) are helpful guides to the planning of questions and items for use in evaluation. Questions on different levels may be used in interviews, discussions, and other situations to assess outcomes of instruction. Test items may be prepared and developed to fit units of study. The following examples are illustrative of questions and items on the various levels of the taxonomies.

Cognitive Domain

> *Knowledge level*: What are the major landforms?
>
> Draw a line under each of the following that is a major landform: plains, cliffs, plateaus, hills, valleys, mountains.
>
> *Comprehension level*: Can you explain the meaning of nuclear family?
>
> A nuclear family includes *A*. Parents and their children, *B*. Parents only, *C*. Parents, children, and cousins, *D*. All people related to the parents.
>
> *Application level*: How can we use the concept cluster "major landforms" to compare our country and Brazil?
>
> Read the paragraphs below and use the concept cluster "major landforms" to find the landforms common to both Brazil and

our country. (Provide paragraphs that present data on land-forms in both countries.)

Analysis level: Why has Japan become a leading industrial nation even though she is not richly endowed with natural resources?

Analyze Japan's productive capacity in terms of the concept cluster "factors of production: resources, labor, capital, and management."

Synthesis level: What shall we include in our reports on Japan?

Formulate original hypotheses about production possibilities in Japan after you have studied the tables and charts on the chalkboard. (Provide tables and charts on factors of production.)

Evaluation level: How can we improve our reports on Japan's arts and crafts?

Which of the following are most important in improving our discussions? *A*. Clarifying the topic, *B*. Speaking clearly, *C*. Taking turns, *D*. Preparing ahead of time, *E*. Making a good summary.

Affective Domain

Receiving (attending) level: Did you notice any instances in which we did not listen to the views of others?

List three ways you can show respect for the views of others.

Responding level: What parts of the story of the fishing village were most interesting?

Make a check by each of the following that you enjoy doing in class:

————Reading stories about people in Japan
————Discussing stories with others
————Finding out about the author
————Telling about the author

Valuing level: Did you feel that you should do something to help the fisherman's family? Tell about it.

Make a check by each of the following that you try to do to understand Japanese ways of life:

————Think of what I would do if I lived there
————Find the reasons why they eat and dress as they do
————Try to understand why their holidays are important to them
————Find out why they do other things the way they do

Organization level: Why should we judge people in different areas in terms of the behavior of individuals?

Which of the following pictures and cartoons present stereotypes of the Japanese that you find objectionable? Tell why. (Present pictures and cartoons and have students find and tell about stereotypes.)

EVALUATION OF THE INSTRUCTIONAL PROGRAM

In addition to using data gathered from tests and analyses of students' work, teachers may use various criteria to appraise the instructional program. The following are directly related to new trends and developments in social sciences education:

Foundations
Are history and the social sciences used as primary sources of content and processes of inquiry?
Is direct attention given to human problems and societal conditions?
Is knowledge of child development and learning used to facilitate instruction?

Structure
Are overall conceptual structures of history and the social sciences defined in terms of themes, concepts, concept clusters, and/or generalizations?
Are conceptual structures in units and courses clearly defined?

Inquiry
Are models of inquiry identified and used flexibly in instruction?
Are techniques of inquiry incorporated in units and courses?

Purposes
Are purposes behaviorally defined in relation to:
Knowledge, concepts, concept clusters, generalizations?
Models and techniques of inquiry?
Basic skills needed for inquiry?
Attitudes, values, appreciations?

A complete program
Is the program balanced in terms of the overall K-12 sequence?
Is the program balanced in terms of adequacy of attention to foundation disciplines?

Teaching strategies

Are active inquiry and discovery by students provided in ways that are consistent with styles of thought employed in the foundation disciplines?

Are different approaches used, depending upon purposes of instruction and the disciplines being given primary emphasis?

Are models and techniques of inquiry incorporated in teaching strategies?

Are various instructional media selected and used to further inquiry?

Evaluation

Is evaluation an integral part of instruction conducted by teachers with the assistance of specialists?

Are devices and items designed on various levels of complexity to assess all outcomes of instruction?

Is self-evaluation a basic part of the program?

Teacher education

Is continuing growth of teachers provided through varied in-service activities that are related to foundation disciplines as well as new curriculum developments?

Are teachers directly involved in selecting, planning, and trying new approaches?

Are consultant services available to teachers?

Continuing revision

Is provision made for ongoing revision of the program in order to incorporate new ideas from the disciplines and from new curriculum developments?

Are systematic efforts made to identify and assess new developments as the program is improved?

REFERENCES

Bailey, Wilfred, & Rice, Marion J. *Development of a sequential curriculum in anthropology for grades 1–7.* Athens, Ga.: University of Georgia, 1965. Basic units and teaching guides.

Bloom, Benjamin S. (Ed.) *Taxonomy of educational objectives: cognitive domain.* N.Y.: McKay, 1956. A classification of objectives according to level of complexity.

Bruner, Jerome. *Toward a theory of instruction.* Cambridge, Mass.: Harvard, 1966. Description of a pilot course in chap. 4.

Buros, Oscar K. *The sixth mental measurements yearbook.* Highland Park, N.J.: Gryphon Press, 1965. Information on achievement tests in social studies published between 1959 and 1964; reviews of earlier tests in preceding volumes.

California. *Social studies framework for the public schools of California.* Sacramento: State Department of Education, 1962. Outline of a K-12 program; listing of generalizations from eight disciplines.

Carpenter, Helen M. (Ed.) *Skill development in social studies.* Thirty-third Yearbook, National Council for the Social Studies. Washington, D.C.: National Education Association, 1963. Principles and procedures for developing the full range of skills used in the social studies.

Clements, H. Millard, Fielder, W. R., & Tabachnick, B. R. *Social study: inquiry in classrooms.* Indianapolis: Bobbs-Merrill, 1966. Readings on history and other topics in part IV.

Dunfee, Maxine, & Sagl, Helen. *Social studies through problem solving.* New York: Holt, 1966. Description of the traditional problem-solving approach.

Educational Services Incorporated. *Research and development in the social studies.* Watertown, Mass., 1965. Mimeographed report on units in history and the social sciences.

Fenton, Edwin, & Good, John. *A high school social studies curriculum for able students.* Pittsburgh, Pa.: Carnegie Institute of Technology, 1965. Course materials for students and teachers.

Greater Cleveland Educational Research Council. *Social science program.* Cleveland, Rockefeller Building, 1965. Teaching guides and students' materials.

Hill, Wilhelmina. (Ed.) *Curriculum guide for geographic education.* Normal, Ill.: NCGE Publications Center, Illinois State Normal University, 1962. Suggestions for a K-12 program of instruction.

Jarolimek, John. *Social studies in elementary education.* New York: Macmillan, 1967. Principles and procedures for social studies instruction.

Joyce, Bruce. *Strategies for elementary social science education.* Chicago: Science Research Associates, 1965. Methods of teaching and other topics.

Krathwohl, David R., Bloom, Benjamin S., & Masia, Bertram S. *Taxonomy of educational objectives: affective domain.* New York: McKay, 1964. A classification of objectives according to degree of internalization.

Lee, John R., & McLendon, Jonathon C. *Readings on elementary social studies.* Boston: Allyn and Bacon, 1965. Selections on foundation disciplines, curriculum planning, and methods and materials of instruction.

McCutcheon, Samuel P. "A discipline for the social studies," *Social Education,* February, 1963, 27, 61–65.

Michaelis, John U. *Social studies for children in a democracy.* Englewood Cliffs, N.J.: Prentice-Hall, 1963. New trends and developments in various phases of social studies instruction.

Michaelis, John U. The social studies. *New curriculum developments.* Washington, D.C.: Association for Supervision and Curriculum Development, 1965. Review of current projects.

Michaelis, John U. *Teaching units based on the social sciences.* Chicago: Rand McNally, 1966. Three paperback volumes containing units of study for grades K-2, 3–4, and 5–6.

Michaelis, John U. *Changing Japan*. Berkeley: Asian Studies Project, Department of Education, University of California, 1967. A unit of instruction for the middle grades.

Michaelis, John U., & Johnston, A. Montgomery. *The social sciences: foundations of the social studies*. Boston: Allyn and Bacon, 1965. Nature of eight foundation disciplines and a review of new projects and developments.

Morrissett, Irving. (Ed.) *Concepts and structure in the new social science curricula*. Lafayette, Ind.: Social Science Education Consortium, 1966. Examples of structure given for economics, history, geography, and political science.

Muessig, Raymond H., & Rogers, Vincent R. *Social science seminar series*. Columbus, Ohio: Charles E. Merrill Books, Inc., 1965. Six booklets on the nature of various disciplines.

National Task Force on Economic Education. *Economic education in the schools*. New York: Joint Council on Economic Education, 1961. Recommended concepts and policies for providing instruction on economics.

New York City. A history and social studies curriculum for the future, *Curric. & Mat.*, Fall, 1965, **20**, 1–7. Generalizations from disciplines and an outline of a K-12 program.

New York State. *Tentative flowchart of the elementary social studies program*. Albany: State Education Department, 1965. Sequence of themes and topics for grades K-6.

Phenix, Philip H. *Realms of meaning*. New York: McGraw-Hall, 1964. A philosophy of curriculum development with sections on history and social sciences.

Price, Roy, Hickman, Warren, & Smith, Gerald. *Major concepts for social studies*. Syracuse, N.Y.: Social Studies Curriculum Center, University of Syracuse, 1965. Thirty-four substantive, value, and methodological concepts for use in curriculum planning.

Rader, William D. *Elementary school economics program*. Chicago: Industrial Relations Center, University of Chicago, 1964. Reading materials for students and guides for teachers.

Sanders, Norris M. *Classroom questions*. New York: Harper, 1966. Questions for each level of the taxonomy of objectives.

Senesh, Lawrence. *Organizing a curriculum around social science concepts*. Lafayette, Ind.: Social Science Education Consortium, Purdue University, 1966. Outlines of the structure of five disciplines.

Soc. Educ., April, 1965, **30**, 228–281. Entire issue devoted to economic education.

Taba, Hilda, and Hills, James L. *Teacher handbook for Contra Costa social studies, grades 1–6*. San Francisco: San Francisco State College, 1965. Rationale of a program in which main ideas are stressed.

West, Edith. *Preparation and evaluation of social studies curriculum guides for grades K-14*. Minneapolis: University of Minnesota, 1965. Materials for teachers prepared in a current project.

Wisconsin State. *A scope and sequence plan for the social studies in Wisconsin schools.* Madison: State Department of Education, 1964. A list of generalizations from basic disciplines and outlines of units for a K-12 program.

CURRENT PROJECTS IN WHICH ELEMENTARY SCHOOL MATERIALS ARE BEING DEVELOPED

Civic Education Project. c/o Henry Toy, Jr., Council on Civic Education, 300 E. 33d Street, New York, N.Y.

Development of a Comprehensive Curriculum Model for Social Studies, Grades 1–8. c/o Hilda Taba, San Francisco State College, San Francisco, Calif.

Development of Guidelines and Resource Materials on Latin America for Use in Grades I–XII. c/o Clark Gill, College of Education, University of Texas, Austin, Tex.

The Development of Instructional Materials Pertaining to Racial and Cultural Diversity in America. c/o John S. Gibson, Tufts College, Medford, Mass.

Development of a Sequential Curriculum in Anthropology for Grades 1–7. c/o Wilfred Bailey and Marion J. Rice, College of Education and Department of Sociology and Anthropology, University of Georgia, Athens, Ga.

Elementary School Economics Program. c/o William D. Rader, Industrial Relations Center, University of Chicago, Chicago, Ill.

Elementary School Social Science Project. c/o Harold Berlak, Graduate Institute of Education, Washington University, St. Louis, Mo.

Elkhart Indiana Experiment in Economic Education. c/o Lawrence Senesh, Department of Economics, Purdue University, Lafayette, Ind. (Materials available from SRA.)

New Approaches to and Materials for a Sequential Curriculum on American Society. c/o John Lee, Social Studies Curriculum Study Center, Northwestern University, 1809 Chicago Avenue, Evanston, Ill.

Preparation and Evaluation of Social Studies Curriculum Guides and Materials for Grades K-14. c/o Edith West, College of Education, University of Minnesota, Minneapolis, Minn.

Preparation of Teaching Guides and Materials on Asian Countries for Grades I-XII. c/o John U. Michaelis, Department of Education, University of California, Berkeley, Calif.

A Program of Curriculum Development in the Social Studies and Humanities. c/o Elting E. Morison, Educational Services Incorporated, 108 Water Street, Watertown, Mass.

Social Science Program. c/o Raymond English, Educational Research Council of Greater Cleveland, Rockefeller Building, Cleveland, Ohio.

The Social Sciences Education Consortium. c/o Irving Morrissett, Department of Economics, Purdue University, Lafayette, Ind.

Chapter Nine

HEALTH EDUCATION

GOOD HEALTH HAS BEEN defined in the constitution of the World Health Organization of the United Nations as "a state of complete physical, mental and social well-being and not merely the absence of disease and infirmity." Good health involves the capacity, or inner strength, to meet a variety of situations. It is based not only on normal functioning of the body, but also upon an understanding of principles of healthful living, positive attitudes, adjustment to conditions in one's environment, and social and emotional health.

The need for health education is great. First of all, while the health of the American people has improved in the past few decades there is still need for specific attention to heart disease, mental disorders, cancer, physical fitness, dental problems, and the large number of accidental deaths that occur each year. Many individuals are the victims of misconceptions, superstitions, fads, and quackery. World-wide conditions are such that poor health conditions in one country can affect health standards in another. The high incidence of illness and disease in other parts of the world is a problem of importance everywhere. Modern concepts of good citizenship make it imperative that each person develop the competencies needed to maintain a high level of personal and community health.

The need for health education can also be considered in relation to the major purposes of education. Self-realization calls for the highest possible level of healthful living. Human relationships cannot be maintained on a high level unless personal and community health are given attention. Economic efficiency depends upon a broad program of healthful living involving the individual, his coworkers, and the community. Civic responsibility can reach a high level only if each person has the capacity to discharge the responsibilities that are guaranteed by our basic freedoms. The development of rational processes, a central purpose of education, is influenced by one's physical, social, and emotional well-being.

A COMPLETE SCHOOL HEALTH PROGRAM

Different aspects of a complete school health program are shown in Chart 9–1. The many links to national, state, and community health programs include ideas and services available from various public and private agencies. The four main facets of the school health program are coordinated so that learning, use of health services, and healthful school living are maximized. The foundation disciplines are drawn upon to improve all phases of the program.

Not shown in Chart 9–1 are the many different individuals involved in a complete health program. The instructional staff includes teachers and

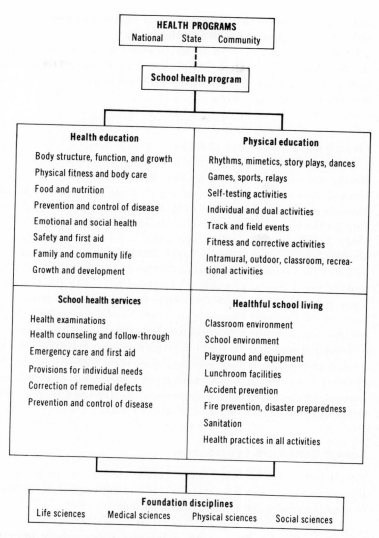

HEALTH PROGRAMS
National   State   Community

School health program

Health education

Body structure, function, and growth
Physical fitness and body care
Food and nutrition
Prevention and control of disease
Emotional and social health
Safety and first aid
Family and community life
Growth and development

Physical education

Rhythms, mimetics, story plays, dances
Games, sports, relays
Self-testing activities
Individual and dual activities
Track and field events
Fitness and corrective activities
Intramural, outdoor, classroom, recreational activities

School health services

Health examinations
Health counseling and follow-through
Emergency care and first aid
Provisions for individual needs
Correction of remedial defects
Prevention and control of disease

Healthful school living

Classroom environment
School environment
Playground and equipment
Lunchroom facilities
Accident prevention
Fire prevention, disaster preparedness
Sanitation
Health practices in all activities

Foundation disciplines
Life sciences   Medical sciences   Physical sciences   Social sciences

Chart 9–1.   A complete school health program.

coordinators or supervisors who are assisted at times by specialists. Specialists include the school physician, the school nurse, dentists, and dental hygienists. The school nutritionist and the custodial staff bring their competencies to bear upon selected aspects of the program. In some school systems members of the state or local health council and the health coordinator help to plan and coordinate the program and keep a close liaison with public and private health agencies.

Primary attention is given to health education in the remainder of this chapter. Physical education is considered in Chapter 10. Detailed information on school health services and healthful school living is contained in the end-of-chapter references.

FOUNDATION DISCIPLINES

Health education is rooted in medical sciences, life sciences, and social sciences as shown in the following examples. From medical sciences are drawn concepts and principles related to healthful living and care of the body, and data on the causes, treatment, and prevention of diseases. From studies of public health problems, safety, and accident prevention are drawn ideas related to family and community health practices, safety education, and other topics. From such life sciences as physiology, bacteriology, botany, and zoology are drawn concepts and principles related to the functions of organs, structure of the body, bacteria, fungi, poisonous plants, and other areas of instruction. From anthropology, sociology, psychology, political science, and other social sciences are drawn data and ideas related to health customs and traditions, cultural differences, health conditions and problems, legal requirements, human relations, individual differences, developmental characteristics, learning, and motivation. Like science education and social sciences education, health education may be classified as primarily in the realm of empirics as defined by Phenix (1964).

Concept Clusters and Generalizations

Health instruction is replete with concept clusters drawn from foundation disciplines. The following examples are illustrative of those typically found in teaching guides and instructional materials:

> *Physical needs*: **food, water, rest, sleep, activity, protection from disease, care of the body**

> *Social-emotional needs*: **acceptance, belonging, security, love, growing independence, intellectual stimulation, success, sense of worth, faith**

> *Basic food groups*: **meat, fish, poultry, eggs; cooked and raw vegetables and fruits; milk, cheese, butter, margarine; bread and cereals**

> *Food nutrients*: **proteins, fats, carbohydrates, vitamins, minerals**

Disease prevention and control: rest, food, cleanliness, immunization, examination, precautions, care during illness, causes of disease, use of medicines and drugs

Social-emotional health: self-respect, respect for others, acceptance of reality, self and group discipline, social skills and standards, being a leader and follower, individual and group problem solving, release of tensions through activity

Growth and development: individual differences, importance of diet, activity, and sleep, relationships with others, functioning of body systems of circulation, respiration, and elimination, body changes, effects of tobacco, alcohol, and narcotics

Community health: local conditions and problems, local, state, and national agencies, safety and health practices, contributions of leaders, careers

Illustrative of generalizations drawn from foundation disciplines are the following which are emphasized in units of study:

Personal appearance tends to affect the way we feel about ourselves and how others feel about us.

Nasal breathing filters and conditions the air we breathe.

Nutritional needs of the body can be met through the eating of basic foods.

Activity, rest, and sleep are essential to optimum health.

The organs of the body serve special functions yet work together as a unit.

Health habits are determined by a variety of personal, social, and economic factors.

Health needs are met through the family, other institutions, and individual activities.

Legal requirements have been established to promote safe and healthful living.

The services of specialists and agencies are essential to healthful living.

Individual and group efforts are needed to solve such current problems as air and water pollution.

OBJECTIVES OF HEALTH EDUCATION

The central goal of health education is the development of the optimum physical, mental, and social well-being of each student. Each individual should make steady growth in his ability to protect and to improve both personal and community health. Given below are specific objectives as reported in recent teaching guides.

Information, Concepts, Generalizations

Scientific knowledge, concepts, and generalizations constitute the basis for sound health practices. Specific purposes in the cognitive domain are to develop:

> **A concept of health as physical, social, and mental well-being**
>
> **Understanding of the contributions of knowledge and physical activity to physical fitness**
>
> **Understanding of the values of rest, sleep, exercise, cleanliness, grooming, recreation, a balanced diet, health habits, immunization, and care of one's body**
>
> **Knowledge of the structure and functioning of the body and the prevention and control of disease**
>
> **Understanding of individual and group responsibility in family, school, and community health**
>
> **Knowledge of principles and practices essential to safe living and to accident prevention**
>
> **Insight into individual differences and ways of maintaining mental and emotional health**

Attitudes, Appreciations, Interests

Affective outcomes are of primary importance in healthful living. The following are emphasized in all phases of the school health program:

> **An interest in finding out how one's own body functions, grows, and changes and can be used effectively in different activities**
>
> **Concern for oneself and for others coupled with a feeling of responsibility for the health and safety of oneself and others**
>
> **Appreciation of the contributions of scientists, doctors, dentists, nurses, and other health workers**
>
> **Appreciation of the importance of mental and social well-being as well as of physical well-being**
>
> **Appreciation of the role of the home, school, governmental agencies, and other groups in promoting healthful living**
>
> **A wholesome attitude toward health, safety, and physical activities**
>
> **An interest in and desire to practice good health and safety habits and to participate with other individuals and agencies in promoting good health for all**

Functional Skills and Habits

A major outcome of the health education program is the development of skills and habits that are consistent with scientific knowledge and positive attitudes. In fact, skills and habits cannot be separated from knowledge and attitudes except for purposes of discussion. Of central importance, therefore, are behavioral manifestations of cognitive and affective goals which can be used to help each student:

> **Use correct procedures in personal grooming and in caring for the face, hands, and fingernails.**
> **Select appropriate clothing and take proper care of it.**
> **Use effective methods in caring for the teeth, eyes, ears, nose, and throat.**
> **Practice sound habits of rest, relaxation, and sleep.**
> **Participate in active play and games and get adequate amounts of sunshine, fresh air, and exercise.**
> **Take precautions in avoiding disease and preventing the spread of disease.**
> **Use safety precautions in daily activities and take appropriate steps when accidents and emergencies occur.**
> **Select and eat balanced meals and abstain from the use of tobacco, alcohol, and narcotics.**
> **Put effective human relations skills to work and seek to improve his own mental health and that of others.**
> **Use his body effectively in various play and work situations and recognize his strengths and limitations.**
> **Use the services of health specialists and agencies, and respect health laws and regulations.**

STRUCTURE OF THE HEALTH EDUCATION CURRICULUM

Most current health education programs are structured in terms of major topics and related concepts and generalizations. A new development is to structure the program around conceptual statements which contain key concepts and integrate substantive elements. The substantive elements may be viewed as clusters of lower-order generalizations related to the conceptual statement, which is a higher-order generalization. Examples of both types of structure follow.

Structure in Terms of Topics and Related Concepts

Major topics and related concepts are used to define the structure of health instruction in many courses of study and in instructional materials for students. The underlying principle is to relate concepts and generalizations to those topics believed to be most important as organizing centers for instruction. The summary below includes topics widely used at the present time; each topic is followed by selected concepts to illustrate the content of units of study and instructional materials.

Body structure and functions: senses, organs, respiratory and other systems, glands, digestion, body changes, growth and development

Fitness: physical, mental, social, emotional, care of the body, posture

Cleanliness and grooming: care of the body, appearance, personal responsibility, personal and social values of grooming, values and customs

Care of eyes, ears, and nose: protection from foreign objects, need to keep fingers away, proper light and posture, listening and viewing habits

Rest and sleep: regular bedtime need for rest, relaxation and sleep, alternation of activity and rest or relaxation, signs of fatigue

Food and nutrition: regular eating habits, variety and balance in meals, cleanliness, basic foods, digestion, effects of emotions, weight control

Dental health: care of teeth, importance of food choices, regular dental care, structure and functions of teeth, prevention of decay, causes of decay

Prevention and control of disease: keeping objects and fingers out of mouth, examinations, health services and workers, immunization, symptoms, causes, spread and control of diseases, use of medicines and drugs

Mental health: responsibility to others, self-control, relations with others, solving individual and group problems, making choices, relation to physical condition, friendship, acceptance of others, facing reality

Family living: cleanliness, harmonious relations, roles, care of members, recreation, settling disputes, safety, concern for others

Community health: traffic, litter, use of fountains and rest rooms, control of pets, health workers and facilities, health agencies, health problems

Safety: home, pedestrian, playground, classroom, and other areas, fire drills, fire prevention, laws and regulations, physical activities, community, summer activities

A Structure Based on Key Concepts, Concepts, and Subconcepts

A structure for a kindergarten-grade 12 program has been outlined in a current health education project (Sliepcevich, 1966). The structure highlights the logical relationships among three basic elements—three key concepts, ten concepts (generalizations), and subconcepts. Notice in the following examples that the concepts are directly related to the key concepts and that physical, mental, and social dimensions are outlined for each statement. Behaviorally stated long-range goals related to three domains—cognitive, affective, and action—are also given for each concept.

KEY CONCEPT: GROWING AND DEVELOPING

Concept: **Growth and development influence and are influenced by the structure and function of the individual.**

Subconcept: **Body routines, environmental conditions, and use of certain substances are key factors. Physical dimensions include nutrition, rest, disease. Mental dimensions include affection, security, and other factors in personality development. Social dimensions include such sociocultural forces as poverty, disease, and lack of opportunity.**

Long-range goals: **Cognitive—The student knows that body parts and systems work together to affect development. Affective—The student recognizes the importance of feelings as factors in development. Action—The student improves personal body routines.**

KEY CONCEPT: INTERACTING

Concept: **There is a reciprocal relationship between man, disease, and environment.**

Subconcept: **Some diseases which impair health are caused by microorganisms. Physical dimensions include the effect of disease organisms on the structure and/or function of organs. Mental dimensions include the spread of diseases as related to conditions in the environment.**

Long-range goals: **Cognitive—The student knows that microorganisms cause some diseases. Affective—The student recognizes the need for social controls of many diseases. Action—The student seeks immunization as recommended by a physician.**

KEY CONCEPT: DECISION MAKING

Concept: **Personal health behavior is affected by often-conflicting forces.**

Subconcept: **Choices made by an individual affect well-being. Physical dimensions include personal health care, which influences appearance and well-being. Mental dimensions include attitudes and values related to health care. Social dimensions include the impact of group approval and acceptance on personal health care.**

Long-range goals: **Cognitive—The student knows that activity produces need for rest and relaxation. Affective—The student feels the need for balance among activity, rest, relaxation, and sleep. Action—The student appraises his personal health habits, retaining sound habits and eliminating unsound ones.**

The Structure in Units of Study

How the proposed structure of key concepts, concepts, and subconcepts is used in unit planning is shown in the following excerpts (Sliepcevich, 1966, pp. 6–10). The first section includes an example of a key concept, a concept, subconcepts, and related goals that are used to guide planning and teaching. This is followed by excerpts from a teaching-learning guide designed for use in level I (primary grades) of the progression sequence. Next is given an example drawn from a teaching guide for level II (middle grades). Notice that the same basic ideas are brought to higher levels of development in the middle grades.

SEQUENTIAL DEVELOPMENT OF CONCEPTS

Sequential development of concepts is handled in two important ways. The first provides for continuing instruction from grade to grade on each of the major topics that serve as strands for defining the structure of the program. The second provides for a cycling of units of study in different grades so that students have recurring encounters with key concepts on succeedingly higher levels of complexity.

Level-to-level Sequencing

The following examples show how there is a buildup from level to level for three selected topics:

Body functions and structure. In the early grades attention is given to the senses of sight, hearing, touch, and taste, functions of the teeth, need for activity, rest, relaxation, and exercise, height and weight differences, and the contributions of foods. In grades 2 and 3 new material is introduced on the senses, teeth, body needs, height and weight gains,

Growing and Developing   Interacting   Decision-Making

Concept: UTILIZATION OF HEALTH INFORMATION, PRODUCTS, AND SERVICES IS GUIDED BY VALUES AND PERCEPTIONS

Subconcepts	Dimensions		
	Physical	*Mental*	*Social*
1. APPRAISAL, SELECTION, AND USE OF HEALTH INFORMATION, PRODUCTS, AND SERVICES ARE INFLUENCED BY ONE'S PAST EXPERIENCES AND THE ENVIRONMENT	One's past or present state of health (e.g., body structure and function, freedom from disease and disorders, progress toward attainment and maintenance of optimal health, and general level of wellness).	Feelings about and emotional reactions to health information, products, and services (e.g., indifference or misconceptions); perceptions and interpretations of past experiences (e.g., recall of pain associated with a visit to the dentist or the degree of confidence one has in a medical advisor).	Values of family, economic and educational status, and effects of communication media and health education experiences.
2. SOURCES AND EVALUATION OF HEALTH INFORMATION, PRODUCTS, AND SERVICES INFLUENCE THEIR SELECTION AND USE.	Use of criteria in selection of health information, products, and services (scientific vs. nonscientific basis); the resulting effect on an individual's well-being (e.g., self-diagnosis and self-treatment, values of early diagnosis and treatment vs. dangers of delayed diagnosis and worthless treatment).	Emotional appeal as it influences the selection of health products and services (e.g., promise of easy and fast cures, emphasis on physical attractiveness or popularity with the opposite sex).	Organizations, agencies, and individuals that provide information and suggest criteria on which evaluation of health information, products, and services can be made (e.g., authoritative sources and sound criteria vs. unreliable sources and testimonials).

EXCERPTS FROM LEVEL I TEACHING LEARNING GUIDE

Behavioral objectives and content	*Teacher and student materials*
NAMES FAMILIAR PEOPLE WHO PROMOTE, PROTECT, AND MAINTAIN HEALTH 1. *Father and mother* and other family members such as grandparents and brothers and sisters, help to protect and maintain good health. 2. *School Workers,* such as the principal, teacher, cafeteria manager, and custodian, are interested in health and health protection. 3. *The Physician* spends many years going to school in order to help people to keep healthy and to take care of them when they are sick. 4. *The Dentist* goes to a special school to learn about the teeth and mouth and to find out how to treat people to keep their teeth in good condition. 5. *The Nurse* is specially trained to help physicians to take care of sick people. There are several different kinds of nurses, including those who work in schools. 6. *The Pharmacist* goes to a school where he learns about the things that go into medicine. He learns how to mix the medicine, and sells the medicine that the physician wants his patients to take. 7. *Specialists,* such as the eye doctor who learns all about eyes and how to help people take care of their eyes, help protect health. 8. *The Dental Hygienist* takes special courses so that she can assist the dentist in helping people to take care of their teeth.	Record references in this column pertinent to the content of each lesson from (1) selected titles on resource list; (2) student textbooks; and (3) supplementary references provided with guides.

Learning opportunities*	Evaluation procedures
Vocabulary	Observe attitudes toward personal visits to the physician, interview sessions and visitations to the class by outside people.

Vocabulary

cafeteria	medicine	prescription
custodian	nurse	promote
dentist	patient	protect
health	pharmacist	sickness
maintain	physician	specialist

Show a film on the physician. Discuss ways in which the physician is a friend. Use a committee to interview a physician to find out how long he had to study to become a doctor. Allow students to report committee findings to the class. (3)

Invite a dentist to talk to the class. Before he comes make a list of questions through class discussion to ask about his special training and work. (4)

Have students collect and display pictures of nurses on the bulletin board. Talk about ways the nurse helps the physician and those who are sick. Interview the school nurse in class. Ask her about her training and work. Let students draw pictures of nurses helping at school, nursing people, or helping a physician. (5)

Visit a drug store pharmacy. Talk to the pharmacist. Find out how he mixes medicines. Ask to see a prescription form and have the pharmacist explain how it is used. Find out what special training he needed in order to do his job. (6)

Use role playing to dramatize a mother and child visiting the eye doctor. Plan the scenes, choose the characters, and develop the props to be used as a class project. Discuss some of the reasons why the eye doctor and other specialists are important. (7)

Encourage students to make a health scrapbook, individually or in small groups. Have them collect and mount pictures, word lists, stories, and other documents pertaining to people who help promote, protect, and maintain health. (1–8)

Evaluation procedures

Observe attitudes toward personal visits to the physician, interview sessions and visitations to the class by outside people.

Check contents of the health scrapbooks and other written or construction work. Note outstanding individual work.

Observe student behavior and attitudes brought out in dramatic play, such as role playing and acting out experiences.

Construct and administer a knowledge test about familiar health advisors and something of their work. This might be done by matching pictures with descriptions as indicated:

Picture	Description
Physician	He takes care of us when we are sick.
Dentist	He helps to take care of our teeth.
Nurse	She assists the physician and his patients.
Pharmacist	He mixes medicine the physician wants patients to take.
Mother	She cares for the family at home.

* *The numbers in ( ) after each item are coded back to the "behavioral objectives and content" column.*

EXCERPTS FROM LEVEL II TEACHING LEARNING GUIDE

Behavioral objectives and content	*Teacher and student materials*
NAMES DIFFERENT MEDICAL, DENTAL, AND HEALTH SPECIALISTS AND IS AWARE OF THEIR ROLE IN HEALTH SERVICES.	Record references in this column pertinent to the content of each lesson from (1) selected titles on resource unit; (2) student textbooks; and (3) supplementary references provided with guides.

1. There are a number of related health professions that help to protect the consumer as well as various specializations within these professions.

2. Competent and ethical health advisors should be distinguished from those who are unreliable.

3. Medical, dental, and health specialists should be known and their role in health services:
   a. Dentist and oral hygienist
   b. General practitioner, obstetrician, and pediatrician
   c. Pharmacist
   d. Oculist, ophthalmologist, and optometrist
   e. Laboratory workers
   f. Public and school health nurses

4. Hospitals, clinics, and other facilities utilize the services of various health specialists in many ways.

Learning opportunities*	Evaluation procedures
Vocabulary	Use a check list of dental and medical specialists and other health personnel which were discussed in class to gain evidence of student understanding.

competent	license	optometrist	prescription
contribution	medical	pediatrician	profession
dental	obstetrician	personnel	specialist
ethical	oculist	pharmacist	therapeutic
hospital	ophthalmologist	practice	unreliable

Learning opportunities	Evaluation procedures
Invite a physician to discuss his daily work, the writing of a prescription, ethical standards, and the local requirements for a license to practice medicine. Have students construct posters illustrating various other medical specialties. Post them in the classroom and in other school locations with brief references as to job description. (1, 3)	Check all assigned written and construction work. Record data on an appraisal form developed for each assignment.
Identify and describe as a class the special work of different kinds of health specialists. Write riddle-type questions with a caption of "Who am I?" to pertain to different specialists and health advisors. (3)	Observe individual and group reactions to visiting dental or medical personnel and other guest speakers. Note individual and group reactions, questions, enthusiasm, and participation.
As a class project write to the local or state chapter of the American Cancer Society for information concerning cancer quacks and cures. Discuss why the specialist is important in dealing with cancer problems. (2)	
Help the class develop and participate in a role-playing situation. Pretend that a child has a cold. Show the place of the family physician, pharmacist, grandmother, FDA official, and others in handling the problem. (3)	Evaluate student awareness of the role of selected health workers as expressed through oral participation.
Display pictures of gadgets and devices sold by quacks or real objects which might be obtained from the Food and Drug Administration or other groups. Use small groups to indicate the role of health personnel in halting such quackery and fraudulent health practices. (1, 2)	Perceive student reactions to display materials, posters, and other items developed by the class or on an individual basis.
Provide for investigation of some of the developments and advances in health and medicine which have come about due to specialization. Have students relate these to increased life expectancy and better health, or discuss this as a class. (3)	
Interview a dentist, nurse, pharmacist, or health specialist. Use a panel group to organize and ask questions concerning their role in health promotion, protection, and care. (1, 3)	
Discuss in class the contributions of various medical, dental, and health specialists as they relate to their places of employment. Have students talk about a visit to the hospital or doctor's office. Identify some of the problems and ways in which they might be solved. (4)	

* The numbers in ( ) after each item are coded back to the "behavioral objectives and content" column.

nerves, the heart and other organs, and the functions of muscles and bones. In grades 4-6 instruction includes deeper studies of the foregoing plus the nervous system, the digestive system, function of glands, and the effects of tobacco, alcohol, and narcotics.

Food and nutrition. In the early grades attention is given to needs for milk and fruit juices, an adequate breakfast, foods for lunch, between-meal snacks, importance of a pleasant atmosphere for eating, development of a taste for variety, and cleanliness. In grades 2 and 3 material is introduced on the nutritive value of dairy products and margarine, protein in the diet, balanced meals, food preparation, elimination, and basic food groups. Building on the foregoing, the program in later grades includes food production and preservation, nutrients in an adequate diet, digestion, effects of emotions, balanced diets, and weight control.

Mental health. In the early grades attention is given to taking turns, sharing, being kind, adjusting to disappointments, learning consideration for others, discussing feelings with others, using simple courtesies, and controlling oneself. The foregoing are continued in grades 2 and 3, and attention is given to growth in friendliness, courtesy, kindliness, concern for others, adjusting to unfortunate happenings, accepting responsibility, welcoming newcomers, controlling anger and other feelings, admitting mistakes, releasing feelings through art and other activities, accepting handicapped individuals, facing difficulties, and talking problems over with others. With a focus on individual differences, attention in later grades is given to reasons behind behavior, expression of emotions, personal and social needs, peer-group relationships, relationships between physical con-

Chart 9–2. The learning program in health education.

Areas of instruction	K	1	2	3	4	5	6	7	8
Care of the body and its parts	×	×		×			×	×	
Dental health		×			×			×	
Vision and hearing	×	×		×					
Prevention and control of disease	×	×			×				
Foods, nutrition, and digestion		×	×			×			×
Habit-forming substances							×		×
Physical fitness and movement					×				×
Safety education	×	×		×	×			×	
Health and the physical environment			×					×	×
Health services and facilities	×						×		
Mental health	×	×		×			×		×
Family health	×		×			×	×	×	
Consumer health		×	×		×				
Health in the rest of the world						×			

dition and feelings, effects of feelings on body processes, facing reality, respecting oneself and others, and solving problems.

Cycling of Units of Study

In many programs there is a cycling of units on major topics in selected grades. The underlying theory is to develop deeper understanding each time a topic is presented. Incidental instruction may be provided on the topic in grades where a unit is not taught. Chart 9–2 shows the grades in which it is recommended that selected units be taught in one program (Sacramento County, 1965, p. 26).

TEACHING STRATEGIES

Many of the strategies used in science and social sciences education are also used in health education. In fact, such units as "How our Body Works" and "Vital Organs" may be taught in either the science or the health education program. And such units as "Safety in the Community" and "Health Workers and Services" may be taught as part of the social sciences or health education program. The strategies and techniques presented in preceding chapters, therefore, should be viewed as applicable to health instruction. In this section are presented examples that show specific applications to units and topics in health education.

Experiments

The experimental model is a useful strategy because children can discover key ideas for themselves as they engage in firsthand observation of phenomena under controlled conditions. Defining the problem or question clearly, stating hypotheses, outlining procedures, observing critically, organizing and interpreting data, and formulating and checking conclusions are key ingredients in effective experiments. The following are illustrative of experiments included in health instruction:

> *Growth of bacteria.* **Prepare three cultures; use sterile dishes and seal them. In the first, place fingernail dirt on a moistened piece of bread; in the second, place dirty water; and in the third, place sterile water. Use a magnifying glass to observe growth of bacteria daily for three days.**
>
> *Need for refrigeration.* **Cover two sterile glasses in which milk has been poured. Place one in the refrigerator and the other on a nearby shelf. Observe and compare changes during the week.**

> *Food decay.* Select two apples as near alike as can be found. Make a break in the skin of one and leave the other intact. Observe and compare the decay process over a period of several days.
>
> *Effects of washing.* Sprinkle salt on the hands of selected children who have washed their hands. Have each child wipe his hands with paper towels and then determine if he can taste salt by touching the tip of his tongue to his hand. Next, have the children wash their hands, dry them, and determine if they can still taste the salt.
>
> *Effects of contamination.* Rub a piece of boiled potato with dirty hands, and another piece with washed hands. Place the pieces of potato in two sterile jars. Put lids on and observe the difference.

Demonstrations

Demonstrations are useful in concept development, application of principles, clarification of appropriate behavior, motivation of learning, and initiation of units. The following are illustrative of demonstrations that may be conducted by the teacher or selected students:

> *Cleanliness and grooming.* Demonstrate washing and drying of hands, cleaning of fingernails, the use of a handkerchief or tissue to blot the nose, how ordinary soap disperses oil more effectively in warm water than in cold.
>
> *Community health and safety.* Demonstrate proper way to use drinking fountains, cross at intersections, get on and off buses, dispose of paper and other litter, care for pets.
>
> *Care of the eyes.* Show proper ways to sit while reading, carry objects that might be injurious, remove objects from the eye, control lighting by means of shades, use a magnifying glass, participate in vision screening tests.

Problem Solving

The problem-solving model is used extensively in health instruction because it is an effective means of dealing with concerns of students and with many topics in the program of instruction. As in other areas of the curriculum, problem solving in health education includes recognizing and defining a problem, gathering and interpreting data, and formulating and applying conclusions. Illustrative problems are:

> **What foods should be eaten to promote healthful growth?**
> **What are sound ways of preparing and preserving foods?**

What steps can be taken to minimize tooth decay?
How can the spread of disease be kept under control?
How can we obtain the use of community health services?
What should we do to promote good relations with others?

Field Study

Field trips and surveys may be used to observe health and safety practices, to gather data on problems, to see demonstrations, and to confer with health service workers. They may be conducted in the school, home, neighborhood, or broader community. The skills involved in planning, observing, interviewing, note-taking, mapping, evaluating, and other activities are applied to health questions and problems. Study trips may be taken to such places as the school nurse's office, cafeteria, food market, dairy farm, water purification plant, and health department. Surveys may be made of such problems and topics as safety hazards, eating habits, safe street crossings, types of food eaten, types of illness, and daily amount of exercise.

Developing Generalizations

Generalizations may be developed through direct instruction that begins with an introduction or opener, proceeds through a series of developmental activities, and concludes with experiences in which students formulate a generalization. For example, the generalization "The human body needs foods containing vitamins, minerals, proteins, fats, and carbohydrates" may be developed as shown in the following abbreviated outline:

Opener: Discuss what is meant by a balanced diet, using pictures of food arranged on the bulletin board. Have the students recall ideas they have about food elements all of us need. List their responses on the chalkboard.

Development: Begin by showing a filmstrip or having the group read a section in their health books that presents information on basic food elements.

Discuss the functions of vitamins. Make a summary of foods that are rich in different vitamins.

Continue in the same manner with minerals, proteins, and other food elements.

Organize the information in a chart that shows the relationship between foods and vital nutrients.

Plan shopping lists and menus that include foods with essential nutrients.

Have individuals investigate and report on rickets and other diseases that result from poor diets.

Conduct an experiment to show the effects of rich and poor soil on the growth of plants.

> *Conclusion:* Have students summarize the main idea in their own words. Have a group make a mural or individuals make posters which illustrate the generalization. Provide for application by having students keep records of foods they eat.

Using Questions to Guide Inquiry

Independent and group study in health education can be improved by devising questions that lift thinking to the higher cognitive processes included in *Taxonomy of Educational Objectives: Cognitive Domain* (Bloom, 1956). For example, the following questions move progressively from the knowledge level to the evaluation level:

> *Knowledge:* What food nutrients do all of us need? In what foods may they be found?
>
> *Comprehension:* Can you explain in your own words why we need vitamins and minerals? What problems may arise if the soil in which food plants are raised is not fertilized?
>
> *Application:* How can we use what we have learned to improve our eating habits? How can we check to be sure we have a balanced diet?
>
> *Analysis:* What is meant by the statement that this cereal contains one-half of the minimum daily requirements? Who can analyze this menu to find out if essential nutrients are included?
>
> *Synthesis:* Who can organize what we have learned about vital nutrients into a set rule for good eating habits? What soil conditions are necessary to produce vegetables that contain vitamins and minerals?
>
> *Evaluation:* Are the claims in this advertisement consistent with what we have learned about vitamins? Which of the three dinner menus on the chalkboard is best in terms of our criteria for balanced meals?

Questions that illustrate ways in which various levels of the affective domain (Krathwohl, Bloom, & Masia, 1964) may be approached are:

> *Receiving:* How did you feel as you read about beriberi? Did you notice anything surprising in the film on vitamins and growth?
>
> *Responding:* Do you eat vegetables because you have to or because you want to? In what ways do you feel it was helpful to make rules for good eating habits?

Valuing: Why are vital nutrients important to us as individuals and as a country? Why should all of us be concerned about soil conditions?

Organization: Who can describe the plight of individuals suffering from malnutrition? How would you feel if you were in a country where it was difficult to have a balanced diet?

Characterization: How do you feel about changing your eating habits as new data become available? What place should health values have in one's view of the good life?

Developing Safety Behaviors

The importance of safety education as an essential part of the health education program cannot be overemphasized. Accidents are the primary cause of death and permanent injury to children of elementary school age. The instructional program should be designed to meet the school's extensive responsibility for promoting behavior conducive to the child's safety in school, in playgrounds and streets, at home, and elsewhere. Goals of safety instruction include the following:

Development of self-responsibility and attentiveness to one's personal safety

Understanding of needs for safety regulations and adherence to such regulations

Consideration at all times for the safety and welfare of others

Care in the use, handling, and storage of tools, appliances, and other articles

The enumeration of general goals such as these and specific objectives relevant to particular age levels or activities makes it evident that safety education must develop both attitudes and behaviors conducive to safe living. Children in the elementary school should be helped to develop an awareness that daily activities involve some dangers, a desire to be attentive to such dangers and to take adequate precautions, a sense of responsibility for one's own safety, a commitment to the value of safety procedures, and the organization of a value system related to safety of oneself and others in all situations. Specific behaviors consistent with safety in particular situations must be taught and reviewed and practiced consistently so that they may become habitual.

Strategies for the development of understandings and attitudes leading to habitual safety behavior utilize techniques similar to those described on the preceding pages. Steps in a safety development strategy might include a problem-focused, attitude-encouragement clarification of specific behav-

iors, practice of behaviors, and evaluation, as described below. Problem situations of concern in the elementary school include such examples as
pedestrian safety, safe places to play, use of specific tools, safety in sports
activities, kite safety, rules for safe public transportation, and, of course,
many others.

Focus. The specific situation to be considered may be brought to the
attention of the class by pupils or by the teacher as the result of a particular incident or as part of the systematic program of safety instruction.
Attention is focused on the situation by means of verbal description by
children or teacher, use of role playing for reenactment of an incident
or presentation of a story, or through vicarious examples in films, story-
books, records, or newspaper articles.

Understandings and attitudes. After the problem situation has
been described, children should be guided to recognize the potential dangers
in the situation and to understand and accept the need to identify appropriate
safety procedures. These understandings and attitudes may be developed
through discussion directed by the teacher's questions, with reference
to the focus situation and to experiences of the children in similar activities.

Clarification of behaviors. Using a progression of questions, such
as those based on taxonomies of cognitive and affective objectives as outlined in the preceding section, teacher and pupils can discuss ways of
meeting the safety hazards they have identified. Demonstrations may be
used to test suggested procedures or to teach those already proved. As
agreement is reached on specific behaviors or on the total sequence of
procedures, these should be recorded on charts such as those shown in
Chart 9–3. This process enables children to develop favorable attitudes
and a sense of self-responsibility as they work out their own safety rules
or analyze and understand reasonable rules set by others.

Practice of behaviors. Use of safety procedures begins with classroom enactment by some pupils during the previous instructional step.
Whenever possible, the entire class should have the opportunity to immediately enact the procedure in a simulated situation in order to clinch
behavior changes, instead of terminating the lesson at the level of ver-
balization. The behaviors should then be habituated through repeated
practice in real situations.

Evaluation. As procedures are developed or analyzed in the preceding steps, children engage in evaluation of their efficacy. Charts drawn
up during safety lessons should be kept for future reference and review.
Some lists of safety-procedures related to school, playground, and classroom activities may be permanently posted in an appropriate location.
For example, rules for use of tools should be posted where the tools are
stored. The teacher should observe children's behavior to ascertain the
extent to which each student has developed the attitudes and habits that
promote continuous and consistent adherence to safety procedures. Children

Safety to and from school	**Safety on a bus**
1. Cross streets only in cross walks.	1. Wait on the curb until the bus door opens.
2. Walk across streets.	2. Go straight to your seat so others can get on.
3. Obey the traffic patrol.	3. Remain seated at all times.
4. When possible, use a corner where there is a signal.	4. Keep arms and head inside.
5. Watch for cars backing out of driveways.	5. Do not disturb the driver.
6. Leave dogs and other animals alone.	6. Watch your step when getting off.
7. Do not accept rides with strangers.	7. Be careful in crossing the street before boarding and after leaving the bus.
8. Walk on the left side of the road facing traffic if there is no sidewalk.	

Passing safely	**Using doors safely**
1. Watch where you are going.	1. Use the knob to open.
2. Always walk, never run.	2. Open slowly so as not to hit anyone passing by.
3. Watch out for opening doors.	3. Keep hands away from the opening on both sides of the door.
4. Look out for others.	4. Watch out for others when closing the door.
	5. Take turns in passing through the doorway.

Safe fire and disaster drills	**A safe playground**
1. Act quickly and quietly when the alarm is sounded.	1. Walk to the area assigned to you.
2. Walk quietly without talking.	2. Keep hands off others.
3. Go to the place assigned to your class.	3. Use playground equipment correctly.
4. If in the toilet at the time of the alarm, join the nearest line going out.	4. Walk around the play areas of others.
5. Be alert for direction from the teacher.	5. Keep equipment and other objects out of play areas.
	6. Look out for others
	7. Report accidents to the teacher.

Chart 9–3. *Examples of safety procedure charts.*

should engage in continuing self-evaluation of behavior and group evaluation as needs arise. Chart 9–3 illustrates points to keep in mind during evaluation.

GUIDELINES FOR THE TEACHER

The teacher may play a variety of roles in health education ranging from director of systematic experiences that develop attitudes and habits of safety essential to group welfare to arranger of situations in which students discover for themselves key ideas from basic sciences. The multiple instructional approaches recommended by experts in health education clearly indicate that many similarities exist between teaching strategies in this area and those employed in science education and in social sciences education. What is unique about health instruction is the focus on personal and group aspects of healthful living. Strategies are selected, adapted, and devised to guide the attainment of objectives related to a broad concept of good health. The following guidelines are recommended by health education specialists.

Provide systematic health education instruction that is viewed as an integral part of the total school health program. Administrators, teachers, school nutritionists, and custodians provide and maintain conditions for healthful school living. The teacher is particularly responsible for safe arrangement of classroom furniture, safe condition of classroom equipment, and attention to adequate lighting and healthful ventilation in the room. In some schools, specialists are available for physical education, but in others this may be the teacher's responsibility. In either case, there are times when the teacher will need to conduct games, exercise, dances, or rhythmic activities in the classroom. School health services are provided by medical specialists, but the classroom teacher's daily observation of the children is an important part of this aspect of the health program. A major area of the total program is the development of cognitive and affective objectives related to health and safety. No staff member is so well equipped and so well placed as the classroom teacher for the provision of systematic and continual health instruction designed to develop understandings, positive attitudes, and specific behaviors conducive to the child's safe and healthful living. Several health education experts suggest that provision of two periods each week in the primary grades and three periods each week in grades 4 through 6 helps to ensure systematic and meaningful learnings in health and safety.

Utilize every possible opportunity for incidental health and safety instruction. No other area of study is so close to the child's personal needs or so permeating in his total experience as is the subject matter of health education, for it is concerned with the child himself. Therefore, systematic health and safety instruction must be supplemented by instruction that meets the needs identified as children raise questions or recognize problems, take health examinations, encounter safety hazards, or exhibit any behavior that seems to be detrimental to the health or safety of the individual or group. Meaningful incidental instruction may also be initiated by current events or by questions arising from studies in other subject areas.

Try to integrate health instruction with the child's daily activities and home conditions. The teacher can provide more adequate and relevant instruction if some knowledge can be obtained about home conditions related to the child's diet, schedule of activities, sleep, health habits, etc. The teacher may gather needed information from school records, home visits, interviews with parents, or questionnaires sent to the home. The teacher should make it possible for parents to be aware of the ongoing health program in the school, and whenever necessary, work with parents to plan appropriate schedules, activities, or conditions for the child's healthful living at home. The teacher should observe the clothing worn by pupils to ascertain that shoes are comfortable, glasses fit properly, and clothing is adequate and appropriate for the weather.

Observe children carefully for symptoms of illness or referral to health specialists. The classroom teacher is sometimes responsible for testing pupils for visual and auditory acuity. Even when specialists handle these tests, the teacher should be alert, throughout the school day, to any indications of visual and auditory difficulties evidenced in a pupil's behavior. As the person who sees the child for several hours every school day, the teacher provides for the health of individuals as well as the entire class by careful observation of each child in order to detect symptoms ranging from generally poor health to the beginnings of serious illness or disability. Check lists are available which direct the teacher's attention to specific signs and symptoms in regard to general appearance, behavior, eyes, ears, and nose and throat. Examples of symptoms in these areas are as follows:

> *General*: **pale complexion, overweight, tires easily, poor posture**
>
> *Behavior*: **nervousness, undue restlessness, excessive use of lavatory**
>
> *Eyes*: **squinting, frequent headaches, inflamed eyes, crusted lids**
>
> *Ears*: **dullness and inattention, watches speaker intently, discharge from ears**
>
> *Nose and throat*: **persistent mouth breathing, frequent colds or sore throat**

Measurement of pupils' weight and height is often conducted in the classroom and can readily be incorporated in other subject area studies.

Try to correlate health and safety instruction with learning experiences in other subject areas. Judiciously planned activities can augment health learnings and provide realistic, meaningful applications for subject area understandings and skills. A few possible examples are as follows:

> *Language arts*: **writing reports; applying study skills to the gathering and processing of data in health and safety studies**

Reading: using health education materials of high personal interest to motivate reading; using health and safety charts developed by the children as materials in an experience-based reading program

Foreign language: learning words for parts of the body; learning names of foods in clusters based on nutritional groups; noting the health implications in practice dialogues dealing with meals, bedtime, and family activities

Social sciences: community, national, and international health services; health and safety responsibilities related to responsible citizenship; health practices in other times and places

Science: biological studies; contributions of life sciences and medical sciences to health understandings; conducting health experiments

Mathematics: recording height and weight measurements; using measurements and other health statistics in mathematical operations

Music: expressing health or safety ideas and catchphrases as chants or as songs composed by the children

Art: application of design principles to posters promoting important ideas about health and safety

Use appropriate multisensory instructional aids. In addition to films, recordings, trade books, and other media widely utilized by effective teachers in all subject areas, the following materials are useful in health and safety instruction:

Models: use of commercial biological models or models made by children to illustrate health principles or demonstrate processes

Advertisements for health-related products: application of critical thinking skills to analysis of advertising claims, using known principles of good health as criteria for evaluation

Charts and records: use of standardized health record forms and height-weight charts in the classroom, as continual records kept by the children themselves

Many types of free or inexpensive instructional materials are available from commercial sources and nonprofit organizations. Some of the end-of-chapter references include addresses of such sources.

EVALUATION OF INSTRUCTIONAL OUTCOMES

As indicated in the preceding sections, teacher observation of pupil behavior is an important aspect of continuous evaluation in health and safety education. Observation of behavior may be guided by check lists and recorded in anecdotal records. Information about the health history of children taken from cumulative record cards can be useful in planning individualized learning experiences and assessing long-term changes in health attitudes and behaviors. Teacher-pupil interviews, paper and pencil tests, questionnaires, interest inventories, and samples of pupil's reports and other work are examples of evaluative tools.

Cognitive Domain

In addition to check lists for behaviors conducive to safe and healthful living, cognitive outcomes may be assessed with questions and tasks such as the following:

> *Knowledge level*: **factual information related to principles of health and safety procedures**
> **Why is it wise to include milk in our daily diet? What procedure do we follow in a fire drill?**

> *Comprehension level*: **interpretation of learnings in relation to one's own health and safety; expression of understandings in nonverbal forms**
> **Explain in your own words the reasons why good posture is important to your health. Design a poster to show other children how to be safe on the playground.**

> *Application level*: **use of health principles in the child's daily life; adherence to safety regulations**
> **Keep a record of the foods you eat for an entire week. List everything you do when you want to go across a street.**

> *Analysis level*: **understanding of the relationships between various health principles; ability to detect relevant and irrelevant information in statements about health and safety; understanding of relationships in safety rules**
> **How does the amount of sleep you get at night affect your work in school?**
> **Which sequence of procedures (of three or four alternative sets) would be most effective for our daily dismissals?**

> *Synthesis level*: **the pupil's own organization of ideas related to good health and safety procedures**

How can we help the first-graders to follow safety rules in and around the school? Write a short story that illustrates an important health idea.

Evaluation level: application of criteria for safety and health to one's own habits; self-appraisal in regard to adherence to health and safety habits
I get eight hours of sleep at night _____ (always, often, sometimes, never).
How effective and fair are our rules for the use of playground equipment?

Affective Domain

Affective outcomes may be assessed by means of check lists, attitude inventories, and interviews with children and their parents. Illustrative questions and items are:

Receiving level: awareness of the difference between good and poor health; willingness to learn health and safety principles
What does "good health" mean to you? Can you think of any reasons why we have rules for behavior on the playground?

Responding level: satisfaction in development of health habits; voluntary participation in learning activities
Do you wear boots or rubbers in wet weather? *A.* When I am reminded to. *B.* Without being told. *C.* I don't like to. *D.* I never wear them.

Valuing level: acceptance of the worth of adhering to health and safety procedures; commitment to the value of practicing good health and safety habits
The school-crossing guard should not be obeyed if he is not one of your friends. *A.* Yes. *B.* No. *C.* I'm not sure.

EVALUATION OF THE PROGRAM

An important criterion for a good school program is the level of the students' adherence to health and safety principles, as assessed above. The following are examples of additional criteria to be used in evaluating health and safety instruction:

Foundations
Is content drawn from children's needs as well as from dependable sources of health information?

Are the health understandings developed in the program consistent with knowledge and principles of foundation disciplines?

Structure

Is health information organized for instruction in a manner that enables the child to grasp the relationship between relevant health practices and characteristics of his own good health?

Inquiry

Have children learned the values of health and safety procedures by participating in discussions, demonstrations, experiments, and exploration of alternative possibilities?

Objectives

Are objectives clearly defined in terms of understandings, positive attitudes, and specific behaviors?

Is emphasis given to development of safety habits?

Complete program

Does the school provide for specific health and safety instruction, healthful school living, health services, and physical education?

Are these aspects of the program closely integrated?

Teaching strategies

Are varieties of appropriate techniques utilized?

Are provisions made for adaptation of instruction to the specific needs of all students?

Evaluation

Is evaluation continuous and an integral aspect of instruction?

Is emphasis placed on pupil self-evaluation?

Teacher education

Are in-service programs and materials provided to keep the teacher up-to-date on health standards and information as well as on effective teaching techniques?

Are specialists available to provide health services and advise on health education activities?

Program revision

Are teachers and health specialists involved in continuous program evaluation and revision?

REFERENCES

American Association for Health, Physical Education, and Recreation. *Health Concepts, Guides for Health Instruction.* Washington, D.C.: National Education Association, 1967. Background information on current health problems.

Bloom, Benjamin S. (Ed.) *Taxonomy of educational objectives: cognitive domain.* New York: McKay, 1956. Sample objectives and test items on six levels of complexity.

Bucher, Charles A., & Reade, Evelyn M. *Physical education and health in the elementary school.* New York: Macmillan, 1964. Chapters on various phases of health education.

Buros, Oscar K. *The sixth mental measurements yearbook.* Highland Park, N.J.: Gryphon Press, 1965. Information on tests published between 1959 and 1964; review of earlier tests in earlier volumes.

Clarke, H. Harrison, & Haar, Franklin B. *Health and physical education for the elementary school classroom teacher.* Englewood Cliffs, N.J.: Prentice-Hall, 1964. Suggestions for a complete school health program.

Inlow, Gail M. *The emergent in curriculum.* New York: Wiley, 1966. Mental health discussed in chap. IV.

Krathwohl, David R., Bloom, Benjamin S., & Masia, Bertram B. *Taxonomy of educational objectives: affective domain.* New York: McKay, 1964. Sample objectives and test items arranged in terms of degree of internalization.

Los Angeles County. *A guide to curriculum development and course of study for elementary schools of Los Angeles County.* Los Angeles: County Superintendent of Schools, 1965. Outline of a complete school health program in chap. 9.

Moss, Bernice R., et al. *Health education.* (5th ed.) Washington, D.C.: National Education Association, 1961. A standard reference jointly developed by NEA and American Medical Association.

Nemir, Alma. *The school health program.* Philadelphia: Saunders, 1965. Background material on health problems as well as material on the instructional program.

Oberteuffer, Delbert. Health education and physical education. *New curriculum developments.* Washington, D.C.: Association for Supervision and Curriculum Development, 1965. A review of current curriculum projects and studies.

Phenix, Philip H. *Realms of meaning.* New York: McGraw-Hill, 1964. Review of disciplines in six realms of meaning. Relates health education and physical education to the arts of movement in chap. 14.

Sacramento County. *Basic course of study for elementary grades.* Sacramento: County Superintendent of Schools, 1965. Pp. 24–27. Outline of health and safety program.

Schneider, Robert E. *Methods and materials of health education.* (2d ed.) Philadelphia: Saunders, 1964. Principles and procedures for a complete program in grades 1–12.

Sliepcevich, Elena M. *School health education study: experimental curriculum materials project.* (rev.) New York: Educational Services Press, 1966. Materials prepared in a current project.

Smolensky, Jack, & Bonvechio, L. Richard. *Principles of school health.* Boston: Heath, 1966. Detailed treatment of various aspects of a complete program.

Vannier, Maryhelen. *Teaching health in elementary schools.* New York: Harper, 1963. Methods and materials for different phases of health instruction.

Veenker, C. Harold, *Synthesis of research in selected areas of health instruction.* Washington, D.C.: National Education Association, 1963. Reviews of research in various areas of health instruction.

Willgoose, Carl E. *Evaluation in health education and physical education.* New York: McGraw-Hill, 1961. Principles and procedures for assessing outcomes of instruction.

Willgoose, Carl E. *Health education in the elementary school.* (2d ed.) Philadelphia: Saunders, 1964. Principles and procedures for a complete school health program.

Wilson, Charles C. (Ed.) *Healthful school living.* Washington, D.C.: National Education Association, 1957. Recommendations for a healthful school environment prepared by NEA and AMA joint committee.

Wilson, Charles C. *School health services.* (2d ed.) Washington, D.C.: National Education Association, 1964. Recommendations for health services prepared by joint committee of NEA and AMA.

Chapter Ten

PHYSICAL EDUCATION

P<small>HYSICAL EDUCATION</small> is that part of the educational program designed to promote the child's physical, social, emotional, and mental development through physical activity. Play, movement, big-muscle activity, neuromuscular skills, coordination, timing, sportsmanship, respect for oneself and for others, and regard for rules of the game are emphasized. Physical activity is recognized as a primary means of attaining worthy objectives, thus distinguishing physical education activities from closely related activities in other areas of the curriculum.

Three basic functions of physical education have been cited by Cowell and France (1963). The social function is to transmit values and standards that are consistent with societal needs and ideals. The biological function is to develop well-rounded fitness. The integrative function is to coordinate a rich program of human development. These functions are kept in balance in high-quality programs of physical education, and their fulfillment re-

Chart 10–1. *A structure of physical education.*

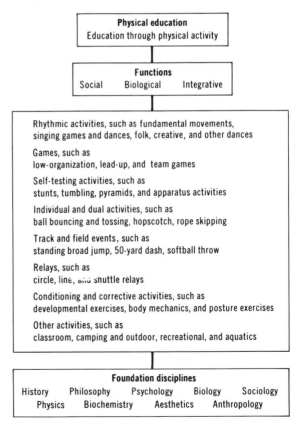

Physical education
Education through physical activity

Functions
Social   Biological   Integrative

Rhythmic activities, such as fundamental movements, singing games and dances, folk, creative, and other dances

Games, such as low-organization, lead-up, and team games

Self-testing activities, such as stunts, tumbling, pyramids, and apparatus activities

Individual and dual activities, such as ball bouncing and tossing, hopscotch, rope skipping

Track and field events, such as standing broad jump, 50-yard dash, softball throw

Relays, such as circle, line, and shuttle relays

Conditioning and corrective activities, such as developmental exercises, body mechanics, and posture exercises

Other activities, such as classroom, camping and outdoor, recreational, and aquatics

Foundation disciplines
History   Philosophy   Psychology   Biology   Sociology
Physics   Biochemistry   Aesthetics   Anthropology

quires a structure of activities and the selection of ideas from several disciplines, as shown in Chart 10–1.

The biological function of physical education has been highlighted during the past decade. The President's Council on Physical Fitness has issued bulletins and carried on activities that have spurred interest in the development of fitness of children, youth, and adults (President's Council, 1961). Currently, fitness is broadly defined to include mental, social, and emotional well-being as well as physical well-being. Physical well-being is defined as freedom from disability and disease, capacity to perform and to recover, and possession of a reservoir of energy for prolonged tasks (Hunsicker, 1963). Specific characteristics of physical fitness include strength, power, endurance, agility, flexibility, speed, balance, and coordination (Dauer, 1965). Fitness includes these and other characteristics that are the outcome of the total educational program and of home and community life. Physical education contributes much to physical fitness and, along with other areas of the curriculum, to total fitness.

Mental, emotional, and social outcomes are not overlooked in physical education. Indeed, such outcomes are given high priority and the separation of physical and mental development is deplored by leaders (Boyer, 1965; Williams, 1964) who point out that physical education is education *through* the physical and not *of* the physical. As shown in later sections, physical education is anchored in a variety of foundation disciplines, includes basic concepts and generalizations, and is designed to attain multiple objectives.

FOUNDATION DISCIPLINES

A surprisingly large number of disciplines may be noted in the writings of specialists who deal with the foundations of physical education (Cowell & France, 1963; Oberteuffer & Ulrich, 1962; Paterson & Hallberg, 1965; Williams, 1964). The study of history gives perspective to the importance of physical activity from the time of ancient Greece to the present, highlights changes in instructional programs and the emphasis on different activities, and clarifies issues and problems of significance today. Principles and values are derived from such schools of philosophy as idealism, naturalism, and pragmatism. The biological, social, and integrative functions of physical education are analyzed in terms of inquiries into the nature and function of democratic societies. Guidelines and concepts from the arts are used to explain and describe rhythms, the dance, and other artistic aspects of creative physical activity. Instructional implications of changes in society and the human condition are derived from sociological studies. Information on the nature and importance of play and physical activity in different cultures is drawn from anthropology. Concepts and principles regarding the nature of human growth and development and the conditions of learning are drawn from psychology and from physiology and anatomy. Principles and procedures for use in various phases of instruction and evaluation are drawn from studies of motor skills, conditions of stress, physical development, and performance of children at various age levels. Such concepts as force, leverage, equilibrium, structure, function, adaptation, and balance are drawn from physical and life sciences and used to analyze, explain, and describe physical activities. Indeed, even a cursory review of foundation disciplines reveals that physical education has roots in nearly all the realms of meaning discussed by Phenix (1964).

Concept Clusters and Generalizations

Because physical education is rooted in many different disciplines a variety of concept clusters may be identified in current programs. These clusters range from those related to common physical needs of human beings to types of physical activity believed to be essential in a complete program of instruction. Many of the clusters noted in Chapter 9 on Health Education are directly related to physical education and will not be repeated in this section. The following examples highlight other concepts that are typically included in materials for teachers:

> *Motor skills*: movement, as in running, jumping, and dodging; eye-hand coordination, as in throwing, catching, and bouncing a ball; eye-foot coordination, as in kicking and punting a ball; balance, as in hopping and stunts; timing, as in rhythms and dances; kinesthetic perception, as in awareness of position of arms, legs, and other body parts in an activity
>
> *Play*: types—active, passive, intellectual; contributions—new experience, adventure, recognition, security, participation, satisfaction, learning
>
> *Total fitness*: physical, mental, emotional, social, and spiritual well-being
>
> *Paths to physical fitness*: proper diet, exercise, play and recreation, rest and relaxation, medical and dental care, satisfying work
>
> *Activities*: individual, dual, group, team; games and sports, dances and rhythms, developmental or conditioning, self-testing, stunts, story, classroom, aquatics, track and field, camping and outdoor, social-recreational, leisure time

Dances and rhythms: fundamental, dramatized, folk dances, singing games, creative or interpretive dances, mimetics

Leisure-time activities: camping, fishing, hiking, swimming, riding, dancing, bicycling, sailing, skating, bowling, tennis, golf, archery, softball, badminton

Posture faults: forward head, round upper back, round shoulders, hollow back, lateral deviation

Among the many generalizations that are drawn from supporting disciplines and put to use in planning and developing the physical education program are the following:

For every action, such as batting or kicking a ball, there is an equal and opposite reaction.

The amount of oxygen needed by the body is directly proportional to the amount of energy released by the body.

Muscles become stronger through use; they become weaker with disuse.

Mental health is influenced by one's state of physical well-being.

Man's cognitive, affective, and psychomotor capacities are interrelated in physical education activities.

Play is a means of learning, adjusting, and satisfying personal-social needs in cultures around the world.

Guided cooperation and competition contribute to individual development and group accomplishment.

Performance in games and other activities involves such aesthetic qualities as form, style, taste, and organization.

Self-activity, self-analysis, and practice are key elements in the attainment of motor skills.

Developmental Characteristics of Children

The following developmental characteristics of children and related implications are cited in many of the end-of-chapter references:

Kindergarten and grade 1. Five- and six-year-olds are active, imitative, curious, individualistic. Their attention span is short, and they are easily fatigued; they are interested in finding out what they can do with their arms, legs, and bodies. Large muscles are more developed than small ones, and game skills are not developed. Fundamental movements, rhythms, singing games, story plays, mimetics, simple stunts, skills such as throwing and tossing a ball, and learning to use apparatus are recommended.

Grades 2 and 3. Seven- and eight-year-olds are active, developing longer attention spans, becoming more interested in group activities, and developing motor skills to higher levels. They enjoy physical contact, vigorous and active games, and the development of motor skills. Big-muscle activities, group activities, simple team games and relays, refinement of skills developed earlier, lead-up games, and rhythmic activities involving partner and group patterns are recommended.

Grades 4–6. Girls grow more rapidly than boys, interest in team and group activity is high, coordination is improving, a desire to excel and a competitive spirit emerge, interest in specific techniques is high, and self-responsibility is growing. The program is expanded to include seasonal sports, selected track and field events, a variety of team games, and other activities. Boys and girls are separated for certain activities, and different norms are used for fitness tests.

OBJECTIVES

The objectives of physical education continue to be viewed in terms of the contribution of physical activities to basic outcomes of education (Boyer, 1965; Bucher & Reade, 1964). The physical aspects of the program are the means of achieving objectives; they are not the ends. The substantive aspects of the program are designed to provide an understanding of the nature of physical activities, of one's own capabilities, and of such concepts as fair play and respect for others. Physical, social, emotional, and intellectual development are emphasized as shown in the following summary of specific objectives.

Knowledge, Concepts, Understandings

The teacher attempts to give the child an understanding of the relationships between physical activities and basic concepts from biological, physical, and social sciences. Specific attention is given to the development of:

> **Insight into the relationships between organs and systems of the body and posture and body mechanics**
> **Knowledge of terms, concepts, rules, and principles involved in physical activities and major sports**
> **Understanding of the abilities involved in different activities**
> **Understanding of the contributions physical activities make to fitness**
> **Insight into relationships between physical fitness and mental health**

Knowledge of the rules and specific aspects of individual and group sports

Knowledge of standards of safety and accident prevention related to physical activities

Functional Skills and Abilities

Skill in basic motor activities, physical fitness, and self-understanding are emphasized, with specific attention to the development of:

Competence in both individual and group activities and in using body mechanics in daily activity

Ability to use one's body efficiently and gracefully in daily activities as well as in sports

Competence in evaluating one's own strengths and weaknesses and those of others in physical activities

Development of coordination, balance, rhythm, organic power, initiative, and neuromuscular skills

Ability to control oneself and one's emotions in both individual and group activities

Skill in serving as a leader at times and as a follower at other times

Ability to rest, relax, and engage in leisure-time physical activities

Attitudes, Appreciations, Interests

Objectives in the affective domain include the development of such attitudes, appreciations, and interests as:

Attitude of inquiry toward body capabilities and movement

Appreciation of the importance of developing competence in physical activities

Appreciation of the competence of others and of creative self-expression through physical activity

Interest in undertaking new activities and in developing new skills

Respect for individuals who differ in ability, who are handicapped, and who do not meet or who exceed achievements of the group

Appreciation of physical skill and performance from the viewpoint of a spectator

Willingness to submit to the discipline of team effort and to assess group activity in the light of rules and standards

A COMPLETE PROGRAM

A complete program of physical education may be viewed in two different ways. The first is a broad view of the major components of the program. The second is a specific view of types of activity included in the program.

The component parts of a complete program have been outlined in terms of three areas (Bucher & Reade, 1964). The first is the required program that includes the games, mimetics, dancing, rhythms, and other activities that are taught through class instruction. The second is the adapted program that includes corrective, conditioning, and other activities designed to meet the special needs of individual pupils. The third part is the intramural program in which opportunities are provided for students to use basic skills in games, sports, and other competitive activities.

The specific elements in a complete program include individual, partnership, small-group, and large-group activities. Although classifications of specific activities vary somewhat from writer to writer, the following types are typically included in the elementary school program:

Dances and rhythms: fundamental movements; creative, folk, square, social

Mimetics: imitation of animals, wooden soldiers, bucking horses

Story plays: on Halloween, a turkey for Thanksgiving, Easter bunnies

Activities on equipment: jungle gym, ladder, rings, bar, swings, slides, seesaws

Low-organization games: dodge ball, circle tag, endball, ringmaster

Individual and dual: hopscotch, ball bouncing, rope jump, tetherball

Self-testing: dog walk, elephant walk, rabbit jump, jumping jack

Relays: circular, shuttle, line, kangaroo, basketball, soccer dribble

Classroom games: yarn ball, dodge ball, lone ranger, Simon says

Developmental: jumping jack, wheelbarrow, pull-ups, push-ups

Lead-up games: circle kickball leading to soccer; paddle ball leading to badminton and tennis; netball leading to volleyball; bat ball leading to baseball; captain ball leading to basketball

Team sports: softball, soccer, touch football, speedball, volleyball

Track and field: broad jump, softball throw, dash, basketball free throw

Stunts and tumbling: stick jump, animal walks, headstand, making a bridge

Holidays and special events: the witch, turkey pass, reindeer, May Day

Intramural: activities drawn from the instructional program, as well as special activities, organized into play days, sports days, tournaments

In the next section additional examples are given of specific activities. Notice that there is a steady progression from low to high organization from level to level.

SEQUENCE OF ACTIVITIES

Courses of study in physical education are designed in terms of developmental growth characteristics of children. The child's physical, social, emotional, and intellectual development is a prime determiner of the grade placement of activities. The following sequence adapted from the Los Angeles *Course of Study for Elementary Schools* (1964) is illustrative of current practice. The program begins in kindergarten with an emphasis on small-group activities, use of big muscles, and rhythmic activity. In subsequent grades more complex activities are introduced in accordance with the developmental characteristics of children. At each level the teacher introduces selected activities, stresses the development of specified skills, and guides the development of social, physical, and intellectual outcomes. Physical fitness, body efficiency, leadership and followership, and emotional stability are given appropriate emphasis at each level.

KINDERGARTEN

Activities: individual, parallel, and dual activities appropriate for five-year-olds

Balls and beanbags: simple uses with attention to handling skills

Apparatus: correct usage with attention to rights of others

Games and rhythms: simple singing games and rhythmic activities

Fitness: planned activities appropriate at this level

GRADE 1

Games: selected group games appropriate at this level

Rhythms: simple singing games and a variety of rhythmic activities

Fitness: activities appropriate for group participation

Controlled use of ball: underhand toss, side toss, arm catch, hand catch, rolling with accuracy, kicking a stationary ball

GRADE 2

Games: simple team games in various game areas

Rhythms: greater complexity, partner and group cooperation

Fitness: appropriate individual and group activities

Skills and rules: for games and activities introduced at this level

Ball skills: kicking, throwing, hand batting, serving with bounce serve

GRADE 3

Major games: fist ball, zone soccer, zone basketball, progressive dodge ball, long ball, prisoner's ball, diamond handball, field-ball, ring tennis

Game skills: bat, throw, catch, block, pass, punt, shoot, free throw, serve, field, feint and dodge, as appropriate with different balls

Track: dash, jump and reach, basketball free throw, soccer kick for goal, softball throw for accuracy, shoot and recover, relays —rescue, round the post, shuttle, over the head, over and under

Physical fitness: rings and ladder, sit-up, push-up, rope jumping, stunts, running

Rhythms: fundamental, interpretive, dramatized, marching

Dances: Shoo Fly, Seven Steps, Yankee Doodle, El Molino, Oh Dear, Pawpaw Patch, Clap and Tramp, Patty-cake Dance

Dance skills: walk, run, skip, bleking, through the arch, dishrag turn, single progression to new partner, trio formation, slide, step-hop, tap, heel-toe, pat-a-cake, clapping with partner

Other activities: four squares, hopscotch, shuffleboard, tetherball, table games, block ball, kickball, headman, zigzag catch, wall stride ball, cowboys and Indians, Newcomb

GRADE 4

Major games: dodge ball, section soccer, section basketball, socco, softball, one bounce (volleyball) Chinese handball, pass ball (football), paddle handball

Game skills: pat, throw, pitch, run and dodge, kick, dribble, punt, pass, catch, block, shoot, free throw, guard, paddle serve, receive, return, and carry different balls as appropriate in various games

Physical fitness: ring and ladder, sit-up, push-up, rope jumping, stunts, running

Track: dash, basketball free throw, soccer kick for goal, jump and reach, softball throw for accuracy, shoot and recover, relays

Rhythms: fundamental, interpretive, dramatized, marching

Dances: Bingo, Gustaf's Skoal, La Costilla, Hitchhiker, O Susanna, La Palmadilla, Flip

Dance skills: chug, grand right and left, two couples together, arch formation, turning partner, square patter, step-hop, rock, balance, jump-stride-jump

Other activities: apparatus, four squares, hopscotch, shuffleboard, tetherball, table games, block ball, prisoner's ball, headman, fist ball, zone soccer, Red River, snatch the bean bag, zigzag catch, overhand and underhand throw at target, long ball, Newcomb, wall stride ball

GRADE 5

Major games: kickball, soccer, basketball, bat ball, softball, netball, rotation handball, pass touch football, paddle tennis, indoor games

Game skills: throw, catch, kick, pitch, block, dribble, punt, shoot, free throw, pass, catch, serve, receive, return, and carry various balls as appropriate in different games

Track: dash, jump and reach, basketball free throw, soccer kick for goal, softball throw for accuracy, various relays

Physical fitness: rings and ladder, sit-up, push-up, rope jumping, stunts, running

Rhythms: fundamental, interpretive, dramatized, marching patterns

Dances: Circassion circle, Pop Goes the Weasel, Red River Valley, Tenton Mountain stomp, Solomon Levy, Jolly is the Miller, Dixie, Polly Wolly Doodle

Dance skills: buzz swing, cross-arm swing, right-hand star, banjo and sidecar positions, progression to second person, draw step, allemande left, girl-twirl, right-arm swing

Other activities: apparatus, four squares, hopscotch, shuffleboard, socco, tetherball, table games, block ball, pass ball, fist ball, dodge ball, kick and run, headman, section soccer, section basketball, Red River, one bounce, hit through short, work up, diamond handball, handball volley, in and out handball, Chinese paddle handball, base football, soccer punt for accuracy, wall stride ball, cowboys and Indians, Newcomb

GRADE 6

Major games: hit-pin kickball, soccer, basketball, bombardment, softball, volleyball, handball, pass touch football, paddle tennis

Game skills: throw, catch, kick, hit, pass, dribble, block, punt, field, serve, pitch, receive, return, center, and carry various balls as appropriate in different games

Track: dash, jump and reach, basketball free throw, soccer kick for goal, softball throw for accuracy, shoot and recover, relays

Physical fitness: rings and ladder, sit-up, push-up, rope jumping, stunts, running

Rhythms: fundamental, interpretive, dramatized, marching patterns

Dances: All-American Promenade, Chihuahua, Sicilian circle, Dance of the Bells, Camino al Baño, Oxford Minuet, Spinning Waltz, La Varsoviana

Dance skills: two-step, waltz balance, three-quarter walk, right and left through, ladies chain, twirl, wheel turn, Varsoviana step patterns, tandem two step, controlled pivoting

Other activities: table games, tetherball, four squares, dodge ball, fist ball, socco, section, soccer, number soccer, diagonal pass, section basketball, headman, diamond handball, one bounce, endball, netball, Red Rover, hit through short, work up, target practice, volleyball, set-up, Chinese handball, rotation handball, kick and run, bat ball, base football, Chinese paddle handball

GRADE-LEVEL EMPHASIS AND TIME ALLOTMENTS FOR ACTIVITIES

General guidelines are provided in some courses of study to show the relative emphasis and time allotment by grades for different types of activity. Chart 10–2 shows the grade emphasis in terms of informal experience, introduction, intensive study, and maintenance and increased facility (Sacramento County, 1965, p. 51) Chart 10–3 gives approximate indications of the amount of time allotted to different types of activity (Sacramento County, 1965, p. 52). Notice the shift in some time allotments from grade to grade, with delayed introduction of certain types of activity and the dropping of others. (Under California requirements a period of at least twenty

Chart 10–2. The learning program in physical education.

Content areas	K	1	2	3	4	5	6	7	8
Physical skill development									
Mimetics and story plays									
Rhythmics									
Games, simple to highly organized									
Stunts, tumbling, and self-testing									
Relays									
Physical conditioning, body mechanics, and tests of physical fitness									
Athletic sports and individual athletic events									

Key:

▭ Informal experience		▨ Intensive study	
▨ Introduction		▧ Maintenance and increased facility	

Activities	K	1-2	3-4	5-6	7-8
Physical skill development _____	15	10	10	10	
Mimetics and story plays _____	20	10			
Rhythmics _____	40	35	35	25	15
Games, simple to highly organized _____	15	25	25	15	
Stunts, tumbling, and self-testing _____	10	10	10	10	10
Relays _____		5	10	10	10
Physical conditioning, body mechanics, and tests of physical fitness _____		5	10	15	35
Athletic sports and individual athletic events				15	30

Chart 10–3. Percentage allotment of time to different activities.

minutes must be provided daily, exclusive of recesses and the lunch period, for every pupil except those who are excused in accordance with state law.)

TEACHING STRATEGIES

Active inquiry, exploration, discovery, and application on the part of children are stimulated by teaching strategies in physical education. Observation skills, a sense of timing, direct involvement, and immediate feedback are involved as children experiment and use physical skills in different activities. Probably no other area of the curriculum exceeds physical education in the degree of direct involvement of students.

Teaching strategies are designed to capitalize on this high degree of involvement. A pattern of demonstration, time for exploration and discovery, application of new learnings, and practice through activities may be noted in most teaching strategies. The examples that follow are illustrative of specific strategies that are used in different activities.

Teaching Basic Skills

The following example is illustrative of how a variety of ball movement, handling, and other skills may be taught. Notice the progression from exploration of the movement, to discovery, and to use in a game (Boyer, 1965, pp. 28–29).

TEACHING VERTICAL JUMPING SKILLS

Explore: Children are scattered in play area to explore vertical jumping. They enjoy having their own "little space," "home," "garage," "hangar" to which they frequently return throughout the exploratory period. (This aids in class control without formal organization.) "Can you bounce like a ball and still keep your feet on the ground? (floor)." "Good!" "What helped you be so bouncy?"

Discover: Discussion leads to the use of the knees, "toes" (balls of the feet), ankles. Typical responses: "My knees bend and push." "My toes push." "My knees are springy." "They all bend and push."

Teacher: "Now try to bounce lightly. Let your feet leave the floor. Bounce, bounce, bounce, bounce. Some of you sound like small rubber balls and some like big, heavy basketballs. Listen to the sound of this ball." (Use a small rubber ball to hear its sound.) "Now—a big basketball." (Use a basketball so they can hear it.) "What do you suppose caused the difference in sound?"

Discover: Discussion leads to first learnings. "Too big a jump." "Knees did not bend when I was a basketball hitting the floor." "I landed on my toes when I was the little ball but forgot when I was the big ball."

Explore: Continue the exploration to help children understand how the principles of jumping apply to various kinds of jumps, big or little.

Suggestions: Look for spring from the feet. A common problem on the big jump is kicking their feet up behind them and then landing flatfooted. Emphasize *springing—bouncing*. Use further imagery to help to develop vertical jumping. To ask "What else goes up and down in a jumpy way," produces responses such as these: "Jack in the box." "A pogo stick." "A Mexican jumping bean." "A jumping jack."

Note: The question may also introduce animal jumps which then leads into horizontal jumps or jumping for distance. If this happens use it. It is considered later in this design, but if it comes up here it is a good place for the children to examine the difference.

Use: Jumping up and over an object.

Teacher: "Pretend you have a small block. Place it in front of you. Jump over it. Walk a few steps forward and put a medium-sized block down. Show us how high it is. Jump over it. Now walk a few more steps and put down a bigger block. Can you jump over it? Run back to your own little space. Now walk to the first block, *stop*, and jump over it. Walk to the medium-sized block, *stop*, and jump over it. On to the big block, *stop*, and jump over it. What did you have to do each time your jump became higher?"

Discover: In addition to continued need for use of feet, ankles, knees, and hips, the children discover the importance of swinging the arms *up*, to help pull the body up, and after swinging up the arms go out and down, which helps to give balance to the landing.

Use in game: Jack Be Nimble.

Games of Low Organization

Games of low organization are taught in the early grades in a progression that builds on skills taught earlier and moves to more difficult skills. The following game is illustrative of those taught to young children. It is recommended that it be followed by call ball and ball stand so that a progression in skill development may be achieved (Bucher & Reade, 1964, pp. 122–123).

TEACHER BALL

In the game of Teacher Ball one child acts as the teacher and stands a few feet in front of his squad of from four to seven other children.

```
  1    2    3    4    5    6    7
  x    x    x    x    x    x    x
  _____
                              Children


              x
         _____
          Teacher
```

The distance from the teacher to the squad members depends on the capabilities of the children. Each teacher must judge this according to the children. The teacher tosses the ball to child number *one*, who tries to catch it, and then toss it back to the teacher. Next the teacher tosses the ball to child *two*, and so on, until each child has received the ball from the teacher and returned it to the teacher. The teacher may then go to the end of the line if the children are interested in playing it again. Child *two* would become the new teacher. This game may progress until each child has had a chance to be the teacher if interest warrants. The interest of the children will determine how long it should be played.

The skills involved are tossing and catching. Attitudes involve sharing equipment and playing together. From Teacher Ball we may progress to Call Ball.

Dances

In some courses of study directions are given for the organization of dance formations and for the steps of the dance that is being taught. Dances are typically taught in a sequence that enables children to use known steps as they learn other steps in a new dance. In the following example, notice the clear-cut directions which are essential for demonstrating the steps and for communicating the movements to children (Cincinnati Public Schools, 1962, p. 314).

LA CUCARACHA (MEXICAN) 2/4 TEMPO

Recording: EPA 4134

Formation: Couples side by side, girl to right, all facing front; girls hold skirt out to side, boys have hands behind their backs holding back their serapes.

Action: Dancers may move in same direction or in opposite directions; boy to left, girl to right.
Moving to the right—step to right (1–2). Close left to right (3). Repeat.
Circle to the right three steps beginning right, and finish with a stamp left (1–4).
Repeat all three more times, left, right, and left.
Cross right over left (1). Lean right shoulder over right foot.
Step back on left foot, straightening up (2).
Step on right foot near to the left foot (3).
Repeat crossing left foot over right (1, 2, and 3).
Repeat all for 8 full measures of the music.

Summary of Procedures

Several procedures related to each of the main types of physical activity may be used to develop the instructional program. To be sure, the rules for each game, the steps for each dance, and the specific characteristics of each activity must be known. However, the following have wide applicability as different activities are provided.

Rhythm and dances: Clarify the beat and have children clap it, demonstrate new movements or steps and review ones taught earlier as needed, select children to demonstrate the new movement or step, form the group and teach a part at a time, try the step without music and then with music, give individual help, add other parts, finally combining them into the complete activity.

Apparatus and equipment: Teach uses of each type; clarify safety practices, establish rules for sharing and use, have children demonstrate proper use, organize groups for use, check daily to see that equipment is safe, avoid use during bad weather because of safety hazards.

Low-organization games: Know the rules and have all equipment ready for use; begin the game with a minimum of explanation or demonstration so children can learn by doing; teach as the game is played and as children ask questions; end the game with review, designation of winners, or other appropriate activity while interest is high.

Individual and dual activities: Use group instruction to introduce, have individuals or couples demonstrate, give individual help and have students assist each other, stress cooperation.

Self-testing and stunts: Put safety first and observe the activity critically; introduce with pictures or sketches and demonstration by teacher or students; have students work at own speed, giving help as needed; avoid competitive situations; use only for a short time during the play period.

Story plays: Keep them interesting and short, start the activity immediately after briefly setting the stage, move from part to part without delay, get suggestions from children for some parts, participate as needed to keep the story moving, have a reasonable and logical ending.

Fitness activities: Provide progressive exercises appropriate at each level, start with short time periods followed by gradual increase to build endurance, adjust to individual differences, use modified exercises for girls, clarify the value of particular exercises.

Lead-up activities: Show how they are related to games; demonstrate basic skills involved, with help of students as appropriate; answer questions; give individual help; have appropriate individual, couple, or small group practice in catching, dribbling, or other skills; when using relays, score for first, second, etc., so that all teams earn points.

Team games: clarify positions of players by means of sketches or diagrams; review or teach rules as needed; briefly point out or show how skills in lead-up games can be used; observe as the game is played, giving tips as needed; when feasible use students as umpires so that two or more groups may play; have skilled students help others; encourage cooperation.

Track and field: Arrange for safety and clarify precautions; designate ball throwing and other areas; select appropriate events in terms of age and sex; organize participants by age, weight, and sex; avoid excessive competition.

Adapted or corrective activities: Follow a physician's recommendations, adapt regular activities to individual needs so that students can participate with others, use recommended exercises to improve posture and other defects, suggest appropriate home exercises.

GUIDELINES FOR THE TEACHER

The following guiding principles are indicative of key responsibilities of the teacher in providing high-quality instruction in physical education.

Provide a balanced program. Keep the social, biological, and integrative functions in balance, selecting and adapting both indoor and outdoor activities that contribute to the development of the objectives specified for physical education. Include attention to cognitive, affective, and psychomotor outcomes as long-range and daily plans are made. Check plans systematically to assure a well-rounded program of physical activities for all children.

Provide for progression. The progressive development of motor skills and other outcomes of physical education should be emphasized within grades as specific activities are taught and between grades as children's capabilities are brought to increasingly higher levels. Plan and guide activities that are linked to the child's capabilities and past experience and lead to higher levels of competence. Use conditioning and rhythmic lead-up and other activities to provide a sequence of development as outlined in current teaching guides.

Adapt and individualize the program. Meet individual differences of children through adaptation of activities, teaching techniques, and evaluation of outcomes. Select activities in terms of observed characteristics and needs of children. Provide for differing interests and abilities of boys and girls as they mature and for different rates and levels of development of all children.

Use strategies that maximize student involvement.   Creativity, discovery, exploration, application, practice, and self-evaluation should be facilitated. Select procedures and techniques that fit each type of activity and use them in ways that develop self-responsibility and initiative. Involve students in the planning, demonstrating, and evaluating of activities so that they will learn from one another.

Begin activities without undue delay.   Explanations, demonstrations, directions, and background information should be clear and to the point. Motivation may be lowered, learning through discovery may be hampered, and the benefits of the activity may be decreased if preliminary activities are overextended. After clear and brief instructions, children need to learn through doing, obtaining further instruction as they get a feeling for the activity and as questions and problems arise.

Use positive and intrinsic motivation.   Constructive suggestions, praise for effort and accomplishment, and encouragement should be given as needed by individual children. Comparisons, embarrassment, and a series of failures should be avoided. Each child will find activities to be intrinsically interesting and enjoyable if he has the opportunity to develop skills, make improvement, and play with others in an atmosphere of mutual respect. Because of children's natural interest in physical activities there is no need for extrinsic rewards.

Direct the use of equipment and facilities.   Close direction should be provided to maximize learning and to minimize accidents. Instructions on use, safety first, adherence to rules, staying in designated areas, removal of glasses and jewelry, appropriate dress, and supervision at all times are essential. All equipment and facilities should be inspected regularly, repaired or replaced as needed, and used in accordance with the purposes they are designed to serve.

Relate the program to other areas.   The close links between physical education and other aspects of the complete school health program have been mentioned. Attention should be given to such items as games and rhythms in other lands in social studies, measuring distance and time in arithmetic, and concepts of force and momentum in science. Related activities in art and music should be identified as May Day activities, play days, folk dances, singing games, and rhythmic activities are undertaken. Reading can be used to gather ideas on games, sports, and other activities and to participate vicariously in the play experiences of other children and in the activities of athletes admired by students. Oral and written expression can be used to share the excitement and joy of children's own experiences, as well as those of others, and to report on ideas gleaned through reading, observation, and firsthand participation.

Seek assistance on special problems.   Children with physical deficiencies should have adapted or corrective programs. The advice of doctors and other specialists should be obtained and used in planning adequate programs for them. In some cases, there may be need for a broad program of development that includes dietary changes, special therapy, and other provisions. The teacher's role is to make referrals, help in gathering data, and carry out the recommendations of specialists.

Assist in intramural programs.   The competitive tendency that emerges as children progress through school should be guided constructively through intramural competition, not interschool competition. Play and sports days that include individual, dual, and group activities from the regular physical education program are recommended. Grouping of children according to age, size, and sex, getting maximum participation of all children, providing a variety of activities, stressing teamwork and sportsmanship, and supervising of events are key ingredients in successful play days and tournaments. The assistance of teachers is needed in planning and conducting intramural programs in order to assure beneficial outcomes for all participants.

EVALUATION OF OUTCOMES OF INSTRUCTION

Evaluation of outcomes of the physical education program is greatly facilitated by the heavy emphasis on physical activities. Directly observable changes in behavior may be noted by both the teacher and students. Informal observation during activities, directed observation guided by charts and check lists, and systematic observation during special testing and self-testing activities are dominant features of evaluation.

Self-evaluation by students is another feature of evaluation that is dominant in physical education. Because of the direct involvement of students, the nature of physical activities, the responsibility each student has for his own performance, and the individual form and style that are developed, students themselves inevitably make continuing assessments of their progress. As in art education, the student is expressing himself in a highly individualized way and is making changes and adjustments in terms of his own evaluation. Self-assessment, therefore, in which the teacher promotes each student's ability to explore, discover, and use his physical capabilities creatively and effectively is a hallmark of sound evaluation.

Both informal and formal testing to assess knowledge, attitudes, and skills are included in complete programs of evaluation. A variety of tests of knowledge and inventories of attitudes and interests may be found in the literature (Buros, 1966; Willgoose, 1961). Teacher-made tests and inventories geared to the instructional program make it possible to assess specific objectives that are being emphasized.

Positive and constructive approaches are essential in all phases of evaluation. During sharing and discussion of problems and difficulties, attention should be given to ways to improve, to promising characteristics that can be nurtured, and to steps to be taken to develop basic motor skills. Students themselves well may share in commending others for their successes, demonstrating ways to improve, and suggesting procedures that they have found to be most helpful. By all means, realistic objectives should be set for each child so that at no time is he faced with insurmountable tasks that can only result in negative and defeatist attitudes and a turning away from physical activities.

Illustrative Evaluation Devices

The check lists given below and Charts 10-4–10-6 are illustrative of devices that are highly recommended for use in the elementary school. In each example, behaviors are listed as guides to observation. Check marks may be made by behaviors in which growth has been observed, letter or numeral ratings may be used as judgments are made, or check marks may be made to indicate behaviors in need of improvement. Notice that several examples contain a cluster of related behaviors, thus showing how concept clusters can be used to devise evaluative devices.

A variety of charts, check lists, and rating devices can be constructed by the teacher and by the children. A key principle is to identify the specific behaviors that are to be assessed. This may be done by checking courses of study, teaching manuals, and other sources. Key behaviors also may be identified through discussions in which students suggest items to be evaluated. The following summary of key behaviors related to various activities includes examples that can be used in their present form for evaluating outcomes or can be incorporated in charts and other evaluative devices.

> *Muscular coordination in story plays:* _____ **Throws** _____
> **Bends** _____ **Twists** _____ **Runs** _____ **Jumps**
> _____ **Stretches**
>
> *Balance beam:* _____ **Walks forward** _____ **Walks backward** _____ **Makes turns** _____ **Kneels** _____ **Cat walks** _____ **Balances object on head while walking** _____ **Tosses and catches ball while walking**
>
> *Rhythmic movements:* _____ **Walks** _____ **Runs** _____
> **Jumps** _____ **Hops** _____ **Slides** _____ **Claps**
> _____ **Trots** _____ **Gallops** _____ **Marches** _____
> **Waltzes** _____ **Two-steps**
>
> *Ball control:* _____ **Tosses** _____ **Rolls** _____ **Bounces**
> _____ **Throws** _____ **Kicks** _____ **Uses arm catch**

_____ Uses hand catch _____ Bats _____ Serves
_____ Bats with hand

Zone soccer: _____ Kicks moving ball _____ Blocks _____
Passes _____ Punts

Zone basketball: _____ Shoots from field of play _____
Passes _____ _____ Catches _____ Guards _____
Makes free throws

Bat ball: _____ Bats with fist _____ Throws _____
Catches _____ Runs bases _____ Tags a moving target
_____ Dodges

Softball: _____ Throws overhand _____ Throws under-
hand _____ Throws side arm _____ Catches _____
Fields ground ball _____ Fields fly ball _____ Pitches
_____ Bats _____ Runs bases

Pass touch football: _____ Passes forward _____ Passes
laterally _____ Punts _____ Place kicks _____
Centers the ball _____ Runs _____ Feints _____
Dodges

Volleyball: _____ Serves _____ Returns _____ Hits
returned ball _____ Shifts _____ Develops strategy

Basketball: _____ Shoots _____ Makes free throws
_____ Passes _____ Pivots _____ Dribbles _____
Catches _____ Guards _____ Uses pattern plays _____
Develops plays _____ Plays position

Soccer: _____ Kicks _____ Punts _____ Blocks
_____ Passes _____ Dribbles _____ Develops plays

Passing skills: _____ Passes underhand _____ Passes overhand _____ Passes from chest _____ Passes from shoulder _____ Passes overhead _____ Bounce passes
_____ Hook passes

Sportsmanship: _____ Plays fair _____ Participates
_____ Follows directions _____ Leads _____ Follows
_____ Loses cheerfully _____ Wins gracefully _____
Accepts decisions _____ Shows concern for others _____
Has self-control _____ Respects others

Physical Fitness

Many tests of physical fitness have been developed during the past several
years. The President's Council on Physical Fitness, state departments of
education, and other groups have devised tests (Clarke & Haar, 1964;

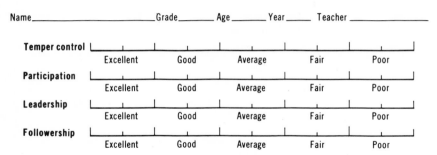

Name_____Grade_____ Age _____ Year_____ Teacher _____

Chart 10–4. *A rating device.*

Chart 10–5. *Check list for evaluating team sports.*

	Names of students
Sportsmanship	
Accepts decisions	
Obeys the rules	
Has self-control	
Respects others	
Participation	
Begins promptly	
Tries to improve	
Encourages others	
Takes his turn	
Team Effort	
Plays for the team	
Plays own position	
Follows instructions	
Wins or loses gracefully	

Chart 10–6. *Charts for self-evaluation.*

Leadership	Sportsmanship	Bat Ball
Are directions clear?	Do I play fairly?	__ Bat with fist?
Is safety emphasized?	Do I look out for others?	__ Throw accurately?
Are all treated fairly?	Do I follow the rules?	__ Catch the ball?
Are rights respected?	Do I accept decisions?	__ Tag a moving target?
Do all have turns?		__ Dodge effectively?

Hunsicker, 1963; Willgoose, 1961). The most widely used tests are the AAHPER (American Association of Health, Physical Education, and Recreation), the California, the New York State, the Marine Corps, and the Kraus-Weber (Collins & Hunter, 1965). The Oregon test is also widely used and has been cited in many of the references included at the end of this chapter.

A preliminary screening test is recommended by the President's Council for identifying underdeveloped students. Three tests are included: pull-ups (modified for girls), sit-ups, and squat thrusts. A normal boy in the ten- to thirteen-year age range should be able to do one pull-up, fourteen sit-ups, and four squat thrusts (in ten seconds).

The AAHPER test includes seven items: pull-ups (modified for girls), sit-ups, shuttle run, standing broad jump, 50-yard dash, softball throw for distance, and 600-yard run-walk. Norms are available for ten- to seventeen-year-olds (Collins & Hunter, 1965). For example, to score "excellent" a ten-year-old boy must do six pull-ups, do sixty sit-ups, throw a softball 122 feet, do the 600-yard run-walk in 2 minutes and 15 seconds, do the shuttle run in 10.3 seconds, do a standing broad jump of 5 feet and 6 inches, and

TABLE 10-1. Physical Fitness Components and Tests

Component	*Selected tests**
1. Arm and shoulder strength	Pull-ups, push-ups, parallel bar, dips, rope climb
2. Speed	50-yard dash, 100-yard dash
3. Agility	Shuttle run, agility run
4. Abdominal and hip strength	Sit-ups, sit-ups with knees flexed, 2-minute sit-ups
5. Flexibility	Trunk flexion standing, trunk flexion sitting, trunk extension (prone position)
6. Cardiorespiratory endurance	600-yard run, half-mile run, mile run, 5-minute step test
7. Explosive power	Standing broad jump, vertical jump
8. Static strength	Grip strength, back lift, leg lift
9. Balance	Bass test, Brace test, tests on balance beam
10. Muscular endurance	Push-ups, chest raising (prone position, hands behind neck, legs held down), V-sit (against time)

* *Norms for many of these tests appear in the citations on tests and measurements and the articles in the Selected Research References (Hunsicker, 1963, p. 30).*

run the 50-yard dash in 7.6 seconds. A ten-year-old girl to score "excellent" must do forty-five modified pull-ups, do fifty sit-ups, throw a softball 69 feet, do the 600-yard run-walk in 2 minutes and 30 seconds, do the shuttle run in 11.2 seconds, do a standing broad jump of 5 feet and 4 inches, and run the 50-yard dash in 8.0 seconds.

Hunsicker (1963, p. 17) has prepared the summary shown in Table 10–1 to indicate the physical fitness components that are assessed by selected tests. (See p. 331.)

EVALUATION OF THE PHYSICAL EDUCATION PROGRAM

Feedback from the evaluation of the effectiveness of instruction activities is a prime source of data for use in evaluating the physical education program. In addition, such criteria as the following may be used to assess the overall program.

Foundations
Are foundation disciplines used as bases for planning the program?
Is the program designed to meet societal needs and conditions?
Is knowledge of child development and learning used to improve instruction?

Structure
Is the program structured in terms of basic physical activities?
Is there a progression from low- to high-level abilities and skills?

Inquiry
Are exploration, discovery, and application emphasized?
Is emphasis given to an experimental and creative approach to activities?

Objectives
Are the social, biological, and integrative functions kept in balance?
Is attention given to key concepts and understandings that underlie physical activities?
Are functional skills and abilities defined behaviorally?
Are attitudes of inquiry, interest in physical activities, appreciations of the importance of fitness, and other affective outcomes stressed?

A complete program
Is the program balanced in terms of required, adapted or corrective, and intramural activities?

Is the program individualized and balanced at each grade level in terms of activities selected to promote the physical, social, mental, and emotional development of children?

Is the program coordinated with other aspects of the school health program and with community recreation programs?

Teaching strategies

Is use made of strategies that promote exploration, discovery, and application on the part of students?

Are specific techniques used to promote growth and development in each of the main types of physical activity?

Are equipment, facilities, and other instructional media available, checked systematically for safety, and used effectively?

Are the attitudes, skills, and knowledge essential to safety stressed?

Evaluation

Is direct observation guided by the use of charts and other devices?

Is self-evaluation guided by the teacher and facilitated through sharing, discussion, and self-evaluative devices?

Are fitness and other tests used regularly to assess achievement?

Is the program of instruction evaluated systematically?

Teacher education

Is continuing growth of teachers provided in order to develop and maintain the competencies needed to offer high-quality instruction?

Are consultant services and special teachers available to give assistance as needed and to handle special activities?

Continuing revision

Are new ideas drawn from the disciplines and used to improve the quality of instruction?

Are new developments assessed systematically in order to determine program changes?

REFERENCES

Boyer, Madeline H. *The teaching of elementary school physical education.* New York: J. Lovell Pratt, 1966. A handbook of activities for elementary grades.

Bucher, Charles A., & Reade, Evelyn M. *Physical education and health in the elementary school.* New York: Macmillan, 1964. Principles and techniques for teaching all types of physical activities.

Buros, Oscar K. *The sixth mental measurements yearbook.* Highland Park, N.J.: Gryphon Press, 1965. Information on tests published between 1959 and 1964; reviews of earlier tests in preceding volumes.

Cincinnati Public Schools. *Intermediate manual.* (rev.) Cincinnati: Board of Education, 1962. Outline of the physical education program in chap. 36.

Clarke, H. Harrison, & Haar, Franklin B. *Health and physical education for the elementary school classroom teacher.* Englewood Cliffs, N.J.: Prentice-Hall, 1964. Principles and procedures for teaching physical activities as part of a complete school health program.

Collins, George J., & Hunter, J. Scott. *Physical achievement and the schools.* Washington, D.C.: U.S. Office of Education, 1965. A study of physical fitness showing the need for continuing improvement.

Cowell, Charles C., & France, Wellman L. *Philosophy and principles of physical education.* Englewood Cliffs, N.J.: Prentice-Hall, 1963. A review of foundational aspects of physical education and a summary of basic principles.

Dauer, Victor P. *Fitness for elementary school children.* Minneapolis: Burgess, 1965. Principles and specific techniques for teaching physical activities.

Espenschade, Anna S. *Physical eduation in the elementary schools.* Washington, D.C.: National Education Association, 1963. A pamphlet containing a statement of objectives and guiding principles for developing a modern program.

Fabricus, Helen. *Physical education for the classroom teacher.* Dubuque, Iowa: W. C. Brown, 1965. Principles and techniques for teaching physical activities.

Hunsicker, Paul. *Physical fitness.* Washington, D.C.: National Educational Association, 1963. A summary of key factors in fitness.

Los Angeles City Schools. *Course of study for elementary schools.* Los Angeles: Board of Education, 1964. Detailed outline of physical activities for kindergarten through grade 6.

Nixon, J. E., & Jewett, A. E. *Physical education curriculum planning.* New York: Ronald, 1964. Principles and procedures for curriculum development; good section on values and their development.

Oberteuffer, Delbert. Health education and physical education. *New Curriculum Development.* Washington, D.C.: Association for Supervision and Curriculum Development, 1965. A review of current curriculum projects and studies.

Oberteuffer, Delbert, & Ulrich, Celeste. *Physical education.* (3d ed.) New York: Harper, 1962. A standard reference on basic principles and procedures.

Paterson, Ann, & Hallberg, Edmond C. *Background readings for physical education.* New York: Holt, 1965. Selected readings on foundations of physical education.

Phenix, Philip H. *Realms of meaning.* New York: McGraw-Hill, 1964. A philosophy of curriculum development including an analysis of disciplines in relation to six realms of meaning. Chapter 14, "The Arts of Movement," deals with dance and sports.

President's Council on Youth Fitness. *Youth physical fitness: suggested elements of a school centered program.* Government Printing Office, 1961. Guidelines for providing fitness activities and for testing achievement.

Sacramento County. *Basic course of study for elementary grades.* Sacramento: County Superintendent of Schools, 1965. An outline of the program of studies.

Sliepcevich, Elena M. *School health education study: experimental curriculum materials project.* (rev.) New York: Educational Services Press, 1966. Materials prepared in a current project.

Willgoose, Carl E. *Evaluation in health education and physical education.* New York: McGraw-Hill, 1961. Principles, techniques, and tests for use in appraising outcomes of instruction.

Williams, Jesse F. *The principles of physical education.* (8th ed.) Philadelphia: Saunders, 1964. A standard reference on basic principles of physical education.

Chapter Eleven

ART EDUCATION

A RT IS THE CREATIVE ORGANIZATION of visual elements to express thoughts and feelings. The visual arts include such forms as painting, drawing, printmaking, sculpture, architecture, industrial design, and types of film making. These arts are a part of the broad realm of aesthetics in which the focus is on a singular particular form (Phenix, 1964). Both expression through art activity and investigation of artistic expression deal with creative organization of visual elements.

A more complete listing of aspects of visual arts would include those which are considered the "fine arts," usually singular creations in comparatively enduring form, and the "applied arts," which produce multiple reproductions of nonendurable forms. Painting, sculpture, and architecture would thus be considered fine arts; industrial design and ceramics would be applied. Because the objectives of art education include development of the child's appreciation of art in daily life, his art experiences in the elementary school include activities related to both fine and applied arts.

Key concepts and generalizations are derived by artists, architects, designers, and art scholars who use methods of inquiry appropriate to the field in which they specialize. Application or reduction to practice in the visual arts is made in relation to the entire range of human activity. Examples of concepts, generalizations, and applications are presented in later sections of this chapter. Before they are considered, attention is given to individual and universal aspects of art. A point to keep in mind throughout this chapter is that the subjective and singular nature of artworks differentiates them sharply from the objective and general nature of scientific works (Phenix, 1964), and therefore individual differences in children's learning experiences tend to be at wider variance than in any other area of elementary instruction.

INDIVIDUAL AND UNIVERSAL ASPECTS OF ART

The unique and distinctive ways in which artists of all ages express themselves constitute truly concrete evidence of individual differences. Goals of expression, perceptions of reality, means of expression, and assessment of one's work are distinctively singular. The artist's interpretations, images, thoughts, and feelings flow from within as media are utilized to express his intentions. The true artist may be aptly characterized as a leading exponent of unique, individualized, genuine self-expression.

Also highly personal is the response of individuals to works of art. The viewer of a work associates thoughts and feelings with the shapes, colors, and patterns that he views. The associations that are triggered for one person may be quite unlike those set off for another. Responses may include feelings of delight, anger, sorrow, joy, or excitement. The individual's past experiences, in general, and his depth of insight into art, in particular, influence his responses.

Along with these highly individualized aspects of art are universal aspects of importance. The urge to express and communicate ideas through the organization of visual elements is noted in cultures of all times and places. The same qualities, elements, and principles of design are interwoven in different art forms. Some symbols and metaphors of the visual arts cross cultures and stir thoughts and feelings that cannot be conveyed by verbal language. Although responses of individuals to particular works of art may differ, responses to any works of art may be universally characterized in terms of positive or negative feelings such as awe, excitement, joy, pleasure, or distaste.

FOUNDATION DISCIPLINES

The field of visual arts which underlies art education consists of both creative activity and the study of artwork. The area of creative expression has generated its own structure of elements, qualities, and principles of design, which guide creative endeavor and form a basis for aesthetics and art criticism. To varying extents in the several fine and applied arts, elements and principles are partly drawn from two areas of physics: mechanics and optics. The reliance of architecture, sculpture, and industrial design upon laws of physics has always been evident. During this century, specific movements within various fields have drawn even more directly upon this foundation discipline; mobiles and kinetic sculpture involve principles of motion and dynamics, while optical principles are explored and utilized in the works of Anuszkiewicz and others of the Op Art movement.

Foundation disciplines in the study of artwork include aesthetics, art history, art criticism, archaeology, and anthropology. From these fields are drawn concepts related to design, periods and styles, and art in the lives of people.

All these disciplines contribute to the subject matter and activities that constitute the art education curriculum. Developmental psychology contributes ideas and principles related to creativity and the developmental stages of art expression.

Concept Clusters and Generalizations

Some of the best examples of concept clusters and generalizations drawn from foundation disciplines are to be found in art education. A primary reason for this close affinity between underlying disciplines and instruction is undoubtedly the specialized nature of art instruction. More than in other subject areas, almost all of the child's learning comes as a result of his participation as an artist. Another reason is the relatively close relationship that many art teachers and supervisors have kept with the art profession in their capacities as artists, critics, and writers on art.

The following concept clusters, drawn from the disciplines, are illustrative of those utilized in recent courses of study:

>*Elements of design*: line, color, light, form, space, texture, movement
>
>*Line*: vertical, horizontal, oblique, curved, precise, broken, bold, thin
>
>*Art history*: styles, movements, periods
>
>*Style in art, industrial design*: De Stijl, Bauhaus, Art Nouveau
>
>*Art movements*: Impressionism, Expressionism, Cubism, Dadaism, Surrealism, Op Art, Pop Art; Classical, Futuristic, Kinetic sculpture
>
>*Ancient art*: Prehistoric, Babylonian-Assyrian, Egyptian, Aegean, Mycenean, Greek, Etruscan, Roman
>
>*European art*: Medieval, Renaissance, Baroque, Rococo
>
>*Cubism*: multiple surfaces, twisting of planes, dislocation of parts, superimposition, geometric lines
>
>*Art criticism*: function, expression, design, media, technique
>
>*Developmental stages*: scribbling, schematic, pseudorealistic
>
>*Architecture*: site, function, materials; post and lintel, arch, cantilever
>
>*Sculpture*: carved, modeled, cast, constructed

Generalizations from basic disciplines which are stressed in art education include the following:

>In all cultures, man expresses his hopes, aspirations, perceptions, and feelings through the language of the visual arts.
>Each work of art is a creative experience for the artist and for those who view it.
>Concepts of design permeate all types of artistic design and aesthetic appreciation.
>Artists vary in the way they communicate through visual arts.
>The meaning of an artwork should be sought in what is uniquely expressed through the creative organization of elements and materials.

Deep appreciation of some artworks requires an understanding of the settings in which they were created.

Much can be learned about a culture by studying its artworks, because art in any culture reflects in part the general characteristics of that culture.

In many contemporary art activities, an important criterion of appropriate design is that form follows function.

Many other generalizations will be discerned in the preceding sections of this chapter. Other generalizations and concept clusters are highlighted in the sections that follow, particularly in discussions of qualities, principles, elements of design, and stages of creative development.

STRUCTURE IN ART AND ART EDUCATION

The concept of design is at the very heart of expression through art. Good design may be viewed as the best that designers of a given time and place have produced according to art experts. Design may be evaluated in terms of classical, contemporary, or other standards that an individual or group believes to be most important. Art educators tend to view design, or composition, in terms of elements, principles, and qualities which are relevant to all the media that are a part of the program of instruction. Design may be defined as the utilization of elements in accordance with principles and qualities to produce artworks by means of specific processes and materials. Each of these aspects of design may be defined in various ways. The terms in Chart 11–1 and the definitions that follow are drawn from recently published courses of study.

Elements

Elements are those components of a work of art which have tangible or objective existence and visible or tactile characteristics, such as hue, size,

Chart 11–1.   Components of design.

Elements	Processes and materials	Artworks
Movement, line, texture, color, light, form, space	Painting, drawing, print making, photography, film making, carving, modeling, casting, constructing, sewing, weaving, pasting, mosaics	Paintings, prints sculpture, buildings, collages, murals, stage design, furniture, illustrations, ads, apparel, tapestry, stained glass, appliances, films
Principles		
Balance, rhythm, contrast, emphasis, proportion		
Qualities		
Unity, clarity, harmony		

and texture, which may be described in terms universal to all observers. Elements may be considered analogous to concepts in academic disciplines. Principles and qualities are statements about the relationships of elements. As verbal descriptions or criteria, their existence lies in the eye, and mind, of the beholder. While the specific elements are distinguishable by certain characteristics, they cannot be physically isolated, because, except for light, various elements of an artwork combine to generate other elements. For example, in two-dimensional design, color is the result of light reflection, line may be formed by the sharp change from one color area to another or the boundaries of dark and light, and space is defined in part by line and color. In three-dimensional design, light on surfaces enables perception of form, while light, form, and movement combine to define space.

Line refers to the path of vision and the direction it takes: vertical, horizontal, oblique, or spiral. Lines may be curved, straight, broken, continuous, delicate, bold, dynamic, static, precise, blurred, tense, relaxed.

Texture is the "feel" or appearance, real or apparent, of surface treatment, which may be rough, smooth, furrowed, wrinkled, even, irregular, soft, shiny, dull.

Light in two-dimensional design is the pattern of light and dark referred to as "chiaroscuro." In three-dimensional design, it is the pattern of light, shade, and shadow without which form could not be perceived. The element of light is used even more directly in such forms as stage design, architecture, films, stained glass, and sculptures that include incandescent lamps or neon tubing as part of their construction. Light may be intense, dim, steady, varying, direct, diffused.

Color refers to the reflection of light and is described in terms of hue (name), intensity (brightness or dullness), and value (lightness or darkness of the color). The colors of natural light are classified as primary (red, yellow, blue), secondary (orange, green, violet), and intermediate. Neutral colors are black and white. Colors may also be referred to as complementary (opposite), analogous (adjacent), warm, or cool.

Form refers to the shapes seen in two-dimensional design and to the shape of a three-dimensional object or its component parts. Form may be solid, amorphous, suggested, defined, simple, complex.

Space refers to the area between and around forms. In two-dimensional design, an illusion of three-dimensional space may be provided by means of perspective, positional relation of forms, or "advancing" and "receding" colors. In three-dimensional design, space is defined by form, and in kinetic or mobile sculpture, by form and motion. The relationship of space, form, and motion may be referred to as *volume*. Space may be real, apparent, open, closed, static, dynamic.

Movement is the direction of vision over or around the work, directed by line, color, and form in two-dimensional design, and form itself in sculpture and architecture. In kinetic sculpture, air currents or motors produce movement as a change of position of the total work or its component parts. Movement may be rhythmic, repetitious, sporadic, smooth, abrupt, intersecting, oscillating, revolving, radiating.

Although works of art are observed in *time*, the duration of time usually depends upon the observer. However, in kinetic sculpture and films, time is an integral element because its duration, or the duration of movement patterns, is fixed by the artwork, not the observer.

Principles

Principles of design are concepts relating to the ways in which elements are employed to create art objects that possess design qualities. *Emphasis* refers to the use of dominance and subordination to make some colors, shapes, or line directions stand out while others are subdued. *Contrast* refers to opposition: dark against light, differing colors, change in planes, differences in form or texture. *Balance* refers to the distribution of each element in an artwork and the degree to which this distribution, in connection with emphasis and contrast, maintains equilibrium within the work. *Proportion* refers to the relation of parts to the whole and of parts to each other within the physical limits of the work. *Rhythm* refers to apparent movement within the work and may be expressed through repetition of lines, forms, colors, and other elements, or continuity of direction of vision between components of the work.

Qualities

Qualities are concepts which go beyond elements and relationships to include the materials and function of the art object. *Unity* refers to integrity in the use of materials and the relation of form to function. *Clarity* refers to the idea that all functional parts should be visible, all visible parts functional—effects achieved in the unification of form and function. *Harmony* refers to the relationships within and between the components of a work, the degree to which parts fit together, and the way in which the work fits into a larger ensemble.

Inquiry and the Creative Process

Inquiry in any academic discipline leads to the production and organization of knowledge relevant to that field. The creative process, which is an inquiry process in the discipline of art, leads to the production of artworks which constitute unique forms or organization of knowledge in the realm of aesthetics. As in other disciplines, this process follows a type of problem-solving procedure.

The artist's creative effort is a response to a recognized problem. The problem may be to determine the design possibilities inherent in a material, to experiment with effects produced by various elements, to express an idea or specific message, to produce a specific design or pattern, to meet a specific function, as in the design of a building, or, at times, to solve problems cutting across or combining categories of exploration, expression, and function. In order to meet the problem he has set, the artist selects appropriate materials and processes, sometimes experiments with them to explore their design-producing possibilities, utilizes them to produce elements which are combined in accordance with principles to create a solution to the problem in the form of an artwork. This characteristic mode of inquiry of the artist is the same procedure that the child follows in his art education experiences. As children become familiar with elements, discover principles, qualities, and symbols, explore materials, experiment with processes, and create a variety of products, they come into direct contact with the structure of art and develop insight into design concepts.

Aspects of the creative process include such activities and thinking skills as the following:

> **observation, imagination, visualization**
> **perception, analysis, spatial organization**
> **classification and utilization of elements**
> **invention and utilization of symbols, real and abstract**
> **manipulation of materials and skill in using them**
> **exploration of various processes**

Specific examples of these activities and skills are found in the sections dealing with developmental stages, the complete program, and teaching strategies. It should be borne in mind that it is often difficult to distinguish these skills individually because of their close interaction. For example, discovery or invention of new materials or new processing techniques can lead to new forms of art products, and the special characteristics of a desired product may stimulate the artist to seek new materials and explore new techniques.

DEVELOPMENTAL STAGES

Programs of instruction in art education have been greatly influenced by studies of child growth and artistic development. In fact, art educators have led the field in relating instruction to stages of development. A knowledge of developmental stages is essential in overall planning and in daily instruction. Although different writers have used different terms to categorize specific stages, the following examples, with typical years of age in parenthesis, indicate that there is broad general agreement regarding the sequence of growth:

Lark-Horovitz: (1939)	Lowenfeld and Brittain: (1964)	DeFrancesco: (1958)
Scribble (3–5)	Scribbling (2–4)	Manipulative (2–5)
	Preschematic (4–7)	Presymbolic (5–7)
Schematic (6–11)	Schematic (7–9)	Symbolic (7–9)
	Dawning realism (9–11)	Inceptive realism (9–11)
Mixed schematic (11–13)	Pseudorealistic (11–13)	Analytical realism (11–13)
True-to-appearance (early adolescence)	Period of decision (adolescence)	Projective realism (13–15)
Representation in space (adolescence)		Renascence (15–20)

Developmental stages are outlined for eight different art activities in the New York City guide (1964). The following examples are illustrative of the consistency of movement from the manipulative and exploratory stage to higher levels of expressive design:

Painting and drawing	Clay and crafts
1. Manipulative and exploratory	1. Manipulative and exploratory
2. Intuitive design (painting) Circular configuration (drawing)	2. Intuitive design
3. Conscious design (painting) Schematic (drawing)	3. Conscious design (clay) Deliberate design (crafts)
4. Planning and organizing	4. Preplanned design
5. Expressing near and far	5. Modified design
6. Increased realism and expressive design	6. Craftsmanship and expressive design

It should be recognized that the stages do not coincide with grades or with ages of children. Rather, each child develops in accord with his own growth pattern and may be at one stage in painting and another in handicrafts. Some of the more important growth patterns and their relationships to instruction are summarized in the following discussion of specific stages.

Manipulative, Exploratory, Scribble Stage

During the first stage of development children explore and manipulate materials to get the feel of them. The motor activity is more important to them than the visual result. The child strokes with a whole-arm movement, making a tangle of line and using masses of color. Longitudinal strokes followed by a circular emphasis emerge after some experience. Clay is pounded, kneaded, rolled, and smoothed as the child experiments with different shapes. Blocks and pieces of wood are piled, stacked, and arranged in different ways. The child's manipulation and exploration are his way of learning how to handle various media. Although children have no conscious design in mind, the day soon arrives when they comment on their work or name it. Their comments should be accepted and received without interpretations by the teacher. Any comments or questions from the teacher should be in the direction of the child's story or remarks about his work. Encouragement to experiment with materials should be given. Materials should be selected that involve the use of large motions by the child. Appropriate activities widely used during this stage include water painting at the chalkboard with a wide brush, easel painting with one color at first and others added as needs arise, use of large black crayons and, then, colored crayons, block building, torn and cut paper work, and modeling with plasticine.

Preschematic, Presymbolic, Intuitive Design Stage

During the ages of five to seven, children typically move to a beginning semblance of order or intuitive design. A shape such as a circle may be used in drawing or painting to represent a person, an orange, or some other object. Lines may be attached to represent arms and legs. Shapes may be repeated in drawings; large masses of color appear in paintings; and clay work may consist of simple arrangements with varied surface treatments. Colors are used in terms of the child's desires, not in terms of reality. Designs that are related to real or imagined objects are evident in the work of some children. Content is related primarily to the child's self. Self-expression is helped by a discussion of experiences and of ideas of interest to the child. Appropriate activities include finger and easel painting, drawing with chalk and crayons, painting with tempera, simple stenciling, paper and wood construction, simple weaving, and clay modeling. Large thick brushes and large pieces of absorbent paper should be provided for painting.

Schematic, Symbolic, Conscious Design Stage

During the schematic or symbolic state characteristic of many seven- to nine-year-olds, children use circles, ovals, and rectangles to portray people, houses, trees, and other objects. Lines and shapes are used in a repetitive manner, and colors are selected in relation to objects. Some children begin to bring out realistic details, others give subjective interpretations, and some use a combination of the two. Features important to the child may be exaggerated, e.g., a truck driver proportionally larger than the truck. Features unimportant to the child may be omitted entirely, e.g., the steering wheel of a car. Details important to the child may be shown even though they cannot be seen in reality as they are drawn, e.g., houses on both sides of the street, a table top "folded up" to show what is on it, and "X-ray" or transparent pictures to show both the inside and outside of a house. The base line is discovered and used, although objects may be placed along it without clear reference to size and space relationships. Objects made of clay show greater variation in shape, proportion, and surface treatment. Work with paper and cloth is indicative of a shift toward conscious design, as assorted colors and textures are used and varied shapes are created. Children are beginning to perceive their environment more clearly and tend to portray objects in accord with their perceptions. They are stimulated as they discuss their experiences, share their reactions, and respond to such questions related to their work as: What did you do? Where did it happen? What took place? What was most exciting? Essential materials and activities include colored crayons, chalks, large paper, tempera and poster paints, clay, sponge and potato printing, simple stenciling, paper and wood construction, work with cloth and yarn, simple weaving, the making of collages, and poster making.

Preplanning, Representational, Beginning Realism Stage

Nine- to eleven-year-olds grow in their ability to observe and visualize their environment with greater realism. The urge to portray perceptions realistically increases, but clarity of detail may be lacking and can be noticed in clothing drawn without folds or wrinkles, parts missing from objects, and the like. The attempts of some children to draw photographically and without creativity should be guided in such a way that freedom of expression of former years is retained. Copying, routine repetition, and somewhat rigid representation may be evident in the work of some children; this may be due to a lack of confidence, a desire to please others, an overemphasis upon the product, or failure of others to accept the child's own work. An important discovery for many children is the space between the base line and the horizon. Objects are placed within this space in better relationship to each other, and the sky is brought down to the base line. Space and distance relationships are given more attention, as indicated by children's efforts to show objects that are near and far. This may be done by having some objects overlap others. Lights and darks, textures, and colors are used by some children to highlight the overlapped parts. Lines are used with increasing effectiveness to show perspective, to emphasize central features, and to give a feeling of rhythm. Colors are selected more deliberately for realism and expression of the child's emotional responses. Decorative touches may be added to designs. A tendency develops to select materials that fit the child's purpose and are appropriate in terms of function. A variety of materials and activities are useful at this stage, including crayon etching, crayon batik, watercolors and tempera painting, colored chalks, poster making, collages, murals, block printing, monoprinting, stenciling, weaving, stitchery, papier-mâché, plaster crafts, soap and wood carving, clay, wire and metal crafts, paper and wood construction, and the making of mobiles and stabiles.

Increasing Realism, Expressive Design Stage

From eleven to thirteen years of age, children grow in the ability to perceive and portray realism, although they are not fully aware of many details. The human body takes on more realistic proportions, arms and legs are jointed, bodily action is more definite, and clothing is colored, shaded, and draped more realistically. Line, form, color, texture, and shading are used with greater control and meaning to show action, space, distance, and mood. Composition, perspective, proportions, and foreshortening become significant problems for some children. More meaningful use of the horizontal line is evident and three-dimensional relationships are shown with greater clarity. Colors are selected more conventionally to express moods and ideas. Crafts are approached with great interest and provide rich opportunities to develop concepts of design. Self-criticism, techniques, content, and the product assume greater importance, and guidance and assistance from the teacher are needed to maintain confidence, emphasis on the process, and continuing growth to higher levels. Children are stimulated by dramatic situations, descriptions of action, posing to highlight bodily movements, demonstrations of processes, sharing and discussion of work, questions that clarify problems, guided observation, preplanning and experimentation, consideration of color in relation to feelings, and wide experience with the artwork of others. Watercolors, poster paints, mixed techniques, such as watercolor and tempera, pen and ink drawings, crayon resist, cartooning, poster making, charcoal, chalk, and group murals are effective for a variety of purposes. Printing activities include linoleum and wood block, stenciling, silk screen, monoprints, and rolling pin and rubber. Other activities include weaving, ceramics, sculpture, marionettes, mosaics, mobiles, stabiles, collages, montages, leather work, and wood construction.

OBJECTIVES OF INSTRUCTION

There has been a remarkable consistency in the objectives of art education during recent years. The development of creativity has been an important and persistent goal, along with the nurturance of an appreciation for the beautiful in both the natural and the social environments. A discernible trend is to give increasing attention to cognitive aspects, with particular attention to concepts and principles of design. Another trend is to view with greater importance those objectives related to the development of appreciation of representative works of art that are a distinguished part of our cultural heritage. Although these two trends are more pronounced at the secondary than at the elementary level, they are evident at both levels. A fundamental objective is provision for the child's creative self-expression; this is brought about through attainment of the following specific objectives which are currently emphasized:

> To develop insight into elements, principles, and concepts of design, understanding of varieties of art forms and processes, and an appreciation of the application of concepts and principles to all art activities
>
> To develop insight into the potentialities of various media and to develop levels of skill in use of art processes appropriate to the child's capacity
>
> To develop understanding, creativity, and confidence in using a variety of art media to communicate thoughts and feelings, and to stimulate the use of imaginative and inventive approaches to the solution of art problems
>
> To engender feelings of interest and dedication needed for continuing growth in artistic expression, understanding, and appreciation
>
> To develop facility in using appropriate vocabulary in the language of art to express responses to art objects, explore problems, investigate topics, and share ideas and experiences
>
> To increase perceptual power, including ability to observe imaginatively, use visual and tactile senses for original expression, and interpret observations creatively, and to develop resourcefulness in utilizing personal interpretations of firsthand, vicarious, and imagined experiences as inspiration for artistic expression
>
> To develop competence in using guidelines for self-evaluation, for constructive response to the work of others, and for improvement of the quality of art in daily activities
>
> To stimulate the discovery of aesthetic elements in nature and daily life and to help children become discriminating producers and consumers of art and decoration through development of personal standards of aesthetic taste
>
> To provide creative and appreciative experiences that will stimulate enduring interest and enjoyment of art in its myriad forms and serve as a foundation for lifelong applications to leisure activity
>
> To develop an appreciation of art as a universal means of expression that is carried on in a highly individualized manner,

and an appreciation of the art of all ages and areas as the
cultural heritage of all mankind

To help the child to develop insight into the intentions, styles,
distinctive characteristics, and cultural background of great
artists and to discover how such insight may enhance appreciation and understanding of their works

These objectives are directly translated into the activities of art education programs such as those outlined in the following section.

THE COMPLETE PROGRAM IN ART EDUCATION

Provision for achievement of the foregoing objectives is accomplished
through a program of art activities which, when complete, includes several
aspects. In the past there has been a tendency to emphasize one or more
aspects at the expense of others. For example, in some schools art activity
has been almost entirely included in the social studies. While there is a
real place for art expression in the subject areas, this is only one aspect
of a complete program. In other schools little or nothing has been done
to introduce children to the great art heritage created in recent and earlier
periods. Other inadequacies may be noted in connection with the use of
art to enrich daily living and the development of sensitivity to aesthetic
elements. What, then, constitutes a complete program? Five aspects, interrelated at every grade level, may be noted.

> *Understanding of concepts of design*: Developing an understand-
> ing of elements, principles, and qualities of design, and the
> use of appropriate vocabulary, as part of the experiences
> provided in each of the other aspects of the program, and
> in the activities that follow.

> *The developmental program*: Exploring various media and de-
> veloping facility in using processes involved in such activities
> as drawing, painting, sculpture, mosaics, constructing, arrang-
> ing, lettering, weaving, stitchery, bookmaking, and other
> crafts. Examples of sequential development in some of these
> activities are outlined in "Art Activities or Media as Cur-
> riculum Strands," later in this section.

> *Art in daily living*: Applying learnings in the above-mentioned
> aspects to appreciation of the many uses of aesthetic principles
> and art materials in daily living and the use of art media and
> objects to enhance and enrich daily living in home, school,
> and community; finding sources of inspiration in nature and
> in man-made objects.

Art in other subjects: Using the artworks of a culture or period as a source of information about the history, customs, beliefs, and appearance of the people who produced the work; special publications, such as those prepared for schools by the Denver Art Museum (1963), aid this type of study; using art objects to stimulate discussion and verbal expression in language arts instruction; using an art activity as a learning process, as when children practice a process or work with materials typical of a particular culture, illustrate ideas, reports, or stories written in various subject areas, and record observations pictorially.

Appreciation of selected masterpieces, art history: Extensive and guided viewing of a variety of masterpieces selected for children from all periods of man's artistic endeavor from prehistoric times to the present; visiting museums and galleries, using books, reproductions, films, filmstrips, and exhibits in the school.

The activities involved in each of these aspects of the art education program are planned in accordance with developmental stages in children's creative growth, as seen in the examples that follow.

Art Activities or Media as Curriculum Strands

Basic art activities are used as strands to define the developmental program of instruction in New York City (1964). Nine basic activities are outlined in a developmental sequence that begins with manipulative and exploratory experiences and moves on to intuitive design, conscious or deliberate design, preplanned design, more refined design, and increased realism combined with expressive design. Exploration of materials and an understanding and use of qualities, elements, and principles of design are an inherent part of each activity. The nine basic activities and illustrative experiences at differing grade levels follow:

Painting
K-2   water painting, one- and two-color painting, design painting, finger painting
3-4   two- and three-color painting, color-mixing experiments, design painting, blocking in work with a variety of colors and brushes, storytelling painting
5-6   experimentation with a variety of colors and brushes, storytelling painting, color mixing, design painting

Drawing
K-2   crayons, chalks, design drawings, storytelling drawings

3-4   crayons, chalks, felt-nib pens, cray-pas in 16 colors, varied papers

5-6   extension of preceding experiences, color over color, using color for contrast, balance, repetition, emphasis

Clay modeling

K-2   manipulative experience, simple figures and objects, using slip to fasten parts together

3-4   continued experimentation, designing with lumps and slabs, welding and scoring

5-6   extending the preceding, coil method, combining lump, slab, and coil methods

Poster making

K-2   simple posters with one or two words

3-4   cut paper posters, experimentation on newsprint paper, lettering on strips, cut paper letters in 4

5-6   extension of above, using varied slogans and symbols, lettering as a part of design, adding tridimensional material

Paper work

K-2   experimentation with a few shapes and strips, folding, curling, bending, twisting, pleating, cutting, making favors and other objects

3-4   extending the preceding, fanfolding, fringing, scalloping, notching, boxes, booklets, other articles

5-6   extending the preceding, stage properties, costume accessories for puppets and plays, paper sculpture

Cloth, yarns, fibers

K-2   stitchery with burlap, dixie mesh, tapes, rick-rack, monk's cloth, fabrics, yarns, ribbons, tinsel, beads, buttons

3-4   stitchery continued, weaving with the above materials and with leather strips, cords, raffia, shells, etc., sock toys, pattern making

5-6   stitchery and weaving, hooking with the above materials and jute, using nylon mesh, buckram, stocking strips, pipe cleaners, reeds, etc., pattern making

Block building

K-2   experimentation and simple construction with ready-cut wood, beads, popsicle sticks, disks, wooden and plastic containers

3-4   extending the preceding, greater skill in using tools to construct wagons, boats, trains, other objects

5-6   extending the preceding, greater variety of construction, using various finishes

Puppetry

K-2 dramatic play with paper bag, cloth square, stick, flat-jointed, sock or mitten puppets

3-4 papier-mâché puppet heads, painting of puppets, costumes, stage backdrops

5-6 extending the preceding, jointed puppet construction, refinement in painting, costume, and staging

A second example of strands that run through the art program is taken from the Sacramento County *Basic Course of Study for Elementary Grades* (1964). Media or processes are used to define the scope and sequence of instruction. Emphasis is given to individualization of instruction in terms of the child's stages of development in using the following:

Chalk	Murals	Three-dimensional
Crayons	Modeling	construction
Finger paint	Pottery	Printing
Paint (tempera,	Carving	Posters
powder, poster)	Design	Stitchery
Water color	Design	Weaving
Pasting and	principles	Art in everyday
gluing	Composition	living

Each of the above media or processes is outlined in a sequence that begins with simple manipulative experiences and moves to more complex and refined techniques. Concepts of design, although outlined separately, are viewed as an integral part of experiences with each media.

TEACHING STRATEGIES

Use of the discovery approach and inductive concept attainment, strategies highly valued in all areas of the elementary curriculum, are essential techniques in the art education program. Opportunities are provided for children to examine and compare commonly held concepts and ideas and for each child to discover and develop modes of expression, insights, and appreciations that are his very own. The following examples, drawn from recently published courses of study, illustrate the current emphasis upon discovery and inductive learning.

Discovering elements and principles of design. Children observe real objects, artworks, and their own creative efforts and are guided to discern the visual components that characterize the object they view. For example, line qualities may be observed within the classroom, in changing body motions, in natural objects, and in man-made designs and patterns.

Color hues are identified through discrimination and comparison, and later the child is able to make refined distinctions regarding intensity and value.

Discovering the potentialities of media and processes. At every developmental stage, children experiment with appropriate media to discover the inherent design possibilities of various materials and to explore ways of working with such materials. Individual discoveries are shared and modified from one child to another. Exploration activities may be prefaced with group discussions of inherent properties of each medium, so that efforts may be focused on potentially useful processing techniques, rather than completely haphazard trial and error. Demonstrations by the teacher should follow, not precede, such activity and should be suggestive rather than prescriptive. As children explore media and processes, they may discover ways in which to use them to express their own ideas and feelings.

Discovering symbols and their uses. Children in the primary grades typically utilize semirealistic symbols to represent their observations; a blue line across the top of a picture is the sky; circles, triangles, and lines are combined to show figures. Stereotyped symbolic forms should be eliminated as children are guided to refine their observations and to experiment with new forms. Abstract symbols may be discerned in the art and artifacts of cultures studied at each grade level. Attention is drawn to common forms which constitute symbols, sources for the symbol's design are sought, and the meaning of the symbol is inferred. Examples are the lotus and papyrus blossoms in ancient Egyptian art, halos in medieval portraits of saints, and the yin-yang symbol of Buddhist cultures.

Discovering information about individuals, cultures, events. Children may gain understanding of the problems of various periods by observing and discussing works that deal with societal problems, by such artists as Hogarth, Daumier, and Orozco; characteristic outlooks of a particular time, as in the works of Bosch, David, Degas, and Hopper; the interests of a period, as depicted by El Greco, Boucher, and Toulouse-Lautrec; or personal reactions to particular conditions and events, as in Chagall's "Green Violinist," Goya's "Third of May," Picasso's "Guernica." Guiding questions may be used in the observation and discussion of such works: What subject is depicted? Why did the artist select the subject or topic? How does he use specific elements, principles, or symbols to convey his intentions? Teachers may find source material and suggestions in a recent series of volumes on *Man through His Art* (New York Graphic Society, 1965). Trends and styles in architecture, sculpture, clothing, transportation vehicles, furniture, and other artifacts reveal much about the customs and outlook of various cultures and times. Children may note the design characteristics of various objects, and the materials utilized, in order to make inferences about the characteristics of the culture that produced them. This is, of course, a strategy used in archaeological and historical study. Children may gain insight into the life of a period and a feeling for the characteristics of a culture by examining culturally distinctive artifacts and art objects. Tastes and values are understood as children compare examples in ancient Grecian sculpture of the attic, classic, and tanagra styles, or compare the Japanese style categories of shabui and hade. Further understandings can be developed in studies of the artistic aspects and symbols used in festivals, ceremonies, and special activities.

Discovering uses of art in daily living. Children develop taste and values as they plan ways to adorn the classroom, prepare decorations and objects for holidays and special events, design and execute sets, costumes, and lighting for dramatic presentations, produce posters and illustrated announcements, make charts, maps, and illustrations for subject-area activities, plan bulletin-board displays, and arrange exhibits of their collections, schoolwork, or artwork.

Discovering and using criteria for art criticism. As children discern concepts of design, they begin to apply these concepts to analysis of their own work and the work of others. Criteria are developed through group discussion, comparison, and observation. The order in which criteria will be stated, the complexity of the statement, and the concepts deemed most important at a particular time will vary in accord with the developmental stages and art activities of each class. Examples of criteria include:

> **The suitability of materials selected by the artist**
> **The compatibility of medium and technique used**
> **The relationship of form to function**
> **How well the design unifies all parts of the work**
> **How well the work commands and holds interest**
> **How color, line, and movement are used to convey mood**
> **The quality of the work in comparison with similar works**
> **The quality of the work in terms of its personal or social uses**
> **The characteristics of the work in light of the artist's intentions**
> **The originality of the work or of its components**

GUIDELINES FOR THE TEACHER

Although skills and understandings in art can come about only as a result of the child's direct and active experiences, the teacher has a definite role to play in art education. He plans appropriate activities, and as he observes children at work, the teacher may raise a suggestive question, make an encouraging comment, help a child clarify a problem through discussion, or demonstrate a process in order to add to children's knowledge after their own explorations. However, there is no place for overdirection in which problems are set for the child, he is told what technique to use and how to use it, or, even worse, difficult aspects of the work are done for him. A key principle that must be kept in mind is that genuine art is the creative expression of the artist; it is his very own. The teacher's role should be defined in accord with this idea. Although art educators differ somewhat on details, a review of their writings reveals several guidelines for teachers:

Create an atmosphere that encourages creativity. Work with the children to maintain a classroom atmosphere that stimulates creativeness in both expressive and appreciative activities. Children and teacher should accept, respect, and encourage honest expression in artwork and recognize that, in art education activities, the experiences of the creative process are more important than the product. Confidence and creative ability grow and enjoyment and understanding of the work of others increase in an atmosphere of respect and acceptance.

Use knowledge of developmental stages for planning and evaluation. General overall planning is most effective when consideration is given to characteristics and interests of children at various developmental levels. In each class, this consideration should be augmented by the teacher's recognition of individual deviations from general growth patterns. Be sensitive to these differences, and provide experiences that nurture individuality.

Pace introduction of materials with children's development. Introduce materials and processes as children evidence readiness for them, but avoid introducing too much at one time or children will become confused. Ample time must be provided for children to manipulate and explore materials and experiment with processes. Bear in mind that there will be variations in the amount of time most suitable for each child.

Plan working time and space effectively. In early grades, arrange materials, tools, work space, and time allotments so that routine management problems are minimized and children are free to do creative work. In the upper grades, children can assume more of a share in such planning. Workmanship skills and responsibility for the care of tools and materials are valuable concomitant learnings.

Utilize children's work constructively to develop design understandings. Techniques and design concepts become more meaningful to children when seen in relation to their own work, rather than in an abstract presentation. Use guiding questions to help children to note similarities and make constructive comparisons in order to attain concepts, and to help them to clarify design problems and discover solutions.

Emphasize enjoyment of art. Guide children to discover the use of art products in daily living. Provide experiences in which they encounter varieties of forms and styles in art. Encourage them to observe and comment constructively on the best or most appealing features of each other's work.

Use a multimedia approach to stimulate interest and inspiration. Take the children on study trips to museums, galleries, and studios. Provide prior classroom experiences that will prepare them for the exhibits they will see. Discuss and evaluate observations after the trip. Invite artists and craftsmen to the school to demonstrate processes and display their works. Have classroom exhibits of art books, magazines, art objects from different cultures, reproductions representing different styles and periods, and examples of natural objects with aesthetic qualities. Other examples of natural and man-made objects may be shown through films, slides, filmstrips, and overhead projections.

EVALUATION OF PUPIL PROGRESS

Evaluation of artistic expression is informal, highly individualized, and very closely integrated with all phases of instruction. Emphasis is on self-evaluation and other constructive techniques that help each student solve problems and discover ways to achieve his intentions. A fundamental principle is to guide self-evaluation so that each student develops confidence, self-reliance, and constructive attitudes. The teacher helps each student to consider his work in terms of what he wishes to accomplish with the media he is using and the background of experience and skill that he has developed. Close identification with the student is essential so that his work may be seen from the student-artist's point of view. Questions and comments made by the teacher are framed in relation to problems confronting the individual student, problems which the student recognizes and needs to solve in order to continue his growth in artistic expression. Therefore, guided self-evaluation which the teacher utilizes to promote each student's ability to explore, experiment, and create in his own way is a hallmark of effective evaluation.

The role of the teacher in guiding self-evaluation varies with the artistic maturation of the child. Young children are guided in the selection of media, given praise and recognition, encouraged to experiment, guided to share work constructively, and assisted in learning basic routines that facilitate creativity. The teacher is a keen observer who notes the child's needs for suitable materials: a wider brush, a larger paper, a different color, a change of subject or media. Samples of children's work may be kept at all grade levels and periodically reviewed by the teacher to discover growth and to identify needs for additional experiences with certain media, processes, and problems. Self-evaluation is sharpened in later grades as the teacher continues to stress positive, constructive attitudes. Care must be taken to prevent self-evaluation from slipping into destructive self-criticism. Special attention should be given to helping each child to recognize his successes, to develop new skills and techniques commensurate with his aspirations and abilities, and to set realistic goals in terms of his capabilities and the limitations of available media, for when the level of aspiration far exceeds one's capabilities, there is a tendency to turn away from art. It is extremely important to guide students to set standards for themselves that are children's, not adults', standards. As each student faces a problem he should have the opportunity to discuss it with the group, to invite suggestions, and to choose and adapt suggestions to his individual modes of expression.

A similar stance is taken during group discussions of artwork. Each individual plays a leading role as his work is shared with the group. Emphasis is placed on his intentions, the ways in which he has expressed his thoughts and feelings, his solutions to problems, and discoveries he has made. Unique and distinctive qualities are highlighted in much the same manner as when professional artists exchange ideas related to their work. Respect for self-expression, self-reliance, ingenuity, and integrity of expression are nurtured. The teacher's role in maintaining a constructive and creative atmosphere is of critical importance if genuine and useful evaluation is to be attained.

Emphasis in group discussions is given to successful aspects of creative expression of ideas or feelings in each work. The successful and distinctive characteristics of a particular work are discovered, noted, and shared in appreciative terms that stimulate further creativity but do not convey the notion that others should copy these characteristics or techniques. It is highly unrealistic and out of step with the character of creative expression to engage in such activities as finding "the *best* picture" or selecting "the *best* artist." Such arbitrary and meaningless judgments have no place in the effective art education program. Instead, each individual's work is viewed in light of its distinctive qualities, and each child is encouraged to explore the use of elements, arrangements, and media in ways that he, as an artist, feels are appropriate for himself. Thus goodness or badness, right or wrong, are not judgments handed down by the class serving as a jury; they are highly *personal* judgments that the artist makes in light of his own intentions and capabilities.

Although evaluation in art education is primarily informal and individualized, the teacher may structure evaluation of pupil growth and understanding in terms of the objectives of the program or the use of taxonomies of objectives (Bloom, 1956; Krathwohl, Bloom, & Masia, 1964). A check list along the lines of such objectives enables the teacher to evaluate different levels of behavior by means of pupil responses in discussions, written expressions of ideas and opinions, and examples of pupils' work. Examples of such levels are given in the following sections.

Cognitive Domain

Knowledge level: Knowledge of art terminology; specific facts such as color names and information about famous artists; knowledge of design concepts, categories of art history periods, and classifications of art forms and styles. This level of knowledge can be expressed verbally and is therefore susceptible to comparatively formal testing. Evaluation may also be conducted through informal interviews and group discussions.

Comprehension level: Recognition of the use of symbols in the art of differing periods; recognition of major ideas and generalizations about art structure and the role of art expression in various cultures. Although comprehension represents a broader level than knowledge, it may be evaluated in a similar manner.

Application level: Application of knowledge of design concepts and processes to the production of work. At this level, the focus of evaluation is on particular knowledge or skills as these are evidenced in the artwork of the student. Children's application of aesthetic criteria to appraisal of artworks may be evaluated through discussion or children's written critiques. Application of concepts of the role of art to learnings about other cultures may be similarly evaluated through children's discussion or written reports. Evaluation at this level must allow for a broad range of differing individual responses.

Analysis level: Analysis of the components of a work of art, the relationship of these components, and the effects these relationships achieve in the work of children and adult artists; analysis of the relevancy and relationships of facts and concepts in art history which leads to interpretation, explanation, and inferences; analysis of an artist's purposes or of the limitation of materials with which the student works. As in the case of application, evaluation at this level must be individualized and informal and may be carried out by means of teacher observation guided by check lists of analytical thinking skills. The acquisition of such skills, rather than the content expressed, is the focus of such evaluation.

Synthesis level: The essential art activities—exploration of media and processes, discovery of techniques of expression, individual response to art problems, creative production of works of art. Evaluation of creative behavior involves teacher observation of the individual at work and a highly individualized appraisal of creative efforts in relation to the background and capacities of the particular child.

Affective Domain

Pupil behavior classified as affective is evaluated informally and individually through observation by the teacher.

Receiving level: Willingness to listen to the views of others and to share differing ideas and opinions regarding creative efforts in the classroom and the work of other artists and other cultures.

Responding level: Willingness to respond with one's own reactions and opinions. In art education, constructive response and sharing of ideas enables children to examine and accept differences among people as these differences are manifested in art objects, artifacts, techniques, and aesthetic values.

Valuing level: Children make constructive comparisons, develop evaluative criteria, and develop appreciation for one another's thoughts and values. The feelings and ideas of others, as manifested in their artworks, are accepted as of equal worth, apart from considerations of the aesthetic qualities of the work (Templeton, 1965).

Organizing level: In art education, this level is close to the valuing level, as children develop value systems of their own, along the constructive and mutually accepting lines of criteria evolved in the classroom. Important qualities are acceptance of individual differences and appreciation of unique characteristics.

Characterization level: The aggregate of the individual's interests, attitudes, and values which constitute his generalized system of values. This broadest level involves the child's total outlook and is evaluated in terms of his total behavior, rather than a single subject area.

EVALUATION OF THE INSTRUCTIONAL PROGRAM

In order to maintain its effectiveness, the art education program should be continually evaluated and revised as needed. Some foci for evaluation of the program include the following:

Foundations
Do the aspects of the complete program reflect the use of major fields of art and related disciplines as sources of instructional activities and learnings?

Is knowledge of child growth and developmental stages of creative expression used to plan the scope and sequence of instruction?

Structure

Are the structural elements of art—design concepts, media and processes, art forms, concepts of art in culture—identified and incorporated in learning experiences?

Are processes and media utilized honestly in accord with their inherent qualities and limitations?

Does the child learn to function as an artist, using the creative process as a unique form of inquiry and expression?

Objectives

Are objectives clearly defined in behavioral terms related to:
Knowledge of art structure?

Experience with a variety of media and processes?

Development of positive attitudes, interests, and values?

Complete program

Does the scope of the program include both creative and appreciative experiences?

Are provisions made for learnings in the area of design concepts, art in other cultures, and art in daily living?

Are children provided with experience in a variety of processes and media?

Is the program designed to achieve appropriate objectives?

Teaching strategies

Are learning techniques consistent with the essence of art as an individual creative process?

Are varieties of experiences provided to achieve each purpose?

Is emphasis placed upon pupil activity rather than descriptive knowledge?

Are concept clusters used appropriately as tools of inquiry in learning processes, design techniques, art history, and appreciation of art in other cultures and in daily living?

Pupil evaluation

Is evaluation an integral part of instruction?

Is evaluation individualized?

Is constructive self-evaluation encouraged and developed?

Is evaluation based upon realistic standards developed in accord with child growth and developmental stages?

Is the emphasis in evaluation upon individual growth in expressive ability and development of positive attitudes, rather than upon the art product?

Program evaluation

Are provisions made for continuous evaluation and revision of the program?

Teacher preparation

Are teachers provided with opportunities for in-service education related to foundational art disciplines as well as up-to-date curriculum developments and instructional techniques?

Are teachers directly involved in program planning and evaluation?

Are specialists available for consultation by teachers?

Are adequate and varied instructional materials available?

REFERENCES

Anderson, W. A. *Art learning situations for elementary education.* Belmont, Calif.: Wadsworth, 1965. Practical suggestions for activities, with attention to concept formation related to structure in art.

Barkan, Manuel. *Through art to creativity.* Boston: Allyn and Bacon, 1960. Specific suggestions for developing creative experiences in relation to levels of development.

Bloom, Benjamin S. (Ed.) *The taxonomy of educational objectives: cognitive domain.* New York: McKay, 1956. Classification of objectives and examples of test items.

Chicago Public Schools. *Art teaching guide.* Chicago: Board of Education, 1963. Outlines of activities for a complete program.

Conrad, George. *The process of art education.* Englewood Cliffs, N.J.: Prentice-Hall, 1964. Principles and procedures for a complete program.

DeFrancesco, Italo L. *Art education: its means and ends.* New York: Harper, 1958. Discussion of nature of art, art development, and procedures for developing a complete program.

Denver Art Museum and Denver Public Schools. *Vision trails through art no. 1: America's cultural heritage* and *Vision trails through art no. 2: North American Indians.* Denver: Denver Public Schools, 1963. Pamphlets designed to develop anthropological and historical understandings by means of artworks and artifacts in the museum's collections.

Dewey, John. *Art as experience.* New York: Minton, 1934. A classic statement which highlights the relationships between art and life.

Gardner, Helen. *Art through the ages.* New York: Harcourt, Brace, 1959. Background information on art history and principles.

Hausman, Jerome J. (Ed.) *Report of the commission on art education.* Washington, D.C.: The National Art Education Association, 1965. Summary of development of art education and recommendations for the elementary program.

Hofstadter, Albert, & Kuhns, Richard. (Eds.) *Philosophies of art and beauty.* New York: Modern Library, 1964. Background information on philosophies of art and aesthetics.

Kaufman, Irving. *Art and education in contemporary culture.* New York: Macmillan, 1966. Discussion of cultural influences on artwork of children and professional artists and suggestions for art instruction and development of good taste in contemporary culture.

Krathwohl, David R., Bloom, Benjamin S., & Masia, Bertram S. *Taxonomy of educational objectives: affective domain.* New York: McKay, 1964. A classification of objectives and sample test items in the area of attitude and value development.

Lark-Horovitz, Betty. *Graphic work diagnosis.* Cleveland: Museum of Art, 1939. A classic study of developmental stages.

Lark-Horovitz, Betty, Lewis, Hilda, and Luca, Mark. *Understanding children's art for better teaching.* Columbus, Ohio: Merrill, 1967. Development of instructional guidelines drawn from the characteristics of artwork and aesthetic responsiveness of average, disadvantaged, and exceptional elementary school children.

Lewis, Hilda. (Ed.) *Child art: The beginnings of self-affirmation.* Berkeley: Diablo Press, 1966. Contributions by Read, Kellog, Arnheim, Schaefer-Simmern, Stern, Barron, Lowenfeld, D'Amico, and Heckscher; examples of children's work in various countries and at various stages of development.

Linderman, W. H., & Herberholz, D. W. *Developing artistic and perceptual awareness.* Dubuque, Iowa: W. C. Brown, 1964. Principles and techniques for providing art activities.

Los Angeles City Schools. *Course of study for elementary schools.* Los Angeles: Board of Education, 1964. Sequences of activities for a K-6 program; examples of concept clusters.

Lowenfeld, Viktor, & Brittain, W. L. *Creative and mental growth.* (4th ed.) New York: Macmillan, 1964. Detailed analysis of stages of development.

McFee, June K. *Preparation for art.* Belmont, Calif.: Wadsworth, 1961. Discussion of cultural and psychological aspects of art as well as art activities.

Merritt, Helen. *Guiding free expression in children's art.* New York: Holt, 1964. Techniques for providing varied activities.

Michael, John A. (Ed.) *Art education in the junior high school.* Washington, D.C.: National Education Association, 1964. Rationale and suggestions for art instruction useful to the teacher in middle or intermediate schools and in the upper elementary grades.

Munro, Thomas. *Art education: its philosophy and psychology.* New York: Liberal Arts, 1956. Review of fundamental ideas underlying art education.

National Society for the Study of Education. *Art education.* Sixty-fourth Yearbook, Part II. Chicago: University of Chicago Press, 1965. Background information and useful discussions of various aspects of art education.

New York City. *Art in the elementary schools.* New York: Board of Education, 1964. Detailed suggestions for promoting growth in various art activities.

New York Graphic Society. *Man through his art.* Greenwich, Conn.: 1965. A series of volumes utilizing artworks as sources of information and understanding about man, his history, culture, and activities.

Phenix, Philip H. *Realms of meaning.* New York: McGraw-Hill, 1964. Discussion of the visual arts as a part of the realm of aesthetics in chap. 13.

Read, Herbert. *Education through art.* New York: Pantheon, 1947. A classic work that continues to influence art education.

Sacramento County. *Basic course of study for elementary grades.* Sacramento: County Superintendent of Schools, 1965. Outline of the program in art education.

Smith, Ralph A. (Ed.) *Aesthetics and criticism in art education.* Chicago: Rand McNally, 1966. Essays on aesthetics and art criticism, and guidelines for critical evaluation of artworks useful for teachers and planners of art education at all grade levels.

Templeton, David E. The arts: sources for affective learning, *Educ. Leadership,* April, 1965, **22**, 465–468. Discussion of inquiry in art and of the learner as artist and inquirer.

Chapter Twelve

MUSIC EDUCATION

MUSIC IS THE CREATIVE ORGANIZATION of tonal elements to express thoughts and feelings. In this mode of expression, sounds, which are themselves the clues to meaning, are arranged in an aesthetic sequence. Such tonal elements as melody, harmony, and rhythm are arranged in a form that expresses the composer's intention. As in all arts within the realm of aesthetics, the objective is to express thoughts and feelings in a singular form (Phenix, 1964).

A musical experience for the listener involves direct perception of the particular form or composition that is being presented. The experience is marked by immediate response or reaction to what is heard. Thoughts and feelings well up within the listener in highly personalized ways that are intimately linked to past musical experience.

Although music is singular and particular for both the composer and the listener, it consists in such basic elements as melody, harmony, and rhythm, and has structural characteristics that are clearly discernible. Sequences of tones are arranged in identifiable patterns. Sounds and sequences are recorded in symbolic notation. The work of composers is marked by particular idioms. Compositions may be classified according to style. Music that was dominant in various historical periods may be studied in terms of common elements and distinctive characteristics. The music of different societies consists in the organization of basic elements in culturally satisfying ways. Throughout the range of diverse musical literature of the past and present, there are basic characteristics that reflect man's universal capacity for musical expression (Knieter, 1966).

FOUNDATION DISCIPLINES

The foundation disciplines of music education include a broad range of subject areas. From the field of physics have been drawn concepts of sound that are helpful in clarifying the nature of sound and characteristics of musical tones that are produced by varying means. From applied studies of physics concepts have come principles of acoustics and insight into new and better ways of planning performances, recording, and reproducing music. Anthropology, in general, and ethnomusicology, in particular, have contributed new knowledge of music as a basic part of culture and of music's relation to other aspects of culture. From musicology, history of music, and musical criticism have been drawn concepts and key ideas related to the forms, types, styles, common and distinctive features, and criteria of great works of music. Psychology has contributed ideas related to perception as a key process and the importance of cognitive processes in the development of musicality.

Concepts and key ideas from foundation disciplines are blended and built into the various components of music education. In the overall design of the program of instruction special effort is made to include compositions that meet criteria set by experts. Different types and styles of music are included to provide for a variety of musical experiences. The functions of music in our own and other cultures are highlighted. Efforts are made to utilize knowledge of acoustics and improved ways of recording and reproducing music and to guide students to deeper understandings of the "physics of music." Key concepts and ideas from the disciplines are evident in activities that range from simple experiments with different tone-producing devices to critical study of masterpieces.

Concept Clusters and Generalizations

Music education abounds with concept clusters and generalizations drawn from supporting disciplines. A major reason for the close links to supporting disciplines is that music is a highly specialized area of instruction. Well-designed materials of instruction are in general reflective of the close relationships that some specialists in music education have maintained with the music profession. Courses of study and textbooks tend to include clusters drawn from supporting disciplines as shown in the following examples:

Elements of music: tone, melody, harmony, rhythm, form

Melody: succession of tones, motif or pattern, phrases

Tone: pitch, color (harmonic vibrations), loudness, duration

Rhythm: meter, time signature, tempo, accent, beat; phrases, combinations of phrases

Harmony: consonance, dissonance; chords, dominant, sub-dominant

Form: phrase, repetition, contrast; canon, fugue, sonata; suite, symphony, opera

Texture: harmonic, contrapuntal, polyphonic, monophonic, homophonic

Analysis: accent, contrast, repetition, variation, progression, patterns

Vocal music: song, chorale, oratorio, opera

Notation: clef, key signature, time signature, time value (duration), rests, dynamics (loudness), expression

Instruments: string, woodwind, brass, percussion, keyboard

Instrumental music: solo, chamber ensemble, orchestra, band, drum and bugle corps

Style: baroque, classical, light classical, romantic, postromantic, modern, impressionistic, popular, jazz, folk

Activities: rhythmic response, singing, playing, listening, creating, reading

Concept clusters may be used to outline a structure of music education, as shown in Chart 12–1.

Chart 12–1.   A structure of music education.

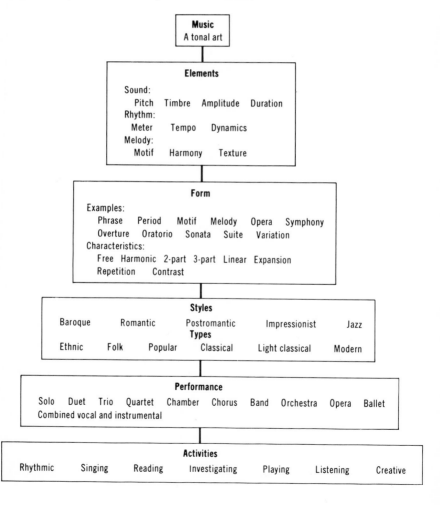

Illustrative of generalizations which may be developed in music education are the following:

> The capacity for musicality is a universal characteristic of mankind.
>
> Folk music is a fundamental mode of artistic expression in many societies.
>
> Much great music has been created in response to spiritual, nationalistic, and aesthetic interests and aspirations.
>
> Distinctive styles of music have been created by musicians in different times and places.
>
> Pitch, rhythm, and tone quality are key elements in musical sounds which can be produced in a variety of ways.
>
> Musical notation is used to communicate melody, rhythm, and harmony in a variety of musical forms.

OBJECTIVES

The central goal of music education is to develop musicality—the capacity to express musical ideas and to grasp musical statements created by others (Palisca, 1964). Toward this end current statements of objectives reflect the importance of developing an understanding of the structure of music and the value of such an understanding in improving appreciation, enjoyment, performance, and creativeness. The following list includes objectives that many children can attain, that some will surpass, that some will not attain, yet which will serve as guidelines for promoting the maximum growth of all.

> *Knowledge, concepts, understandings*
>
> To understand that music is a tonal art consisting of such basic elements as melody, rhythm, and harmony
>
> To develop a knowledge of common tonal and rhythmic patterns, internal relationships, key and meter signatures, musical terms and symbols, notation, harmony, major and minor mode, chromatics
>
> To recognize and understand the music typical of different composers, styles, periods, and cultures, and realize that musicality is a universal capacity
>
> To develop a repertoire of music for use in singing, playing, listening, and rhythmic activities
>
> To develop an understanding of how sound and different tones are produced
>
> To develop an understanding of standards for judging the quality of music and musical performance

Skills and abilities

To develop sensitivity to and awareness of tonal and rhythmic patterns, pitch discrimination, mood, harmony, phrasing, tempo, dynamics

To develop facility in interpreting thoughts and feelings through singing, playing, and rhythmic expression

To develop the ability to sing with natural and expressive tonal quality

To develop skill in responding creatively to music and in creating songs, tunes, descants, melodies, rhythmic movements, embellishments, harmony, accompaniments

To develop skill in playing percussion, melody, and harmony instruments individually and with others, and for some, the ability to play band and orchestral instruments

To identify and recognize preorchestral, orchestral, and band instruments by sight and sound

To develop the ability to read notation and musical terms and to use them in musical activities

To develop discrimination in selecting musical literature and instruments for specific purposes

Attitudes, appreciations, interests

To develop an enjoyment and understanding of music that touches the lives of children, carries over into out-of-school experiences, and enriches daily living

To provide a means of achieving social and emotional satisfaction, relaxation, and wholesome release of feelings

To develop an appreciation of other people through their music and an understanding of the significance of music in the lives of people here and now and in other times and places

To develop sensitivity to music in various forms, idioms, styles, and moods

To contribute shades of meaning and feeling to moral and spiritual values, to enlightened patriotism, and to empathy with others in ways that can only be conveyed through music

To extend children's cultural horizons by acquainting them with the best of different kinds of music and with recognized masterpieces and the composers who created them

A COMPLETE PROGRAM

A clearly defined program of music education is needed to attain the objectives noted above. In general there is widespread agreement among music educators regarding the various phases of a complete program even though

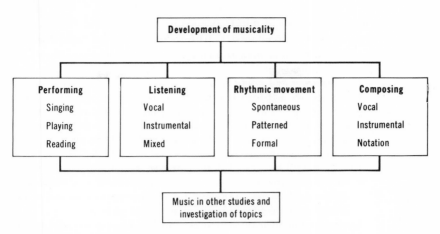

Chart 12–2. *Phases of a complete program of music education.*

there may be disagreement on particular aspects of each phase of the program. A review of recent courses of study, professional textbooks, and recommendations of specialists in music indicates that performing, composing, listening, and rhythmic movement are essential to the development of musicality. (For example, see Palisca, 1964.)

Performing may be broken down into singing, playing of instruments, and reading of music. Composing includes vocal, instrumental, and rhythmic creative activities and the writing of musical notation. Listening includes a variety of ear-training activities ranging from sensitivity to simple rhythmic patterns to discrimination of various musical forms. Rhythmic activities include creative and spontaneous response to music as well as various dance forms. Related to each of these musical activities are uses of music in other subjects and the investigation of topics in music, such as music in the lives of other peoples, how musical sounds are produced, characteristics of instruments, and stories about composers. Chart 12–2 shows these various phases and highlights relationships among them. Basic musical activities are used as strands to structure the curriculum.

RHYTHMIC ACTIVITIES

Rhythmic experiences are an inseparable part of activities in each area of music education. Clustered around the major concept of rhythm are meter, accent, pattern, and syncopation. Tempo is considered in relation to pace, character of movement, and change. Rhythmic movement is used as a vehicle to improve enjoyment and to deepen understanding of rhythm as a basic element of music. Spontaneous, patterned, and formal activities are included as shown in the following summary.

Kindergarten and grade 1

Engaging in self-initiated rhythmic movement as the teacher claps or plays an appropriate accompaniment, responding to music in a free or spontaneous manner, learning singing games, action songs, and fundamental patterns such as skipping and galloping

Recognizing like and unlike patterns, responding to changes in tempo, long and short values, light and heavy tones, and different patterns, participating in interpretive activities descriptive of people, animals, places, and objects

Using rhythm instruments to accompany movements and songs, combining rhythmic movement with singing and instrumental activities, discovering rhythmic patterns in listening activities, developing an awareness of beat, accent, and meter

Grades 2 and 3

Continuing the above as needed, interpreting songs, recordings, and playing of instruments with increasing rhythmic awareness, keeping regular rhythm as in march time and waltz time, and clapping, tapping, and stepping familiar patterns

Learning simple folk dances and new rhythmic patterns as in the polka (step-close-step-hop), learning to conduct in $\frac{2}{4}$, $\frac{3}{4}$, and $\frac{4}{4}$ time, selecting appropriate music to accompany movement

Identifying common rhythmic patterns by notation, such as quarter notes for walking and eighth notes for skipping, interpreting note and rest values, developing increasing awareness of the relation of phrase, accent, and meter to form, creating movements for use in dramatic, singing, and other activities

Grades 4-6

Continuing the above as needed, improving expressiveness in interpreting singing games, creative movements and folk dancing, learning new dance forms and the underlying rhythmic patterns

Changing movements without losing time, identifying basic meters in folk music and poetry, identifying patterns by notation and notating frequently used patterns, using notation to find elements or units in a pattern

Creating new movements and floor patterns, investigating and comparing rhythmic patterns in the music of other cultures, learning to substitute inner response for overt movement in reacting to beat, measure, phrase, and patterns

SINGING

Through singing experiences students develop increasing sensitivity to tonal relationships, melody, harmony, rhythm, song forms, and voice classification. As their repertoire increases, steady growth may be noticed in tonal quality, free voice production, use of the full vocal range, and the blending of one's voice what that of others. With increasing maturity and experience come growth in clarity of enunciation, intonation, and diction, confidence in singing, voice projection, part singing, and use of symbols to improve interpretation. Singing experiences contribute much to the development of musicality as activities such as the following are provided:

Kindergarten and grade 1

Finding one's singing voice by listening and matching tones in calls, tone games, and songs, developing sensitivity to changes in pitch, volume, and melody, singing by phrases, changing the singing voice to fit the mood, and increasing vocal range

Learning the meaning of texts in songs, interpreting songs through rhythmic, dramatic, and other activities, using rhythm instruments for accompaniment of familiar songs, singing with piano accompaniment of familiar songs

Recognizing familiar melodies, marches, lullabies, and simple tonal and rhythmic patterns in familiar songs, interpreting songs expressively, and creating simple songs

Grades 2 and 3

Continuing the above as needed, improving tonal quality, accuracy of pitch, sensitivity to rhythm, and clarity of enunciation, recognizing like and unlike phrases, accent, underlying beat, fast and slow tempo, differing time values, dynamics (loud and soft), and notation of familiar tonal patterns

Adding introductions and codas (endings) to familiar songs, playing a descant to accompany familiar songs, singing simple rounds and descants, playing one- and two-chord accompaniments on the autoharp, building a repertoire of songs

Grades 4-6

Continuing the above as needed, refining beauty of tone, sensitivity to phrasing, tempo and dynamics, pitch discrimination, awareness of rhythmic patterns, interpretation of mood, and breath control and intonation

Learning common key and meter signatures and how to find the key chord, *do*, and the starting tone for a song, learning descants, how to harmonize by ear, and how to do vocal chording, learning two- and three-part songs, singing in the school chorus

Singing from notation in textbooks and on charts or the chalkboard, increasing the repertoire of songs for use in a variety
of situations, playing accompaniments on the autoharp, piano,
and other instruments, creating original descants and songs
and related accompaniments, investigating favorite composers,
voice production, and other topics

PLAYING INSTRUMENTS

Effective programs include the playing of a variety of instruments in all
grades as an extension of singing and rhythmic experiences. At first, opportunities are provided for children to experiment with instruments and
to discover the sounds that can be made by playing them. This is typically
followed by experiences in which simple instruments are used to produce
rhythms, melodies, and accompaniments. Group instruction is provided in
some schools in piano and instrument classes. Concepts and concept clusters are developed, links to other phases of the program are highlighted,
and growth in musicality is extended as shown in the following summary
of instrumental activities:

Kindergarten and grade 1
Discovering sounds made with one's hands and feet and by
striking metal, wooden, and glass objects, experimenting with
melody bells, tuned bottles or glasses, and percussion instruments
Learning to play rhythmic patterns appropriate for such fundamental movements as walking, running, skipping, and galloping, playing tunes and melodies on melody bells, playing
accompaniments to songs on percussion instruments
Strumming the autoharp, recognizing common instruments by
sight and sound, selecting and playing instruments to enrich
songs, creating rhythmic patterns and melodies

Grades 2 and 3
Continuing the above as needed, playing accompaniments,
melodies, and tonal patterns with increasing skill, finding the
pitch and demonstrating up and down, high and low, step-
wise and skipwise intervals, and repeated tones
Using percussion and melody instruments to add introductions,
interludes, and codas to songs, recordings, rhythmic activities
and dramatizations, playing simple descants while the class
sings
Taking group instruction in piano and instrumental classes,
reading notation while playing simple percussion and melody
instruments, recognizing additional band and orchestral instru-

ments, developing increasing awareness of harmony, using instruments creatively to add embellishments and to accompany musical activities, making simple instruments

Grades 4-6

Continuing the above, developing increasing facility in playing percussion, melody, harmony, recorder-type and other instruments, using melody bells or the piano to check pitch, find the starting tone, improve part singing, play descants and deepen understanding of intervals, harmony, and other concepts, using the autoharp for accompaniment

Recognizing and identifying the tone and timbre of band and orchestral instruments, developing sensitivity to forms of instrumental music ranging from solo and chamber to band and orchestra, finding out about instruments used in other lands, making and playing selected instruments such as claves, bongo drum, guiro, maracas, and cabacas, taking group instruction in piano and instrumental classes, investigating how instruments produce tones, and learning to identify the instruments included in chamber, band, and orchestral music

LISTENING

Listening is an indispensable part of musical experience because music is a tonal art and tones are perceived through listening. And listening is basic to other phases of the program. Getting the beginning tone for a song, sensing a rhythmic pattern, improvising a coda, discovering patterns and their variations, identifying instruments, and discovering harmonic changes are illustrative of the key importance of listening. Listening is the major mode of perception of musical experiences that range from discovery of tonal patterns and melodic design to the enjoyment of tone poems and sonatas. Because of its basic importance the developmental program of listening experiences includes such activities as the following.

Kindergarten and grade 1

Identifying sounds and tones, matching tones, developing sensitivity to tones that are high and low, loud and soft, and fast and slow, and recognizing simple tonal and rhythmic patterns

Interpreting the feeling, mood, or story through pantomime or rhythmic movement, responding to different rhythms by walking, running, skipping, galloping, and other fundamental movements

Becoming acquainted with such great literature as Saint-Saën's *The Swan* and Brahms' *Lullaby*, building a beginning listening repertoire of folk music and other selections, identifying percussion, melody, and common orchestral instruments such as the violin

Grades 2 and 3

Continuing the above as needed, matching tones, and repeating tonal and rhythmic patterns with greater facility, distinguishing like and unlike rhythmic and tonal patterns, recognizing changes in tempo and meter

Interpreting moods, descriptions, and stories through movement, dramatization, art media, and language activities, gaining greater understanding and enjoyment of descriptions and stories in program music

Becoming acquainted with great literature such as Debussy's *Corner Suite*, Grieg's *March of the Dwarfs*, and Haydn's *Surprise Symphony*, increasing the listening repertoire, identifying common instruments

Grades 4-6

Continuing the above as needed, following the melodic line in repeated and altered form, recognizing themes and their repetition and variation, distinguishing major and minor mode, recognizing the different parts and voices in part singing, recognizing harmony in vocal and instrumental music, identifying instruments according to tone, and recognizing the group to which they belong

Interpreting mood, description, and story through varied means, developing greater understanding of melody, rhythm, harmony, dynamics, arrangement, form, and style, developing increasing ability to concentrate on the music itself without extramusical stimulation

Building a larger listening repertoire of program and absolute music, associating selected works with stories, descriptions, composers, styles, periods, themes, and forms of composition, investigating composers, forms of music, families of instruments, and how tones are produced, recognizing different forms such as two-part, three-part, variation, free, sonata, overture, opera, oratorio, suite

CREATIVE ACTIVITIES

Creativity takes many forms in music education as children express their own intentions in original ways. Creative interpretation of the music of others, self-expression of responses to music through various activities, selection of music in relation to various purposes, improvisation of melodies and rhythmic patterns, arrangement and rearrangement of accompaniments, and construction of instruments are widely used to tap the creativity of children. Most completely creative of all activities is the composition of original songs for which words, music, and accompaniment are created by children. The following summary of activities is illustrative of ways in which creativity may be sparked at various levels of instruction:

Kindergarten and grade 1

Interpreting music about people, animals, and activities through dramatic play, rhythmic movement and impersonation, responding to different rhythms and moods through finger painting, movement, and dramatization, selecting rhythm instruments to fit a mood, to play a rhythmic pattern, to produce special effects, and to accompany rhythmic activity

Improvising a tune on melody instruments, making a jingle or chant to use with a tonal or rhythmic pattern, creating a tune for a rhyme or poem, creating lines for a familiar melody, creating a line to a song after a question or line is sung by the teacher, composing words and music for a short song after a study trip or other exciting experience

Grades 2 and 3

Continuing the above as appropriate, interpreting folk, patriotic, and other music, adding introductions, interludes, and codas to familiar songs, responding to moods and descriptions in music through rhythmic language and art activities, devising and combining rhythmic patterns and movements, producing special effects on instruments, making instruments, arranging instruments for accompaniments

Creating songs, movements, and melodies related to units of study, the seasons, holidays, and special events, writing new verses for a familiar song, improvising melodies on tone bells and the piano, experimenting with harmony (such as thirds), devising accompaniments on the autoharp, creating songs with verse and related accompaniment

Grades 4-6

Continuing the above as appropriate, interpreting songs with greater originality and understanding of the composer's intention with attention to phrasing, breath control, tone quality, mood intonation, and dynamics, devising variations or embellishments, rhythmic movements, and dance steps, selecting music in major or minor mode in relation to mood and to special topics in social studies and other subjects, selecting poems or stories to be set to music or that express the mood of familiar music

Improvising melodies on various instruments, making and playing instruments for use in units of study on other lands, making charts of original music, rhythmic and tonal patterns,

themes and variations and chord progressions, working out
harmonic accompaniments and arranging parts in vocal and
instrumental activities, combining musical selections and
dramatization into a playlet, creating songs, chants, rounds,
descants, obbligatos, harmonic embellishments, rhythmic movements, and dance steps

UNDERSTANDING AND READING MUSIC

This phase of music education is clearly on the cognitive side of learning.
Concepts of music are clarified and understanding of notation is developed
as visual perception of musical terms and symbols is used to enrich aural
perception of melody, rhythm, harmony, and form. Rich experiences in
singing, listening, and other phases of music education constitute the context in which the understanding and reading of music are developed. Efforts
are made to maintain the intrinsic qualities of positive affective response
to music activities as the intellect is challenged to develop insight into the
structure of music and ways in which musical ideas are communicated. The
many contributions that this phase of the program may make to the
development of musicality are illustrated in the following summary of
activities.

Kindergarten and grade 1
Developing readiness for music reading through singing, playing, listening, rhythmic and creative activities, associating
tonal direction with high and low tones and arm movements,
associating rhythmic patterns and meter with fundamental
movements, recognizing like and unlike phrases, playing tunes
on tone bells by ear and later by numeral
Discovering that notes are written on lines and spaces, developing the meanings of terms such as fast and slow, soft and
loud, high and low, heavy and light, starting tone, phrase,
tune, melody, march, gallop, trot

Grades 2 and 3
Continuing the above as needed, following notes in textbooks
and on charts or the chalkboard while singing, recognizing
notes of differing duration, associating notes with syllables,
numeral notation and letter notation, identifying meter in
music that moves by twos, threes, and fours, using notation
to play phrases and melodies
Relating note and chord sequences to piano chording, learning
notation in group instrumental instruction, notating phrases
and original music on charts and the chalkboard with assistance as needed, developing the meaning of terms such as

notes, chord, beat, lines and spaces, pitch, staff, stanza, measure, accent, bar line, double bar, key and meter signatures, clef

Grades 4-6

Continuing the above as needed, playing instruments by reading notation, using notation for writing, singing, and playing original music, phrases, rhythmic patterns and chords, following parts in two- and three-part songs

Recognizing marking and directional terms and key and meter signatures, increasing facility in independent sight reading, investigating and comparing different scales such as diatonic and pentatonic, notating melodies, descants, thirds, sixths, basic chords and chord sequences, learning the meaning of such terms as descant, coda, interlude, theme, harmony, modulation, cadence, dominance, sharps, flats, basic and tonic chords, major and minor modes, solo, quartet, crescendo, retard, bass, sonata, opera

MUSIC IN OTHER STUDIES

Anthropologists and ethnomusicologists have studied the place of music in a variety of cultures, revealing much that is relevant to curriculum planners. People everywhere have made music a significant part of activities ranging from ceremonies and dancing to politics and warfare. There is music of work, play, love, worship, rest, travel, heroes, battles, hopes, fears, and a myriad other human activities, thoughts, and feelings. Because music is such an important part of the lives of people, it inevitably is made a part of learning experiences in the social studies. Because of its many links to other arts and to science it is appropriately included in studies outside the developmental program of music education. A guiding principle is to include musical experiences in ways that contribute to the development of musicality. The following examples are illustrative of ways in which music is made a part of selected subjects.

Social sciences education: learning lullabies, folk and art songs, and work and recreation songs related to family and community studies; exploring music of Indians, Hawaiians, and others; learning state and national songs and folk games and dances; learning to utilize ethnic and national music and the music of differing periods as sources for information and understanding of other times and cultures; making and playing authentic instruments; hearing recordings, seeing dances, and hearing music performed by local, national, and international artists; selecting music for culminating activities, discovering that the capacity for musicality is universal; discovering intercultural influences in music

Language arts: writing creatively as music is played, selecting background music for individual or choral reading and storytelling, selecting music to fit the mood of poems and stories, composing music to use in singing original poems, hearing great works related to heroes in literature, hearing poems that have been set to music

Science: learning how pitch is changed in relation to length of a bar, string, or tube, discovering how thickness of bars and strings alters tone, finding how heat, moisture, and paint change the tone produced by striking drumheads, bars, clay pots, and gourds, learning how a megaphone, violin box, or gourd reinforces vibrations and gives resonance

Art: drawing, painting, or sketching as music is played, using drawings, paintings or pictures to illustrate songs, using pictorial materials to direct and motivate listening, making and decorating musical instruments of different cultures, discovering that rhythm is a basic element in art as well as in music and poetry, discovering that there are similar styles in both art and music, sometimes within a time period, as in the paintings of Watteau and the music of Mozart, and sometimes cutting across periods, as in the paintings of Mondrian and the music of Bach.

TEACHING STRATEGIES

Many different teaching strategies are used in music education, ranging from directed rote singing and listening to guided discovery of elements of music and inquiry into selected topics. With increasing attention to elements of music as key concepts in the development of musicality has come greater emphasis on strategies that highlight ways in which rhythm, melody, and harmony are organized in various forms to express musical ideas. The teacher's role is primarily one of guiding the learning of students in a series of performing, listening, creating, and investigating experiences. Throughout the program high premium is placed on creative expression and response as students are given opportunities to interpret, enjoy, and compose music in genuinely original ways. Specific teaching techniques are used to develop competence in various activities as shown in Chart 12–3. Summarized in the following sections are examples of strategies used in connection with various musical activities.

Discovering rhythmic patterns	A folk dance
1. Have children demonstrate walking and running patterns as the class claps the rhythm.	1. Listen to catch the rhythm.
	2. Clap the rhythm or play it on rhythm instruments.
2. Have the class listen as a record with a galloping rhythm is played.	3. Watch the foot pattern as it is demonstrated.
	4. Match the foot pattern to the beat and accent.
3. Discuss how the rhythm is different from running and walking rhythms.	5. Sing or say the rhythm steps as the music is played: Step-step-step-hop.
4. Have a child demonstrate the movement he thinks is appropriate.	6. Do the steps to music.
5. Have others demonstrate the movement as the record is played.	7. Practice as needed.

Listening activities	Reading music
1. Know the music thoroughly.	1. Place several measures on the board.
2. Discuss purposes for listening.	2. Review the types of notes to be sung.
3. Present the selection.	3. Discuss the meter and clap the time.
4. Use pictures, poems, or other devices to highlight mood.	4. Clarify the time for different notes.
	5. Discuss the key signature and give the starting tone.
5. Discuss discoveries which students enjoyed.	
6. Provide for repetition to increase enjoyment and understanding.	6. Have a student give the syllables for each note in the first measure.
7. Provide for follow-up activities related to objectives.	7. Have one student sing a measure followed by others.
8. Respect the views of students.	8. Have the class sing the entire song from notation.

Rote singing	The autoharp
1. Use a pitch pipe to sound starting tone.	1. Use a single chord at first.
2. Sing the song for the class with a clear diction.	2. Locate the key to be depressed with the left hand.
3. Sing it again as children listen to note the time and phrases.	3. Get the rhythmic pattern.
4. Clarify the meaning of new words.	4. Depress the key with the left hand and strum with the right.
5. Have the group sing with you.	
6. Have the group sing each phrase.	5. Try a two-chord accompaniment, following a similar procedure
7. Listen as the group sings.	
8. Review and practice as needed.	

Chart 12–3.   Illustrative teaching techniques.

Using Varied Approaches

The use of different approaches is recommended in a California teaching guide (California, 1963). In recognition of the fact that the various phases of music education are highly interrelated, the guide urges teachers to begin with rhythmic or singing or other experiences and to devise such sequences as the following:

1. Begin with rhythmic activity and move to related singing, playing of instruments, listening, and reading
2. Begin with singing and move to related rhythmic activity, playing, listening, and playing of instruments
3. Begin with listening and move to rhythmic expression accompanied by playing of instruments
4. Begin with the playing of instruments and move to related rhythmic movement and listening
5. Begin with the notation of a pattern on a chart or on the chalkboard and move to singing and playing of the pattern
6. Begin with a pattern created by the students and move to rhythmic movement, the playing of an accompaniment, and listening to a taped recording of the activity
7. Begin with inquiry into a selected form of music and move to listening, singing, or playing of selected patterns, and on to further listening

The beginning and the sequence may be varied as needed by the teacher. A guiding principle is to relate each succeeding activity to others so that various dimensions of understanding and feeling are engendered. When this is done children have opportunities to respond in a variety of ways and thus gain insight into the relationships among elements of music as a part of different activities. Furthermore, individual differences can be met as each child is guided to participate in the various activities that are included in the sequence.

Rhythmic Activities

Strategies in this phase of music education range from providing opportunities for spontaneous response to music through movement to direct teaching in which elements of music are emphasized. The following examples are illustrative.

Fundamental rhythmic movements. Teachers of young children frequently provide opportunities for pupils to walk, skip, or gallop in a spontaneous manner as music is played. One or two children may respond to a selection and others join them as the music is played. The movement is changed as the tempo of the music changes. At other times, the music is changed to fit the movement of children. Rhythm instruments, clapping, the piano, the autoharp, or recordings may be used for accompaniment.

Creative movement. One strategy is based on creative response to music in which children create rhythmic movements that are sparked as music is played. One or two children, or a group of four or five, may initiate the activity by moving about the room or by swaying, bending, or using other axial movements. Later, other children create movements which they feel are expressive of the mood of the music. A second strategy is based on children's expression, and music is selected to fit the movements. Children create movements or dance steps, and an accompaniment is improvised on the piano, autoharp, or percussion instruments.

Discovering rhythmic elements. The focus of this strategy is on the use of rhythmic activity to highlight patterns that are discovered through listening activities. Music is selected to reveal elements of music that can be expressed rhythmically. Children listen to discover ways in which they can express one or more of the following through rhythmic activity: story, mood, tempo, accent, metric beat, melodic and rhythmic patterns, and form. Individuals and small groups give interpretations, followed by others in the class.

Singing

The teaching of songs includes the use of both aural and visual approaches. In the aural approach children listen as the teacher or a child sings or as a recording or an instrument is played. Repeated listening experiences may be provided so that children can learn the melody and discover the rhythmic pattern. Special attention is given to phrases that are alike and different. Children then hum or sing the melody as they listen, sing repeated phrases, sing with and without music books, sing with and without listening to the teacher or recording.

In the visual approach, notation is provided to guide listening. Children watch the notation and listen critically in order to discover like and unlike phrases, ascending and descending passages, small and large melodic intervals, and rhythmic patterns. Selected parts may be highlighted as children watch the notation while someone sings or plays the song. This may be followed by having the class sing various phrases, clap the time, tap the rhythm of the melody, or play repeated patterns on simple instruments. The children next sing the song as accurately as they can as they watch the notation. As shown in the foregoing example, the visual approach is supplemented by aural and rhythmic activities. This appears to be essential in the early stages of the development of musicality. It probably should be stressed at all stages for most students, because music is primarily a tonal art.

Part singing calls for strategies that may combine both aural and visual approaches. Preparatory experiences should be provided in which children sing as a descant or alto part is sung or played, embellishments are added to familiar songs, rounds are sung or played, and harmonic accompaniments are provided by means of the piano, autoharp, or recordings. Instruction should include the singing of descants and rounds, harmonizing the ending of songs, listening to parts sung or played by others or played on a recording, singing in parallel thirds or sixths, listening to one or two parts while singing another, following the notation while listening and while singing, and the learning of several two- and three-part songs. Current textbooks contain a variety of part songs that have been graded in difficulty and can be used to develop competence to a high level.

Listening

Different strategies are used for program and absolute music. Listening to program music is guided so that children may discover ways in which stories or descriptions are portrayed. Listening to absolute music is guided so that they may discover melodic and rhythmic patterns, form, and other musical elements without reference to story or descriptive material. Both types of listening call for discovery on the part of children, and both are guided inductively to elicit responses from them.

Program music. After the teacher has made introductory comments regarding the selection and composer, children are asked to listen in order to find out how a story or description is suggested through the use of rhythm, melody, or other elements. Questions about the selection are asked in a way that does not give clues to the answer so that children themselves will use the music for clues. If a story is suggested, children are asked to tell which parts are the best clues and to explain why they chose them. Replaying may be done as needed as children discover and tell in their own words the story suggested by such a selection as Weber's *Invitation to the Dance* in which the first measures suggest an invitation and later measures indicate acceptance, the dance, and the ending.

Absolute music. Children are asked to listen to musical content in order to discover creative ways in which selected elements of music are used. Introductory comments may include information on the selection and the composer in order to set the stage for listening. Themes to be heard may be played, and attention may be called to rhythmic, melodic, or harmonic characteristics of special importance in the selection. The teacher or student may identify the theme or other elements as they appear if such behavior does not detract from listening. Children express their reactions, demonstrate patterns they have discovered, and discuss other elements after the listening experience. For example, after listening to a selection they may play or hum the theme and discuss the variations that resulted as different instruments or varied accompaniments were used in the composition.

Instrumental Activities

Strategies in this phase include a combination of creative experimentation and direct instruction. Self-instruction through practice is a key to continuing progress. Strategies vary somewhat for rhythm, melody, and other instruments as shown in the following examples.

Rhythm instruments.   The introduction of rhythm instruments typically begins with exploratory activities so that children can discover the clicking, rattling, swishing, clanging, and booming qualities of sticks, claves, blocks, maracas, triangles, cymbals, drums, and gourds. Opportunities are provided for children to select and use them to accompany activities, to set the mood for activities, to improvise rhythmic patterns, and to demonstrate patterns discovered through listening.

Melody instruments.   Diatonic and chromatic bells fastened to a frame and resonator bells on separate blocks may be introduced by playing the starting tone of songs, playing a phrase, or playing a simple tune. Children need opportunities to experiment with them and, after discovering how they are played, to use them for a variety of purposes. Simple melodies, descants, rounds, duets, and embellishments may be played. Pitch may be checked, new melodies may be created, melodies may be played by ear, and chords may be played to strengthen harmonic concepts. Reading letters and numerals in order to play melodies and chords is helpful in developing understandings and skills that are useful in playing other instruments.

Other instruments.   Instruction on the autoharp includes guidance in following chord markings in song books, playing a single chord and then two or more different chords for accompaniment, changing chords, and stroking to fit rhythmic patterns, the metric beat, and fast and slow tempo. Flute-type instruments (recorders, tonettes, song flutes) are used in individual and group instruction to teach concepts of melodic movement, to improve music reading, to help uncertain singers, to clarify a part in part singing, to create interest in learning to play orchestral instruments. Individual and group instruction in orchestral and band instruments is provided in a systematic sequence by a teacher who has had appropriate preparation. Various instruments are used in the classroom to acquaint children with their sound and appearance, produce different musical effects, demonstrate phrasing and rhythmic patterns, play obbligatos and parts, improve music reading, accompany musical activities, and introduce transposition.

GUIDELINES FOR THE TEACHER

The teacher has a specialized role to play in music education. Teachers who carry out this role effectively are well grounded in music as a field of study, have insight into the structure of music, plan and carry out a variety of musical experiences, and are continually developing higher and higher levels of musicality as individuals. No longer should it be assumed that anyone can be a teacher of music. Rather, the view is dominant that special preparation is needed if music education is to reach a level of quality that is essential to the attainment of current objectives. Among the guidelines which teachers may use to reach a high level of quality are the following which are drawn from teaching guides and professional textbooks.

Provide a planned program of musical experiences designed to develop musicality to higher and higher levels throughout the year and from year to year. Contributions to the objectives of music education may be made by providing developmental activities in seven basic areas: singing, listening, rhythmic expression, playing instruments, creating music, reading music, and music in other subjects. The overall program in the elementary and secondary schools should be designed as a whole. The integrity of music as a tonal art should be maintained throughout the program as every effort is made to develop attitudes, appreciations, interests, understandings, and abilities that will have lasting value in the lives of students.

Select music of different types in relation to its intrinsic worth and its value in contributing to the development of musicality. Different kinds of music are needed to acquaint children with man's rich musical heritage, to provide a broad base for the development of tastes and appreciations, and to take children far beyond the musical fare that they experience at home.

Employ creative approaches to musical experiences in ways that involve children actively as both producers and consumers of music. Avoid the exclusive use of a "consumer's approach" which inevitably limits learning. Through creative approaches to producing, performing, and enjoying music, children bring out their own thoughts and feelings, express them in different ways, begin to understand that music is a means of communication, develop a desire to learn how others have expressed their ideas, and are motivated to develop understanding and skills that are essential to growth in musicality.

Develop concepts, skills, and appreciations in the context of the music the children are experiencing under the guidance of the teacher. The development of musicality should be rooted in musical experiences appropriate to students' backgrounds at each level of instruction. In the context of such experiences it is possible to guide students to develop insight into the structure of music, learn to read music for purposes important to them, and use terms and symbols to interpret the music of others and to express their own thoughts and feelings. Appreciation and enjoyment may be extended and new avenues of learning may be opened as children develop increasing understanding of the basic elements of music and increasing ability to read notation.

Challenge each student to develop in all dimensions of musicality. Well-rounded musical growth can be attained by providing varied experiences even though some children are more successful in one mode of expression or enjoyment than another. At the same time differing aptitudes for music and for particular modes of expression should be accepted, satisfying participation should be provided for each student, and every student should be challenged to the limit of his capabilities. Both individual and group activities should be used to meet individual differences.

Obtain and use basic equipment and instructional media that are essential to the development of high-quality instruction. Available in each classroom should be the following: a pitch pipe, an auto-harp, chromatic tone bells, a record player, basic textbooks with accompanying manuals and recordings, supplementary books, a staff liner, and staff rule paper for notation. Available as needed should be a library of recordings, a piano, a tape recorder, picture sets of instruments, instruments for demonstration, a radio, and a television receiver. Instruments made by students are useful for many purposes but in no way should be viewed as a substitute for basic equipment and instructional media.

Encourage students to use what has been learned in music education and to engage in musical activities outside the classroom. A desired outcome for students is sensitivity to the wealth of music that is around them and how it can enrich daily living. This may take a variety of forms, such as keener interest in one or more types of music, greater discrimination in selecting musical fare, participation in community activities, taking private lessons, making a record collection, and enjoying music on radio and television.

Seek the assistance of specialists in order to provide for continuing improvement of instruction in all phases of music education. Consultants in music education can demonstrate effective techniques, assist in obtaining equipment and instructional media, advise on special problems, and suggest creative approaches to teaching. Special teachers who give instruction on band and orchestral instruments, group piano lessons, and the school choir are a valuable source of ideas and help. Many classroom teachers have special musical competence that can be tapped through the use of team teaching, the swapping of classes, and the combining of classes for various musical activities.

EVALUATION OF INSTRUCTIONAL OUTCOMES

A primary mode of evaluation in music education is direct observation of each student's musical performance and his responses to music. The behavior of students as they sing, play, engage in rhythmic activities, and express musical ideas is immediately perceivable by the teacher. How students respond to music in listening activities is less directly perceivable but may be assessed by observing reactions and by providing follow-up discussion and rhythmic and other expressive activities.

Evaluation may be facilitated through the use of observational guidelines as noted in the following section in which behaviorally stated outcomes are listed under different activities. A key principle to keep in mind is that observation check lists should be designed to fit instruction in each classroom. The following sample check lists illustrate the range of objectives in music education; they conclude with the heading "other," which is followed by space to write in other outcomes sought by the teacher.

Rhythmic activities: _____ Knows fundamental rhythms _____ Recognizes different patterns _____ Moves to music _____ Selects music to fit movement _____ Creates movements _____ Recognizes beat, meter, and accent _____ Plays and distinguishes rhythm instruments _____ Selects accompaniments _____ Knows dance patterns _____ Substitutes inner response for overt movement _____ Other _____

Singing: _____ Matches tones _____ Is sensitive to changes in pitch, melody, and volume _____ Is sensitive to phrasing _____ Sings with accompaniment and selects accompaniment _____ Interprets mood _____ Enunciates clearly _____ Recognizes lullabies, marches, and other types of music _____ Sings rounds, descants, parts _____ Sings from notation _____ Is building a singing repertoire _____ Other _____

Playing instruments: _____ Plays simple melody and percussion instruments _____ Selects instruments for use in other activities _____ Uses autoharp for accompaniments _____ Adds introductions and codas _____ Enjoys group and individual instruction _____ Recognizes woodwinds and other types of instruments _____ Identifies instruments by sound and sight _____ Investigates how sounds are produced and other topics _____ Other _____

Listening: _____ Identifies sounds and tones _____ Interprets feeling or mood _____ Enjoys listening to music _____ Responds in various ways _____ Catches the mood _____ Discusses listening out of school _____ Detects rhythm, melody, harmony _____ Identifies instruments _____ Detects phrases, beat, independent melodies _____ Recognizes overture and other forms _____ Is building a listening repertoire _____ Investigates composers and other topics _____ Other _____

Creative activities: _____ Responds to music in original ways _____ Expresses responses through art and other activities

_____ Improvises tunes and rhythmic patterns _____
Experiments with instruments to devise special effects
_____ Creates embellishments _____ Creates songs and
related accompaniment _____ Sets poems and stories to
music _____ Other _____

Reading music: _____ Associates tonal direction with arm
movements _____ Associates rhythmic patterns with fundamental movements _____ Recognizes notes of varying
duration _____ Associates notes with syllables _____
Associates notes with numeral and letter notation _____
Plays tunes by ear, numeral and letter notation _____ Uses
notation to sing and to play _____ Notates phrases and
original music _____ Understands musical terms _____
Reads by sight _____ Other _____

Using the Taxonomies to Improve Evaluation

The taxonomies of educational objectives (Bloom, 1956; Krathwohl, Bloom, & Masia, 1964) are suggestive of items and questions that may be used to improve evaluation. With increasing recognition of the importance of the cognitive side of music education has come increased attention to assessment of conceptual outcomes. Assessment of affective components of the program can be sharpened by devising evaluative items and questions on the various levels identified in the taxonomy. The cognitive and affective domains are intimately interrelated.

Cognitive Domain

Knowledge level: knowledge of musical terminology, information, and forms of music; knowledge of vocal music; recognition of musical works
What instruments are included among woodwinds? Mark a *W* under each of the pictures that shows a woodwind instrument.

Comprehension level: ability to read music and to understand and explain musical principles
Can you explain how sound is created by a violin? Make a sketch or drawing that shows how sounds are produced on a string.

Application level: ability to apply musical knowledge and comprehension to the selection of appropriate music in varying situations; ability to understand and classify new musical works or instruments when these are heard
What rhythmic pattern is best for marching? Listen to the following rhythmic patterns and select the one that is best for marching.

Analysis level: understanding of the relationships of parts of musical forms

In what ways is the melodic phrase varied in this composition? Keep a record of the following as you listen: (1) the number of times the melodic phrase is repeated, and (2) the number of times it is varied.

Synthesis level: production of original musical works or creative organization and utilization of existing works

How shall we combine the songs, rhythms, and accompaniments in our program on Indians?

Play on the melody bells a tune that can be used to set this poem to music.

Evaluation level: use of criteria to evaluate quality of a composition or performance

How can we improve the accompaniment to the folk dance? Listen critically and rank the following compositions according to the power of the underlying rhythmic pattern.

Affective Domain

Receiving (attending) level: Can you tell when the music sounds like a rooster crowing?

Change from walking to skipping as the music changes.

Responding level: What parts of the recording made you feel happy? Sad?

Make a check by each of the following that you would like to have more time to do: _____ Singing _____ Playing instruments _____ Folk dancing _____ Listening to records

Valuing level: After hearing a song that you enjoy very much, do you try to find out about the singer? The composer?

List the main reasons you would include in a letter to a radio station to convince them to play the kind of music you like.

Organization level: Can you tell why you like this type of music?

As you listen to music that does *not* tell a story or describe something, which of the following do you do? _____ Identify the theme _____ Discover how the theme is varied _____ Find rhythmic patterns _____ Identify instruments _____ Hear unusual harmony _____ Find new uses of instruments

EVALUATION OF THE INSTRUCTIONAL PROGRAM

Data gleaned from assessment of outcomes of instruction are useful in evaluating the instructional program. In fact, continuing changes should be made to improve daily instruction. In addition, attention should be given to systematic appraisal of the overall program in terms of guidelines such as the following:

Foundations

Are all phases of music education rooted in foundation disciplines?

Is the program geared to the musical capabilities and backgrounds of children?

Structure

Are the structural elements of music clearly defined?

Are structural elements made a part of each phase of the program?

Are provisions suggested for making honest and sincere musical expression and study the core of the program?

Objectives

Is the development of musicality viewed as a central objective?

Are specific objectives clarified for each phase of the program?

Are relationships among different phases of the program clear?

Is attention given to cognitive and affective outcomes?

A complete program

Are the following phases outlined in a developmental sequence? _____ Rhythmic activities _____ Singing _____ Listening _____ Playing _____ Creative activities _____ Understanding and reading music _____ Music in other studies

_____ Are investigative activities included?

_____ Are needed equipment and materials provided?

Teaching strategies

Are teaching techniques consistent with the practices of musicians?

Are both discovery and directed learning approaches used in relation to differing objectives ?

Are approaches varied in terms of objectives, type of activity, and backgrounds of students?

Evaluation

Are observation guidelines developed for individualized assessment of outcomes?

Is evaluation of cognitive and affective outcomes planned in terms of levels of complexity and internalization?

Is the program of instruction evaluated continuously and systematically?

Teacher preparation

Are teachers of music well grounded in foundation disciplines and methods of instruction?

> Are specialists available to provide instrumental and other
> aspects of instruction?
> Are teachers and specialists involved in trying out new materials
> and approaches?
>
> *Continuing revision*
> Are continuing efforts made to improve the program?

REFERENCES

Arberg, Harold W. *Music curriculum guides.* Washington, D.C.: U.S. Office of Education, 1964. Brief annotations of guides from all sections of the country.

Bloom, Benjamin S. (Ed.) *Taxonomy of educational objectives: cognitive domain.* New York: McKay, 1956. Examples of objectives and test items of six levels of complexity.

California. *Teachers guide to music in the elementary school.* Sacramento: State Department of Education, 1963. Detailed suggestions for using varied approaches to all phases of music education.

Crocker, Richard L. *A history of musical style.* New York: McGraw-Hill, 1966. Review of style from the Gregorian chant to the present; useful for enriching teachers' backgrounds.

Ernst, Karl D., & Gary, Charles L. (Eds.) *Music in general education.* Washington, D.C.: Music Educators National Conference, 1965. Concise review elements of music, form or design, interpretive aspects, and other components of the program of instruction.

Garretson, Robert L. *Music in childhood education.* New York: Appleton-Century-Crofts, 1966. Procedures for developing experiences in singing, rhythmic experiences, listening, instrumental music, creative activities, and reading.

Hartsel, O. M. *Teaching music in the elementary school.* Washington, D.C.: Association for Supervision and Curriculum Development, NEA, 1963. Practical answers to a variety of questions about music education for children.

Hartshorn, William C. The study of music as an academic discipline, *Music Educ. J.*, January, 1963, **49**, 25–28. Review of music as a discipline with attention to content and inquiry.

Kaplan, Max, & Steiner, Francis J. *Musicianship for the classroom teacher.* Chicago: Rand McNally, 1966. Practical presentation of rhythm, melody, and other structural components of music.

Knieter, Gerald L. Musicality is universal, *Teach. Coll. Rec.*, April, 1966, **67**, 485–491. Discussion of stages ranging from receptivity and understanding to explanation, synthesis, and wholeness.

Krathwohl, David R., Bloom, Benjamin S., & Masia, Bertram B. *Taxonomy of educational objectives: affective domain.* New York: McKay, 1964. Objectives and test items arranged by levels in terms of degree of internalization.

Los Angeles City Schools. *Course of study for elementary schools.* Los Angeles: Board of Education, 1964. A grade outline of musical activities; examples of concept clusters at teacher level.

Myers, Louise Kifer. *Teaching children music in the elementary school.* (3d ed.) Englewood Cliffs, N.J.: Prentice-Hall, 1961. Includes a chapter on the role of music in understanding other cultures, with suggestions for studying non-Western styles of music.

National Society for the Study of Education. *Basic concepts in music education.* Fifty-seventh Yearbook, Part I. Chicago: University of Chicago Press, 1958. Discussion of basic aspects of music education.

Nye, Robert E., & Nye, Vernice T. *Music in the elementary school.* (2d ed.) Englewood Cliffs, N.J.: Prentice-Hall, 1964. Principles and procedures for all types of musical activity.

Orff, Carl. *Music for children.* (Adapted by Doreen Hall and Arnold Walter.) New York: Associated Music Publishers, 1960. Principles and procedures in Orff's approach, which is receiving increased attention in many schools.

Palisca, Claude V. *Music in our schools.* Washington, D.C.: U.S. Office of Education, OE–33033, 1964. Report of Yale seminar on ways of improving music education; examples of concept clusters and structure of the music program.

Phenix, Philip H. *Realms of meaning.* New York: McGraw-Hill, 1964. Discussion of music as part of realm of aesthetics in chap. 12.

Ratner, Leonard G. *Music: the listener's art.* (2d ed.) New York: McGraw-Hill, 1966. Application of musical elements to analysis of music from medieval to modern; useful for enriching teachers' backgrounds of understanding.

Richards, Mary H. *Threshold to music.* San Francisco: Fearon, 1963. Examples of Kodaly's methods of instruction.

Swanson, Bessie. *Music in the education of children.* (2d ed.) Belmont, Calif.: Wadsworth, 1964. Principles and procedures for developing all types of musical activity.

Wilson, A. Verne. *Design for understanding music.* Evanston, Ill.: Sumy-Birchard, 1966. Discussion of relationship of music to other arts; background material for teachers.

CHALLENGES AND PROBLEMS

THE CURRENT CURRICULUM reform movement has brought new challenges and problems to curriculum builders. These range across every aspect of curriculum adoption, implementation, and evaluation, the continual cycle of curriculum building in every school system. There is no dearth of potentially valuable curriculum designs and materials available for incorporation into local programs, but while a few offer materials for in-service education, most do not deal with considerations of implementation beyond provision of teaching manuals. How are guidelines developed for curriculum change and implementation? How may planners distinguish between substantial innovations and those which are untested but attractive fads? Current emphases in objectives call for new focus on content structured in accord with foundation disciplines, and they require teaching strategies that develop children's skills as inquirers. Are new professional skills needed? What preparation in terms of academic knowledge and approaches to new strategies may be necessary to enable teachers to carry out new programs? How should in-service training be organized? Are newer teaching procedures difficult for teachers who have no inquiry experience of their own? New curriculum designs call for new types of supportive media, and many new materials and media systems are available from diverse sources. What guidelines are needed for incorporation or coordination of these media? Which are appropriate, and what specific objectives do they support? Finally, the many changes in new curriculum designs have provoked a need for a broader range of evaluative techniques. How may we measure the child's attainment of understanding at higher cognitive levels? How may inquiry skills be assessed? What techniques, beyond pupil achievement tests, will permit evaluation of the full range of outcomes of new instructional programs?

These are but a few examples of the challenges, problems, and questions that confront curriculum builders as they adopt or adapt, put into practice, and determine the effectiveness of new curriculum designs. In this concluding chapter attention is given to some challenges and problems of immediate concern to those interested in improving the instructional program in elementary schools. These considerations will be discussed in the framework of the interrelated curriculum-building processes of incorporation, implementation, and evaluation of new curriculum designs.

INCORPORATION AND ADOPTION OF NEW CURRICULUM DESIGNS

The first consideration in planning the elementary school curriculum is the development of the overall curriculum structure—the framework that indicates the strands or fields of study to be included within and across grade levels. Curriculum workers need to develop criteria that enable them to determine which fields of study must be included in order to provide a complete and balanced curriculum. Attention to the disciplines as sources of curriculum design presents a challenge to the curriculum worker to explore the ways in which knowledge may be organized, since these may serve as sources for the development of criteria for balance in the curriculum.

The section on "Classifications of Knowledge" in Chapter 1 discusses some examples of the organization of knowledge as proposed by Cassidy, Broudy, and Thelen. A particular elementary curriculum may be evaluated to determine whether it includes studies representative of each of the categories included in a proposed organization. Phenix's classification of knowledge in accordance with different ways of acquiring meaning or understanding provides a framework in another dimension. He suggests that the curriculum at every level should include studies drawn from disciplines representative of each of the six realms of meaning (Phenix, 1964).

In a discussion of the problem of the organization of the total curriculum, Bellack (1964) pointed out the importance of examining relationships among allied disciplines, relationships among broad areas of knowledge (such as those exemplified in the classifications cited above), and relationships of knowledge to human affairs, in order to plan a complete and balanced curriculum. Such considerations would help curriculum workers avoid a fragmented or incomplete curriculum by facilitating the selection, coordination, and incorporation into a balanced program of curriculum designs and projects focused on learnings in a single discipline. As a basis for curriculum planning, he suggested that two views of the relationships between fields of knowledge should be utilized. One view emphasizes conceptual structure and modes of inquiry associated with broad fields of knowledge, such as the natural sciences, the social sciences, mathematics, and the humanities. The other view emphasizes modes of thought that cut across the boundaries of the individual fields: the analytic, empirical, aesthetic, and moral modes.

Another preliminary consideration in curriculum building is the determination of those who should participate in various phases of the process. The planning phase, which includes examination of new curriculum designs, should involve people of several professional responsibilities. Curriculum supervisors and specialists are able to offer guidance and coordination through all phases of the process. Administrators, teachers, and such supportive personnel as librarians and instructional materials specialists, as the people who will be directly responsible for implementation of the program, should certainly be involved in its planning. Scholars from the disciplines and from schools or departments of education may provide leadership, guidance, and assistance in planning, implementation, and research related to evaluation.

New curriculum designs and related materials need to be scrutinized in regard to the nature of their objectives, planning, utilization of foundation disciplines, scope and sequence, teaching strategies and materials, evaluation of instructional outcomes, relation to total curriculum, and feasibility of use. Problems and questions in each area will be considered below in this sequence. Useful sources of criteria for evaluation of new curriculum projects and designs will be found in several end-of-chapter references (Ammons and Gilchrist, 1965; Gilchrist, 1963, pp. 1–10; Fraser, 1962; Michaelis, 1963, p. 169).

Objectives

Curriculum builders will need to identify the objectives of new designs and materials, compare them with those of the school system, and consider their suitability for the school population. Such questions as the following should be raised:

> **What are the objectives of the design? Are they specified in behavioral terms that include understandings in a structural framework related to the disciplines; skills in the areas of thinking, inquiring, learning; and attitudes? Are the objectives meaningful to teachers? Will teachers encounter difficulties in their implementation?**

> **In what ways, or to what extent, do the objectives fit in with and support the overall educational objectives of the school system? How do they match or augment specific objectives for each grade level or curriculum area?**

> **How does the school population compare with tryout groups (if any were used)? For what groups or types of learners are project or materials objectives best suited? What modifications can be made to suit new designs to the needs of specific groups within the school system?**

Planning of Designs and Materials

Criteria related to the planning and production of new curriculum designs are reflected in such questions as these:

> **How was the design initiated? Under whose auspices (foundations, public institutions, commercial organizations, etc.) was the design produced? What are the qualifications of those who planned the design or materials? Were diverse specialists (scholars in academic disciplines and education, teachers, curriculum specialists) involved? To what extent was each of these special competencies represented?**

Have the designs or materials been tried out in appropriate classroom settings? What evaluative information is available? Is further information needed?

What assistance is available from scholars and other curriculum producers for implementation of new designs? How can the benefits of their assistance be maximized or maintained over long periods of time? If revisions are planned, how are these communicated to the school system?

An important point to note here is that close cooperation between curriculum producers and school systems in the planning of new designs and materials can enhance the suitability of the design and produce a variety of "spin-offs" of value in improving curriculum development. A key spin-off should be increased research on teaching and learning as new curriculum materials are tested in different situations. Among the other possibilities are increasing support of curriculum development from the academic community, new knowledge of ways to use structure and modes of inquiry from the disciplines in improving instruction, new insights into concept overlap and other relationships among the disciplines, clearer notions of the value of separate-discipline and multidiscipline approaches, and new conceptions of teaching and learning theories that are grounded in classroom studies. Such outcomes can be obtained only if programs of evaluation and research are extended far beyond the present plans of curriculum project producers. Sorely needed are large-scale efforts that will involve scholars, curriculum specialists, measurement and other experts, and school personnel in a series of related studies designed to explore in depth the many issues, problems, and outcomes of current curriculum designs.

Foundation Disciplines

A major challenge is to develop insight into the structure of the disciplines. The outlines of structure that have been prepared by those scholars who are involved in curriculum development are clearly the most helpful. A good beginning can be made by studying the examples of structure presented in preceding chapters. Special attention should also be given to the related references in which the disciplines are reviewed and additional examples of structure may be found. It is strongly recommended that intensive efforts be made to identify key concepts, concept clusters, and generalizations that are used in units of study as well as those which outline the overall structure of a discipline or a program of instruction. In determining the outlines of structure that are most useful in curriculum planning, designers should also give attention to the microstructures used in units, as these are concrete indications of how ideas are related in a form immediately useful in the instructional program.

Special efforts should be made to draw out the major modes of inquiry (experimental, historical, case study, survey, etc.) that constitute the syntactical aspects of structure. Specific methods of investigation employed (interviewing, mapping, observing, etc.) should also be identified. If the focus in curriculum design is exclusively on the substantive, conceptual aspects, the dynamic processes that are key ingredients in inquiry may be neglected. Both content and process should be considered as disciplines are reviewed and curriculum is planned. A model for reviewing disciplines is presented later in this chapter as a guideline in developing a unified curriculum from several sources and materials.

Closely related to these considerations is the problem of making appropriate forms of inquiry an *integral* part of instruction. A variety of proposals have been made, ranging from inquiry based on questions posed by students, to which the teacher should reply either yes or no, to free-wheeling experimentation in which little or no teacher direction is provided. The authors take the stand that primary attention should be given to the use of modes and techniques of inquiry drawn directly from the disciplines. Special inquiry procedures designed outside the context of fundamental ways of knowing and producing knowledge cannot be expected to pay off in the long run. Nor will a single mode of inquiry, anymore than a single view of learning, have much mileage in curriculum planning. In short, the view is taken that curriculum builders should draw upon the full array of processes of inquiry in current use in disciplinary and cross-disciplinary studies in order to select and use the most appropriate modes and techniques of inquiry as units or programs of study are planned.

Another problem posed by the use of inquiry in the classroom is reflected in the argument that, since teachers are not inquirers (in the sense that they are not usually trained to the point of specialization and investigation in physics, linguistics, anthropology, or other disciplines), they cannot possibly teach inquiry procedures. The authors reject this argument flatly, provided certain conditions obtain. First, teachers can make inquiry a part of the program if well-designed materials with adequate teaching guides are provided. A major effort of current projects is directed to devising inquiry-oriented materials and guides. Critical study and use of such materials will go a long way in helping teachers to provide experiences in inquiry provided they are not put off by the bugaboo of "teacher-proof materials." The authors have found that one of the quickest ways to find out how an economist or mathematician or other inquirer handles questions and problems is to examine materials specifically designed for school use. Second, teachers can teach inquiry if they will take a stance that may be epitomized in the question: How can we find out? Such a stance leads to a consideration of multiple-inquiry approaches and the selection and use of what appear to be the most useful approaches. Third, teachers can teach inquiry if they will engage in in-service and self-study activities that focus on modes and techniques that can be put to use in the classroom. Experimentation, content analysis, interviewing, field studies, and the like can be embedded in usable contexts from the teacher's point of view. In addition, a good start can be made by considering examples presented in the preceding chapters and related references.

The following questions, then, might be used to evaluate the structural aspects of new curriculum designs:

> **What outlines of structure are found in curriculum designs and materials? Are there conflicts between the approaches of various designs, or are differences reconcilable as the content of one design supplements that of another? Are conceptual frameworks suitable to the learning needs of children for whom the designs or materials are intended?**
>
> **What inquiry modes and specific techniques are incorporated in the design? How appropriate are these procedures for classroom use at intended grade or learning levels? Are suggested inquiry procedures clearly described and consistent with the syntactical structure of foundation disciplines, or are they vaguely set forth, overly generalized, or not stated at all?**

Scope and Sequence of Curriculum Designs

The current emphasis on the use of the disciplines as foundations for the elementary curriculum has been pointed out and exemplified in earlier chapters. Much of the discussion of substantive and syntactical structure in the preceding paragraphs bears directly on the scope of new curriculum designs. It is important to recognize, of course, that adherence to structure drawn from the disciplines does not mean concomitant neglect of the needs of individual learners. If the aim of education is, after all, to develop necessary understandings and thinking skills on the part of all learners, then appropriate means must be found to present all learners with the content, materials, and sequences of experiences that will achieve this aim most effectively. Attention must be given to ways in which the structural aspects of curriculum content and experiences meet the needs of culturally different groups within the school system, different learning styles, and differing rates of comprehension and skill attainment.

In analyzing or planning the sequential organization of the curriculum, designers should employ both logical and psychological aspects of curriculum planning, giving increasing attention to logical sequencing of instructional materials. There is no need for any debate over logical versus psychological planning. Both aspects are evident and mutually supportive in new curriculum designs. Logical planning should be evident in the arranging of facts, concepts, generalizations, skills, and methods of inquiry in sequences related to outlines of the structure of disciplines. The use of logical processes should be apparent in the modes of instruction in many designs, involving such elements as deducing hypotheses, categorizing and classifying data in terms of criteria, systematic testing of conclusions, and critical analysis of evidence and proof. Psychological aspects of planning should be evident in the attention given to such cognitive processes as classifying, generalizing, and evaluating, and in using methods that move students to higher levels of thinking in a teaching sequence.

Questions such as the following may be employed in analysis of the scope and sequence of curriculum designs:

> **Is the content of the design or materials representative of essential aspects of the structure of the field of knowledge? Is the content supportive of modes of inquiry and modes of understanding appropriate to the field? Is the content organized in a framework and sequence that will enhance children's understandings and encourage inquiry and independence in learning?**
>
> **Does the content represent an improvement over present programs in the effectiveness of its organization? Does it replace outmoded content?**
>
> **Are provisions made for modification of scope and pace of sequence to meet the needs of individual learning differences? Are special materials provided for various groups of learners?**

Teaching Strategies and Instructional Media

Some new curriculum designs include a coordinated "package" of content outlines, teaching plans, and instructional media. All designs specify appropriate supportive media, even when these are not included within the project materials themselves. Other materials are produced independently. Guidelines for teaching strategies and use of materials are provided, to varying extents, in the form of manuals and unit or lesson plans. These guidelines for teachers should be, in general, directive without being prescriptive. Teachers should be free to alter and improve them to meet local needs and conditions. Guidelines and directives should be set up to highlight relationships among objectives, content, key concepts and generalizations, learning activities, instructional media, and evaluation.

Teaching strategies should involve inductive approaches in which students are guided in analyzing and synthesizing information. New programs should employ some form of inductive approach in which questions embodying key concepts are used to guide study, problems are analyzed, independent study is emphasized, and students themselves organize data and formulate generalizations. Conceptual models in the form of questions should be used to guide study of different problems or topics. Cognitive processes involved in handling content and values should be stressed. Processes of conceptualizing, hypothesizing, inferring, generalizing, and evaluating should be emphasized. Taxonomies of cognitive objectives may be used to identify process objectives and to build a series of questions on varying levels of cognition.

Multimedia approaches and coordination of media should be considered in curriculum planning. Although reading materials are dominant in most new designs, a variety of related instructional materials are being prepared: transparencies with overlays for overhead projection, single-concept films, films, filmstrips, and slides (some with accompanying tapes), kits that include artifacts and models, sets of pictures on selected topics, graphic and tabular materials, charts, and diagrams. There appears to be a strong effort in many designs to bring the instructional media together in a teaching system that is accompanied by detailed teaching plans.

Some relevant questions include the following:

> **What strategies are suggested? How clearly are these described? Are they based on teaching-learning theories consistent with those of the school system? What balance is there between adequate guidance for teachers and freedom to adapt to special needs?**
>
> **What materials are required? Do they support the goals of the overall curriculum design? Do they develop content in a form consistent with structural outlines? Do they develop inquiry processes?**
>
> **What materials are provided with the overall design? Are other suitable materials available? Are any materials called for which are already utilized in local programs? Are the materials provided in new designs and projects appropriate to the needs of learners for whom they are intended?**

Evaluation of Instructional Outcomes

Evaluation of instructional outcomes should be concerned with the full range of possible outcomes beyond the measurement of academic achievement. Attention should be given to assessment techniques that will reveal data on development of skills, attitudes, and values. Evaluation may be improved as projects and designs build appraisal devices into instructional materials and as new instruments are developed. A variety of techniques and devices for evaluating outcomes of instruction may be found in project materials: summarizing questions and test items in students' materials, self-checking programmed material, check lists, charts, questions to guide self-evaluation, questions and items to guide teacher evaluation of learn-ing, and end-of-unit tests. The preceding chapters present examples of eval-uative procedures and instruments.

Questions such as the following may be used in reviewing evaluation provisions in new designs:

> **What instructional objectives are identified for evaluation? Are tests and other instruments provided? Are guidelines given for construction of evaluative materials?**
>
> **Does the design provide activities and materials that permit continuous evaluation? Are materials provided for pupil self-evaluation?**
>
> **What outcomes may be anticipated, in addition to those identi-fied in design or project materials?**

Feasibility of Adoption and Implementation

Important considerations in the analysis and review of new curriculum de-signs are those related to the feasibility of their use in the local school sys-tem. Of course, all the preceding questions refer to the suitability of the design or materials for the learners in a particular system, and suitability is the primary requisite for adoption. However, that which is desirable must also be feasible to implement if it is to be adopted. Questions such as the following should be considered:

> **What competencies are required of teachers? What relevant background preparation do the system's teachers have? Will teachers be able to understand, and be willing to meet, the changes to be made?**
>
> **What in-service training will be necessary? What assistance for such training is provided by curriculum producers? What time, facilities, and personnel are available in the system to meet in-service training needs?**
>
> **What organizational changes, if any, need to be made? Are changes required in class size, vertical school organization, responsibilities of teachers? Are adequate plant facilities and equipment available?**
>
> **To what extent is the local community aware of needs for cur-riculum change? What changes does the community favor? What efforts must be made to inform the community about proposed changes? Is there sufficient financial support to thoroughly implement the program?**
>
> **Are administrative and supervisory personnel available to guide implementation of the program? Can the program be given**

an experimental tryout? Are time, instruments, and personnel available for adequate evaluation of all aspects of the program?

Adopting, Adapting, and Utilizing New Designs

As projects have multiplied in different areas of the curriculum, local groups have been confronted with issues that are more difficult to decide than any they have faced before. With competing new programs of instruction, plus revised traditional programs, a decision must be made whether to stick with the old, move to one of the new, build a different program that is a combination of new designs, or combine old and new elements into a single program. The designing of a combination program is especially difficult. For example, given a certain structure with related content and materials selected to develop key ideas in the structure, how can local groups "restructure" a mixture from two or more programs and still have a logically defensible program? Where attempts are made to build such a combination, experts on the structure of the supporting disciplines should be involved. In no other way can curriculum workers be sure of the quality of a combination program from the standpoint of its fundamental structure.

The opportunities to design combination programs are especially bright in the social studies, science, language arts, and fine arts. As one moves from mathematics and natural science to the social sciences and humanities, structure is less rigorously defined and there is increasing diversity of viewpoints. The large number of new projects in the social studies and language arts will force a search for combinations. For example, different approaches and materials in the fields of history, geography, economics, and area studies should be examined carefully in order to select those parts which are most useful in a local program. In the language arts, best ideas from projects related to the use of linguistics in improving instruction might well be incorporated with sound ideas drawn from traditional programs. Such combinations appear to be more feasible at the present time than do combinations that would be designed from various mathematics programs, although, to be sure, the possibilities here should be explored in depth.

In reviewing new designs and planning programs, one must compare the outlines of structure of foundation disciplines represented in curriculum materials. What is needed is a model for analyzing disciplines, setting up points of comparison, and using the results of the analysis. The following proposed model includes the elements that the authors believe to be fundamental to the design of programs of instruction.

A MODEL FOR REVIEWING DISCIPLINES

What is anthropology? (or botany, geometry, etc.) Provide a succinct definition that clarifies the domain of study. In some cases, scholars use more than a single definition.

Why study the discipline? Indicate reasons, objectives, or major values to be attained; include values from the student's as well as the scholar's point of view.

What basic questions are investigated? Indicate the major questions of concern in this domain of study.

How may the conceptual structure be specified? Explore various ways in which key concepts, concept clusters, generalizations, and themes may be presented. Select the way or ways that are most useful to curriculum workers.

How may the syntactical or process aspects of structure be indicated? Outline modes of inquiry and techniques of investigation that are used, giving examples that can be used in curriculum planning.

What are the relationships between this and other disciplines? Indicate relationships to other disciplines both within the same broad field and those in other categories. Include examples of conceptual or syntactical similarities, or areas of concern, that can be used in cross-disciplinary studies.

What applications can be made at various levels of instruction? Suggest actual examples of how concepts, clusters, generalizations, and modes of inquiry may be used in units and courses. Include examples both for separate-discipline and cross-discipline units.

What conditions of instruction are basic? Indicate teaching strategies, instructional media, organizational patterns, and evaluation procedures that are believed to be most useful.

What references are recommended for further study? Suggest references that will be most useful to curriculum builders.

Notice that this model includes curriculum planning elements as well as elements for analyzing a discipline. The assumption is that scholars and curriculum specialists need to work in a way that focuses on the ultimate task at hand, building a program of instruction. As indicated earlier in this chapter, scholars and curriculum specialists should work together in all phases of planning. The authors reject the notion that scholars should only outline the structure of their disciplines and then leave the remainder of curriculum planning to others.

IMPLEMENTATION OF NEW CURRICULUM DESIGNS

Implementation of instructional programs is not a single activity. It is an interwoven network of varying activities involved in translating curriculum designs into classroom practice. The implementation phase of curriculum development is defined by questions such as these: What must teachers do to carry out this particular program or effectively utilize these materials? What do they need to know to do this? How can they be prepared? What supportive personnel are needed? What kinds of instructional materials and facilities are most helpful? What forms of school and class organization are required? Is the community informed of needs for change, and is it in favor of the changes made?

Curriculum change is most effectively implemented when the community understands and supports it, when facilities are available for desirable school organization and learning activities, when appropriate materials are at hand, and when supportive personnel assist teachers. But it is the classroom teacher who is the key to curriculum implementation, for in the last analysis, in plain terms, the curriculum is what the teacher makes of it. The curriculum is described in the teacher-pupil interaction of each classroom. Therefore, the professional preparation of the teacher will be considered first in this discussion, although it is understood that all the other elements of implementation contribute to what the teacher does with curriculum designs in the classroom.

Teacher Preparation

Before any program can be implemented, teachers must be aware of needs for change and should be informed about the directions of change. Ideally, teachers should be involved in preliminary phases of curriculum planning and experimentation. The close links between curriculum development and in-service education must not be overlooked. Teachers, as well as other school workers, need in-service education in order to utilize new curricula, and an excellent in-service activity is participation in the preparation and tryout of guides and materials. Because of the accelerated pace and variety of educational innovations today, in-service education programs for teachers, supervisors, and administrators have become increasingly important and, at times, urgent.

Few classroom teachers have experienced, in their own education, the structure-based organizations of knowledge in the forms represented by new curriculum designs. A major problem is the development of a grasp of structure and greater depth of understanding in the disciplines that are most fundamental to planning and teaching each of the elementary school subjects. The outlines of structure that have been prepared by scholars are helpful in this regard. The model for analysis of disciplines presented in the preceding section is a tool for use in studying such outlines.

In-service education must also include preparation for the use of teaching strategies that develop children's inquiry skills. The preceding section of this chapter includes some guidelines for the development of such teaching competencies.

Another important problem for in-service education is the preparation of the teacher for changes in instructional roles. Traditionally, the teacher has been prepared for the role of sole (or at least primary) determiner of all curricular activities in all subjects in a single classroom at a specified grade level. This role is changing in many ways. To begin with, the teacher who genuinely develops children's inquiry skills has assumed a role of less-than-complete determination of all phases of the child's learning experiences. Changes in instructional media have further altered the teacher's role from selector and coordinator of a variety of independently produced media to that of a member of an instructional system whose other interactive elements are a package of coordinated data, media, and guidelines for instruction. A further example of change is seen in the greater attention being given to utilization of special competencies of teachers who have depth of preparation in different school subjects, as teachers are grouped into teaching teams. The responsibilities of the team teacher are at once limited and extended in comparison with the traditional role—limited to one, or just a few, of the school subjects and extended to the instruction of varying groups of children in a wider range of grade or achievement levels.

As new curriculum designs are adopted (or adapted), resultant needs for in-service education must be assessed.

> **What specific skills or understandings need to be developed? Do all teachers need the same program? What provisions should be made for differing teacher backgrounds and needs?**
>
> **What are the most effective procedures for the in-service program? What time allotment is required in the teacher's day and school year?**
>
> **What materials are needed? Are materials and guidelines for in-service activities supplied by the curriculum producers? Are members of curriculum planning groups available for consultation if needed? Can demonstrations or observations**

of classroom activities be arranged? Are adequate reference materials available in the system's professional or school libraries?

In-service education is only one aspect of adequate teacher preparation. No less than their pupils, teachers differ in regard to their academic and experiential backgrounds and in the specific talents they bring to the instructional task. Self-directed activities can greatly augment each teacher's competencies. In addition, teachers may explore new ideas and materials even when no system-wide revision is in progress. The following are possible ways of developing insight into the content and processes needed to utilize new developments:

> **Obtain, examine, and try out (if feasible) materials still under development in various projects. Administrators may write to project directors to obtain materials and be placed on the mailing list for project bulletins.**
>
> **Formulate objectives in behavioral or operational terms. Study examples presented in current materials, such as those cited in the preceding chapters. Use behavioral statements in unit and lesson plans.**
>
> **Begin now to make the classroom a laboratory for the development of competence in inquiry. If there is one common element in the many new curriculum developments across the board, it is the emphasis on the involvement of students in inquiry.**
>
> **Examine current materials to find examples of structure and inquiry. Look for key concepts, concept clusters, generalizations, modes of inquiry, and specific techniques of inquiry in new units of study, textbooks, films, and other materials. Compare them with the examples presented in this volume. Begin to guide students to use concepts, clusters, and generalizations to structure their learning.**
>
> **Examine so-called "teacher-proof" or "teacher-safe" materials for the express purpose of finding out how specialists structure ideas, ask questions, stimulate inquiry, and assess outcomes. Much can be gained by analyzing these materials for good ideas; much can be lost by condemning them for being assertedly "teacher-proof."**
>
> **Try out selected teaching strategies presented in this volume and in new curriculum materials. Modify and adapt them to fit your style, the capacities of your students, and local conditions. By all means, try to keep in mind that the spirit and intent of various strategies is to involve students as intensively as possible in learning experiences.**

Give particular attention to the kinds of questions used, striving for those which spur inquiry on the part of students. Study guidelines for framing questions as reported in current materials and cited in examples in the preceding chapters.

Assume the role of teacher-observer in the classroom in order to diagnose needs, to plan next learning experiences, to evaluate outcomes of instruction, and to study ways in which children carry on inquiry and cluster ideas.

Make evaluation a basic part of instruction from initial through concluding phases. Use a variety of devices and procedures ranging from questions and items on various levels of the taxonomies of educational objectives to check lists and tasks related to multiple outcomes. Give attention to both cognitive and affective outcomes.

Participate in professional activities that bear directly on new developments. Identify courses (both academic and professional), National Defense Education Act and other institutes, workshops, meetings, and conferences that are specifically designed to familiarize school personnel with new programs and materials in various areas of the elementary curriculum.

Many school systems have instituted programs designed to improve teacher competence in the areas of mathematics and foreign language instruction, and attention is being extended to science and social sciences education in the elementary school. Programs in the humanities appear to be next in line. Perhaps some of the tribulations encountered by school personnel in the "new math" in-service programs can be avoided in the future if steps are taken now to keep abreast of new developments through communications to teachers and suitable in-service courses.

While the needs of teachers in service are met by in-service and self-directed activities, the needs of the school system require a third vital aspect of teacher preparation: the pre-service education of teachers. Implementation of new curriculum designs and effective learning by elementary pupils are greatly facilitated when there is close communication of ideas and coordination of efforts in teacher preparation among curriculum project developers, school systems, and teacher education institutions. An example of efforts in this direction may be found in proposals made by the American Association of Colleges of Teacher Education (LaGrone, 1964). In-service programs will always serve the function of keeping experienced teachers abreast of new developments, but the demands on the school system's in-service personnel and resources are less staggering when pre-service education provides the beginning teacher with an understanding of the rationale underlying curricular innovations in addition to providing contact with specific new designs and materials.

Supportive Personnel and Services

Pre-service and in-service education provide preparation for effective program implementation, but supervision and consultation must take up implementation responsibilities where these leave off, in the continuous assistance and provision of supportive services needed daily in the classroom. The challenge to supervisors and principals has been especially great because the national curriculum projects have not dealt with problems of supervision and consultation to any great extent.

One aspect of this challenge is the identification of the types of supportive services needed and the provision of suitable training for the personnel who will provide these services. Just as the role of the teacher has undergone changes, the responsibilities and roles of supervisors, curriculum specialists, school administrators, and central staff personnel are being redefined as new curriculum developments affect the kinds of leadership each one provides in all phases of curriculum planning and implementation. For example, the roles of the school librarian and audio-visual coordinator tend to merge as the impact of new designs and materials turns the school library into an instructional materials center where children find books, films, tapes, or programmed materials for individual or group study and teachers obtain resource materials and equipment for classroom use.

Other ways in which school systems have met the challenges posed by new designs have included provision of such supportive services as closed-circuit or intersystem educational TV, institution of team-teaching procedures and nongraded organization, construction of elementary schools with flexible interior partitions to permit varying groupings and activities, and exploration of ways in which programmed instruction and computer technology can free teachers to devote more of their time to creative and individualized aspects of instruction.

Instructional Media

New developments in the design and use of instructional media have posed a further set of challenges and problems to curriculum workers. In the past, teachers and administrators have evolved ways of utilizing new materials in support of instructional programs within an approach that regarded each new item as a supplementary aid to the central components of instruction, the teacher and the textbook. There is a growing tendency now for curriculum planners to go beyond listing recommended materials and to produce a package of materials that constitutes an integral, not a supplementary, part of the total curriculum design. When the design is implemented, the teacher, employing the materials in the sequence and manner prescribed in the curriculum design, is functioning as a part of a total instructional system. The teacher needs to understand the rationale for the organization of the system in order to be able to utilize it most effectively, and this means knowing how to modify the system to meet specific, local instructional needs. Attention should be given to pre-service and in-service programs that acquaint the teacher with appropriate approaches to the uses of educational media systems and permit teacher selection and coordination of separate materials to reach more effective levels.

The Community and Curriculum Implementation

Effective implementation of new curriculum designs is dependent on at least two factors related to the neighborhood and school system community. First, financial support, despite state, Federal, or foundational assistance, is still requisite for the provision of needed educational facilities and services. Second, though equal in importance, is the community's theoretical support for changes. Educators can bring about changes most effectively if a climate of understanding and encouragement prevails in the community. Especially important are the attitudes held by parents, for these are invariably transmitted to the children for whom the changes are intended. Preceding sections have touched on the tremendous range and accelerating pace of new developments in curriculum design and materials and the challenges to educators to keep abreast of these developments and, of course, to go beyond merely maintaining such awareness by initiating curriculum innovation activities themselves. But at the same time, school personnel should recognize that the supportive community must not be left behind. Despite the time and effort devoted to information and curriculum development within the school system, some time and effort must be expended to keep the community aware of the changing conditions and needs perceived by educators. School-community communication should go beyond mere information; it should include the maintenance of a continuous dialogue that enables the community to understand rationales for change, to understand the educational problems and procedures involved, and in many instances to provide direct assistance for curriculum implementation in the form of resource persons, school volunteers and aides, and any number of other personal forms of contribution to the efforts of the schools.

EVALUATION OF NEW INSTRUCTIONAL PROGRAMS

Preliminary evaluation of instructional programs has been carried on primarily by project staff members. After materials are developed, they are tried out in the classroom, critical reactions are obtained, test data are

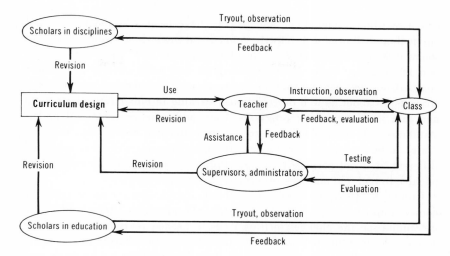

Chart 13–1. *Preliminary classroom evaluation of new curriculum designs.*

analyzed, and needed revisions are made. This process, a subsystem in the total implementation process, may be conducted in the ways diagramed in Chart 13–1.

Following this phase, more formal evaluation is developed and is conducted along the lines diagramed in Chart 13–2.

There is a need to identify all the objectives and outcomes that may be evaluated. This means going beyond mere assessment of pupil achievement as measured by paper-pencil tests, to an evaluation of a full range of cognitive, affective, and psychomotor outcomes through a variety of instruments. The attitudes and effectiveness of teachers and other supportive personnel, the value of various materials, media systems, and strategies, the

Chart 13–2. *Formal evaluation of new curriculum designs.*

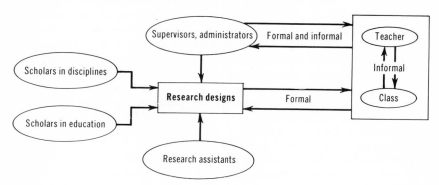

extent to which better scope and balance have been achieved in the total curriculum—all need to be clearly defined and properly assessed before any sound judgment can be made of the effectiveness of new curriculum designs and innovations. Under limited procedures and techniques of evaluation, comparisons between old and new programs have in general revealed that students do about as well on traditional learning in either type of program and that students in new programs "gain additional insights and understandings." A key difficulty is to get measurement instruments that are "fair" to both new and traditional programs. Because objectives are quite different, it is not possible to define appraisal criteria that are equally applicable to both old and new programs.

Cronbach (1963) has proposed evaluation guidelines for use in studying course improvements. Multiple measures of outcomes, item analysis to determine specific changes, getting clues to needed revisions, comparative studies of programs with different objectives, using essay tests and open-ended items, direct observations, and assessing aptitude for learning new material are discussed in Cronbach's recommendations. Guba (1965) has suggested that a full range of evaluation of instructional programs may be facilitated when experimental research is complemented by "aexperimental" research (field study). The preceding chapters include check lists of questions for the evaluation of curriculum improvement in specific curriculum areas. Other lists that aid in definition of questions to be evaluated may be found in end-of-chapter references. There is agreement on the part of all concerned with program evaluation that, to be meaningful, evaluation must be continuous.

REFERENCES

Alexander, William M. *Changing curriculum content.* Washington, D.C.: Association for Supervision and Curriculum Development, NEA, 1964. Brief summary of viewpoints on emerging curriculum content.

Ammons, Margaret, & Gilchrist, Robert S. *Assessing and using curriculum content.* Washington, D.C.: Association for Supervision and Curriculum Development, NEA, 1965. Useful guidelines for curriculum workers.

Bellack, Arno A. *The structure of knowledge and the structure of the curriculum. A reassessment of the curriculum.* New York: Bureau of Publications, Teachers College, Columbia University, 1964. Discussion of curriculum questions related to the structure and relationships of the disciplines.

Broudy, Harry S. *Building a philosophy of education.* Englewood Cliffs, N.J.: Prentice-Hall, 1954. Pp. 144–196. Sections on elements to be mastered in any logically organized field or discipline.

Cassidy, Harold C. *The sciences and the arts.* New York: Harper, 1962. Discussion of relationships between sciences and humanities.

Cronbach, Lee J. Course improvement through evaluation, *Teach. Coll. Rec.*, May, 1963, **64**, 672–683. Guidelines for evaluation as programs are developed.

Elam, Stanley. (Ed.) *Education and the structure of knowledge.* Chicago: Rand McNally, 1964. Essays on structure in relation to curriculum organization.

Ford, G. W., & Pugno, Lawrence. (Eds.) *The structure of knowledge and the curriculum.* Chicago: Rand McNally, 1964. Essays on structure in various disciplines.

Fraser, Dorothy M. *Current curriculum studies in academic subjects.* Washington, D.C.: National Education Association, 1962. Guidelines for using curriculum projects in last chapter.

Frazier, Alexander. Making use of national curriculum studies, *Educ. Leadership*, November, 1964, **22**, 101–106. Analysis of steps in developing new curriculum materials.

Gilchrist, Robert S. (Ed.) *Using current curriculum developments.* Washington, D.C.: Association for Supervision and Curriculum Development, NEA, 1963. Guidelines for curriculum workers, review of curriculum developments.

Goodlad, John I. *School curriculum reform in the United States.* New York: Fund for the Advancement of Education, 1964. Review of early tendencies in the current reform of the curriculum.

Guba, Egon G. *Methodological strategies for educational change.* Columbus, Ohio: School of Education, Ohio State University, 1965. Mimeographed. Suggestions for evaluation of instructional programs.

Hillson, Maurie. *Change and innovation in elementary school organization.* New York: Holt, 1965. Selected readings on grouping, team teaching, nongrading.

LaGrone, Herbert F. (Dir.) *A proposal for the revision of the pre-service professional component of a program of teacher education.* Washington, D.C.: American Association of Colleges of Teacher Education, 1964. Suggestions for teacher education related to curriculum innovations.

Lange, Phil C. (Ed.) *Programed instruction.* 66th Yearbook of the National Society for the Study of Education, Part II. Chicago: University of Chicago Press, 1967. A critical review of principles and procedures.

Leeper, Robert R. (Ed.) *Curriculum change: direction and process.* Washington, D.C.: Association for Supervision and Curriculum Development, NEA, 1966. Collection of four addresses on problems and procedures in curriculum change.

Michaelis, John U. *Social studies for children in a democracy.* (3d ed.) Englewood Cliffs, N.J.: Prentice-Hall, 1963. Chapter 5 includes guidelines for curriculum evaluation applicable to all subject areas.

National Society for the Study of Education. *The changing American school.* Sixty-fifth Yearbook, Part II. Chicago: University of Chicago Press, 1966. Chapters on the changing role of the teacher, the curriculum, instructional resources, school organization, and school plant facilities.

NEA Project on Instruction. *Education in a changing society; Deciding what to teach; Planning and organizing for teaching.* Washington, D.C.: National Education Association, 1963. Three booklets on principles and procedures for instructional planning.

Phenix, Philip H. *Realms of meaning.* New York: McGraw-Hill, 1964. A philosophy of curriculum development.

Rev. Educ. Res., June, 1966, **36**, 339–398. Entire issue devoted to review of literature on curriculum planning and development, 1963–1966.

Thelen, Herbert. *Education and the human quest.* New York: Harper, 1960. Pp. 31–75. Discussion of domains of knowledge.

Trow, William Clark. *Teacher and technology.* New York: Appleton-Century-Crofts, 1963. Review of new instructional media and suggestions for utilization of media and systems.

Unruh, Glenys G. (Ed.) *New curriculum developments.* Washington, D.C.: Association for Supervision and Curriculum Development, NEA, 1965. Review of developments in all subject areas. Chapter on instructional technology.

Wilhelms, Fred T. (Ed.) *Evaluation as feedback and guide.* 1967 Yearbook, Association for Supervision and Curriculum Development. Washington, D.C.: National Education Association, 1967. Guidelines for using evaluation constructively.

Witty, Paul A. (Ed.) *The educationally retarded and disadvantaged.* 66th Yearbook of the National Society for the Study of Education. Chicago: University of Chicago Press, 1967. Guidelines for improving programs of instruction.

INDEX

INDEX